Devotional Visualities

Bloomsbury Studies in Material Religion

Series editors: Birgit Meyer, David Morgan, S. Brent Plate, Crispin Paine, Amy Whitehead, and Katja Rakow

Bloomsbury Studies in Material Religion is the first book series dedicated exclusively to studies in material religion. Within the field of lived religion, the series is concerned with the material things with which people do religion, and how these things – objects, buildings, landscapes – relate to people, their bodies, clothes, food, actions, thoughts and emotions. The series engages and advances theories in 'sensuous' and 'experiential' religion, as well as informing museum practices and influencing wider cultural understandings with relation to religious objects and performances. Books in the series are at the cutting edge of debates as well as developments in fields including religious studies, anthropology, museum studies, art history, and material culture studies.

Buddhism and Waste, edited by Trine Brox and Elizabeth Williams-Oerberg
Christianity and Belonging in Shimla, North India, Jonathan Miles-Watson
Christianity and the Limits of Materiality, edited by Minna Opas and Anna Haapalainen
Figurations and Sensations of the Unseen in Judaism, Christianity and Islam, edited by Birgit Meyer and Terje Stordalen
Food, Festival and Religion, Francesca Ciancimino Howell
Islam through Objects, edited by Anna Bigelow
Material Devotion in a South Indian Poetic World, Leah Elizabeth Comeau
Museums of World Religions, Charles D. Orzech
Qur'anic Matters, Natalia K. Suit
The Religious Heritage Complex, edited by Cyril Isnart and Nathalie Cerezales
Sensational Piety, Murtala Ibrahim
Textual Amulets from Antiquity to Early Modern Times, edited by Christoffer Theis and Paolo Vitellozzi

Devotional Visualities

Seeing Bhakti *in Indic Material Cultures*

Edited by
Karen Pechilis and Amy-Ruth Holt

BLOOMSBURY ACADEMIC
LONDON • NEW YORK • OXFORD • NEW DELHI • SYDNEY

BLOOMSBURY ACADEMIC
Bloomsbury Publishing Plc, 50 Bedford Square, London, WC1B 3DP, UK
Bloomsbury Publishing Inc, 1385 Broadway, New York, NY 10018, USA
Bloomsbury Publishing Ireland, 29 Earlsfort Terrace, Dublin 2, D02 AY28, Ireland

BLOOMSBURY, BLOOMSBURY ACADEMIC and the Diana logo
are trademarks of Bloomsbury Publishing Plc

First published in Great Britain 2023

A catalogue record for this book is available from the British Library.

A catalogue record for this book is available from the Library of Congress.

ISBN: HB: 978-1-3502-1418-7
PB: 978-1-3502-1422-4
ePDF: 978-1-3502-1419-4
eBook: 978-1-3502-1420-0

Series: Bloomsbury Studies in Material Religion

Typeset by Deanta Global Publishing Services, Chennai, India

For product safety related questions contact productsafety@bloomsbury.com.

To find out more about our authors and books visit www.bloomsbury.com
and sign up for our newsletters

Contents

List of Illustrations vi
Note on Transliteration and Translation x

Introduction: Looking Again at Devotion *Karen Pechilis and Amy-Ruth Holt* 1

Part I Materializing Memory

1 The Beginnings of Mass-Produced Devotional Prints in Calcutta *Richard H. Davis* 41
2 Expanding Meanings of *Bhakti* in Bengali American Home Shrines *Ashlee Norene Andrews* 63
3 Merchant Patronage and Royal Hanumāns: A Modern Devotional Visuality *R. Jeremy Saul* 85
4 Evolving Material Authority: Devotion, History, and the Svāminārāyaṇa Museum *Shruti Patel* 108

Part II Mirroring and Immaterializing Portraits

5 Kabīr in Indo-Muslim Visual and Literary Culture *Murad Khan Mumtaz* 137
6 The Devotional Role of Paintings and Photographs in the Puṣṭi Mārga *Shandip Saha* 164
7 The Iconic Sūrdās *John Stratton Hawley* 186
8 The Visual Multiplicity and Materiality of Guru Nityānanda's Portraits *Amy-Ruth Holt* 210
9 *Darśan* in Twelve Ways: Portraying the Divine in Early Svāminārāyaṇa Art *Ankur Desai* 235

Part III Shaping the Return Look

10 *Bhakti* and Looking at What We Do Not Want to See *Karen Pechilis* 261
11 Mīrā's Iconography: From Miniature to Movie *Heidi Pauwels* 285

Notes on Contributors 311
Index 314

Illustrations

Figures

1.1 *Debi Kally* (Kālī of Kalighat), *c.* 1865 45

1.2 *Śrī Śrī Kālī*. Chromolithograph, *c.* 1880s 47

1.3 *Kṛṣṇa-Kālī*. Lithograph, *c.* 1878–83 52

1.4 *Kṛṣṇa as Kālī*. Painting, *c.* 1830 53

1.5 Durgā slaying the buffalo demon depicted on a stand and surmounted on a *toraṇa* decorated with smaller figures of demon kings and Hindu gods. Transfer lithograph, *c.* 1860s 55

1.6 Durgā slaying the buffalo demon with other deities, set in a *toraṇa*. Coloured lithograph, *c.* 1870s 56

2.1 Sita's shrine, December 2014 64

2.2 Shushmita's shrine, June 2019 70

2.3 Father's glasses, inside Sushmita's shrine, June 2019 72

2.4 Subrata's shrine, July 2019 75

2.5 Nina's shrine, July 2019 77

2.6 Kālī's feet, July 2019 79

3.1 Bālājī, Icchāpūrṇ Bālājī temple, Sardar Shahar 86

3.2 Poster of Bālājī, Salasar 92

3.3 Poster of Bālājī, Mehandipur 95

3.4 Bālājī, Ghata Mehandipur Bālājī temple, Ratangarh 97

3.5 The monkey construction foreman, Icchāpūrṇ Bālājī temple, Sardar Shahar 103

3.6 Kubera, Icchāpūrṇ Bālājī temple, Sardar Shahar 104

4.1 Stone umbrella (*chatrī*) with sculpted footprints (*caraṇārvinda*) of Sahajānanda mark a sanctified space (*prasādīnī jagyā*) 116

4.2 Printed footprints (*caraṇārvinda*) and sandals of Sahajānanda are examples of sanctified objects (*prasādīnī vastu*) 119

4.3 Exterior view of Akshar Bhuvan, which was created to house and display Sahajānanda's materiality (*prasādī*) 121

4.4 Interior view of the display and storage of Sahajānanda's *prasādī* (sacred objects and images) 121

4.5 Courtyard and neem tree on estate (*darbār*) of Dada Kachar, devotee and patron of Sahajānanda 123
4.6 Exterior view of the "Shree Swaminarayan Museum," 2011 125
5.1 *Kabīr and Kamāl*, *c.* 1680 140
5.2 *Gathering of Ascetics*, *c.* 1655 143
5.3 *Gathering of Ascetics* (detail), *c.* 1655 144
5.4 *An ascetic with two disciples*, *c.* 1610 153
5.5 *Kamāl Das*, *c.* 1720 155
5.6 *Kabīr tending his loom*, *c.* 1760 157
5.7 *A gathering of holy men of different faiths* by Mir Kalan Khan, *c.* 1770 158
5.8 *Kabīr with his wife Loī*, *c.* 1830 160
6.1 The Gopāṣṭamī festival being celebrated in the late nineteenth century by the Nathdwara *mahārāja*, Govardhanlāl (left), using a *citrajī* of Śrīnāthjī, which is placed upon an altar 168
6.2 A home shrine in London, England, with the *citrajī*s of Śrīnāthjī (right) and the river goddess Yamunajī (left), whose waters flow along the banks of Kṛṣṇa's childhood home of Gokul 169
6.3 A photograph of the popular *mahārāja* Devakīnandanācārya (1859–1903) of Kamvan from *Svarūpa Darśan* 175
6.4 A painting of Devakīnandanācārya inspired by the photograph in *Svarūpa Darśan* 175
6.5 *Festival of the Five Svarūpas*. Ghasiram Hardev Sharma, *c.* 1908 177
6.6 Group photograph with devotees next to a *pichvāi* of Śrīnāthjī. Narendra Kumar Paliwal, *c.* 1950s 179
6.7 *Manoratha of Śrīnāthjī*. Artist Khubiram and Sons, *c.* 1950s 180
7.1 Commemorative four-anna postage stamp issued by the Government of India on October 1, 1952, with Sūrdās's name written in Devanāgarī letters beneath the dates ascribed to him, 1479–1586 187
7.2 Sūrdās painted in oil by Kalicharan Verma in 1953–4 188
7.3 Sūrdās sings to Kṛṣṇa *c.* 1965–6 190
7.4 Sūrdās sings to Kṛṣṇa, 1967 192
7.5 Bowing in praise before the Lord's sacred feet. Illustration to "I bow in praise before your lotus feet," *c.* 1700 196
7.6 "They worship Mt. Govardhan with great liberality." Illustration to *govardhan pūjat param udār*, *c.* 1720 203
7.7 Sūrdās, as he appears in the lower left-hand corner of the painting illustrating "Muralī has cast her spell on Krishna, our lad" 204

7.8 "Peacocks have mounted whatever peak they can." Illustration to *sīṣanī saṣaranī caḍ ṭer suṇāyo*, *c.* 1660 205
8.1 Ānandeśvara-Ānandeśvarī (Śiva and Pārvatī as Nityānanda) 211
8.2 Portrait *mūlvar* or "main deity" of Nityānanda (left) with Mt. Meru (center) and goddess Ānandeśvarī *vigraha* (right) 214
8.3 Viṣṇu Room with Śirdi Sai Baba (center), Kṛṣṇa and Rādhā (right), Rāma, Sītā, Lakṣmana, and small Hanumān (left) in the Nithyananda Vedic Temple 216
8.4 Murugaṉ and his two wives 220
8.5 "Cut-out" of Guru Paramahaṃsa Nityānanda 221
8.6 Portrait of Guru Paramahaṃsa Nityānanda with *Tat Tvam Asi* (*You Are That*) hung over the sanctum 229
9.1 On left, *Caraṇārvinda* (footprints) of Sahajānanda Svāmī, *c.* 1820–30. On right, sculpted *caraṇārvinda* (footprints) of Sahajānanda Svāmī, *c.* early twentieth century 243
9.2 On left, Kṛṣṇa as Śrīnāthajī, *c.* late eighteenth century. On right, Sahajānanda Svāmī in *dvibhuja* (two-armed) form, *c.* mid- to late nineteenth century 245
9.3 Print of Śrī Sahajānanda Svāmī, with Śrī Bhaktimātā and Śrī Dharmapati, from a cast attributed to Nārāyaṇajī Hīrajībhai Suthāra, *c.* 1828–30 247
9.4 Śrī Sahajānanda Svāmī, attributed to Nārāyaṇajī Hīrajībhai Suthāra, *c.* 1823–8 249
9.5 On left, Śrī Sahajānanda Svāmī, attributed to Nārāyaṇajī Hīrajībhai Suthāra (possibly), *c.* 1823–8. On right, Raja Sangram Pal of Basohli, *c.* mid- to late seventeenth century 250
9.6 On left, *mūrti* of Sahajānanda Svāmī as Śrī Harikṛṣṇa Mahārāja, 1824. On right, *mūrti* of Śrī Gopīnāthajīdeva Mahārāja, 1828 252
10.1 The many faces of Kāraikkāl Ammaiyār 267
10.2 Shilpika Bordoloi as Kāraikkāl Ammaiyār in *Katyayani's* "O," conceptualized and directed by Sohaila Kapur, 2012 276
10.3 The Descent of the Ganges or Arjuna's Penance rock relief at Mahabalipuram, Tamil Nadu, seventh to eighth century CE 277
11.1 Cover of the 1930 booklet *Bhakta Nārī* by Hanumān Prasād Poddār 287
11.2 A commemorative postage stamp on Saints and Poets: Mira, fifteenth to sixteenth century 291
11.3 Bilingual poster of the Punjabi film *Matwali Mira*, directed by Prafulla Roy with Mukhtar Begum in the title role, 1940 296

11.4 Mīrā fondles her image. Screenshot from the Tamil film *Meera*, directed by Ellis R. Dungan, 1945 296
11.5 Domestic scene with Bhoj (Vinod Khanna) and Mīrā (Hema Malini) sewing an outfit for her deity. Screenshot from the Hindi film *Meera*, directed by Gulzar, 1979 296
11.6 Young Mīrā (Aashika Bhatia) and her Giridhar from the Hindi TV serial *Meera*, directed by Mukesh Kumar Singh, aired 2009–10 on NDTV's Imagine channel 296
11.7 Promotional poster for the Telugu film *Meerabai*, directed by B. N. Rao, 1940 297

Tables

8.1 Nityānanda's Life Bliss Mediation 215
8.2 The Nityānanda Pañca Bhūta Temples in the United States 223

Note on Transliteration and Translation

Within this volume, many of the authors are noted translators within their various fields. To highlight the academic significance of their works and for standardized access across disciplines and multiple languages, we have followed the practice of transliterating Indic languages using diacritics for terms as well as names of saints, teachers, and gurus. We italicize the term *bhakti* to emphasize its definition according to the various works and images discussed in this volume and not as a common English word. For Bengali, Gujarati, Hindi, Tamil, Sanskrit, and Urdu terms, the standard diacritic schemes are applied; however, Sanskrit equivalents with a's, such as *dharma* for *dharm*, are kept so as to provide continuity throughout the volume for religious terminology with the exceptions of the more common *darśan* being used instead of *darśana* and *bhajan* instead of *bhajana*. In specific cases, such as place names and film titles, we have followed the practice of using their common Romanized English forms without diacritics.

Introduction

Looking Again at Devotion

Karen Pechilis and Amy-Ruth Holt

Devotion expressed in the regional languages of India, which has existed for at least 1,500 years and spans the regions of the subcontinent, introduced and promoted a shared participatory culture of involvement that included an emphasis on creative endeavor in the arts such as literature, fine arts, performing arts, and music. This shared participatory culture of devotion through the arts encouraged and encourages ordinary and not-so-ordinary people to engage interestedly in observing, locating, and responding to their conditions and those of the world they inhabit. The premise of this volume is that such engagement has centrally involved "practices of looking" (Sturken and Cartwright 2018 [2001]); however, to date the range of such visual practices as they have generated, shaped, advanced, and redirected devotion has been overlooked in scholarship. The authors contributing to this volume are committed to analyzing devotion's participatory impulse based on human concern to identify the diversity of logics and practices of looking in Indic devotional visualities that are rooted in specific times, places, and traditions yet interact and are comparable across them. And, given that devotion is a category across religions more widely, our study of Indic devotional visualities has broader comparative applicability suggested by, but not overtly explored in, this volume.

Visuality is also a comparative category. It is a term with a complex history (Mirzoeff 2006), from Carlyle's coining of the term with influential discussion in the 1830s to the prominent Dia Art Foundation symposium on the topic in 1988 (Foster 1988). Key theoretical insights on visuality are provided by Alexa Sand, who, as an art historian of western medieval art history, seems especially relevant since there was a critical mass of devotional activity in the arts in medieval India from which devotees in subsequent eras continuously draw. She points to visuality as "the element of visual experience that is contingent on culture" and its instability, and that it is constituted by "physicality wed to immateriality," including both embodiment and spirituality, before concluding that "In a sense then the whole project of visuality is medieval, in that it prods at the places where visual experience comes loose from rational explanation, and vision serves as a bridge between the unspeakable, invisible, and sublime realm of the sacred, and the physical, visible, and tangible essence of bodily life" (Sand 2012: 89, 93–4).

Foregrounding cultural practices of looking, the intermingling of physicality and immateriality, and the making visible of devotion, the essays in this volume examine the workings of devotional visualities in a number of arenas such as the crafting of god images in the contexts of pilgrimage, home shrines, and success in business (Davis, Andrews, and Saul chapters); representing saints in painting, film, and drama in ways that make them speak to a variety of people from specific communities to a mass audience (Hawley, Mumtaz, Pechilis, and Pauwels chapters); and instantiating the vitality of the guru in images from sculptural to digital as well as in everyday objects (Patel, Saha, Desai, and Holt chapters). However, since our aim is to foreground processes in the material visualities of Indic devotion, the bringing together of these chapters into one volume is meant to highlight not the devotional object, in which god, saint, and guru would be the headings, but instead aspects of human agency and reception via visual and material strategies that make visible, circulate, and shape human concerns: materializing memory (Davis, Andrews, Saul, and Patel chapters), mirroring and immaterializing portraits (Mumtaz, Saha, Hawley, Holt, and Desai chapters), and shaping the return look (Pechilis and Pauwels chapters).

These strategies are individually explained more fully as we introduce each chapter at the end of this introduction. But to begin, we set our volume into theoretical context in order to highlight its many interventions through overlapping challenges: to the scholarly focus on modernity in studies of Indic visuality; to the predominance of textual studies of regional-language *bhakti*; to the assumption that study of Indic religious imagery has to designate and segregate religious identities; and to any separation of visual culture and material culture as modes of study, which we approach in this volume as a defined interdisciplinary inquiry. In a later section of this introduction, we expand our theme of challenge to show significant ways in which devotional practices have challenged influential established ways of seeing in Indic tradition.

In the scholarship on Indic visualities there has been a preponderance of studies situated in the nexus of image-making, modernity, and the nation (Dwyer and Pinney 2001; Ramaswamy 2003a; Pinney 2004; Dwyer 2006; Davis 2007). These studies serve as an excellent foundation for further studies of visuality, given their focus on practices of looking; for example, as characterized by Sumathi Ramaswamy: "patriotism or nationalism in India is an intensely ocular ideology and set of visual habits, grounded in the practice of seeing the nation, and being seen in turn adoring and worshipping the nation. These acts of seeing, akin to *darshan*, are facilitated by different kinds of patriotic visual practices ranging from painting, poster art and maps, to film and video" (Ramaswamy 2003b: xxiii). The late colonial era has a dominant place in such analyses, with its explosion of image-making and its extensive documentation, yet the "pull of nation" has its limits: "The image and discursive practices . . . become meaningful only when they reveal contests over the nation-space" (Sinha 2007: 215). Collectively, such studies show us that devotion was repurposed to be directed toward the nation, although the workings of devotion are not their focus. Our volume places devotion at the center of analysis to show how images were made devotional and ways in which such new legibilities of images were created by expanding the meanings of devotion. For example, a photograph of a deceased man requires that his eyeglasses be nearby in a home shrine (Andrews); the dramatized sculptural image of a female saint gazes critically at society (Pechilis); a contemporary guru fuses with material images in multiple media (Holt); and an 11,000-kilogram *laḍḍū* (a type of sweet) makes legible the merger of the divine's highest level of efficacious miracles with the large and growing prosperity of a devotional merchant community (Saul).

The long history of Indic devotionalism provides us with a defined lens to analyze visualities across the early modern, modern, and postmodern eras as "an integral element of history in the making" (Pinney 2004: 8). The essays in this volume analyze materials in distinctive time periods, including early modern (Mumtaz and Hawley chapters), modern (Davis, Desai, Pauwels, and Saha) and present (Andrews, Holt, Pechilis, Patel, and Saul), but the inquiry is in most cases not limited to that time period. For example, early modern images are brought into dialogue with a current singer (Mumtaz) and images from the internet (Hawley); modern images resonate with those of the present day, in both film (Pauwels) and painting (Saha); and objects preserved from the past are collected today to display authority (Patel). The histories that devotional images create are "useable pasts" that make a powerful past palpable in the present. Authorized by Indic devotionalism's long history of enjoining participatory engagement, people create, relate, and participate with the images considered herein, which makes visible the diversity of contributions to public culture. Our interest is in the fields of vision they open up, revealing the ways in which images have agency as well as the people who mobilize and shape devotional visualities to intervene in their world. Both images and people are visible participants. Sandra Freitag's (2014b: 400) observation about modern visuality is applicable to the longer history of devotional visualities: the "expansion of participants underscores a major value to the 'visual turn'; it highlights the multiple ways in which meaning is made, suggesting the experiential insights that viewers contribute when they interact with artefacts of visual culture."

All of the essays in this volume engage images associated with *bhakti*, or "devotional participation." *Bhakti* imagery is not confined within one faith community. As a term, *bhakti* is more descriptive than technical, since what it signifies has been differently imagined in overlapping ways in multiple traditions, including Buddhism, Jainism, and Hinduism, and within Hinduism there are numerous distinctive groups that identify with *bhakti*, each investing it with their own specific meanings and practices (see Pechilis 2011). The Sikh Ādi Śri Gurū Granth Sāhib includes texts attributed to a number of *bhakti* saints, including Nāmdev, Ravidās, and Kabīr as well as the Chishtī Sufi saint Shaikh Farīd. The essay by Murad Khan Mumtaz in this volume discusses Sufi interpretations of Kabīr and his son Kamāl, illuminating a distinctive Indo-Muslim situatedness in a shared devotional context. This volume recoups the generative nature of *bhakti* images of gods, gurus, and saints as a history of diverse local and affective devotional "narratives of human belonging" (Chakrabarty 2008: 71). Our documentation of these narratives presents an alternative to other scholarly views of *bhakti*, including those that emphasize its connections with communalist politics from 1857 into the present (Schofield 2015: 118), as well as those that emphasize its imbrication with Sufism to pose a significant attempt to decenter the constructed division between Hindu and Muslim, such as Panjabi (2011). Any specific devotional perspective is developed in a complex Indic context in which it shapes and is shaped through interactions with other perspectives. It is to keep the reality of this interactive process and its multiplicity of results to the forefront that we use the term "Indic" to frame this collection. While each chapter acknowledges distinctive religious locations, taken as a whole the essays in this volume illuminate transformative visual practices that engage *bhakti* imagery across Indic devotionalism.

Bhakti poetry and hagiography in regional languages constituted a major participatory intervention in Indic culture, and it is not surprising that most studies to date have focused on its textual dimension. Hindu *bhakti* poems in the regional language of Tamil began to be composed in the late classical era (500–900 CE), which are our earliest examples of such vernacular literature characterized by a named speaker, theistic orientation, observational stance, and promotional impetus for engaged participation. This style of poetry and hagiographies of the poet-saints accelerated in the post-classical era with regional-language literature composed in Tamil, Kannada, and Telugu in south India; and Hindi, Rajasthani, Gujarati, Marathi, Bengali, and Kashmiri in the north. In many of these regions, *bhakti* poetry is among the first writings in the vernacular, contributing to a "new *cosmopolitan vernacular*" (Pollock 2006: 322) from about the ninth century that challenged the Sanskrit cosmopolis that had been dominant for more than 1,000 years. Late in the post-classical era and into early modernity, *bhakti* and Sufism, which had a long history in the Middle East, generatively interacted in the Indic context (Behl 2007; Burchett 2019).

Bhakti literature's emphasis on visual imagery and engaged participation has encouraged scholars to be cognizant of its relationships to material culture prior to the recent emergence of "visual culture" and "material religion" as overt theoretical perspectives in religion studies. Studies of *bhakti* literature have questioned "the inward-centered, mentalistic approaches of religion that . . . dematerialize scholarly analysis" (Meyer 2014: 209), as well as the premise in much of religion studies that textual materials are "putatively more sophisticated forms of knowledge" (Uehlinger 2015: 388; see also Dubuisson 2015: 301). In discussing the history of the scholarly designation of belief as "an interior spiritualized religiosity" that is central to defining religion and its neglect and even denigration of the material aspects of religion, Birgit Meyer and Dick Houtman point to Protestantism "as its main exponent" (2012: 1). The influence of Protestant definitions in Orientalist scholarship on *bhakti* has been noted and critiqued in scholarship (Sharma 1987; Prentiss 1999; Pintch 2003; Hawley 2022) in favor of an emphasis on *bhakti*'s attention to embodied experience (Prentiss 1999; Holdrege 2015; Holdrege and Pechilis 2017).

Instead of describing a dematerialized interiority, studies of Indic devotional literature have emphasized its sensory language of presence—for example, the hypotyposis-like qualities of Tamil *bhakti* poetry's vivid descriptions of deity and landscape (Hopkins 2002; Venkatesan 2010; Pechilis 2012), and Sufi poetry's emphasis on connection with "historical memory as preserved and handed down in writing" so that "individuals were also able to enter into a relationship with the grand figures of the past. The dead saints were vicariously able to speak to and create new followers, even centuries after their deaths" (Green 2004: 139). Leah Comeau (2021) has centralized the visual and sensual imagery of *bhakti* poetry in her monograph analyzing material religion and literary landscape in the poetry of a ninth-century Tamil *bhakti* poet-saint. Scholars have analyzed the stories of *bhakti* poet-saints to discuss ritual practices, such as diversities of worship made visible in a Kannada hagiography but rendered invisible in later texts (Ben-Herut 2018), and Marathi stories of food and eating as a locus of debate on egalitarianism and community (Keune 2021). Studies of Indic devotionalism have also been attuned to multisensory experiences, especially in their analysis of song (Qureshi 1986; Peterson 1987; Pechilis 2006; Hess 2015; Jackson 2016) and the performing arts (Frazier 2010; Panjabi 2011). *Bhakti* poetry continued to be written into the modern period, such as the eighteenth-century Rajput prince Sāvant Singh of Kishangarh's devotional compositions aimed at reconstituting his court (Pauwels 2017) and the early twentieth-century reformer Kumāran Āśān's *bhakti*-inflected poems in Malayalam that critique caste in Kerala (Pati 2019). Recent scholarship has demonstrated that people have continuously engaged regional-language *bhakti* poetry in modernity up to today to create an image of devotional subjectivity (Pechilis 2012), a contemporary public (Novetzke 2008), a visible regional community (Shukla-Bhatt 2015), and a nation (Schultz 2013; Hawley 2015; Bhatia 2017a and 2017b).

Yet to date there has been no volume dedicated to *bhakti* visualities. Our specific intervention in this volume is to address that gap. In an initial inquiry, we had put together a special issue titled "Contemporary Images of Hindu Bhakti: Identity and Visuality" (Holt and Pechilis 2019). The present volume contributes to the growing scholarship that views "*bhakti* traditions in their broader context," which is the focus of the Regional Bhakti Scholars Network (RBSN). The studies in this volume had their genesis in a collaborative full-day symposium on "*Bhakti* Visualities: Imaging Devotion in the Visual Arts," sponsored by the RBSN at the 2019 Annual South Asia Conference at the University of Wisconsin-Madison (https://www.regionalbhakti.org/bhakti-visualities/), which expanded the scope of the RBSN symposium format into a central focus on visualities. Some of the essays in this volume engage the texts of *bhakti* poet-saints, notably in order to support their focus on imagery. What we are showing is that there are multiple ways to engage *bhakti* visually, not that all interpretations themselves are *bhakti*; for example, Karen Pechilis's chapter discusses ways in which a recent dance performance repurposes the biography of a classical female *bhakti* poet-saint in order to raise issues related to contemporary concerns about violence against women.

Bhakti images are distinctive from texts in many ways, including that the latter are often canonized and thus investigating change related to them often involves identifying distinctive uses of their stable content. Images, on the other hand, often themselves show us change. In this volume, Jack Hawley shows that an iconic image of Sūrdās easily found over the internet today has a very long and largely documentable history of change intertwined with continuity. If there is a textual analog, it may be that of other people composing songs in the name of a poet-saint, such as Mīrābāī, as contributors to the creation of iconicity; however, how to document such activity remains a question (see Hawley 2005). Devotional visual practices of looking, on both individual and community levels, create, shape, and are shaped by interactive processes. It is a different orientation than the formulation, "[t]he power to see, the power to make visible, is the power to control" (Levin 1993: 7, cited in Ramaswamy 2003b: xiv). Instead, devotion provides distinctive narratives and histories of belonging that contrast with modern political movements that co-opt religious precepts and devotional modes in an effort to erect and enforce control, because iconicity happens over time by the interest of diverse people.

Like *bhakti*, visual practices are not confined within one faith community, although they may originate in one. An important case study is Woodman Taylor's (2002) analysis of the use of *darśan* and *naẓar* practices of looking in modern Indian commercial films. *Dṛṣṭi/darśan* is associated with Hinduism; it refers to human viewing and in turn being viewed by a concentrated source of sacred power, such as in a divine image, a guru, or a natural object such as a mountain. *Naẓar* is associated with Islam; it is, depending on context, a look of love or a covetous "evil eye" gaze. Woodman shows that in the romantic genre of film, which supplanted the "mythologicals" genre in modern India, the filmic gaze engages the practice of *darśan* to lead to the look of love, or *naẓar*, in order to convey romantic devotion. "This correlation of visual performance between the experience of *darshan* and the visual foreplay leading to the exchange of *nazar* is indicative that the operations of *nazar* in a South Asian context often incorporate aspects of a visuality based on the practices of *darshan*" (2002: 310). In a similar vein, Shaila Bhatti and Christopher Pinney propose a "networked" approach to visuality that would "draw attention to the role of contingency in the constitution of practice, rather than the effects of supposedly suprahistorical forces such as Hinduism or Indian-ness." This accords with the view of *bhakti* imagery pursued in the present volume, in its quest "to understand the contemporary changing idioms through which questions of visuality make themselves apparent in India" and beyond (2011: 232).

Belonging is a constructed relationship. As noted earlier, in devotional traditions relationships to god, guru, and humanity are not fixed and formulaic but instead experiential, interested, and expressive. What is demanded is personal concern and involvement. As such, devotional traditions are never finished, since they must continually be enacted. We can add that devotional traditions operate by a logic of voluntary association, involving choices and transformation. We can also add that images are not finished either: "figures [in the sense of 'an expressive form'] do not merely represent, but enable perception, sensation and understanding, and in so doing take part in effecting reality" (Meyer and Stordalen 2019: 7). Ashlee Andrews's essay in this volume foregrounds belonging in her discussion of Bengali American women's home shrines. The women choose what objects to display, and then the display itself transforms their sense of self and situatedness. Amy-Ruth Holt's essay shows that the guru Nityānanda's use of multimedia for his self-portraits blurs embodiment with energy as a mechanism for conveying and transmitting his sacred power to devotees. As discussed by Shandip Saha, photographs of the *mahārājas* in the Vallabha tradition were intended to enhance the leaders' status, but devotees responded to the circulation of such photographs by having photos or paintings made of themselves in worshipful poses before two-dimensional images of Kṛṣṇa.

Our cover image, Siona Benjamin's *Finding Home (Fereshteh) #75 "Lilith"* (2005), speaks to our themes of visual networks and belonging through the creative repurposing of Indic devotional imagery. The female figure is in a traditional devotional posture with her eyes lowered and hands held together in the *añjali mudrā* of honor and humility. It is a human gesture made to a respected other, including people and deities. The figure's thoughts, "You must save us from their wrath," seems a petition to a respected other, but who the "you" and "us" are must be filled in by the viewer based upon their own understanding of the image. The figure also invokes the Hindu iconography of divinity in that it is colored blue, which commonly indicates Kṛṣṇa in Indic painting. Further, part of the title of the painting is *fereshteh*, a Persian and Urdu word for "angel" that is etymologically linked to a Sanskrit term (*preṣyatā*). The cloth gracefully wrapped over the head has multireligious connotations, including the iconography of the Virgin Mary; the Jewish prayer shawl (*tallit*) as per the depicted blue bands, which is traditionally worn by men but today also by women if they choose; the head covering that Muslim women wear to pray (*ḥijāb*); and it resonates with women pulling the end of the saree (*pallu*) over their heads.

In a historical key, the painting seems to reclaim Lilith, Adam's exiled first wife, who is a controversial figure in Jewish tradition. The lettering at the bottom of the image (not shown on the cover) is "Lilith" spelled in Urdu-like script. Here, the figure is self-composed and steadfast amid a violent explosion depicted in a retake of Roy Lichtenstein's *Blam* (1962). The bold lines and colors of the composition bring its classical elements of Indian painting into the present day, where it intersects with the personal history of the artist, who is a Jewish Indian American who grew up in Bombay in a Marathi-speaking Bene Israel Jewish community (Benjamin n.d.). According to Benjamin, her style in this painting is also informed by the Bombay movie posters and Amar Chitra Katha comic books of her youth (Soltes 2015: 48). The color blue of the figure has an additional resonance for the artist: "Blue skin has become a symbol for me of being a Jewish woman of color" (Soltes 2015: 47). Her paintings provoke and complicate issues of her, and our, multifaceted identities of belonging through imaging.

This volume is an interdisciplinary venture in which analysis of logics and practices of looking is performed by historians, some of whom are professionally located as historians with a focus on religion (Andrews, Davis, Hawley, Patel, Pauwels, Pechilis, Saha, and Saul) and some of whom are art historians (Desai, Holt, and Mumtaz). There is an emerging scholarly literature on interdisciplinarity in the study of Indic materiality (Chatterjee, Guha-Thakurta, and Kar 2014) and visuality (Freitag 2014a; Motrescu-Mayes and Banks 2018). This volume is distinctive in its defined interdisciplinarity that brings together the history of religion and art history as well as its distinctive intervention in bringing together the fields of material culture and visual studies. There has been something of a bifurcation of the fields with historians of religion mainly gravitating toward studies of material culture and art historians gravitating toward studies of visual culture.

Both material culture and visual studies or visual culture have their own nuanced histories in the study of religion and art. Scholarship on material culture stems from key theoretical interventions on things, their agency, and circulation in anthropological and sociological works by Appadurai (1986), Latour (2005), and Miller (2005). For religion studies, this has meant an emphasis more on experiential encounters with religious objects that are not limited to their symbolic meanings, as demonstrated by both comparative studies (Arweck and Keenan 2006; Vásquez 2011; Houtman and Meyer 2012; Whitehead 2013; Plate 2014) and studies focused on Indic objects (Davis 1997; Flood 2009; Pintchman and Dempsey 2015; Narayanan 2015; Aktor 2017; Flueckiger 2021). Visual culture or visual studies emerged from a long history of interdisciplinary thinking, and as such, its genealogy is imagined in different ways (Elkins, Frank, and Manghani 2015). Many agree that key interventions include works by art historians Hal Foster (1988) and W. J. T. Mitchell (1994 and 2005), the anthropologist Alfred Gell (1998) on the agency of images, and the media studies scholar Nicholas Mirzoeff (1999) on counter-visuality.

Religion studies, in contrast, has had a "delayed cooperation" with visual studies (Dubuisson 2015). The editors of *Material Religion* journal (2009) noted two trends in studies of visual culture: one is to expand the range of materials considered to include more than objects deemed fine art, and the other approach does more to shift the object-centered focus of earlier methods toward a networked understanding more in tune with material culture. Both comparative (Plate 2002 and 2014; Morgan 2005 and 2012; Meyer and Stordalen 2019) and Indic-focused studies (Waghorne 2004; Pinney 2004; Dwyer 2006; Jain 2007; Davis 2009; Dehejia 2009; Freitag 2014a and 2014b; Holt and Pechilis 2019a and 2019b) illuminate this more interactive perspective on visuality and religion. The overlap between visual culture and material culture studies is apparent in that they both strive to reveal the situatedness of things, especially their networked quality, in which they contribute, derive, and display their power. The essays in this volume pay particular attention to this overlap, standing at the intersection of both these fields in their focus on the devotional visualities of Indic material cultures.

Devotion and Established Practices of Looking: *Rasa* and *Darśan*

In keeping with Indic devotional traditions' emphasis on participation, they authorize involvement. Historically, devotional participation sought to disrupt established practices of looking in order to assert the immediacy, directness, and validity of a devotee's experience. Two examples are devotion's intervention in the *rasa* theory of the arts and its different imaging of the gaze in the context of the established visual practices of *darśan*. In these instances, devotional perspectives transformed established practices of looking into agentive embodied participation, thus making visible and challenging the limitations of established practices.

Devotional traditions have inspired creativity in all forms of the arts, which engage their religiously transformative objectives with the affective transformations articulated by aesthetic theory. The *rasa* (taste; juice) theory of the arts was a complex Indic discourse on aesthetics by intellectuals writing in Sanskrit that originated circa 300 BCE with a foundational text on drama by Bharata (the *Nāṭyaśāstra*) and continued by turning the discussion toward literature for a millennium and a half before it "came to an end" in the early modern period (Pollock 2016: 39–41). It has endured as a way of understanding the arts. The multiple theories of *rasa* were modernized in the late colonial-nationalist movement period (Bhushan and Garfield 2017) and remain generative today across a wide spectrum of practices considered art (*kala*) in India (Schwartz 2004; Chakrabarti 2016). Though initial theories centralized the aesthetics of seeing drama (*dṛśyakāvya*) and subsequently were dominated by the concern with the aesthetics of hearing poetry (*śṛavyakāvya*), drama and poetry were not envisioned as entirely separate, since a drama can be read and a poem "depending upon the intrinsic qualities like powerful image-creative description, etc., will tend to become nearly, if not exactly, equal to a Dṛśyakāvya" (Hardikar 1994: 267). One of the key principles in the aesthetic analysis of *kāvya* is that the foundational emotion should be suggested by carefully crafted verbal imagery, rather than being directly stated such as in a *manoratha* or "desire/object of the mind" (see Saha and Pauwels chapters in this volume).

The central image of both devotional traditions and *rasa* theories is the human heart, and they offer distinctive ways to "see" via the heart. For devotional traditions, love of God is a habitation that in a transformative manner inspires, guides, and evaluates everything in view toward enabling the savoring of divine bliss. In *rasa* theory, the aim is to inhabit the experience of aestheticized emotional savoring: "Indian aesthetic theory was founded upon representation of human emotion in the literary artwork and our capacity not just to find the representation 'beautiful' but to *get inside* it" (Pollock 2016: 2). The person who could get inside it is theorized to be the *sahṛdaya*, literally "one of similar heart," such as the ideal spectator, connoisseur, or cultured audience who fully appreciates the aestheticized sentiment of a drama or poem. Discussing a commentary of Abhinavagupta (*c.* 1000), A. R. Hardikar states that a *sahṛdaya* is "made, not born" since that person has been acquainted with literature, has reflected on it, has assimilated the emotions represented by the character, and, thus, "whose stable emotions are capable of being triggered into a sympathetic resonance with the emotions portrayed" (Hardikar 1994: 265). Chakrabarti provides a contemporary description of the *sahṛdaya*:

> But even when suggested by absence, a durable sentiment is not yet the fully relishable savor called *rasa*. Only when this sentiment is delinked from any egotistic worldly pragmatic concern and depersonalized, then a certain heart, resonating in sympathy with other similar hearts, loses itself completely in the wondrous subjective self-savoring of the sentiment. *Notice that it is not the stable sentiment that re-emerges* out of the alchemical cuisine of determinants, consequents, and transient states, which is called *rasa*, but only the intuitive experience of it. One or more of these stable sentiments are transmuted into one

> or more of the nine *rasa*-experiences, the special aesthetic genres of the Erotic, the Comic, the Pathetic, the Furious, the Heroic, the Terrible, the Wondrous, the Hideous, and the Serene. (Chakrabarti 2016: 8)

The incorporation of the ninth *rasa* (*śānta*, the "Serene"), an addition to the original eight and inclusive of devotion, was elaborated and contested, in part because religious literature and artistic literature had long been separated in the *rasa* intellectual discourse (see the extensive literature on this contestation in Cahill 2014). Abhinavagupta authoritatively accepted the addition and located devotion in the Serene aesthetic genre. The calm clarity of the *śānta rasa* is achieved by the connoisseur's awareness of a reflexive consciousness in which "one recognition moves the witness from private experience (*bhava*) to a universal experience (*rasa*)," followed by a second recognition that "moves him from a world that merely appears *to* him (i.e., seems to *be* before him), to one that is essentially his contemplation of it (e.g., one that is *for* him)" (Gerow 1994: 192).

The *rasa* theory was used by devotional groups to create mutually informing texts and practices. A Sufi example illustrates the application of the theoretical principles in a transformed manner. Sufi master Shaikh Quṭban Suravardī's *Mirigāvatī* (1503) is "the perfect instance of the Sufis' use of the Sanskritic technology of the sublimation of desire into divine love in order to express their own ideology of Islamic monotheism" (Behl 2012: 36). The text describes a journey through the emotions to progress on a defined path to higher stages of mystical awareness. "In a sense, each episode asks the listener with heart (*sahṛdaya*) to understand the nature of that particular emotion and to turn it around, moving on to the next stage when a particular lesson is learned" (Behl 2012: 37). In this volume, Mumtaz's chapter illuminates Sufi interpretations of love (*prem-rasa*).

Also in the sixteenth century, the intervention of intellectuals from the Bengali Gauḍīya Vaiṣṇava tradition changed the *rasa* theory with a distinctive theologizing of the *rasa* aesthetic (Haberman 1988: 30–9). This had been precipitated by the circulation of the *Bhāgavata Purāṇa*, celebrated for both its literary and devotional qualities, from the tenth century onward. Rūpa Gosvāmin's theologizing authorized real-world devotees to become in essence the original characters in the *Bhāgavata Purāṇa*, who constitute a source for the *rasa* experience. "Rūpa's greatest task . . . was to devise a *sādhana* that would enable the *bhakta* to enter and participate in the dramatic world of the Vraja-līlā, thereby generating the essential *sthāyi-bhāva* of love for Kṛṣṇa, the foundation of the ultimately meaningful experience of *bhakti-rasa*, Kṛṣṇa-prema" (Haberman 1988: 39; see also Okita 2017). Scholarship that engages ethnography shows the enactment of this real-world performance in contemporary times, through the ritual role-playing, singing, and somatic visualization of *bhakti rasa* among Bengali devotees (Haberman 1988; Sanford 2008). The body of the *bhakta* is repositioned at the center of the genesis and realization of *rasa*, in the context of a community of god and devotees. The multisensory image of experiencing the *bhakti rasa* of love for Kṛṣṇa is one of a community of belonging through one of the five *bhakti rasa* modes: neutrality (*śānta*), love, parentage, friendship, and servitude. In this volume, one or more of these five traditional modes of *rasa* engagement with the divine are noted in the essays by Pauwels, Saha, and Desai, and one of the traditional nine *rasas*, disgust (or the Hideous), is further expanded upon in the essay by Pechilis.

Bhakti's performative visuality in particular challenged other established practices of seeing, contrasting, for example, with the hierarchically mediated and charged experience of *darśan*. A temple practice since classical times (Willis 2009), *darśan* attracted scholarly attention in the 1980s (Eck 1998 [1981]; Babb 1981) and quickly gained the status of a metonymic representation of Hinduism and perhaps even of India (Vidal 2006 and 2016). As such, *darśan* has received recent critical attention from scholars, including, for example, a study discussing the centrality of yogic *dṛṣti* (focused gaze) rather than the related *darśan* in Jain temple practice (Cort 2012) and a study focusing on the physical appearance, especially ornamentation, of icons in Hindu temples (Packert 2010). More helpful for our purposes here are studies that focus on new ways of *darśan* as a practice of looking. While it is "problematic" to consider *darśan* as "a unique Hindu manner of seeing" (Vidal 2016: 54), *darśan* in Hindu temples is institutionally enacted on a daily basis across the subcontinent; for this reason, a number of the images in this volume typically are found in temple or shrine settings, and their analysis engages the concept of *darśan*. The term encompasses a status differential between the participants. The traditional homologizing of king and deity plays out in the *darśan* practice of seeing, both of whom represent the superior participant in the *darśan* encounter between unequal participants. "The relation between beings of such different status as the ones who come into contact on the occasion of *darshan* should be normally more distant" (Vidal 2006: 5), suggesting that what is central to *darśan* is the perception of a constructed intimacy across the structures of distance operative in the temple or the ceremonial viewing of a royal figure.

This practice could be described by ocularcentrism, a concept developed in theorizing western visual practices: "in the objectivist paradigm generated by traditional ocularcentrism, the subject is invariably positioned either in the role of dominating observer or in the role of an observable subject, submissive before the gaze of power" (Levin 1993: 4). The *pūjā* ceremony's careful staging limits liberal access to the main icon to the priests, who work with care and coordination. Simultaneously, the devotees are in the hall, crowded and jostling for the line of sight to the icon. This is a controlled ritual of "reciprocal recognition" (Elison 2018: 18), producing a visibility that hopefully prefigures good things but whose scopic regime is structured around distance with the divine giving *darśan* (*darśan dena*) and the devotee taking it (*darśan lena*), which lends itself to a political homology of submission and potentially a gaze of opprobrium. Drawing on Sophie Hawkins's discussion of *darśan* as a technique of control, Christiane Brosius identifies a coercive capacity to *bhakti* when it is used to make nationalist claims in Hindu fundamentalist videos (Hawkins 1999; Brosius 2005: 107–10).

When the *darśan* visual practice is recontextualized outside of the *pakka* (perfected) Hindu temple, its ritual visuality is challenged and changed by other ways of seeing. At urban wayside shrines, the processes of ordinary humanity enframe the icons. Devotees can publicly perform their own *darśan* at their own convenience. The material visibility of the shrine is situated in and disrupts "a socially embedded vision" of order, cleanliness, and social distinction (Larios and Voix 2018). Instead, these religious structures are embedded in a visual culture of mass-produced images that compete with religious images that might also be found in a temple; they are publicly recognized yet lack authorization; and they make the survival of communities of the marginalized visible (Elison 2018: 81–3). In another example, villagers' practices of looking at mass-produced two-dimensional images in their homes are characterized by a sensory "corpothetics" as related to the images' iconic "non-absorptive directness," the villagers' customizing of them, and their ritualized treatment of the images, including disposal of them (Pinney 2004: 191–7). In this volume, essays profile different *darśan* spaces and modes such as home shrines (Andrews), selfless ritual worship (*sevā*) that transforms pictorial representations into living objects of devotion (*citrajī*s) (Saha), the complex simultaneity of portrait and *mūrti* in images of Sahajānanda Svāmī of the Svāminārāyaṇa community (Desai), and modern media images of a contemporary guru (Holt).

Visualities of the cinema (Pauwels) and the museum (Patel) are also analyzed in this volume. In terms of the visuality of the cinema (which is the original domain of C. Metz's theory of the "scopic regime" [1982 (1977)] that Jay [1988] adapted to typologize modern visual conventions in art), there is an interocularity between the gazes of *dṛṣṭi* and *naẓar*, with the former enacted via camerawork to encode the intensity of *darśan* for the spectator and the latter voyeuristically encoding the erotic gaze of lovers suggestive of, but not portraying, physical contact (Taylor 2002). Intriguingly, a shared convention is to start the gaze at the feet of the icon or lover and pan upwards (see Desai and Pechilis chapters this volume). In terms of the visuality of the museum, Shaila Bhatti has argued for museums in the Indic context—her example is Lahore Museum—to bring in cultural practices of looking, instead of locking them out:

> consumption is less about viewing an object/image as evidence of historical chronology or cultural authenticity and more about emotional engagement based on other experiences and idioms that recontextualize the objects and museum as part of an interocular culture. . . . Spectatorship in South Asia, once relocated within indigenous ways of seeing (*darshan/dekhna/nazar*) in various visual arenas, demonstrates that the audience is attracted by objects inviting them into a visceral and interested interpretation, which expands and extends beyond the objective to incorporate aspects of history, culture, wonder, novelty and fantasy. (Bhatti 2012: 224; see also Bhatti 2021)

Bhakti images do precisely this—they create conditions that authorize "visceral and interested interpretation" through practices of looking. *Bhakti* itself is not represented as originating in temple culture. The ur-text, the Sanskrit *Bhagavad Gītā*, has Kṛṣṇa explain and extol *bhakti* on a battlefield. Even the poet-saints of a so-called *saguṇa* (imagining the divine with characteristics) tradition such as Tamil Śiva-*bhakti* see forms of the divine in named towns beyond simply recording iconographic description (Prentiss 2002). The *bhakti* poet-saints' songs were brought into temple culture over time, in a carefully scripted manner that was clearly marked to support, but not overtake, normative temple ritual proceedings (Prentiss 1999); in part, *bhakti* addressed a question common to all priestly traditions of how to engage people who traditionally are structurally positioned as an audience. We have already seen from the example of *bhakti rasa* that *bhakti* challenges the idea of a segregated and removed audience by its emphasis on diverse forms of agentive embodied participation. The essays in this volume examine the use of *bhakti* images in the creation of devotional visualities. They identify practices of looking that make space for one's own devotional participation, namely, materializing memory, mirroring and immaterializing portraits, and shaping the return look.

While each of these selections draws out an important feature of devotional visuality, the individual studies themselves show several points of intersection and comparative themes not bound by their sectional placement. Readers will likely find much in the cross-comparison of individual chapters outside of these sections based upon their own areas of interest. Some of these intersections may be found in the usage of similar terminologies and ideologies; some in investigations of similar religious institutions or people; some in similar regional or language-based geographies, literatures, and histories; and others through the similar usage, style, creation, or purpose of comparable imagery. These chapters are not bound, other than in the material sense of the printed book itself, to a singular arrangement, and instead, call upon the readers' own abilities to imagine or finish the project that we have started.

Introduction to the Themes and Essays

Materializing Memory

"Materializing memory" is a phrase that emerged from reflection on the essays by Richard Davis and Ashlee Andrews, and its connection to authenticity as amplified in the essays by R. Jeremy Saul and Shruti Patel. A subsequent internet search revealed that a book has been published with that title (Munteán, Plate, and Smelik 2017), which provides a comprehensive review of the literature in its cleverly titled first chapter that reminds us of debates concerning the nature of material items (object vs. thing) and agency as it concludes that

> Memory is thus no longer conceived of as a sole privilege of human beings who use objects to remember but rather as an activity deeply entangled with nonhuman things and processes. Besides foregrounding the role of objects in human practices of memory, our use of the phrase "materializing memory" in the title of this book also indicates our intention to locate and trace memory as a practice *of* and *within* the material world. (Munteán, Plate, and Smelik 2017: 15)

The chapters in this section of the present volume advance such theorizing by showing us a networked multiplicity of circulations of both material images and human beings that establish and provoke memory.

Davis's essay signals the issue straightaway via a quote from an artisan that "everyone knows what the gods look like," which affords a primacy to the images of gods via their ubiquity in material and memory; in fact, the artisan expresses that he feels quite secondary in the process (see also Pauwels, this volume, who provides similar evidence of image currency from a scene in a documentary film). Davis's essay recoups the intertwined agencies of visual image, producer, and consumer in a discussion of the emergence of a "devotional economy" in the earliest development of mechanically reproduced religious imagery by nineteenth-century Calcutta artisans. Pilgrims' desire to remember a temple visit served as a catalyst to transforming hereditary artistic practices toward making indexical images for pilgrims as consumers. Itinerant traditional artisans—"picture showmen" (*patua*)—who settled in the area of the newly constructed Kalighat temple transformed their image-making from scrolls to single sheets in response to pilgrims to the temple who wished to acquire "souvenirs of their religious trip, portable objects of remembrance that referred iconically to the site visited." The single-sheet images produced were not of the temple or crowd scenes, but instead evoked the *darśan* practice of looking directly at the distinctive temple icon of Kālī, rendered with the new materials of watercolor on paper. These images were themselves remembered by other artisans associated with an art firm, Chore Bagan Art Studio, who used a chromolithographic process to create images of the Kālī icon in more detailed and color-saturated fashion, adding to the drama a curtain framing the icon that "owes more to the world of theater then becoming popular in urban India than to the enshrinement of a temple."

Circulations of being there, memory, and production also took other forms that distinctively signaled the widening audience for mass-produced devotional images, creating visual relationships with foreigners and between wealthy and less well-off citizens. The Calcutta Art Studio created a collection genre of the "Scrap Book" that contained multiple images based on mythology labeled in Hindi, Bengali, and English, which "sought to reach a market that extended beyond Bengali Hindus, and could potentially include the many Europeans living in or visiting the capital of British India, and beyond." The simultaneity of colonial and conventional Indic artistic techniques rendered the images legible to a diverse invested audience. "Durgā Pūjā Shrine" images, popular when the festivities were primarily held in the home, situated the frontal iconography of the gods in the home shrines of wealthy landowners, which brought two-dimensional images of their elaborate three-dimensional home shrines to a mass audience for display in their more modest home shrines.

This iconographic-focused mode of memory circulates in expansive practices of looking in contemporary times, as Andrews's essay shows. Her focus is the home shrines of Bengali American women in the greater Chicago metropolitan area, which they personally craft (Andrews with justification calls it "artistry," though she notes that one of the women she interviewed good-naturedly deflected the characterization). Making such shrines is contoured by material realities: "Unlike their mothers, grandmothers, and mothers-in-law who typically inherited ancestral deity images and were eventually given charge of their in-law's pre-existing shrine after marriage, most of the Bengali-American women I worked with immigrated to the U.S. without their in-laws and with very few deity images or *pūjā* implements." Also, the traditional Indian architectural feature of a home *pūjā* room cannot be expected across the United States, so that these women "constructed and worshipped at shrines in their guest and master bedroom closets, in home office bookcases, on bedside tables, or in IKEA cabinets repurposed with extra shelving and track lighting." Material things displayed go beyond iconographical images to include "pictures of ancestors and family gurus, souvenirs from travels in India or around the U.S., gifts from friends and family, and ancestral heirlooms." At least one woman that Andrews interviewed contrasted her mother-in-law's shrine's focus on her favored deity, Gopāl, with her own shrine's focus on her Bengali Hindu identity.

As one hears the voices of the Bengali American women in Andrews's essay, it becomes clear that home shrines are a potent and poignant creative space for women to grapple with issues of concern to them specifically, and to expect help from the material images of deities, ancestors, and memories to clarify and address those issues. In the U.S. context, one of the issues is having an accessible, safe, and validating space to practice Hinduism; one of the women tells of her children's experience with denigrating things being said about Hinduism in school. The photos in the chapter show the deliberative thingness of the home shrines, instantiating an abundance of experiences and connections; another woman tells Andrews that "everything has a story." One gets a sense of the interactive layering of stories as a present and palpable horizon of possibility made real by the diaspora women's artistry, an indexical "I was there" and "I am here."

The chapters by Saul and Patel call attention to the use of memory to create an institution that signals an authenticity of devotion to a broader public. A special issue, "Temple Publics—Religious Institutions and the Construction of Contemporary Hindu Communities," in the *International Journal of Hindu Studies* (2009) raises issues of changes in institutional expressions of "a religion called Hinduism" (Reddy and Zavos 2009: 242). Drawing on Joanne Waghorne's (2004) work on modern temple building in Madras and the diaspora, the editors note a "critical transformation, through which notions of 'public' related to temples emerges: different temples invoke devotees not so much as *subjects* of the sovereign deity, but as a *constituency* within a competitive ritual marketplace" (Reddy and Zavos 2009: 246). Applying this insight to modern temples involves thinking about communities as constructed in various places at various times, instead of as a "natural," ongoing, and reified identity (Reddy and Zavos 2009: 252). The temple is one example of a place where a Hindu community is constructed, as shown in the diverse chapters in the special issue. "The many divergent perceptions, desires, views, needs, and analyses of these publics, and their participation in the discourses of religion, produce not only communities but the space of the temple itself" (Reddy and Zavos 2009: 254).

The chapters by Saul and Patel in this volume advance this discussion by detailing the work of devotion as a discursive project in which communities construct and constitute both their own authenticity and that of material institutions of display—in this case, temples and a museum. Devotional agency that materially shapes temple displays today challenges the traditional script of devotional practice as an ancillary formation that supplements the priests' activities, and the devotional construction of a museum represents a new mode beyond traditional religious space for the community to represent itself. In these cases, devotional motivation claims for itself a foundation in and generative power of an authenticity promoted by participants. This is less a situation of "cultural enclosure" (Reddy and Zavos 2009: 256, citing Mazzarella 2002: 388) than a *bhakti*-framed practice of looking based on a claimed authenticity that innovates and arranges material images as a statement of and reference point for the public display of devotional identity, community, authenticity, and authority.

Saul analyzes "four Bālājī [Hanumān] temples in Rajasthan to discuss how Marwari patronage has materially transformed the visuality of devotion in that region in the last thirty-plus years." The four temples are the Salasar Bālājī temple and a temple that follows its devotional style, the Icchāpūrṇ Bālājī temple, and the Mehandipur Bālājī temple and a temple that follows its devotional style, the Ratangarh Bālājī temple. The Salasar and Mehandipur temples "are the most renowned manifestations of Hanumān in northwestern India," yet they are distinguished by a marker of authenticity: the Salasar temple resides in the traditional ancestral region of the Marwari, whereas the Mehandipur temple, located farther south and east from the other temples considered in the essay, "makes no claim to any aspect of Marwari identity." They thus represent "opposite extremes of Marwari visual engagement."

The complex construction of Marwari authenticity embeds this ancestry within material action that shapes not only the temple but the image of Hanumān itself. As successful merchants, the Marwari community could leverage that identity and wealth to contour religious imagery, often in "collaboration" with priests. In the early twentieth century, Marwari merchants who were based in large cities outside of Rajasthan, such as in Kolkata, built large mansions in their ancestral lands, which Saul sees as a "harbinger" for the merchants' building and patronage of often large-scale temples to Hanumān in the 1990s and beyond. The history of the Salasar temple is instructive. It was a modest structure in the nineteenth and for most of the twentieth century. What changed as the twentieth century concluded was the development of Marwari devotional organizations dedicated to Hanumān/Bālājī in the 1980s, in the midst of the popular rise of devotion to Rāma across India in the 1980s and 1990s and accompanying renewed emphasis on pilgrimage. Members of the Marwari community began to refurbish the Salasar temple, constructing a new passageway for circumambulation and adorning the temple walls with silver plaques, often with Marwari donor names on them and specification of the donor's dual connections with northern Rajasthan and a remote commercial city. A contrast Saul draws with the Mehandipur temple reveals the degree to which Marwari merchants' attention, prominent at Salasar, is a transformative modern expression of devotion in the context of economic liberalization.

The Marwari community perceives its wealth to be tied to the miraculous powers of Bālājī, and its Vaiṣṇava aesthetic of devotion has created a new image of Bālājī that appears at the Icchāpūrṇ temple. Obtaining miracles through Bālājī has become a "core ideology of practice," relating to modern economic liberalization's "promotion of individualistic aspiration requiring miracles." Furthermore, "visual splendor from patronage substantiated Bālājī's reputation for great miracles, since donations are a measure of the efficacy of a deity." The distinctive image of Bālājī at Icchāpūrṇ signifies majesty: it is a larger-than-life-sized anthropomorphic Jaipur marble sculpture seated on a throne and adorned with a large crown. Stories about the donor's visions of this form of Bālājī that precipitated his creation of the temple, as well as visual features of the temple, support the promise of miracles for the public. The new icon and these temple elements visually present the authenticity of Marwari ancestry, wealth, and their strong connection to the power of Bālājī's divine miracles.

Patel's chapter traces the layers of Svāminārāyaṇa *bhakti*, charting shifts in presence, authority, encounter, and display to reveal the changing relationship of history and devotion through materiality. In the nineteenth century, the journeys and activities of the founder, Sahajānanda, and the sanctified materiality or spiritually charged objects, space, and images he handled, encountered, and distributed served as an "unwritten archive" that created a devotional community mediated by materiality alongside doctrine or beliefs. This culture of devotion introduced and integrated Sahajānanda across time and space, chiefly via objects, that created a nonliterate connection, energized by soteriology, emotional affect, charisma, social capital, and access to the past among devotees. It emplotted (placed in context) discrete acts of encounter between Sahajānanda and individual devotees in an emerging narrative of his authenticity and authority. The devotional acts of visiting, gifting, receiving, and then recalling these interactions reflect a community emphasizing forms of history. This challenges the view that texts of *bhakti* frequently invite us to view a formative representation of devotional history, and thus an often-privileged interpretation, as constituted by various literary and linguistic expressions. Yet since devotional culture is oriented to specific audiences, regions, and their conditions, and further, because it is sustained over time in diverse contexts, *bhakti*'s long-term nature rests on incorporating a range of frameworks and practices to suit the historical circumstances. To understand this aspect of change between religious community formation and later adaptations, we must grasp the efficacy of visual and normatively secular modes, not solely the written record or imagery normally circumscribed by religious specialists and space.

Into the twentieth century, the possession as well as display of this legacy of materiality is linked to claims of religious veracity and historical legitimacy. In 2011, the Narnārayaṇ Dev Gādī (Ahmedabad Gādī), which self-identifies as as "The Original Shree Swaminarayan Sampradaya," opened the Shree Swaminarayan Museum in Ahmedabad, Gujarat. The museum continues to braid together history and devotion after two centuries, but it does so differently than before in its presentation of objects on visible display for devotees to take *darśan* while simultaneously presenting them as artifacts that have and establish history as indicated by their framing in glass cases with accompanying explanatory text. The combination reveals how contemporary desires for broader audiences and secular perceptions now inflect foundational narratives. By evoking notions of culture and history, the forum of a museum helps to generate a broader public authorization of a very specific devotional vision.

Mirroring and Immaterializing Portraits

Five of the essays in this volume relate to the topic of portraiture (Mumtaz, Saha, Hawley, Holt, and Desai). Art historian Padma Kaimal has compellingly argued "that portraiture was indigenous to India," against past scholarship that had in essence othered India in a "necessity of accommodating Indian art as some unusual case" (Kaimal 1999: 60, 66). Noting the scholarly discussion of the perceived realism and idealism of portraits as culturally inflected, she points to the "prominent even constitutive role of indexicality in portraiture," since indexicality holds in tension history and present, recognition and suggestion, individual and "extra artistic" features, and representation and aesthetics, which "can . . . be meaningful across cultures" (Kaimal 1999: 65). Contouring the field by limiting it to human subjects and excluding visual stereotypes of human types, gods, and personifications of natural elements and animals, she defines the portrait

> as a visual image composed of a collage of elements selected to capture something of the essential nature of specific human subjects who lived within the span of historical time. In order to function as a portrait, an image need not adhere to any particulars of the subject's original appearance but it must somehow successfully articulate within its own culture its role as an index to that person's extra-artistic reality. (Kaimal 1999: 66)

Kaimal proposes that *bhakti* is the extra-artistic reality that makes sculptures of people on the walls of Tamil south Indian temples in the tenth century legible as portraits (Kaimal 1999: 132). Their physical features and postures of worship differ, as described in her comparison of two portraits side by side in the Gōmuktīśvara temple at Tiruvaduturai, dated to 932 CE (Kaimal 1999: 125), one of which is younger ("his ribs project like those of a quickly-growing young man") and "caught up in fervent prayer . . . [he] closes his eyes, arches his back and raises his hands above his head" (Kaimal 1999: 125). The other is perhaps older, suggested by his "sharp brow line," taller height, and posture: "He inclines his head gently toward the *liṅga* [image for worship] instead of throwing his head back, and he clasps his hands in front of his chest. His hips sway only slightly toward the *liṅgapīṭha*" (Kaimal 1999: 126). *Bhakti* provided both a common rationale for rendering these select people in portraits and a way to distinguish them by their devotional gestures that showed how "[t]he body was the instrument through which one worshipped. Representation of the individual devotee's entire, idiosyncratic body was, then, entirely appropriate on the god's house, especially for a devotee who had helped to build that house" (Kaimal 1999: 133).

Significantly, many of the portraits were positioned such that they would welcome visitors to the temple, modeling recognized gestures of a devotional stance to them (Kaimal 1999: 125, 128). This is a mirroring, in which one is encouraged to see oneself in the image and apply it. Three of the essays relating to portraiture in this volume, those by Mumtaz, Saha, and Hawley, fruitfully advance our understanding of such mirroring. Murad Khan Mumtaz brings us into the world of Indic devotional Islam, identifying ways in which Sufis in India and Pakistan see themselves in *bhakti* poetry, music, and art. The point of entry is a contemporary Pakistani *qawwālī* singer's performance of Kabīr's poetry, including the singer's own commentary, which "gives us insights into how Indo-Muslims have not only identified with devotional ideas shared among Indic spiritualities, but have also used these voices to define themselves." Mumtaz argues for a historical understanding of the prominent poet-saint's significance to the contemporary Indo-Muslim public that can be gained through an examination of literature in Persian and Urdu scripts and north Indian schools of miniature painting, rather than the primary lens of Devanāgarī sources as in past scholarship.

A distinctive view of Kabīr emerges from Sufi Persian and Urdu literature and painting from the late sixteenth century to the first half of the seventeenth century, that he "represent[ed] a legitimate path outside the limits of Islam." For example, a late sixteenth-century hagiography composed by Dehlavi, a Chishtī Sufi, includes Kabīr. Into the seventeenth century, Mughal emperor Shah Jahan's son, Prince Dārā Shikoh, possessed a painting of prominent Sufis, including the prince's spiritual master Mulla Shah in the upper register, Indic saints, and Kabīr and his son Kamāl Das in the lower register. He also composed a book of utterances that situates the sayings of Kabīr as "within the fold of Islamic spirituality, tracing them back to themes found in the Quran and Hadith" by using a Sufi vocabulary to characterize Kabīr's ideas. In the same period, the Sufi poet-saint Naushā wrote poetry that resonates with and responds to Kabīr's, in effect translating his ideas into Sufi philosophy.

The figure of Kamāl Das has received less scholarly attention, but in Mumtaz's argument, he may have served as a closer mirror in which Indic Sufis could see themselves. Paintings into the eighteenth century depict him as a handsome youth wearing a cap, a patchwork cloak, and a black cord, all of which associate him with "Muslim antinomian groups." In one image, he is pictured seated next to Dārā Shikoh as a youth, suggesting a meeting that could not chronologically have occurred. Suggested by the images as well as biographical and musical interpretation, "Kabīr's path finds its perfection in the figure of the youthful, and therefore virginal and virtuous, Kamāl, who then becomes a mirror reflecting Kabīr's own inner state" as a "paragon of the perfect devotee."

Shandip Saha discusses the developmental usage of devotional images rendered in painting, drawing, and photography in the Vallabha community or Puṣṭi Mārga in western India, stemming from and transforming the temple and home worship practices that may have originated with Vallabha (1479–1531) himself. The traditional practices involved the ritual expression of *bhakti* in both private and public temples through selfless acts of devotional service known as *sevā*. The images used in such worship are three-dimensional sculptures made of metal and are understood to be Kṛṣṇa's own form and self-manifestation (*svarūpa*), vivified by the devotional attitude of devotees. In particular, the image of Kṛṣṇa as a child is favored. Vallabha's son and grandson authorized worship with pictorial two-dimensional images (*citrajī*s); by the eighteenth century, selflessly serving such images (*citra sevā*) became popular among royalty and also for large outdoor festivals. The Vallabha tradition stands out for such practices, even using life-sized *citrajī*s of Śrīnāthjī in temples, such as in Mumbai and Rajasthan. Today, use of *citrajī*s also occurs in home worship shrines, and instructional videos on the internet can be found that provide details about the ways in which home worship with pictorial images differs from temple worship with metal sculptures.

Intriguingly, the Vallabha leader *mahārāja* Govardhanlāl (1862–1934) sought to restore the image of the Puṣṭi Mārga after scandal by turning the town of Nathdwara in Rajasthan into "an important center for arts and religious learning." The artisans created a hybrid style of Indian and European techniques to respond to wealthy urban patrons, and portraits of individuals were painted in a photographic style. The *mahārāja*s were prominent subjects of such paintings. Photographs made as the basis of the paintings themselves became popular and were circulated to encourage personal devotion to the *mahārāja*s: "a compilation of photographic *citrajī*s of *mahārāja*s across western India would be published in 1923 with the intent of making the visual argument that the *mahārāja*s were indeed living manifestations of Kṛṣṇa." And this was not the only literal instance of putting oneself in the picture—a mirror of oneself as a mirror of devotion for display to others—that occurred. *Manoratha*s, understood in the Puṣṭi Mārga as a "cherished desire or dream of a *mahārāja* or devotee to perform *sevā* to Śrīnāthjī or another important Puṣṭi Mārga *svarūpa* in a way that reflects the individual's own personal relationship with the image," began to be created. Some of them pictured lavish special *sevā*s by *mahārāja*s, but groups of devotees and families also had themselves photographed or painted in a stance of devotional reverence, standing with hands in the prayerful *añjali mudrā* before a *citrajī*.

John Stratton Hawley's discussion of portraits of Sūrdās, from mid-seventeenth-century illustrated manuscript folios to mid-twentieth-century prints to present-day images on the internet, shows us mirroring in at least two ways: the visual intertextuality of earlier and later images, and the visual shaping of Sūrdās's identity by the cumulative effects of the visual intertextuality that create recognizable visual variations associated with the "same" personage, Sūrdās. Taking as his point of departure two prominent images of the poet-saint on the internet today, one that portrays the poet-saint as contemplative and one that portrays him as singing to a child form of Kṛṣṇa, Hawley traces each historically through multiple modern formats and notes significant details of their rendering.

As to the contemplative image, Hawley considers whether it might have emerged from a specifically Puṣṭimārgi environment, as several of its features at first glance seem to suggest, but in the end, he is struck by visual resonances that connect it to one of the very earliest images of Sūrdās that we have, probably dating to a time before the Vallabhites took up permanent residence in the Mewar region. The image of Sūrdās singing to a child form of Kṛṣṇa has a more elaborate traceable history, which involved much sleuthing. Noting that the motif of the child Kṛṣṇa is by no means the most prominent one among poems that circulated in Sūr's own century, the sixteenth, Hawley is particularly drawn to the first extant illustrated manuscript of "Sur's Ocean" (*Sūrsāgar*), which was made in Udaipur, the capital of Mewar. It is entirely dominated by the child-Kṛṣṇa theme. About that set of paintings Hawley says, "[T]he Amar Singh *Sūrsāgar* was the first to generate a truly stable image of the poet. . . . Sūr is distinctly recognizable as the same person and no page fails to display his image." As Hawley deftly demonstrates, iconicity has a long history.

Ankur Desai and Amy-Ruth Holt's essay subjects have a distinctive relationship to mirroring. At its widest, the issue in this case is how to represent the unseen. This is different from Kaimal's "extra artistic" quality of a human portrait, since she excludes images of the divine from her analysis and the subjects in Desai and Holt's essays are gurus, who straddle the line between human and divine. The nature of the guru also renders these essays different from Birgit Meyer and Terje Stordalen's paradigm-shifting edited volume on "specific figurations and sensations of the unseen across Judaism, Christianity and Islam" (Meyer and Stordalen 2019: 1). What that volume argues against is the common assumption that a "fundamental feature" of these three religions is that they "reject the use of images," supported by "theological and ideological apologies" (Meyer and Stordalen 2019: 2). Instead, the editors' focus is "towards a broader exploration of sets of practices through which humans mediate and sense the unseen, and struggle over legitimate ways in doing so" (Meyer and Stordalen 2019: 5). En route, they raise significant issues such as contextualizing the Second Commandment with other biblical passages and with humanities and social science studies of artifacts; contextualizing visuality with other experiential sensations used to perceive the unseen; and "attending to the ways in which images are employed to conceal as much as they show, depicting the 'real absence' of an unseen God" (Meyer and Stordalen 2019: 3–4).

The essays by Holt and Desai both focus on Hindu traditions. In Hinduism, the majority of philosophies and practices do not make a dramatic separation between seen and unseen—one can get to the sacred through the sensual. A pan-Indian example of this phenomenon is the figure of the guru, a concept of a spiritual master that appears across multiple Indic traditions. The guru or spiritual master is both human and the object of devotion. It is not that the guru is unseen; instead, the guru is "uncontainable" (Copeman and Ikagame 2012). Murad Khan Mumtaz (2020) shows us that devotional practices related to portraits (Persian *shabīh*, "likeness") of Sufi saints served as aids to meditation in seventeenth-century Mughal India. His case study is the daughter of Emperor Shah Jahan, Princess Jahanara Begum, who commissioned portraits of her spiritual master Mulla Shah. In a gendered logic, the portrait allowed the princess to see (*naẓar* and *dīdan* are the terms most frequently used in Sufi treatises and hagiographies) her spiritual master regularly, since his gatherings were of his male devotees and he only rarely met with female spiritual disciples. Via the portrait, she could experience his presence and communicate with him. The practice of looking with portraits also allows "the devotee to witness the transcendent divinity—which in its essential reality is beyond physical representation or likeness—residing in the perfected human being, the *insān al-kāmil*" (Mumtaz 2020). Thus, she used the portrait as a "portal" to access higher spiritual states, such as seeing a sacred gathering in which the Prophet is with his companions and accompanied by saints, and to experience intense love of the divine beloved, who is understood by Jahanara Begum and more widely in Indo-Muslim culture to be the "colorless" beyond the colors of the portrait. The view that there is a strong connection among vision, visualization, and materiality circulated in other traditions as well, such as in the literatures of Tantra (Timalsina 2015; Biernacki 2017).

The chapters in this volume by Holt and Desai advance this discussion by showing practices of looking that immaterialize portraits. As they demonstrate, the issue is not how to represent the unseen by keeping the boundary between seen and unseen intact but to blur the boundary. *Bhakti* prioritizes embodied experience, and displays of *bhakti* to god or guru are bodily. But what about the body of the guru? What visually makes the guru's body signify something other than sameness with devotees? How is the line between human and divine not just crossed but dismantled and reconfigured in the ways in which the guru's body is imagined, performed, and portrayed? (On related issues of in-betweenness, see Pechilis and Dempsey 2016.)

Amy-Ruth Holt analyzes the imagery of the contemporary Tamil guru Paramahaṃsa Nityānanda (or "Nithyananda") at his temples in Columbus (Delaware), Ohio, Los Angeles (Montclair) and San Jose (Milpitas) in California, and on the internet. Resonating with Desai's chapter, Holt also notes that several of the images of deities at the Columbus temple resemble the guru and had their faces carved by him, "suggesting that they were meant to be self-portraits of the guru himself." Comparatively pointing to select art historical examples of painted and sculpted images that have been interpreted to signal both the human and the divine, she underscores the point that the living guru is able to enact a "visual multiplicity" via his material self-portraits and operationalize it to spread his persona and philosophy abroad and bestow his grace upon his viewers. There is a "visual primacy" to Nityānanda's program of self-portraits that he has developed into a core feature of his guru *bhakti* through both traditional and modern-media-related portraiture, which may provide an important link for understanding the historic imagery of gurus more widely.

Holt discusses the deep imbrication of the guru's bodily form with temple sculptures large, small, and onscreen. An unusual element is that a large "cut-out" of the guru, made from a life-sized printed image of his photograph, stands adjacent to the sculptures of the deity in the main sanctum and is simultaneously worshipped. And then there is the guru's live performativity, made accessible to a global audience via the internet, his satellite Nithyananda TV, his main website, podcasts, and videos. A live *satsaṅga* broadcast or an online "Oneness Capsule" video, where the guru dresses to ritually appear as various deities, is understood to transmit the "cosmic energy" or *śakti* of the guru, which may cause devotees to fall into fits of ecstasy or perform various tantric acts such as a hopping-like levitation, blind reading, the transmutation of objects, and healing. The basis of this philosophy is the tantric *siddha* theory of the immaterial subtle body and its yoga-based power centers or *chakra*s that align with select deities in the temple program. The repetitive ritual use of the guru's image moves between the material and immaterial with the aim of breaking down the self-imposed boundaries dividing these two ideals. Before the start of any worship, devotees are told to declare that cosmic energy exists, it is embodied in the guru and images, and that they access this power through worship, entering in and partaking of this cosmic energy, and thus becoming part of the visual multiplicity and cosmic materiality; as in the guru's words, "my mission is not to prove my divinity, it is to prove *your* divinity."

Ankur Desai analyzes early nineteenth-century textual descriptions and painted depictions of Sahajānanda Svāmī (1781–1830), the founder of the Svāminārāyaṇa *sampradāya* tradition. Taking his cue from a hagiographical description of the body of Sahajānanda multiplying into twelve simultaneous forms distinguished by different moods during a festival, Desai argues that images of Sahajānanda reflected "a flexible form of *bhakti*, or a devotional model that did not pit the limitations of worldly or historical existence against the realm of divine possibility, but rather aided in their coalescence." The tradition centers around images of Kṛṣṇa, some of which seem to be an appropriation of stylistic elements from the Śrīnāthjī images of the Puṣṭi Mārga or Vallabha community (see Saha this volume). Sahajānanda is considered by some select adherents to be a manifestation of Kṛṣṇa. As Desai shows, the early Svāminārāyaṇa community composed poetic verses and sermons that extolled the appearance of Sahajānanda, often using the "head-to-toe" format of description known across Indic literatures (see also Pechilis chapter this volume). Such texts may have informed the creation of concrete visual works depicting the guru.

Printed or painted images of Sahajānanda depict him in the idealized stance of the tradition's painted images of Kṛṣṇa, with a full-frontal orientation, splayed feet, and uniform contours. Additionally, Sahajānanda has both a nimbus, signifying divinity, and in some painted images he is flanked by his parents, signifying his humanity. Other pictorial images situate Sahajānanda in the cultural specifics of nineteenth-century Gujarat, especially elite images. In these, he is pictured as both a deity and a sovereign. Seated on a thick and patterned bolster, he is richly adorned with an ornamented turban and wears gemstone jewelry, all signs of royalty. Like a divine icon, both eyes directly face the viewer and to further the resonance he is framed by a nimbus. These double references also occurred in temple sculpture, as images of Kṛṣṇa were "directly modeled after the proportions of Sahajānanda," his "body provid[ing] the *tāla* (unit) measurements for the *mūrti*s, thereby correlating his physicality with the *alaukika rūpa* (transmundane form) of the sculpted image."

Shaping the Return Look

The essays by Karen Pechilis and Heidi Pauwels bring together literature and the visual arts with the performing arts of dance-drama (Pechilis) and film (Pauwels) to analyze the ways in which classical female *bhakti* saints have been imagined in history and the present. This opens opportunities not only to examine the ways in which meanings attributed to female saints and the path of *bhakti* changed across eras but also to view the dramatization of the female poet-saints Kāraikkāl Ammaiyār in dance-drama and Mīrābāī in film and their use of the gaze that returns our look. Theorizing the "female gaze" has moved beyond serving as an opposite to influential psychological theorizing in the 1970s of the dominance and eroticism of the "male gaze" in cinema. In her interviews with contemporary female directors of documentaries from different global locations, Laura French learned that there is a division of view on whether or not a female gaze can be discerned, or whether it is possible to tell if a woman has made a film (French 2021: 56–7). David Morgan has persuasively argued for a more neutral sense of "gaze" in the study of religious images:

> I find the word *gaze* useful: it encompasses the image, the viewer, and the act of viewing, establishing a broader framework for the understanding of how images operate. A gaze is a practice, something that people do, conscious or not, and a way of seeing that viewers share. By *gaze* I mean not just one domain of vision, such as "the male gaze," but rather an entire range of ways of seeing. (Morgan 2005: 5)

Keeping in mind this wider practice of the gaze, as well as questions that deconstruct any gender binary, it remains significant that some contemporary female directors of documentaries do find value in the concept of the female gaze. In such a view, the female gaze enacts female subjectivity with a degree of autonomy in its awareness of difference as chosen or imposed within a context of patriarchy (French 2021: 55), denoting "an understanding of what it means to be female in a patriarchal society" (French 2021: 60). Drawing on filmmaker Joey Soloway's theorizing on fiction, French notes three "markers of the female gaze": "prioritizing the feeling body," "how it feels to be seen or the object of the gaze," and "returning the gaze to take up subjectivity and not be the object of the gaze" (French 2021: 60–1). Returning the gaze is "to claim a place for one's own subjectivity," or, quoting director Agnès Varda, "it's to decide to look, not see the world and oneself through another's eyes" (French 2021: 61).

In the case of Mīrābāī and Kāraikkāl Ammaiyār, their own statements of their devotional subjectivity appear in the poetry they are understood to have written. It is a prominent feature of *bhakti* poetry for the "I" subject to be explicit, and thus for the poetry to read as a practice of looking, the reader or hearer seeing what the poet sees. Pechilis foregrounds a verse of Kāraikkāl Ammaiyār's poetry in which she describes a female ghoul (*pēy*) in detail, creating an image that challenges canons of female beauty. The question is why the poet's and thus our attention is focused on this being. Pauwels notes the "defiance" of images created in Mīrā's poetry, such as imaging herself as a female ascetic and her in-laws as physically threatening her. The question is the extent to which this defiance is suggested in visual representations of Mīrā. Pauwels and Pechilis both note pressures toward domestication of the image of each saint; in Mīrā's case, the visual images of her in modern and late modern film prioritize her submission, in contrast to her poetry and biographical stories, whereas in Kāraikkāl Ammaiyār's case, a contemporary dance-drama undoes the domestication attempted by a medieval biographer, recouping and redirecting the poet's gaze.

Pechilis's essay considers the circulation of Kāraikkāl Ammaiyār's poetic image of a misshapen female ghoul (*pēy*) through a number of perspectives in an attempt to understand why we are asked to look at the figure, including Indian literature that provides "head-to-toe" descriptions (see also Desai this volume), ritual performance inflected by caste, aesthetic theories of disgust, and western theories of the abject. Distinctively from Ammaiyār's poetry, Tamil Śaiva tradition does not view the female ghoul as a vision beheld by the poet-saint but instead as a self-portrait. The discursive project of constructing and understanding the non-beautiful reveals a generative creativity that challenges what is understood to be the naturalized and normative order embedded in the scopic regime of beauty. In late modernity, displaying the abject in the arts, instead of camouflaging what society does not want to see, opens up possibilities for articulating and enacting issues of social justice. A contemporary dance-drama in India rewrote the script of Kāraikkāl Ammaiyār as *pēy*, dramatizing her life as a statement opposing violence against women. The dance-drama channels the poet-saint's challenge but redirects it toward mobilizing on a contemporary social issue. As shown by these interlinked instances, in its focus on what society does not want to see *bhakti* fundamentally promotes a sustained encounter with the challenging, disturbing, and avoided aspects of human social life.

In a detailed tracing of the imaging of Mīrā in a number of pictorial genres (book cover, comic book, postage stamp, posters, and paintings), Pauwels shows that the gaze of Mīrā suggests immersion, whether the image portrays her as a solitary figure, often holding a musical instrument, or as before Kṛṣṇa, mainly in prayerful worship but at times dancing in worship. These images isolate her from a social context, "portraying her in conformity with convention" insofar as they suggest that her *bhakti* is private and, most often, calm and introspective. Promotional posters from nationalist films of the 1930s and 1940s show Mīrā clasping the feet of an icon of Kṛṣṇa, her gaze looking up at him or, in one case, looking outward as though in a defensive posture.

A very successful 1945 Tamil film, *Meera*, brought in a new and influential element, that of a child Mīrā holding the Kṛṣṇa icon as though it were a doll, a posture reproduced by an adult Mīrā in the 1979 film *Meera*, which became "the classic" of the genre. Pauwels shows the wide traction of this image of Mīrā's loving and maternal gaze in contemporary films and television shows, noting its social accommodation to a conservative consumerist milieu in its channeling of female aspirations and expectations toward wealth, home, and submission.

These overlapping modes of devotional visuality—materializing memory, mirroring and immaterializing portraits, and shaping the return look—provide us with critical lenses to re-picture *bhakti* sacred imagery and its greater resonances, revealing the vibrant and intertwined material cultures of devotion that look back and forward as they perform the unfinished work of self and community that make Indic devotional traditions richly contoured and widely relevant.

References

Aktor, M. (2017), "Hinduism: Material Religion," *Oxford Bibliographies Online*. DOI: 10.1093/OBO/9780195399318-0181.

Appadurai, A., ed. (1986), *The Social Life of Things: Commodities in Cultural Perspective*, Cambridge: Cambridge University Press.

Arweck, E. and W. Keenan, eds. (2006), *Materializing Religion: Expression, Performance and Ritual*, Aldershot: Ashgate.

Babb, L. A. (1981), "Glancing: Visual Interaction in Hinduism," *Journal of Anthropological Research* 37 (4): 378–410.

Behl, A. (2007), "Presence and Absence in Bhakti: An Afterword," *International Journal of Hindu Studies* 11 (3): 319–24.

Behl, A. (2012), *The Magic Doe: Quṭban Suravardī's Mirigāvatī*, New York: Oxford University Press.

Ben-Herut, G. (2018), *Śiva's Saints: The Origins of Devotion in Kannada according to Harihara's Ragaḷegaḷu*, New York: Oxford University Press.

Benjamin, S. (n.d.), *The Art of Siona Benjamin*, https://artsiona.com/about-siona-benjamin/.

Bhatia, V. (2017a), "Sisir's Tears: *Bhakti* and Belonging in Colonial Bengal," *International Journal of Hindu Studies* 21 (1): 1–24.

Bhatia, V. (2017b), *Unforgetting Chaitanya: Vaishnavism and Cultures of Devotion in Colonial* Bengal, New York: Oxford University Press.

Bhatti, S. (2012), *Translating Museums: A Counterhistory of South Asian Museology*, London: Routledge.

Bhatti, S. (2021), "Opening the Eyes of South Asian Museums: Making Sense of the Visitor Gaze," *South Asian Studies* 37 (1). Accessed online: https://doi.org/10.1080/02666030.2021.1909324.

Bhatti, S. and C. Pinney (2011), "Optic-Clash: Modes of Visuality in India," in I. Clark-Decès (ed.), *A Companion to the Anthropology of India*, 225–40, Chichester: Blackwell Publishing.

Bhushan, N. and J. L. Garfield (2017), *Minds without Fear: Philosophy in the Indian Renaissance*, New York: Oxford University Press. Oxford Scholarship Online. DOI: 10.1093/oso/9780190457594.001.0001.

Biernacki, L. (2017), "Imagining the Body in Tantric Contemplative Practice," *International Journal of Dharma Studies* 5 (4): 1–15. DOI: 10.1186/s40613-016-0043-7.

Brosius, C. (2005), *Empowering Visions: The Politics of Representation in Hindu Nationalism*, London: Anthem Press.

Burchett, P. (2019), *A Genealogy of Devotion: Bhakti, Tantra, Yoga, and Sufism in North India*, New York: Columbia University Press.

Cahill, T. (2014), "Hinduism: Aesthetics," *Oxford Bibliographies Online*. DOI: 10.1093/OBO/9780195399318-0073.

Chakrabarti, A., ed. (2016), *Indian Aesthetics and the Philosophy of Art*, London: Bloomsbury.

Chakrabarty, D. (2008 [2000]), *Provincializing Europe: Postcolonial Thought and Historical Difference*, Princeton: Princeton University Press.

Chatterjee, P., T. Guha-Thakurta, and B. Kar, eds. (2014), *New Cultural Histories of India: Materiality and Practices*, New Delhi: Oxford University Press.

Comeau, L. E. (2021), *Material Devotion in a South Indian Poetic World*, London: Bloomsbury Academic.

Copeman, J. and A. Ikagame (2012), "The Multifarious Guru: An Introduction," in J. Copeman and A. Ikagame (eds.), *The Guru in South Asia: New Interdisciplinary Perspectives*, 1–45, Abingdon, Oxon: Routledge.

Cort, J. (2012), "Situating Darśan: Seeing the Digambar Jina Icon in Eighteenth and Nineteenth Century North India," *International Journal of Hindu Studies* 16 (1): 1–56.

Davis, R. H. (1997), *Lives of Indian Images*, Princeton: Princeton University Press.

Davis, R. H. (2007), *Picturing the Nation: Iconographies of Modern India*, Hyderabad: Orient Blackswan.

Davis, R. H. (2009), "Material and Visual in South Asia," *Material Religion: The Journal of Objects, Art and Belief* 5 (3): 355–6.

Dehejia, V. (2009), *The Body Adorned: Boundaries Between Sacred and Profane in India's Art*, New York: Columbia University Press.

Dubuisson, D. (2015), "Introduction: Visual Culture and Religious Studies," *Method and Theory in the Study of Religion* 27 (4–5): 299–311.

Dwyer, R. (2006), *Filming the Gods: Religion and Indian Cinema*, Abingdon, Oxon: Routledge.

Dwyer, R. and C. Pinney, eds. (2001), *Pleasure and the Nation: The History, Politics and Consumption of Public Culture in India*, New Delhi: Oxford University Press.
Eck, D. (1998 [1981]), *Darśan: Seeing the Divine in India*, New York: Columbia University Press.
Editors (2009), "Visual Culture and Material Culture: Paradigms for the Study of Religion," *Material Religion: The Journal of Objects, Art and Belief* 5 (3): 355–6.
Elison, W. (2018), *The Neighborhood of the Gods: The Sacred and the Visible at the Margins of Mumbai*, Chicago: University of Chicago Press.
Elkins, J., G. Frank, and S. Manghani, eds. (2015), *Farewell to Visual Studies*, University Park: Pennsylvania State University Press.
Flood, F. B. (2009), *Objects of Translation: Material Culture and Medieval "Hindu-Muslim" Encounter*, Princeton: Princeton University Press.
Flueckiger, J. B. (2021), *Material Acts in Everyday Hindu Worlds*, Albany: State University of New York Press.
Foster, H., ed. (1988), *Vision and Visuality*, Dia Art Foundation; Seattle: Bay Press.
Frazier, J. (2010), "Arts and Aesthetics in Hindu Studies," *Journal of Hindu Studies* 3 (1): 1–11. Accessed online: https://doi.org/10.1093/jhs/hiq011.
Freitag, S., ed. (2014a), "The Visual Turn in South Asian Studies," Special Issue of *South Asia: Journal of South Asian Studies* 37 (3): 398–540.
Freitag, S. (2014b), "The Visual Turn: Approaching South Asia across the Disciplines," *South Asia: Journal of South Asian Studies* 37 (3): 398–409.
French, L. (2021), *The Female Gaze in Documentary Film: An International Perspective*, Cham, Switzerland: Palgrave Macmillan. Accessed online: https://doi.org/10.1007/978-3-030-68094-7.
Gell, A. (1998), *Art and Agency: An Anthropological Theory*, Oxford: Clarendon Press.
Gerow, E. (1994), "Abhinavagupta's Aesthetics as a Speculative Paradigm," *Journal of the American Oriental Society* 114 (2): 186–208.
Green, N. (2004), "Emerging Approaches to the Sufi Traditions of South Asia: Between Texts, Territories and the Transcendent," *South Asia Research* 24 (2): 123–48.
Haberman, D. (1988), *Acting as a Way of Salvation: A Study of Rāgānugā Bhakti Sādhana*, New York: Oxford University Press.
Hardikar, A. R. (1994), "The Aesthetic Appreciator of Sahṛdaya," *Annals of the Bhandarkar Oriental Research Institute* 75 (1/4): 265–72.
Hawkins, S. (1999), "Bordering Realism: The Aesthetics of Sai Baba's Mediated Universe," in C. Brosius and M. Butcher (eds.), *Image-Journeys, Audio-Visual Media and Cultural Change in India*, 139–63, New Delhi: Sage.
Hawley, J. S. (2005), "Mirabai in Manuscript," in J. S. Hawley, *Three Bhakti Voices: Mirabai, Surdas and Kabir in Their Time and Ours*, New Delhi: Oxford University Press.
Hawley, J. S. (2015), *A Storm of Songs: India and the Idea of the Bhakti Movement*, Cambridge, MA: Harvard University Press.

Hawley, J.S. (2004), "Dramas of Estrangement: Christ and Krishna," *Journal of Vaishnava Studies* 13(1): 5–9.

Hess, L. (2015), *Bodies of Song: Kabir Oral Traditions and Performative Worlds in North India*, New York: Oxford University Press.

Holdrege, B. A. (2015), *Bhakti and Embodiment: Fashioning Divine Bodies and Devotional Bodies in Kṛṣṇa Bhakti*, Abingdon, Oxon: Routledge.

Holdrege, B. A. and K. Pechilis, eds. (2017), *Refiguring the Body: Embodiment in South Asian Religions*, Albany: State University of New York Press.

Holt, A. R. and K. Pechilis (2019a), "Contemporary Images of Hindu Bhakti: Identity and Visuality," Special Issue of *Journal of Hindu Studies* 12 (2): 129–269.

Holt, A. R. and K. Pechilis (2019b), "Contemporary Images of Hindu Bhakti: Identity and Visuality," *Journal of Hindu Studies* 12 (2): 129–41.

Hopkins, S. (2002), *Singing the Body of God: The Hymns of Vedāntadeśika in Their South Indian Tradition*, New York: Oxford University Press.

Houtman, D. and B. Meyer, eds. (2012), *Things: Religion and the Question of Materiality*, New York: Fordham University Press.

Jackson, W. J. (2016 [2005]), *Vijayanagara Voices: Exploring South Indian History and Hindu Literature*, London: Routledge.

Jain, K. (2007), *Gods in the Bazaar: The Economies of Indian Calendar Art*, Durham: Duke University Press.

Jay, M. (1988), "Scopic Regimes of Modernity," in H. Foster (ed.), *Vision and Visuality*, 3–23, Dia Art Foundation; Seattle: Bay Press.

Kaimal, P. (1999), "The Problem of Portraiture in South India circa 870–970 A.D.," *Artibus Asiae* 59 (1/2): 59–133.

Keune, J. (2021), *Shared Devotion, Shared Food: Equality and the Bhakti-Caste Question in Western India*, New York: Oxford University Press.

Larios, B. and R. Voix (2018), "Introduction to Wayside Shrines in India: An Everyday Defiant Religiosity," Special Issue of *South Asia Multidisciplinary Academic Journal* 18. Accessed online: https://journals.openedition.org/samaj/4523 (Accessed July 3, 2021).

Latour, B. (2005), *Reassembling the Social: An Introduction to Actor-Network-Theory*, Oxford: Oxford University Press.

Levin, D. M. (1993), "Introduction," in D. M. Levin (ed.), *Modernity and the Hegemony of Vision*, 1–29, Berkeley: University of California Press.

Mazzarella, W. (2002), "Cinty at the Taj: Cultural Enclosure and Corporate Potentateship in an Era of Globalization," in D. P. Mines and S. Lamb (eds.), *Everyday Life in South Asia*, 387–99, Bloomington: Indiana University Press.

Metz, C. (1982 [1977]), *The Imaginary Signifier: Psychoanalysis and the Cinema*, Bloomington: University of Indiana Press. Originally *Le Significant Imaginaire*, Paris: Union Général d'Éditions.

Meyer, B. (2014), "Inaugural Lecture by Birgit Meyer," *Religion and Society: Advances in Research* 5: 205–30. DOI: https://doi.org/10.3167/arrs.2014.050114.

Meyer, B. and D. Houtman, eds. (2012), "Introduction: Material Religion—How Things Matter," in *Things: Religion and the Question of Materiality*, 1–26, New York: Fordham University Press. DOI: 10.5422/fordham/9780823239450.001.0001.

Meyer, B. and T. Stordalen (2019), "Introduction: Figurations and Sensations of the Unseen in Judaism, Christianity and Islam," in B. Meyer and T. Stordalen (eds.), *Figurations and Sensations of the Unseen in Judaism, Christianity and Islam*, 1–18, London: Bloomsbury Academic. DOI: https://doi.org/10.5040/9781350078666.0006.

Miller, D., ed. (2005), *Materiality*, Durham: Duke University Press.

Mirzoeff, N. (1999), *An Introduction to Visual Culture*, London and New York: Routledge.

Mirzoeff, N. (2006), "On Visuality," *Journal of Visual Culture* 5: 53–79.

Mitchell, W. J. T. (1994), *Picture Theory: Essays on Verbal and Visual Representation*, Chicago: University of Chicago Press.

Mitchell, W. J. T. (2005), *What Do Pictures Want? The Lives and Loves of Images*, Chicago: University of Chicago Press.

Morgan, D. (2005), *The Sacred Gaze: Religious Visual Culture in Theory and Practice*, Berkeley: University of California Press.

Morgan, D. (2012), *The Embodied Eye: Religious Visual Culture and the Social Life of Feeling*, Berkeley: University of California Press.

Motrescu-Mayes, A. and M. Banks, eds. (2018), *Visual Histories of South Asia*, Delhi: Primus Books.

Mumtaz, M. K. (2020), "Contemplating the Face of the Master: Portraits of Sufi Saints as Aids to Meditation in Seventeenth-Century Mughal India," *Ars Orientalis* 50: n.p. DOI: https://doi.org/10.3998/ars.13441566.0050.015.

Munteán, M., L. Plate, and A. Smelik (2017), "Things to Remember: Introduction to Materializing Memory in Art and Popular Culture," in M. Munteán, L. Plate, and A. Smelik (eds.), *Materializing Memory in Art and Popular Culture*, 1–25, London: Routledge.

Narayanan, V. (2015), "Matters that Matter: Material Religion in Contemporary India," in K. A. Jacobsen (ed.), *Routledge Handbook of Contemporary India*, 329–46, London: Routledge.

Novetzke, C. L. (2008), *Religion and Public Memory: A Cultural History of Saint Namdev in India*, New York: Columbia University Press.

Okita, K. (2017), "From *Rasa* to *Bhaktirasa*: The Development of a Devotional Aesthetic Theory in Early Modern South Asia," *Journal of Indian and Buddhist Studies* 65 (3): 1066–72.

Packert, Cynthia (2010), *The Art of Loving Krishna: Ornamentation and Devotion*. Bloomington: Indiana University Press.

Panjabi, K., ed. (2011), *Poetics and Politics of Sufism and Bhakti in South Asia: Love, Loss and Liberation*, Hyderabad: Orient BlackSwan.

Pati, G. (2019), *Religious Devotion and the Poetics of Reform: Love and Liberation in Malayalam Poetry*, Abingdon, Oxon: Routledge.

Pauwels, H. (2017), *Mobilizing Krishna's World: The Writings of Prince Sāvant Singh of Kishangarh*, Seattle: University of Washington Press.

Pechilis, K. (2006), "Singing a Vow: Dedicating Oneself to Śiva Through Song," in S. J. Raj and W. P. Harman (eds.), *Dealing with Deities: Religious Vows in South Asia*, 147–63, Albany: State University of New York Press.

Pechilis, K. (2011), "Bhakti Traditions," in J. Frazier (ed.), *The Continuum Companion to Hindu Studies*, 107–21, London: Continuum.

Pechilis, K. (2012), *Interpreting Devotion: The Poetry and Legacy of a Bhakti Female Saint of India*, London: Routledge.

Pechilis, K. and C. Dempsey (2016), "Introduction: Not Quite Divine—Co-stars and Supporting Casts in South Asian Religions," *Journal of Hindu Studies* 9 (2): 163–7. DOI: https://doi.org/10.1093/jhs/hiw017.

Peterson, I. V. (1987), *Poems to Śiva: The Hymns of the Tamil Saints*, Princeton: Princeton University Press.

Pinney, C. (2004), *"Photos of the Gods": The Printed Image and Political Struggle in India*, London: Reaktion.

Pintch, V. (2003), "Bhakti and the British Empire," *Past & Present* 179: 159–96.

Pintchman, T. and C. Dempsey (2015), *Sacred Matters: Material Religion in South Asian Traditions*, Albany: State University of New York Press.

Plate, S. B. (2002), "Introduction," in S. B. Plate (ed.), *Religion, Art, and Visual Culture. A Cross-Cultural Reader*, 1–18, New York: Palgrave.

Plate, S. B. (2014), *A History of Religion in 5½ Objects: Bringing the Spiritual to Its Senses*, Boston: Beacon Press.

Pollock, S. (2006), *The Language of the Gods in the World of Men*, Berkeley: University of California Press.

Pollock, S. (2016), *A Rasa Reader: Classical Indian Aesthetics*, New York: Columbia University Press.

Prentiss, K. P. (1999), *The Embodiment of Bhakti*, New York: Oxford University Press.

Prentiss, K. P. (2002), "Joyous Encounters: Tamil Bhakti Poets and Images of the Divine," in V. Dehejia (ed.), *The Sensuous and the Sacred: Chola Bronzes from South India*, 65–79, Seattle: American Federation of Arts and University of Washington Press.

Qureshi, R. B. (1986), *Sufi Music of India and Pakistan: Sound, Context and Meaning in Qawwali*, Cambridge: Cambridge University Press.

Ramaswamy, S., ed. (2003a), *Beyond Appearances? Visual Practices and Ideologies in Modern India*, xiii–xxix, New Delhi and Thousand Oaks: Sage.

Ramaswamy, S. (2003b), "Introduction," in S. Ramaswamy (ed.), *Beyond Appearances? Visual Practices and Ideologies in Modern India*, xiii–xxix, New Delhi and Thousand Oaks: Sage.

Reddy, D. and J. Zavos (2009), "Temple Publics: Religious Institutions and the Construction of Contemporary Hindu Communities," *International Journal of Hindu Studies* 13 (3): 241–60. Accessed online: https://www.jstor.org/stable/pdf/40608064.pdf.

Sand, A. (2012), "Visuality," in Special Issue on Medieval Art History Today – Critical Terms, *Studies in Iconography*, vol. 33: (Special Issue Medieval Art History Today—Critical Terms), 89–95.

Sanford, A. W. (2008), *Singing Krishna: Sound Becomes Sight in Paramanand's Poetry*, Albany: State University of New York Press.

Schofield, K. B. (2015), "Review (of Panjabi, Trivedi, Venkatasubramanian)," *The Indian Economic and Social History Review* 52 (1): 116–19.

Schultz, A. (2013), *Singing a Hindu Nation: Marathi Devotional Performance and Nationalism*, New York: Oxford University Press.

Schwartz, S. L. (2004), *Rasa: Performing the Divine in India*, New York: Columbia University Press.

Sharma, K. (1987), *Bhakti and the Bhakti Movement: A New Perspective*, Delhi: Munshiram Manoharlal.

Shukla-Bhatt, N. (2015), *Narasinha Mehta of Gujarat: A Legacy of Bhakti in Songs and Stories*, New York: Oxford University Press.

Sinha, A. J. (2007), "Visual Culture and the Politics of Locality in Modern India: A Review Essay," *Modern Asian Studies* 41 (1): 187–220.

Soltes, O. Z. (2015), "Finding Home: The Worlds of Siona Benjamin," *Marg* 67 (1): 44–55.

Sturken, M. and L. Cartwright (2018 [2001]), *Practices of Looking: An Introduction to Visual Culture*, New York: Oxford University Press.

Taylor, W. (2002), "Penetrating Gazes: The Poetics of Sight and Visual Display in Popular Indian Cinema," *Contributions to Indian Sociology* 36 (1–2): 297–323.

Timalsina, S. (2015), *Tantric Visual Culture: A Cognitive Approach*, Abingdon, Oxon: Routledge.

Uehlinger, C. (2015), "Approaches to Visual Culture and Religion: Disciplinary Trajectories, Interdisciplinary Connections, and Some Suggestions for Further Progress," *Method and Theory in the Study of Religion* 27 (4–5): 384–422.

Vásquez, M. A. (2011), *A Materialist Theory of Religion*, New York: Oxford University Press.

Venkatesan, A. (2010), *The Secret Garland: Aṇṭaḷ's Tiruppavai and Nacciyar Tirumoli*, New York: Oxford University Press.

Vidal, D. (2006), "Darshan," School of Oriental and African Studies (SOAS) keyword file at: https://www.soas.ac.uk/south-asia-institute/keywords/file24803.pdf (Accessed July 3, 2021).

Vidal, D. (2016), "Darshan," in G. Dharampal-Frick, M. Kirloskar-Steinbach, R. Dwyer, and J. Phalkey (eds.), *Key Concepts in Modern Indian Studies*, 54–5, New York: New York University Press.

Waghorne, J. P. (2004), *Diaspora of the Gods: Modern Hindu Temples in an Urban Middle-Class World*, New York: Oxford University Press.

Whitehead, A. (2013), *Religious Statues and Personhood: Testing the Role of Materiality*, London: Bloomsbury.

Willis, M. (2009), *The Archaeology of Hindu Ritual*, Cambridge: Cambridge University Press.

Part I

Materializing Memory

1

The Beginnings of Mass-Produced Devotional Prints in Calcutta

Richard H. Davis

"Everybody knows what the gods look like," the Mumbai-based painter J. P. Singhal told Daniel Smith when Smith interviewed him in 1988.[1] Singhal was an artist who began his career by producing painted images for mass reproduction by commercial firms. He was required, therefore, to be sensitive to what an audience of religious consumers would approve as a proper visual depiction of Lakṣmī, Kṛṣṇa, or any Hindu deity. As a popular artist, Singhal had felt constrained by these expectations and complained that they led to repetitive work.

Singhal's statement poses the question: What has determined what "everyone knows" the gods look like? Why do modern Hindu gods look the way they do? Of course, the visual appearances of Hindu deities have long iconographic histories, which art historians and textual scholars have traced in detail. But as the point of departure for this essay, I wish to argue that the greatest determining factor in the visual appearance of Hindu deities in modern India has been the prolific, far-reaching imagery produced by artists like Singhal, Raja Ravi Varma, and many others, producing painted designs that firms like Ravi Varma Press, S. S. Brijbasi, and J. B. Khanna could reproduce on a mass scale. Focusing on the earliest development of this genre of mechanically reproduced religious imagery, I will examine how print artists began to render the deities for a mass audience of Hindu consumers. They created a new type of devotional visual representation. Through this exploration of several early examples from Calcutta artists, we will see ways that the Hindu deities were made more accessible for devotional response, as part of a *bhakti* economy involving artists, publishers, consumers, and the gods themselves.

The Ocean of Prints

From the late nineteenth century to the present, the genre of two-dimensional imagery variously called "calendar prints," "bazaar art," "Indian kitsch," "God-pictures," or "framing pictures" has flooded the visual landscape of Hindu religious life. (I will use the neutral term "God-prints" in this essay.) These ubiquitous images have had profound effects on the expectations of Hindu viewers. The goddess Lakṣmī should look much as Ravi Varma depicted in his famous 1894 print and as many print artists following in his wake have portrayed her.[2] Images of the gods have circulated widely as framed prints, calendar illustrations, advertisements, magazine illustrations, stickers, merchandise labels, container decorations, and holiday greeting cards. In the twenty-first century, they appear in online digital reincarnations. A Google image search for any Hindu deity will summon myriad examples of God-print portrayals of that deity. It is difficult to quantify the profusion of God-print images that have circulated in India. The prolific J. P. Singhal, it is estimated, produced over 2,700 paintings that have been reproduced 800 million times. Similarly, the south Indian painter M. Ramalingkum, writes Stephen Inglis, must be "one of the most published painters in history," for he produced up to a hundred God-print designs a year over several decades, and each design was printed in runs of a hundred thousand or more (Inglis 1995: 66). Singhal and Ramalingkum are just two of many artists who have contributed their designs to this ocean of divine imagery.

The God-print style of visual imagery has drawn from other modes of visual presentation—photography, theater, cinema, advertising, television, and so on—and in turn been drawn upon by them, in "inter-ocular" networks of relationship. Christopher Pinney uses this term to refer to "a visual inter-referencing and citation" similar to verbal "inter-textuality" (Pinney 2004: 34). And God-prints have infused themselves within the devotional ethos of Hinduism, both as reflections of a devotional imagination and as objects of devotional practice.

The aim of this essay is an initial examination of the most important place of origin of the God-print genre. While the work of Ravi Varma and the press he and his brother founded in 1894 have often been seen as the foundation of the genre, it had earlier manifestations in both Maharashtra and Calcutta, as Pinney has shown. Here I will focus on the prints of colonial-period Calcutta in the nineteenth century, since it has the richest and best-documented body of such images. This is an initial exploration of the earliest mass-produced Hindu religious prints, focusing on three primary topics: the technologies of print production, the iconographic presentation of divine subjects, and the devotional reception of the prints. To keep this essay within bounds, I will center the exploration on three main design types: the Kālī image associated with the Kalighat temple, the Kṛṣṇa-Kālī image, and the image replication of the Durgā Pūjā Shrine. My aim here is to engage the question of "*bhakti* visuality" (Holt and Pechilis 2019). What are the ways that the prints examined here functioned within a devotional economy of images?

Technologies: Kālī of Kalighat and the Devotional Souvenir

In nineteenth-century Calcutta, Bengali artisans explored new methods and practices for the rapid production of two-dimensional images, in order to meet a developing consumer market for display prints. They drew on existing technologies and adapted them to new purposes. These techniques include Kalighat painting, woodblock printing, electrotyping, lithography, and various combinations of these.

The first artisans to adapt new methods were the painters who settled around the newly constructed Kalighat temple in the early nineteenth century. Rebuilt in 1809 on a sacred site where, according to myth, the toes of the goddess Satī had fallen to earth, Kalighat housed a distinctive form of Kālī as its central icon. It soon became a popular destination for worshippers, pilgrims, and tourists (see Gupta 2003; Ramos 2015; Moodie 2019). Rural *patua* artists migrated into the neighborhood near the temple and began to adapt their painting to meet the needs and requests of temple visitors. This required a notable transformation in their artistic practice and led to the development of the new genre of painting that we refer to as "Kalighat painting" (see Archer 1971; Jain 1999; Sinha and Panda 2011; and the extensive collection in the Victoria and Albert Museum).

Previously, *patua* artists had worked as "picture showmen," in the apt phrase of A. K. Coomaraswamy and Jyotindra Jain (Jain 1998; Hauser 2002; Singh 1996). They painted sequences of scenes connected by mythical narratives on lengthy rolls of fabric, and they performed by telling and singing the stories while unfurling the painted scrolls. It was largely an itinerant art. *Patua* artists traveled from village to village to perform their works. When they settled in Kalighat, on the outskirts of urbanizing Calcutta, the artists addressed a very different audience. The pilgrims who visited the temple, evidently, were interested in acquiring souvenirs of their religious trip—portable objects of remembrance that referred iconically to the site visited. Long fabric scrolls were not suitable for this, and the *patua* artists developed a new mode of artistic production. They began to produce single scenes or images of single deities, separated from the *patua* sequential narration and performance. They adopted new materials for this, painting on single sheets of mill-made paper with British factory-made watercolor paints.

The *patua* artists were now engaged in selling their artistic objects, rather than performing for fees or donations. For the middle-class and lower-class pilgrim consumers, price was certainly an issue. The Kalighat artists responded by developing working methods and an aesthetic style that allowed for rapid production of inexpensive two-dimensional images. Using an assembly-line workshop system, the master artist would sketch in the main lines of the image, and apprentices would fill in colors and details. Backgrounds were left minimal or absent, and nonessential details were omitted. A workshop of four or five could produce several hundred images in a day, and prices could be kept to an affordable rate. The Kalighat style that emerged was lively and vivid, spontaneous, and expressive.

Subject matter of Kalighat painting initially reflected the religious interests of the pilgrim-consumers. The earliest Kalighat paintings, from the 1830s, focus on Hindu gods and goddesses, scenes from the life of Kṛṣṇa, and epic scenes. Over the following decades, as new media like western theater and photography became more widely present, Kalighat artists also explored secular themes, including satirical takes on the urban culture of the nouveau riche in colonial Calcutta. But most common were paintings directly related to the Kalighat temple. These either depicted scenes from the Satī narrative or, more commonly, represented the distinctive form of the main temple icon, Kalighat Kālī (see Ramos 2015). Evidently, large numbers of pilgrims wished to take home a two-dimensional painted simulacrum of the decorated stone Kālī icon as a devotional souvenir.

The central Kālī icon of the temple is a fearsome and disorienting figure (Figure 1.1). De-anthropomorphized, this black-skinned Kālī has a preponderant head with two large eyes and a third forehead eye, and a bright red lolling tongue. She has four tiny arms, with one holding a cleaver and another holding a severed head. Other hands form the *mudrās* of security (*abhaya*) and generosity (*varada*). She wears a prominent garland of severed heads. Her broad garment extends to the plinth on which she is standing, so most of her body is not visible. She wears a tiara, and a halo of rays extends outward above her head. Some of this iconography is shared with other more anthropomorphic images of Kālī, but the particular form here is distinctive to this temple. This painted image, done by

Figure 1.1 *Debi Kally* (Kālī of Kalighat). Anonymous, Kolkata, *c.* 1865. Painted in opaque watercolor on paper, lithographic outline. Photograph Victoria and Albert Museum (IS.3-1995).

an anonymous Kalighat artist or atelier around 1865, refers unmistakably to the Kālī icon of Kalighat temple.

The *patua* artists settled at Kalighat were not the only artisans to produce two-dimensional prints in nineteenth-century Calcutta to meet the growing consumer demand for inexpensive pictures of divine subjects. In addition to, and in competition with, the Kalighat paintings, old and new methods of mechanical reproduction were adapted to the Bengali religious market. These included woodcut prints, metal imprints, lithography, and chromolithography. But the evidence of the prints themselves makes clear that hybrid techniques were also employed, such as Kalighat artisans using lithographic processes to establish the line-outlines that could then be hand-colored. This can be seen in the illustration here, where faint iconographic lines can be detected, under the watercolor, most clearly in Kālī's garland of heads.

Woodblock printing in India developed within the "small-book" printing industry of nineteenth-century Calcutta, centered in the Battala neighborhood.[3] The earliest printing presses in India were established and controlled by British colonial administrators and European missionaries, but by the early nineteenth century, indigenous Bengali printers had established new independent presses. Some aimed at an elite audience, while others began to cater to a more popular, lower-middle-class readership with inexpensive publications like almanacs, religious and mythological works, and educational materials. According to Anindita Ghosh's careful study *Power in Print* (2006), the small-book industry took off in the 1860s. The printing was mostly done by men of lower-class communities—smiths and artisans—who had migrated into the city from surrounding rural areas.

Almanacs and mythological pamphlets might be illustrated with woodblock images on religious themes. But printers discovered a new market for separate display prints. As Ghosh observes, "when sold as separate picture prints these are far more accessible and manipulable—being easily carried, or hung on walls and thus available for continuous viewing—a part of everyday life" (Ghosh 2006: 140). Woodblock prints could be produced in large batches of up to a hundred prints, and they could readily compete in price with the Kalighat paintings. Costs were kept even lower by using cheap paper. (This, along with the Bengali climate, explains why fewer woodblock prints from this period survive.) They were sold in tens of thousands. From at least the 1860s, if not earlier, printers in Battala created woodblock prints illustrating the same range of themes as the Kalighat artisans. Like the Kalighat painters, they focused on religious subjects and also took on depictions of the urban life of Calcutta. It is not clear whether the Kalighat artists and Battala engravers saw each other as collaborators or competitors, but they certainly marketed their prints to the same audience.

A related technology employed metal plates rather than wooden blocks. In the process of electrotyping, invented in Russia in 1838 and quickly adopted in India, copper plates are made from engraved woodblocks. The plates are then mounted on wood and printed by hand on a flatbed letterpress.[4] Metal plates would last through more pressings than blocks of etched wood and leave sharper images.

Lithography was first used in India in the 1820s and adapted to the production of God-prints around the middle of the century. Numerous small firms in Calcutta experimented with God-printing in the 1870s and 1880s. In many cases, we know only the names, sometimes the addresses, and a few of their prints: Oriental Studio, Jubilee Art Studio, Kansaripara Art Studio, Hindu Art Studio, Chitra Silpi Company, and the National Art Gallery. The earliest examples were single-color lithographs that could then be hand-colored, not too different in technology from the Kalighat use of lithography to create an initial outline. But in the 1870s, some firms began to adopt the more complex method of chromolithography, first developed in France in 1837. In this process, color images are printed from multiple limestone blocks. The results can be striking indeed. As Pinney notes, chromolithographs elicited a mixed response (and still do): "Disparaged by the aesthetic elite, in both Europe and India, . . . they were powerful vehicles for the mediation of faith and sentiment" (Pinney 2004: 14).

Figure 1.2 *Śrī Śrī Kālī*. Chromolithograph. Chore Bagan Art Studio, Calcutta, *c*. 1880s. Collection of Mark Baron and Elise Boisanté.

Lithographers in nineteenth-century Calcutta took on the same religious subject matter as the Kalighat painters and woodblock printers. The firm of Chore Bagan Art Studio created their version of Kalighat Kālī, using a chromolithographic process (Figure 1.2), and it is instructive to compare with other examples of the same theme.[5] The Chore Bagan print follows the iconographic model closely, but also shows a great concern with the detail and colorful clarity of Kālī's adornments: her jeweled tiara, her pendant earrings, her necklaces of pearl strings and severed heads. The severed head in Kālī's lower hand to the right is given a more living presence. The artist has also seen fit to place Kālī in a suitably auspicious setting. Pillars hold up an archway within a green dome, and red curtains hang tethered from the arch. The framing here owes more to the world of theater then becoming popular in urban India than to the enshrinement of a temple. But it has the equivalent effect of highlighting the divine figure within the frame, set against a yellow background. The parasol suspended above Kālī's head also points to her lordly status.

In the Calcutta marketplace of God-prints, these new color lithographs enjoyed some advantages. They offered visually engaging two-dimensional images of gods that surpassed the paintings of Kalighat artists or Battala woodblock prints in richness of color and detail of finish. Due to the economies of mechanical reproduction, they could compete in price. And so, by the 1880s, the chromolithographers were out-competing their rivals in the production of God-prints. In an official report of 1888, T. N. Mukharji reported that "owing to the cheaper coloured lithograph representations of Gods and Goddesses turned out by the ex-students of the Calcutta School of Art having appeared on the market," the painters of Kalighat were being put out of business (Mukharji 1888). We turn to these ex-students in the following section.

Iconographies: Calcutta Art Studio and Kṛṣṇa-Kālī

The iconographic repertoire of nineteenth-century Calcutta prints reflected the distinctive religious ethos of Bengal of that period. The choice of subjects matched what would find favor among Bengali consumers, based on (and helping construct) what the gods looked like for that audience. Some of these subjects are found only in the Bengali region. Starting with the press founded by Ravi Varma and his brother in 1894, and continuing with the large print forms of the twentieth century like S. S. Brijbasi and J. B. Khanna, there has been a conscious effort to reach a pan-Indian or "national" market. The pantheon of gods in print has changed, as have their appearances.

Within the output of nineteenth-century Kalighat painters and Calcutta print-makers, goddesses figure prominently. The goddess Kālī appears abundantly, both in her Kalighat icon form and in her triumphant stance atop a prostrate Śiva. She manifests herself also in a beautiful aspect, as Jagadhātrī, "supporter of the world." Ravi Varma also rendered Kālī, and she appears in many twentieth-century versions, but never so prominently as in the earlier Calcutta prints. The pan-Indian Durgā shows up often in Calcutta prints, both in her common demon-killing pose as Mahiṣāsuramardinī. But she also appears—more distinctive to Bengal—as a young mother (identified with Umā) carrying her infant Gaṇeśa to visit her parents during the autumn festival, Durgā Pūjā. Likewise, particular to Bengal is the Durgā Pūjā Shrine design in which Durgā appears in the center flanked by other deities in a two-dimensional shrine. (We will come back to this image in the next section.) Another set of goddesses who appear prominently in nineteenth-century Calcutta prints but do not seem to travel into twentieth-century Indian God-prints are the Ten Mahāvidyās. This set of ten goddesses reflect a tantric part of the Śākta religious tradition that was especially strong in Bengal (Kinsley 1997).

Calcutta print-makers also favored images of Kṛṣṇa. Of course, the flute-playing divine cowherd of the *Bhāgavata Purāṇa*, the Dwaraka prince of the *Mahābhārata*, the wise teacher and all-encompassing deity of the *Bhagavad Gītā*, and the poetic protagonist of innumerable devotional poets is a deity of pan-Indian scope. But the Kṛṣṇa of the nineteenth-century Calcutta images takes on some distinctive regional features too. Here we focus on a Kṛṣṇa print of the Calcutta Art Studio, the best-known and most successful publisher of God-prints in nineteenth-century Calcutta.

The Calcutta Art Studio was founded around 1878 by five artists affiliated with the Government School of Art in Calcutta.[6] Anand Prasad Bagchi (1849–1905) was a well-established painter, who had enrolled in the school in 1865. He was quickly recognized for his artistic skills, and the school principal, H. H. Locke, assigned Bagchi to accompany the eminent Bengali archaeologist Rajendralala Mitra, in order that Bagchi could make sketches during Mitra's research in Orissa. Lithographic illustrations from Bagchi's drawings appear in Mitra's landmark publication, *Antiquities of Orissa* (1880). After graduating, Bagchi gained a teaching position at the school in 1876. In 1878, he joined with four of his students—Nabakumar Biswas, Phanibhushan Sen, Krishna Chandra Pal, and Yogendranath Mukhopadhyaya—to establish a commercial enterprise that would utilize lithographic technology to publish and sell prints on religious and mythological subjects. The studio undertook other commercial activities such as photography, portrait commissions, and book printing as well. In 1879, Bagchi was appointed Headmaster of the Government School and left the firm to the four former students. By 1920 Nabakumar Biswas's youngest son was the sole partner. The firm continues today occupying its original location on Bowbazar Street (since renamed Bipin Behari Ganguli Street), and its current directors are descendants of Nabakumar Biswas. Though no longer in the religious print business, the firm is justly proud of its past, and the company website features a rotating display of its "heritage collection."

The religious prints of the Calcutta Art Studio reflected the art school training of the founding artists and their interest in multiple print-making technologies. The Government School of Art in Calcutta, one of the earliest such schools in India, was established under British colonial direction in 1864. The aim was to establish an institute for training Indian youth of all classes in the production of "industrial art based on scientific methods." Presumably, the British founders considered the higher category of "fine art" beyond the reach of Indian artisans. The school drew many of its students from the urban *bhadralok* classes, the emerging educated upper class of Calcutta and other cities of colonial Bengal. The "gentlemen-artists" who founded the Calcutta Art Studio were of a different class from the more rural, lower-class artisans of Kalighat and Battala (Mitter 1994).

The "scientific methods" the school sought to impart to its students had largely to do with European artistic conventions of the time. Chief among these was the use of single-point perspective to reproduce visually the objects of the natural world "correctly." The dissemination of photography during the nineteenth century also played a role in stressing pictorial resemblance to a perceived visual reality. But in the hands of the Art Studio print-makers, these techniques and conventions drawn from the European art tradition were employed to render the divine world of the Hindu gods, which Hindus considered equally if not more real. The results could be striking indeed. Christopher Pinney calls this effect the "xeno-real": "a colonial authorized realism that circulated outside its framework of origination" (Pinney 2004: 31). The Hindu gods wander through Alpine settings, display Madonna-like expressions, and wear the voluminous engulfing robes they might need in a chilly European climate. The bodies of the gods, for the most part, are rendered with anatomical realism, yet they bear all the iconographic features—the additional limbs, extraordinary complexions, animal vehicles, and conventional iconic implements—that long-standing Hindu artistic traditions called for and Hindu audiences expected.

In 1883, the Calcutta Art Studio issued a folio of hand-colored lithographic prints of Hindu subjects, entitled *Scrap Book illustrated with Fifteen Hindu Mythological Pictures.*[7] Each print in the folio is labeled in Bengali, Hindi, and English characters, and each is accompanied by a written English explanation of the image on the facing page. The multiple labeling, English explanatory apparatus, and folio format all indicate that the Art Studio sought to reach a market that extended beyond Bengali Hindus and could potentially include the many Europeans living in or visiting the capital of British India and beyond. This "scrap book" provides a glimpse of the Hindu pantheon as envisioned by the art school-trained Bengali gentlemen-artists of the late nineteenth century.

The *Scrap Book* begins with two auspicious goddesses, Lakṣmī and Sarasvatī. Gaṇeśa also receives an independent illustration. Kālī appears in two contrasting forms: as a naked dark figure stepping across the prostrate body of Śiva on a field of battle between the gods and demons, and as the fair-skinned beneficent Jagadhātrī riding a lion through a mountain landscape. The folio does not include a version of the Kālī icon of Kalighat, but it does refer to the pilgrimage site implicitly in its rendering of Śiva Mahādeva carrying the corpse of Satī on his shoulders. Śiva appears in a second print, seated in a forest with his wife Gaurī, probably explaining the secrets of yoga to her. There are two scenes that draw on well-known stories found in the epic *Mahābhārata*, of Nala and Damayantī and of Sāvitrī pleading with the death-god Yama. Durgā appears twice, but not in her demon-killing mode. Rather, the prints show her as a young mother Umā, holding her infant Gaṇeśa, during her joyous arrival home to her parental home ("Agamani") and then her sad departure from it ("Bijaya"). These days mark the key moments of the autumnal Bengali celebration of Durgā Pūjā.

In this set of fifteen prints, four focus on Kṛṣṇa, more than any other individual Hindu deity, no doubt reflecting his high status within Bengali Hindu circles of the time. No other forms or incarnations of Viṣṇu are included. The Calcutta Art Studio artists depict Kṛṣṇa twice as an infant and twice as a youth in forest settings with Rādhā and other *gopīs*. These choices anticipate the two most popular ways that Kṛṣṇa would come to be portrayed in the God-print genre: as a charming and mischievous toddler and as a seductive flute-playing cowherd boy accompanied by his beloved *gopīs* and cows. The Art Studio folio does not include Kṛṣṇa's demon-defeating deeds, such as subduing the snake Kāliya, nor does it show him raising Mount Govardhana to protect his pastoral tribe from Indra's deluge. These had been the most common forms of Kṛṣṇa imagery in medieval sculpture throughout India (Hawley 1979). The Calcutta artists do not show an interest in the Kṛṣṇa of the *Mahābhārata*. Only later, when the popularity of the *Bhagavad Gītā* rose in the early twentieth century as the Indian nationalist "Bible" would prints of Kṛṣṇa and Arjuna on the Kurukshetra battlefield and of Arjuna's awesome vision of Kṛṣṇa's supernal form become popular themes for God-prints (Davis 2015: 115–53 and 200–3).

A dramatic example of the "xeno-real" from the *Scrap Book* is the lithograph labeled *Kṛṣṇa-Kālī* (Figure 1.3). The scene takes place in a forest clearing, with an opening in the foliage to a lake and hills in the distance. In the foreground, a young woman draping crimson head-covering kneels before a standing figure and makes offerings of worship.

Surrounding this pair are seven more women, all fully draped. In the upper right a male figure with a pointing-hand enters the grove. The standing figure, most prominent in the composition, has a dark-blue complexion, a hanging red tongue, and four arms, one holding a cleaver and another a severed head. The figure wears a necklace of detached heads. These are all clear iconographic features of the goddess Kālī. But the figure is male, and he wears the peacock feather and the yellow *dhoti* characteristic of Kṛṣṇa. The main subject, then, appears to be a combined form of goddess Kālī and god Kṛṣṇa, just as the title suggests.

Figure 1.3 *Kṛṣṇa-Kālī*. Lithograph, watercolor (hand-coloring). Calcutta Art Studio, *c*. 1878–83. Collection of Mark Baron and Elise Boisanté.

The English caption on the facing page provides a narrative explanation for this perplexing scene.[8]

> Once upon a time Krishna and his beloved Radhica, were enjoying themselves in a bower. Information of this reached Ayan Ghosh the married consort of the latter, and he rushes in at once in a furious mood where the lovers had resorted. Radhica foresees this and desires Krishna to devise some such stratagem as might prevent their detection. Krishna upon this at once transforms himself into the Goddess *Kali*, of whom the blind husband was a devotee, and the young lady sits in front of the Goddess in an adoring posture, with all the necessary articles of worship. Ayan comes in and is agreeably disappointed in finding his wife, not in the midst of an amorous intercourse with Krishna, which he had expected, but deeply engaged in the pious act of worshipping his own Deity, Kali. (Calcutta Art Studio 1883)

The artist has rendered the moment in this story at which Kṛṣṇa's transformation into Kālī is complete and Rādhā is making her offerings of worship to this goddess, just as her husband arrives on the scene in hopes of discovering her secret tryst with Kṛṣṇa. Kalighat painters had rendered this theme as well. A fine example in the Victoria and Albert Museum is dated to circa 1830 (Figure 1.4).[9] The difference in

Figure 1.4 *Kṛṣṇa as Kālī*. Painting, watercolor and tin alloy on paper. Anonymous, Kalighat, Kolkata, *c*. 1830. Victoria and Albert Museum (IS.225-1950).

treatment, relating to the two methods of production, is striking and instructive. Here the artist has included only the three primary characters: kneeling Rādhā to the left, Ayan Ghosh standing to the right, and a dominant haloed Kṛṣṇa-Kālī at the center. The lack of any background allows a visual concentration on the divine figure, but it leaves the viewer to construct the larger narrative.

That story is distinctive to Bengali religious culture. It seeks to make an ecumenical point about shared divine identity linking the two principal Hindu orientations within nineteenth-century Bengali religious culture, namely Kṛṣṇa-centered Vaiṣṇavism and goddess-centered Śākta. Iconography here works as a means of creating or reinforcing linkages between different devotional communities. It can articulate theological assertions, such as the ultimate identity of different gods in visual form.

Reception: Domestic Devotion and the Durgā Pūjā Shrine

What did the consumers want with the Calcutta prints they purchased from Kalighat painters, Battala printers, or Art Studio presses? How did they intend to use them? The question is one of engagement or reception. The creation of display prints independent of *patua* storytelling and separate from book illustration allowed new possibilities. The prints could be hung on walls for decorative display, always available for household viewing. They could also be framed, enshrined, and incorporated into domestic worship practices. Modern anecdotal evidence for the devotional use of God-prints is ubiquitous, but it is more difficult to assess the question of devotional usage historically for nineteenth-century Calcutta.[10] What kinds of venerative actions were involved? In this section, we consider one design type that was particularly oriented around devotional practice, the Durgā Pūjā Shrine.

Nowadays Durgā Pūjā is an enormous public event in Kolkata.[11] Neighborhood groups construct elaborate pandals, temporary shrines of the goddess, throughout the city. The displays in these transitory pavilions follow a long-standing iconographic scheme, with a standard set and arrangement of deities, but the creators develop new variations and often use the scheme to address contemporary social and political issues. The pandals are considered to be religious shrines, and priests are employed to carry out regular liturgical rites for the deities within them. But for the great majority of the public, the pandals are remarkable decorative displays to be viewed as part of the festive celebration of Durgā Pūjā. This vibrant public festival in the city streets dates back about a century. Dramatic innovations in the design of public Durgā Pūjā pandals were made in the 1920s. Prior to that, the festival was celebrated primarily in domestic settings.

In nineteenth-century Bengal, affluent *zamindar* families could hire artisans to construct elaborate three-dimensional domestic shrines in their homes. For others, this was not feasible. However, two-dimensional prints depicting Durgā Pūjā Shrines could provide an inexpensive way for the less affluent to populate their own domestic altars for the festival. Kalighat painters, woodblock printers, and lithographic artisans all produced the Durgā Pūjā Shrine design type in nineteenth-century Calcutta. It is seldom found in twentieth-century God-prints, to my knowledge. Clay sculptures are more common in domestic Durgā Pūjā celebrations.

The Durgā Pūjā Shrine follows a set iconographic scheme (Figures 1.5 and 1.6.) At the center of the composition, a beautifully dressed ten-armed Durgā stands atop her lion-mount. With one right hand, she holds a long spear that is piercing a male demon below her. At the same time her lion bites fiercely into the demon's chest, and the demon (whose head and upper torso may be emerging from a buffalo body) is on his knees in defeat. The goddess Durgā gazes off to the side with unruffled confidence in her powers. Appearing behind her within the shrine space are four other deities. The goddesses Lakṣmī and Sarasvatī stand on lotuses to the left and right of Durgā, while the smaller male figures of Gaṇeśa and Kārttikeya are seated on their animal mounts. Stretching above all the divine figures is a large semicircular arch supported on pillars, called a *chala*, with decorative illustrations of gods and mythical scenes. The entire composition appears as a portable shrine, elevated from the ground on short feet. In the context of Bengali Durgā Pūjā, the four other deities are considered to be the

Figure 1.5 Durgā slaying the buffalo demon depicted on a stand and surmounted on a *toraṇa* decorated with smaller figures of demon kings and Hindu gods. Transfer lithograph. Anonymous, Calcutta, *c.* 1860s. Wellcome Collection (no. 26170i). Public Domain Mark 1.0.

children of Durgā, in her aspect as Umā, daughter of Himalaya and Mīnā, wife of Śiva. The autumnal festival of Durgā Pūjā is in part a homecoming festival, structured around the arrival of the young wife Umā to visit her parents and her departure four days later. But it also commemorates Durgā's successful defeat of the threatening buffalo demon, Mahiṣāsura. On the final day of public Durgā Pūjā celebrations, Durgā slays the demon, victory over evil is declared, and the pandals are dismantled. The temporary images are processed through the streets and immersed in nearby rivers. The Durgā Pūjā Shrine design, then, highlights the dual identity of the goddess, as both the powerful demon-slaying Durgā and

Figure 1.6 Durgā slaying the buffalo demon with other deities, set in a *toraṇa*. Coloured lithograph. Calcutta Art Studio, Calcutta, *c*. 1870s. Wellcome Collection (no. 26241i). Public Domain Mark 1.0.

the maternal Umā. It shows her both in the act of defeating Mahiṣāsura and accompanied by her four divine children.

Two examples of this design type, now in the collection of the Wellcome Institute in London, illustrate both the iconographic consistency and the artistic flexibility among Durgā Pūjā Shrine prints (Figures 1.5 and 1.6).[12] The first is a relief print made from an engraved woodblock or metal plate, and the second is a hand-colored lithograph printed by the Calcutta Art Studio. Both feature the exact same arrangement of deities, the shrine-like construction, and the overarching *chala*. But the relief print renders the shrine with a kind of medieval stasis. Without color, and with no effort to convey depth, the artisans evince a great delight in the detailed ornamental profusion surrounding the five deities.

In the Calcutta Art Studio lithograph, by contrast, the art school-trained artists have sought a more three-dimensional representation of the shrine, using receding perspective and shading. The deities are treated as fleshy living beings, and the three goddesses have benign expressions a bit like porcelain dolls. The creators in both cases (and in many other treatments of the same design type) have produced inexpensive but visually complex and engaging two-dimensional replications of the elaborate shrines that wealthy *zamindar*s had constructed in their homes of the Durgā Pūjā festival. They are prints well-suited to domestic devotion. I call them "temples in a frame" (Davis 2015).

Before leaving the Durgā Pūjā Shrine, we should note a very similar design type with one highly significant iconographic difference. At the center of "Deva Gostha" (cattle-station of the god) instead of Durgā slaying the buffalo demon, we see the ten-armed goddess in a decidedly maternal aspect. (Two examples may be seen in Davis 2012: Plate 5 on p. 12 and Plate 33 on p. 42.) Seated on her pacified lion, she holds a child on her lap. Her four children still flank her, as in the Durgā Pūjā Shrine. But the child she now holds is young Kṛṣṇa. New figures now crowd the shrine still further: male deities like Brahmā, Śiva, and Viṣṇu. And in the foreground, not part of the shrine, is a group of young cowherd boys and the cows they are tending, Kṛṣṇa's friends in the cattle-station. Much as in the Kṛṣṇa-Kālī design type, this composition unites the Vaiṣṇava and Śākta religious orientations of the Bengali Hindu community, but here the unity is that of a shared family, not one of divine identity.

Toward an Aesthetics of Indian Print Devotion

I would like to conclude with a few reflections on the question of devotional visuality, or in this case, on mechanically produced visual objects as sites of devotional engagement.

In *Art Rethought* (2015), the philosopher Nicholas Wolterstorff offers a critique of the long-standing Kantian tradition in aesthetic theory and the ways this had configured modern western attitudes toward art. He traces a "grand narrative" within which certain forms of art "come into their own" as privileged types of high art; this same narrative has excluded other forms of artistic production from aesthetic consideration. Wolterstorff insists that we view art objects in the context of "long-enduring, ever-changing social practices": practices of creation, practices of performance and display, and practices of public engagement (Wolterstorff 2015: vii). He investigates various types of art that have not fit easily into the grand narrative of art in the modern world, such as memorial art, social protest art, and art for veneration. This last category is the one most relevant to the issues raised by the nineteenth-century Calcutta prints we are considering. By venerative art, Wolterstorff has in mind works that are produced with the intention that they may be venerated by others. For his primary example within the Christian tradition, he examines the century-long debate that took place in eighth and ninth-century Constantinople over the veneration of icons.

For "veneration," in the Hindu tradition we would more readily use terms like "devotion" (*bhakti*) and "worship" (*pūjā*). Devotion and worship directed toward three-dimensional icons, which are understood to participate in some way within the divine reality to which they iconically refer, is an ancient social and religious practice within the Hindu community. Within that context, artisans have produced myriad remarkable works of religious sculpture intended for devotional usage. (We often see these artworks now resituated in modern secular museums for appreciation of their formal aesthetic value.) Image-worship has its own history of critique and defense, going back centuries, and that debate continued in nineteenth-century Calcutta.[13] But here we are concerned with the degree to which new God-prints made by Bengali painters and printers may have functioned within that larger devotional economy. Wolterstorff helpfully distinguishes between the practices of creating works of art and the public engagement with them. It is clear, however, that these two are dialectically related to one another. What an artist creates and how a public comes to engage with it will inform one another. This is particularly the case in the commercial God-print context. A God-print artist like Singhal will feel constrained by commercial parameters to depict the gods in the way that "everybody knows" they look, while the public knowledge of what the gods look like will rest on the depictions of artists like Singhal. But looking at the history of this genre, we can readily see that the visual appearances of gods can and do change. Artists may push the boundaries, as the gentlemen-artists of the Calcutta Art Studio and Ravi Varma selectively appropriated European art practices to Hindu purposes, thereby creating the "xeno-real" images of gods. The choices of consumers will orient the kinds and forms of objects being created; reciprocally, newly created objects can give rise to new consumer desires.

Nineteenth-century Calcutta prints stand at the beginning of a new genre, mass-produced religious prints that would have an enormous impact on the religious landscape of twentieth-century India. We have seen, in this examination of select examples from nineteenth-century Calcutta, several primary directions that this form of venerative art would take in the twentieth century. In a competitive commercial setting, supply and price are important. Calcutta artisans adopted new technologies that would enable the rapid production of devotional prints at a low cost. The recognizability of the gods is important, as J. P. Singhal recognized. Print artists observed long-standing iconographical conventions, even as they altered the style in which the gods were depicted. It is important, within a devotional economy, that deities be accessible for interaction with their worshippers. In the Calcutta prints, we see an emphasis on vivid colors to make a strong visual impact. We see frontal and often hieratic enshrined depictions of the deities. The artisans often sought to emulate the environment of a temple shrine within prints intended for domestic devotion.

In the twentieth century, God-prints became so ubiquitous within the Indian religious landscape that we often fail to register the profound impact this genre of devotional imagery has made. But as H. Daniel Smith observed, "as a popular art genre, the poster gods have fostered a democratic devotionalism, a populist piety, of extraordinary proportions in the present age" (Smith 1995: 37).

Notes

1 H. Daniel Smith unpublished 1988 interview with J. P. Singhal, in H. Daniel Smith Poster Archive, Syracuse University Library.

2 See Davis (2015) on Ravi Varma's "Laksmi" and its offshoots. Jain (2004) documents some of the great variety in the ways God-print imagery has appeared and been recycled. See also Jain (2007) on the history of God-print aesthetics.

3 On Calcutta small-book publishing, see Ghosh (2006). The key study of Calcutta woodcut prints is Paul (1983). Issues of preservation are especially acute for woodblock prints, due to the Bengali climate, poor quality of paper, and perhaps the sense that these cheap objects were of no artistic or social value (Paul 1983: 8 and Hirsh 2016).

4 I am grateful to Mark Baron for alerting me to this process and for background on its use in Calcutta prints.

5 A similar example, also created by the Chore Bagan Art Studio, is now in the MAP Collection, Bengaluru (POP.00099). Active in the 1880s and 1890s, Chore Bagan Art Studio was located at 24 Bhoobun Banerjee's Lane. According to Bengali Directories of the period, the proprietors were Akhoy Kumar Shaw and his two sons, Bijoy Kumar Shaw and Hemanta Kumar Shaw. Amar Nath Shaha also issued prints under his own name from the same address. The largest collection of Chore Bagan prints, forty-three in all, was acquired by the British Museum

from a private library in England in 2003. The original owner had mounted the individual prints on cloth pages to create an album of Hindu subjects.

6 Some portions of this section are drawn from an earlier article on Kṛṣṇa in early prints, Davis (2013). For more detailed literature on the Calcutta Art Studio, see Guha-Thakurta (1992), Mitter (1994), and Pinney (2004).

7 Collection of Mark Baron and Elise Boisanté. All fifteen prints are illustrated in Davis (2012): 13–30, Plates 6–20. Baron believes the images were originally produced as loose prints and subsequently bound into folio form along with explanatory text. This folio was put together at the City Press, Bentinck Street, Calcutta, whose proprietor Thomas Smith may have seen this format as more suited to broad distribution of the prints. Smith worked with dealers elsewhere in India, and he also marketed publications in London (Baron, email correspondence).

8 I am grateful to Rachel McDermott, Gaurika Mehta, Jack Hawley, and Mark Baron for email consultations on the Krishna-Kali theme.

9 See Archer (1971: 45). The Victoria and Albert Museum acquired the print from a Roman Catholic Missionary College in England. Religious missionaries often acquired images of the Hindu gods for use in fundraising.

10 Valuable efforts that look at devotional practices utilizing God-prints include Smith (1999) and Pinney (2004: 182–200).

11 For an introduction and history of Durgā Pūjā in Bengal, see McDermott (2011: 1–5). Guha-Thakurta 2015 looks at the recent developments in this festival and its display aesthetics.

12 The Wellcome Institute collection of early Indian prints was acquired by Dr. Paira Mall (1874–1957). He was sent by the Wellcome Trust to India in 1911 as a collecting agent, primarily to collect medical texts and manuscripts. But during his ten-year stay, he also assembled a large collection of early prints by the Calcutta Art Studio, Chitrashala Press of Poona, and the Ravi Varma Press (Symons 1993).

13 See Davis (2001) on ancient debates. For the nineteenth century, see Rammohan Roy's 1820 tract, "Dialogue between a Theist and an Idolater," in Hay (1964). Hatcher (2008) surveys many of the Bengali debates concerning "idolatry" of the mid-nineteenth century.

References

Archer, W. G. (1971), *Kalighat Paintings: A Catalogue and Introduction*, London: Her Majesty's Stationery Office.

Calcutta Art Studio (1883), *Scrap Book Illustrated with Fifteen Hindu Mythological Pictures*, Calcutta: Calcutta Art Studio.

Davis, R. H. (2001), "Indian Image-Worship and Its Discontents," in J. Assmann and A. I. Baumgarten (eds.), *Representation in Religion: Studies in Honor of Moshe Barasch*, 107–32, Leiden: Brill.

Davis, R. H. (2012), *Gods in Print: Masterpieces of India's Mythological Art*, San Rafael: Mandala Publishing.

Davis, R. H. (2013), "Krishna Enters the Age of Mechanical Reproduction," *Journal of Vaishnava Studies* 21 (2): 31–42.

Davis, R. H. (2015), "Temple in a Frame: God Posters for and of Worship," in C. Brosius, S. Ramaswamy, and Y. Saeed (eds.), *Virtual Homes, Image Worlds: Essays from Tasveer Ghar, the House of Pictures*, 138–49, New Delhi: Yoda Press.

Ghosh, A. (2006), *Power in Print: Popular Publishing and the Politics of Language and Culture in a Colonial Society*, New Delhi: Oxford University Press.

Guha-Thakurta, T. (1992), *The Making of a New "Indian" Art: Artists, Aesthetics and Nationalism in Bengal, c. 1850–1920*, Cambridge: Cambridge University Press.

Guha-Thakurta, T. (2015), *In the Name of the Goddess: The Durga Pujas of Contemporary Kolkata*, Delhi: Primus Books.

Gupta, S. (2003), "The Domestication of a Goddess: Caraṇa-tīrtha Kālīghāṭ, the Mahāpīṭha of Kālī," in R. F. McDermott and J. J. Kripal (eds.), *Encountering Kali: In the Margins, at the Center, in the West*, 60–79, Berkeley: University of California Press.

Hatcher, B. A. (2008), *Bourgeois Hinduism, or the Faith of the Modern Vedantists: Rare Discourses from Early Colonial Bengal*, Oxford: Oxford University Press.

Hauser, B. (2002), "From Oral Tradition to 'Folk Art': Reevaluating Bengali Scroll Paintings," *Asian Folklore Studies* 61 (1): 105–22.

Hawley, J. S. (1979), "Krishna's Cosmic Victories," *Journal of the American Academy of Religion* 47 (2): 201–21.

Hay, S. N. (1964), *Dialogue between an Theist and an Idolater: Brahin Pauttalik Samvad. An 1820 Tract Probably by Rammohan Roy*, Calcutta: K. L. Mukhopadhyay.

Hirsh, F. (2016), "A Rare Kali Woodcut from the Era of the Battala Printers," *Art in Print* 6 (3). https://artinprint.org/article/a-rare-kali-woodcut-from-the-era-of-the-battala-printers/ (accessed March 2022).

Holt, A. R., and K. Pechilis (2019). "Contemporary Images of Hindu Bhakti: Identity and Visuality," *Journal of Hindu Studies* 1: 1–13.

Inglis, S. R. (1995), "Suitable for Framing: The Work of a Modern Master," in L. A. Babb and S. S. Wadley (eds.), *Media and the Transformation of Religion in South Asia*, 51–75, Philadelphia: University of Pennsylvania Press.

Jain, J. (1998), *Picture Showmen: Insights into the Narrative Tradition in Indian Art*, Mumbai: Marg Publications.

Jain, J. (1999), *Kalighat Painting: Images from a Changing World*, Allahabad: Mapin Publishing.

Jain, J. (2004), *Indian Popular Culture: "The Conquest of the World as Picture,"* Kolkata: Apeejay Press.

Jain, K. (2007), *Gods in the Bazaar: The Economies of Indian Calendar Art*, Durham: Duke University Press.

Kinsley, D. R. (1997), *Tantric Visions of the Divine Feminine: The Ten Mahāvidyās*, Berkeley: University of California Press.

McDermott, R. F. (2011), *Revelry, Rivalry, and Longing for the Goddesses of Bengal: The Fortunes of Hindu Festivals*, New York: Columbia University Press.

Mitra, R. (1880), *The Antiquities of Orissa*, Calcutta: W. Newman & Co.

Mitter, P. (1994), *Art and Nationalism in Colonial India, 1850–1922*, Cambridge: Cambridge University Press.

Moodie, D. (2019), "Kalighat and the Fashioning of Middle Class Modernities," *International Journal of Hindu Studies* 23 (1): 11–26.

Mukharji, T. N. (1888), *Art-Manufactures of India*, Calcutta: Superintendent of Government Printing.

Paul, A. (1983), *Woodcut Prints of Nineteenth Century Calcutta*, Calcutta: Seagull Books.

Pinney, C. (2004), Photos of the Gods*: The Printed Image and Political Struggle in India*, London: Reaktion Books.

Ramos, I. (2015), "The Fragmentation of Sati: Constructing Hindu Identity through Pilgrimage Souvenirs," *Journal of Decorative and Propaganda Arts* 27: 12–35.

Singh, K. (1996), "Changing the Tune: Bengali Pata Painting's Encounter with the Modern," *India International Centre Quarterly* 23 (2): 60–78.

Sinha, S., and C. Panda (2011), *Kalighat Paintings*, Ahmedabad: Mapin Publishing.

Smith, H. D. (1995), "Impact of 'God Posters' on Hindus and Their Devotional Traditions," in L. Babb and S. S. Wadley (eds.), *Media and the Transformation of Religion in South Asia*, 24–50, Philadelphia: University of Pennsylvania Press.

Smith, H. D. (1999), "A Contemporary Iconic Tradition: Laksmi, Ganesa, Sarasvati—An Emerging 'New' Hindu Trimurti," in P. K. Mishra, *Studies in Hindu and Buddhist Art*, 11–49, New Delhi: Abhinav Publications.

Symons, H. J. M. (1993), *Wellcome Institute for the History of Medicine: A Short History*, London: The Wellcome Trust.

Wolterstorff, N. (2015), *Art Rethought: The Social Practices of Art*, Oxford: Oxford University Press.

2

Expanding Meanings of *Bhakti* in Bengali American Home Shrines

Ashlee Norene Andrews

Sita invited me into her sprawling home in an affluent Midwestern suburb and guided me upstairs to the home shrine that she created and maintains in the closet of her sons' playroom (Figure 2.1). When she arrived in the United States, she had nothing more than a few pocket-sized lithographs of her most beloved deities, and she could only afford to utilize a cardboard moving box next to her bed to house the images in her tiny apartment. As her household income and home expanded, so did her shrine. She purchased, or was gifted, *mūrti*s (embodiments of divinity) and gave her deities a proper home in this closet-turned-shrine room. Sita had grown up in her ancestral joint-family home outside of Kolkata, and *bārir pūjā* (domestic worship) had been a major routine of her household, particularly for her grandmother and mother. "You couldn't not see it," she told me, referring to her maternal predecessors' daily routines of cleansing, adorning, feeding, and worshipping the deities at home. It was family culture. In contrast, her in-laws—who were deeply influenced by Brahmo Samaj thought—were not interested in *pūjā* (worship). As a result, her shrine is, in her words, "really just for me." "Why do you maintain a shrine?" I asked her. Her answer was immediate: "For me, the number one thing is tradition, you know. It's what I was ever since I was born. It is something that I am. It is very typically, what I am."

In 2014, I began interviewing Bengali American Hindu women like Sita living in the Chicago metropolitan area about their home shrines and the traditions of domestic worship that they have developed, after completing a summer of fieldwork on the same topic with women in Kolkata, India. Unlike their mothers, grandmothers, and mothers-in-law—who typically inherited ancestral deity images and were eventually given charge of their in-law's preexisting shrine after marriage—most of the Bengali American women I worked with immigrated to the United States without their in-laws and with very few deity images or

Figure 2.1 Sita's shrine. Chicago, Illinois. December 2014. Photograph Ashlee Norene Andrews.

pūjā implements. After immigrating, some of these women drastically limited, and a few even rejected, the home shrine traditions their in-laws might have expected them to maintain. Many others, like Sita, developed elaborate deity collections and domestic worship traditions in response to their lives in the United States. These women have constructed and worshipped at shrines in their guest and master bedroom closets, in home office bookcases, on bedside tables, or in IKEA cabinets repurposed with extra shelving and track lighting. At times, women would admit with embarrassment or even regret that their shrines and worship traditions were not as elaborate or old as those of their native childhood homes. Some would laugh at memories of their first attempts at shrine-making on moving boxes and in the small apartments in which they first resided after immigration. For the most part, however, women expressed pride in the unique and wholly personal nature of their shrines and domestic worship traditions that they thoughtfully crafted and maintained in the United States.

My work with these women encouraged me to see the home shrine—not simply the deity image—as *bhakti* visuality and to envision a more expansive meaning for *bhakti* than the now common gloss "devotion to a form of divinity." Beyond housing the embodiments of particular divinities that women care for and worship, shrines can also contain pictures of ancestors and family gurus, souvenirs from travels in India or around the U.S., gifts from friends and family, and ancestral heirlooms. These items visualize each woman's personal histories, relationships, families, and familial traditions. As such, women's creation and arrangement of home shrines and their regular ritual engagements with the shrine—what I call home shrine image-making—enable women to maintain relationships not only with particular deities but also with friends, family members, and ancestors, and to participate in familial traditions. This participation and relationship maintenance in turn enable shrine-makers to inhabit, and then teach to their American-born children, the identities forged through these relationships and traditions, which they often fear losing in the United States. In the course of an interview early on in my research, one woman named Bani reflected to me that her work to find time and energy to perform *pūjā* in the United States as a busy working mother of two was motivated by her desire to maintain the traditions she grew up with as much as any desire to connect to God. Bani described, with great respect, her mother-in-law's deep love for the deity Gopāl. She then compared her mother-in-law's desire to connect with Gopāl through *pūjā* with her own desire to maintain her Bengali Hindu traditions in the United States. After saying this, she thoughtfully reflected "Perhaps I am expanding the meaning of *bhakti*." Her thoughtful reflection planted the conceptual seed for this chapter's analysis of the meaning and visuality of *bhakti* within home shrine image-making.

This chapter will analyze Bengali American women's home shrines as *bhakti* visuality and argue that their home shrine image-making expands the meaning of *bhakti* to include participation in the relationships and traditions integral to familial and ethno-religious identity. I furthermore show how important this participation and relationship maintenance is for women who live in a context characterized by their ethno-religious marginalization and their geographic separation from family and natal household routines. My arguments are founded upon years of ethnographic research with Bengali American women living in Chicago. They are also guided by many of the scholars in this collection, whose work has provided us with a fuller vocabulary to speak about the meanings and objects of *bhakti* beyond the gloss "devotion." For example, Richard Davis has explained *bhakti* as participating in, sharing in, tasting, and being as intimate as possible with the divine being (2002: 28). Karen Pechilis has similarly built upon the gloss "participation," defining *bhakti* as "a stance of I am involved accompanied by a participatory impetus that mobiles intellection, emotion and the body" (2019: 142). These discussions helpfully communicate the depth of the relational intimacy one seeks with the divine being through *bhakti* traditions. Moreover, as Pechilis notes, the rendering "participation" has the advantage of "not resonating with something we think we already know but encourages us to understand the relationships of *bhakti* as represented by its promoters and interpreters in history" (Prentiss 1999: 24). *Bhakti* traditions are shaped and remade by each practitioner and community to respond to their evolving needs and worlds (Holt and Pechilis 2019: 138). Scholarly conceptions of *bhakti* and *bhakti* visuality must, therefore, be flexible and expansive enough to reflect the diverse character and objects of this "participation." For the Bengali American women I worked with, the home shrine is a *bhakti* visuality that they created to fulfill their desire to bridge the gaps between themselves and their deities, families, ancestors, and familial traditions—gaps they experience as augmented living in the United States.

Just as home shrine image-making expands the meaning of *bhakti*, it also makes the subjects of Hindu transactional "looking" more inclusive and the powers of *bhakti* visuality more expansive. *Darśan* (seeing and being seen by a deity) frames visuality as a primary mode of establishing intimacy between deity and devotee (Sahney 2016: 281). The logic of *darśan* certainly informs how most of the women I worked with interpret and experience the deity images within their shrines. However, women also suggested their deity images were inclusive of presence, so that looking at an inherited deity image could also embody and provide connection to ancestral presences. Moreover, women frequently extended the logic of *darśan* to pictures or belongings of deceased family members that they placed within the shrine as well as to the shrine itself. Many women told me they feel their ancestors look upon them and bless them when they look at their shrine, and they frequently expressed pride that they had constructed shrines that embodied these presences. Importantly, however, the shrine's capacity to enable women's relational participation is not limited to its embodiment of divine or ancestral presence. The shrine can also represent family and tradition, and it can visualize personal histories and relationships; when women look at the shrine, it enables them to recall, enjoy, and connect to each of these. Thus, the home shrine both embodies metaphysical presence and represents aspects of existence beyond those presences. In this way, "embodiment" and "representation" are not mutually exclusive categories of interpretation of the nature of this devotional visuality; they are coexisting categories of interpretation that point to the inclusive subjects and expansive powers of visuality within the practice of home shrine image-making.[1]

To be clear, I am not denying that the deity images that women place within their shrines are potent foci of relational intimacy. Indeed, for most women, a primary function of the home shrine is to house the deity images that demand the daily acts of *sevā* (service) that enable the traditional sense of *bhakti* as an intimate and selfless participation with divinity. However, because women's relationships with divinity are embedded within a larger web of human relationships, deity images can facilitate women's relationship maintenance and participation with more than that deity alone.[2] Women's relationships with each deity are often inherited from generations of familial devotion or ignited and developed through women's human relationships. Additionally, women are often gifted or inherit deity images from loved ones. As a result, deity images can visualize and help women to connect to a broad web of human relationships. Ancestral deity images that have been worshipped in a family for generations additionally offer a potent means for women to participate in familial traditions. These human relationships and familial traditions that inform a woman's relationships with particular deities and deity images, in turn, increase the pleasure and significance of worshipping these images, particularly for women living in the diaspora. In other words, for the women I worked with, the deity image not only remains significant as a focus for participation with that divinity, but it also gains significance as a conduit to participate in a web of human relationships and traditions important to shrine-makers.

That being said, if we are to understand home shrine image-making as a *bhakti* practice and how it expands meanings of *bhakti*, we must also expand our scholarly gaze and contemplate the shrine itself. In doing so, we may value images of family members and ancestors, gifts from faraway relatives and dear friends, souvenirs of trips taken to India within home shrines as examples of *bhakti* visuality because they visualize the relationships, histories, and traditions in which women want to connect to and participate. Furthermore, we may value shrine-makers as thoughtful *bhakti* artisans, whose visually stunning, emotionally affecting, and relationally powerful shrines are profoundly important for themselves and their families, and for the maintenance of Hindu traditions in the United States.[3]

Ethnography and Background

From September 2014 to December 2015, I attended meetings hosted by the Bengali Association of Greater Chicago (BAGC) to conduct informal interviews and observe the community. In this same fifteen-month period, I conducted home visits and interviews with eighteen first and second-generation immigrant women from the BAGC community. In order to diversify and expand my data, in 2019, I returned to Chicago for the summer to work with twelve new women and revisited women from the first phase of this study. The women I worked with ranged in age from eighteen to seventy-eight, though the majority of women were middle-aged. All of the women I worked with live in middle or upper-middle-class households in the United States and have lived there for at least twenty years. Additionally, they come from middle-class and upper-caste families in Kolkata. This socioeconomic skewing of my participant pool reflects the general makeup of the BAGC community.[4]

The Bengali word historically used to refer to the home shrine is *ṭhākurghor*, which translates as "God's room" or "God's home." When women referred to their home shrine in English, they most commonly referred to it as a "home temple" and often interchanged this English translation with "*mandir.*" This tendency to refer to the home shrine as a "temple" is significant because it points to an idea that many Bengalis stated explicitly throughout my research: for Bengalis, the home shrine is the Bengali temple. It is the center of an individual's and a family's practice of *pūjā*, and a primary place that Bengali Hindus express and maintain their everyday Bengali Hindu ways of life. Bengali Americans frequently contrast the Bengali emphasis on worshipping at home with what they viewed as a tendency for Hindus from other regions, especially south India, to place greater importance upon worship at the public temple. This generalization is to some degree echoed in the pattern of temple-building in the Chicago metropolitan area, where the largest and oldest public temple communities, like the Hindu Temple of Greater Chicago or the Chicago Balaji Temple, were built by immigrant communities from south Indian states.[5] Folks in the BAGC community frequently, and with great pride, characterized Bengalis as a uniquely progressive and intellectual community, particularly when it comes to religious philosophy and practice. Sometimes in the same breath, they would cite the Bengali preference for home worship as an illustration of the less conservative and more intellectually curious approach to ritual and religion that Bengalis tend to take. For Bengali Americans, the home shrine is, therefore, extremely important for the maintenance of what are viewed as uniquely Bengali approaches to religion.

Like the public temple, the *ṭhākurghor* houses deity images that must be cared for and worshipped. All members of a household can offer some kind of worship to domestic deities each day like bowing in respect, lighting incense, or offering a prayer. However, the more elaborate forms of deity caretaking like cleansing, feeding, adorning, and dressing deities, as well as cleaning and arranging the shrine, have typically fallen to women (Ghosh 1995: 21). I have found this to be the case in both brahmin and non-brahmin families in Chicago and in Kolkata. Even in brahmin families where a male family member is trained in and performs *pūjā* to home deities, the matriarch tends to be the one in the home who maintains and cleans the *pūjā* space, procures all the items necessary for *pūjā*, cooks food offerings for *pūjā*, and performs her own *pūjā*. Some families, particularly non-brahmin families, have historically employed a brahmin priest to perform *pūjā* to domestic deities to ensure that all brahmanical protocols are maintained. In this case, the matriarch of the household tends to be the one in charge of employing and assisting the priest because the deities' care remains her responsibility. Moreover, even in the case that a brahmin priest performs regular *pūjā*, women are likely to still perform their own *pūjā* to domestic deities. In other words, a brahmin's rituals do not usually replace a woman's *pūjā* or her responsibility over the home shrine.

Historically, Bengali women take over care for their in-laws' already-established home shrine after marriage. This responsibility is assimilated with all of the domestic caretaking labors that have historically been regarded as the duties of a *bārir bau* or "daughter-in-law," which also significantly means "housewife" in Bengali (Ghosh 1995: 21). The deities in the shrine are viewed as family members, and some women suggested that Bengali women have historically been the primary home shrine caretakers because women are often deemed (or view themselves) as the natural caretakers of baby Gopāl or Ma Kālī. Women also explained their historical responsibility over the shrine by citing the fact that middle-class men have historically been too occupied by education or careers outside the home to have the time necessary to care for a shrine.[6] Today, however, middle-class Bengali womanhood has evolved in India and the United States so that being educated and pursuing a career are now also highly encouraged for middle-class women. This is particularly so for Bengali American women, who face added pressure as immigrants to achieve significant financial and social success. Thus, the majority of women I worked with in the United States have fruitful careers that demand a great deal of time outside the home. Still, among Bengali American households, home shrine image-making tends to either be done by the matriarch or not done at all. These historical expectations most certainly normalize domestic shrine traditions as female-centered labor, but, as I will show, the Bengali American women I spoke with told me they chose to create and maintain a shrine in the United States primarily to maintain relationships with their deities and families and participate in their Bengali Hindu traditions.[7] It is to three of these women's home shrine image-making that I now turn.

Home Shrine Image-Making in the United States

Shushmita's shrine (Figure 2.2) is large and beautifully adorned. It sits on a cardboard box that takes up the entire length of her guest bedroom walk-in closet in the home she purchased with her husband nineteen years earlier. She

Figure 2.2 Shushmita's shrine. Chicago, Illinois. June 2019. Photograph Ashlee Norene Andrews.

has decorated the largest box with a cherished cloth inherited from her mother, and she uses the silver *pūjā* plates and a few cooking implements that her mother gave to her. At one point, Shushmita had considered purchasing a more traditional wooden altar, or *maṇḍapam*, which would have been more like her mother's back home in Kolkata, but none were large enough and she wanted everyone in the shrine to "have room to breathe." Indeed, over the years, she has grown her shrine beyond the box itself. She had recently been initiated at the Vivekananda Vedanta Society of Chicago, a decision she largely credits to her husband, whose family have been devout Ramakrishna Mission disciples for generations. After initiation, Shushmita created a separate shrine area devoted to Ramakrishna, but she confessed to me that she didn't make time to read any of her swami's writings or attend his lectures at the Vedanta Society.

The peripheral location she has given to this mini-shrine is meaningful. Vedāntic philosophy denigrates *pūjā* as necessary only for the spiritually immature to connect to the ultimately formless, abstract divine.[8] Shushmita performs *pūjā* at home for around an hour every morning, and she told me it gives her the mental peace and strength necessary to make it through the challenges of working motherhood. It is, therefore, not surprising that her shrine image-making does not facilitate her participation with her swami or his teachings.

What, then, does Shushmita give priority to at her shrine? The answer is her father, whose picture and reading glasses she has placed prominently in the center of her shrine. When I met Shushmita, her father had passed away just a few years earlier, and much of our discussions circulated around the acute difficulty of his death and being far from him when he had died. She had boarded a plane to India just three hours after her mother's phone call informing her of his unexpected passing, and she was able to attend all of his death rituals. Nevertheless, at the end of the two weeks of rituals, she had to leave her mother and sister—and her father's cremated body—behind in India. Her father's death had brought the distance between herself and her family into stark focus. A number of women I have worked with in the United States have spoken similarly about the difficulty of losing their parents after immigrating and of the profound feelings of separation they felt both from the loss of their deceased family member and from their living family in India. It is very common for shrine image-makers, in India and the United States, to integrate images of deceased family members and gurus into their shrine image.[9] Women in the United States suggested that the shrine helped them overcome the separation between themselves and their deceased family members, and that this was particularly important because they lived so far from the rest of their living family members.

After her father's death, Shushmita placed her father's picture and glasses in the center of her shrine so she could, as she put it, "see him directly and feel that he was there." This comment is noteworthy and worth reflecting upon. Shushmita suggests that seeing her father's picture and glasses is connected to feeling his presence. Indeed, for a year and a half after his death, she felt his concentrated presence at her home shrine, so much so that, according to Shushmita, her mother asked her one day to "let him go." One function of Hindu death rituals is, after all, to free a soul from its earthly connections so it can move on to another form and life. After the one-year anniversary of her father's death, Shushmita felt her father's presence wane, but today, she still feels he is "here in the shrine." From Shushmita's perspective, she has constructed an image that visualizes her father so well that it houses some part of his actual presence, in much the same way that the *mūrti*s in her shrine embody divine beings. Even as the feeling of her father's presence has waned over the years, Shushmita told me that when she sits in front of her shrine, she feels that her father is looking at her and offering his blessings and the blessings of all her ancestors. In saying so, Shushmita evoked the very logic of *darśan*. On this note, it is significant that of all of her father's possessions, Shushmita has chosen her father's glasses (Figure 2.3) to display along with his picture. Shushmita never explicitly explained to me why she had chosen his glasses, but her choice may be informed by the tradition of *darśan*. A divine being must be able to see to be present in an image, and one may only be blessed by the divine being if they can both see and be seen by it through the divine image (Eck 1998: 7). This is why *mūrti*s are often believed to be fully consecrated only after

Figure 2.3 Father's glasses, inside Sushmita's shrine. Chicago, Illinois. June 2019. Photograph Ashlee Norene Andrews.

the eyes are painted or opened. Her father's glasses are evocative of this tradition of consecration. His glasses help produce her father's presence because they are connected to both his seeing and being seen by his daughter.

Shushmita also frequently visits the Shri Sai Baba Mandir in Aurora and the nearby Chicago Balaji Temple. Neither Sai Baba nor Bālājī were worshipped in her or her husband's families. A decade earlier her eldest child had been diagnosed with a cancerous brain tumor at the age of three, and it was during this time that friends had suggested she begin worshipping Sai Baba and Bālājī and visiting their temples. She partially attributes her son's cancer remission to both these divine figures' intercession. Shushmita also worships Bālājī and Sai Baba at home. Their images are displayed near her father's picture. However, she claims that because the temple *mūrti*s are larger and "more magnificent" she feels their presence in an equally magnified way at the temple. Thus, if she is asking for their assistance on a particular issue in her life, Shushmita prefers to visit these divine beings in their temples. I asked her what, if anything, her own shrine provided her that visits to either temple could not. Her response is significant: "I just feel like my *pūjā* room is *my* area. I have designed it this way. I feel like my dad, his mom, everybody lives here. I feel like they are here with us. It's my space." Her answer emphasizes the personal and intimate nature of a shrine she has designed herself, and the utility of her shrine to embody and connect her to ancestral presence.

As is the case for many first-generation immigrant women, Shushmita's shrine image-making is also a way for her to teach her American-born children about their family and their family's Bengali Hindu traditions. Shushmita will occasionally invite her son and daughter, aged nine and thirteen, to join her for morning *pūjā*, and she has welcomed them to come and sit at the shrine anytime they want. Her broader hope is that by seeing her shrine and helping her with the *pūjā*, her children will feel affinity for their Bengali and Hindu traditions and the identity inherent in these traditions. She views this as particularly important instruction given that both of her children attend a private Baptist school, and each have shared stories of their teachers denigrating Hindu traditions in both covert and overt ways. For example, her son's teacher had recently shown a picture of Gaṇeśa during a classroom presentation and had referred to the beloved deity as a "false" god. Having attended a Catholic school in Kolkata like many middle-class Bengalis, Shushmita was familiar with these kinds of critiques and with the challenge of being Christian at school and Hindu at home. Just as her own mother had done when Shushmita was young, Shushmita relies on her shrine to counter these critiques and teach her children about their family's Hindu beliefs and practices. In her years of ethnographic work exploring newly immigrated

Hindu women's practices of home worship and decoration in the United States, Puja Sahney similarly found that many immigrants view their home shrines, and even the decorative images of deities they place throughout their homes, as pedagogical in nature (2016: 297). Beyond being foci of personal devotion, these images also help teach their American-born children about the deities so central to their family's religious identity. Shampa and Sanjoy Mazumdar have similarly argued that for Hindu families, who sacralize their homes through practices like shrine-making, the home facilitates "religious teaching, expression and identity" (2003: 154). This becomes particularly important for diasporic populations because it makes the home a place, where children can "observe and participate in the practice of their religion without fear" (Mazumdar 2003: 153).

Still, Shushmita worries that her work to help inform her children's religious identity will not be enough for them to want to maintain a shrine when they are older. At one point, after describing the family history of her *pūjā* items, Shushmita thoughtfully reflected, "But I sometimes wonder what will happen to all of this because these kids won't do all of this, I'm sure . . . but we'll see." In saying so, she communicated a common uncertainty expressed by many of the first-generation immigrants I interviewed. To what degree, if at all, would their American-born children create and worship at a shrine? The particulars of second-generation immigrant women's shrine image-making extend beyond the purview of this chapter, but it deserves mentioning that all six of the American-born women I worked with had small shrine images in their bedrooms, apartments, or dorm rooms and irregularly prayed in gratitude and/or reverence to their mini-shrines. Fascinatingly, two of these women expressed uncertainty about the existence of God and all of them a distrust in religion more generally. Despite this, each of them told me that they kept shrines because it helped them to feel connected to their families and to maintain the Bengali Hindu traditions that gave them great pride. Much as Bani suggested, even for women for whom home shrine image-making is not primarily a participation with divinity, the tradition remains significant as a powerful mechanism for women to participate in the Bengali Hindu traditions they fear losing as religious and ethnic minorities in the United States. While this may push the boundaries of *bhakti*, they are certainly boundaries to evaluate if we are to understand immigrant Hindu identity and religiosity.

Subrata's shrine (Figure 2.4) also illustrates the utility of the home shrine as a means of participating in family traditions and the familial identity inherent in them. Subrata and her husband are both professors at a local university, and they moved to the United States nearly thirty years ago. In the center of her shrine, the area given the most significance, Subrata has placed the framed

Figure 2.4 Subrata's shrine. Chicago, Illinois. July 2019. Photograph Ashlee Norene Andrews.

deity images that her mother gave to her when she immigrated. These were the same images that her mother previously worshipped at her own home shrine, and her mother had told her that Subrata needed the images because she was "going far away." Echoing Shushmita, Subrata told me that she preferred her home shrine over the temple because when she looked at these specific, inherited images, she felt she received the blessings of her family members. Beyond conveying ancestral presence and blessing, inherited deity images like these also have utility as a means to participate in family traditions. Subrata told me as much when she continued to explain her preference for home worship:

> Because my home deities have been passed on by my mom I can connect more (than at the temple). And that's why, when I am worshipping at home, be it ten minutes, I think I am connecting more to my past. You understand? It's like, oh my God, like I grew up sitting next to my mom when she used to worship the same picture of Kālī. And she gave it to me. She passed it on to me. So it's that connection.

When Subrata sits and worships at the shrine she created in her suburban Chicago home using the images she watched her mother worship at for years in Kolkata, she connects to the ancestors, the faraway family members who had worshipped the same images, and the familial identity associated with the generational performance of such domestic *pūjās*. What Subrata calls "my past" and "my roots" are references to not only her own childhood memories of watching her mother perform *pūjās* at her shrine but also her familial identity communicated in that memory and her family's continual performance of generational domestic worship. In his study of images of Jesus displayed in Protestant American homes, David Morgan suggests that devotional images that are handed down through generations can shape the family's collective memory and broadcast the religious identity of a family (1998: 19). When the image is displayed in the home—the epitome of everyday identity inculturation—that family's memory and religious identity are remembered and imbibed. Emphasizing the particular power of material culture in Indic contexts, Tracy Pintchman has similarly argued that objects of worship can embody histories and, as such, "help produce a sense of collective identity or tradition even as innovation occurs" (2016: 11). Inherited deity images allow women to maintain a relationship with the deity as well as connect to family members and participate in family histories. This participation in family traditions can, in turn, articulate and affirm familial identity, which becomes particularly important in the diaspora. Much as our first image-maker, Sita, reflected that home shrine image-making was "very typically what I am," Subrata's home shrine image-making enables her to connect to and participate with the familial "roots" and "past" that are core to who she understands herself to be.

Subrata's shrine image also demonstrates how shrines visualize stories about their shrine-makers, much like a deity image visualizes stories about the deity it depicts. Her shrine's visual aesthetic is characterized by abundance. She has included every single deity image she has ever received or collected over her life within her shrine and now struggles to find a space for new items when she receives them. At one point, when I described her shrine-making as an artistry, Subrata laughed off the term "artistry" and remarked, "I don't really see any artistic sense. I just wanted to fit everything." She then explained that it was hard to limit the items in her shrine because "Everything has a story. There is always something associated with each of the things that you see here." Illustrating this, she then began to recall the giver and particular circumstances around items in her shrine. Every item was connected to a person, a relationship, or an event she felt to be significant. To remove an item felt equivalent to denying the significance of the associated person, relationship, or event—like erasing it from her visual story.

Because shrine-makers like Subrata often include items that were given to them from loved ones or inherited from family, the excess of a shrine can reflect the richness of a shrine-makers' relationships. It can also reflect the abundance of a shrine-makers' life: the trips they have taken, the celebrations and holidays they have observed, the special events of their lives, all of which were marked by their purchase, inheritance, or reception of a material item that they then include within their shrine. In his essay analyzing his mother's domestic shrine and *pūjā*, Jayasinhji Jhala similarly observes that because every item within his mother's shrine is associated with people and events in her life, the shrine provides a visualization of the societal networks within which she is embedded (2000: 112). Jhala furthermore argues that gazing at these objects and contemplating the persons connected with the object allow her to "project herself into a spatial domain of association that is not a part of her everyday" (Jhala 2000: 113). When shrine-makers include items within their shrine, they acknowledge the significance of these particular personal histories and relationships associated with each item in their lives. Seeing and contemplating these relationships and events materialized in an abundant visual form can, in turn, produce profound feelings of connection and identification with these histories and relationships. Thus, abundance of a shrine can enhance a shrine's relational power. This is precisely what folklorist and art historian Kay Turner argues in her analysis of mostly Mexican American Catholic women's shrines. Turner characterizes the home shrine as a bridge-building mechanism that "consecrates and serves women's understanding of the power of relationship to overcome separation" (1999: 23) and, furthermore, argues that excess is a part of what she calls the "aesthetic of relationship" that characterizes shrine-making and makes its bridge-building goals possible (1999: 100).

Yet as Nina's simple shrine image (Figure 2.5) demonstrates, shrines need not be elaborate to have profound relational and bridge-building capacity. Nina chose an understated aesthetic intentionally. Her Bengali husband is an adamant atheist, and she felt it would be disrespectful to him for her shrine to be too

Figure 2.5 Nina's shrine. Chicago, Illinois. July 2019. Photograph Ashlee Norene Andrews.

elaborate or take up too much of their home. This is also one reason why she keeps her shrine in her personal home office rather than in their bedroom. She also felt an elaborate shrine to be incongruent with her worldview and her ritual approach. Her life motto, which intentionally echoes Ramakrishna's teachings, is "let people know my religion through what I do for others." Nina completes her work for others as the international director of a nonprofit home and school for girls that she helped establish in Kolkata. She described the humanitarian work as "my religion" and told me she values it over any ritual as an expression of her beliefs. Still, she begins most days by reading a religious text, giving *praṇām* (bowing in respect) and sometimes praying or meditating at her home shrine.

Nina was born in Kolkata, but her family immigrated to Australia in 1974. She grew up in Sydney until the late 1980s when she immigrated with her husband to the United States. The few items she includes in her shrine intentionally reflect the maternal side of her family's affiliation with Ramakrishna Mission as well as her paternal side's deep devotion to Kālī. The top shelf of her shrine, which displays the Ramakrishna Mission trinity—Ramakrishna, Sarada Ma, and Swami Vivekananda—visualizes the centrality of these saints' teachings and examples in her life as well as her maternal ancestors. On the lower shelf of her shrine, she has carefully curated a handful of deity images gifted from family. The Durgā that she has framed and placed on the far left was a gift from her grandfather. He gave it to her at her wedding before she left Australia to move to the United States. On the inside of the card, he wrote, "Even if you are far away, let her *śakti* (power) always be with you." The Kālī image on the far right of the same shelf is a souvenir postcard from the Dakshineswar Kali Temple in Kolkata. She has many fond memories of visiting the temple with her grandmother and father when her family would spend the summers in Kolkata, and her father so loved the temple that her brother spread their father's ashes on the temple grounds.

She has very intentionally placed her shrine in a bookshelf. Her maternal great-grandfather was a professor of medicine in Kolkata and had for some time served as head of Kolkata's Theosophical Society. Not surprisingly, the primary belief that Nina's mother attributed to him, and which Nina herself had internalized as a central theological belief, was that "knowledge is God." Nina cherished a story her mother had told her about her grandfather, where every year during Sarasvatī *pūjā*, he had the children place all of the household's books into an enormous pile. And then they would perform *pūjā* to the books, rather than the traditional image veneration of the goddess of knowledge Sarasvatī. After sharing this story with me, I happened to notice the eclectic mix of books that lined her own bookshelves, and she immediately pointed me to a book she had purposely placed just above her images of the Ramakrishna trinity: Richard Dawkins's *The God Delusion*. She laughed and reminded me of her belief that knowledge is God and then continued saying, "If you believe in Sarasvatī as knowledge, you must be open to all ideas. And God can take it. I believe it. God can take your questions." Nina's shrine powerfully demonstrates the importance of expanding our scholarly vision of *bhakti* and its visuality; even a thoughtfully placed copy of *The God Delusion* can connect Nina to divinity, to her theological beliefs, and to her maternal ancestors.

Alongside her maternal predecessors' universalist and Vedāntic philosophies, Nina holds a deep and thoughtful faith in Kālī. She experiences Kālī as a source of *śakti*, particularly during times of crisis. In light of this, in addition to the Kālī in her shrine, Nina has also placed her favorite image of Kālī adjacent to her main shrine and looking down over her office desk—a sacred site all its own since it is where she completes her humanitarian work. The image (Figure 2.6) depicts Kālī's feet sprinkled with the stars of the universe. Nina finds this image comforting as it reminds her of Kālī's vastness in the face of her own challenges. In speaking of such challenges, Nina told me about an inexplicable experience she had while sitting at her shrine twenty years earlier. Her eldest son had just been diagnosed, as a toddler, with a cognitive disability, and doctors had told her that he was not likely to ever be able to live independently.

Overwhelmed with the diagnosis, Nina fell into morning prayer at her shrine. When she opened her eyes, everything was a brilliant color and she was filled with an inexplicable peace, courage, and optimism. She was certain it was Kālī's presence that filled her shrine and her mind. The event motivated her to become

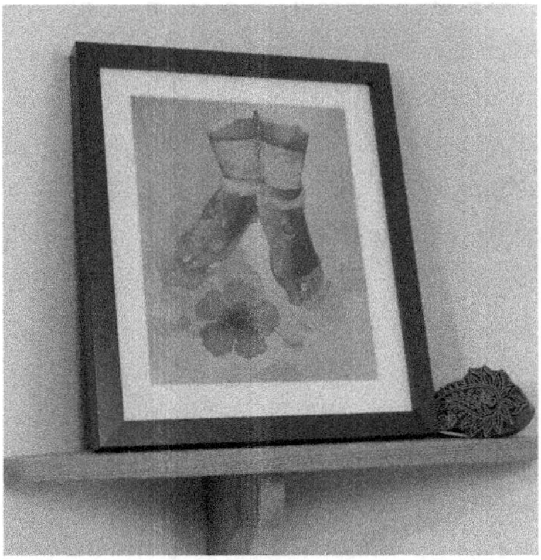

Figure 2.6 Kālī's feet. Chicago, Illinois. July 2019. Photograph Ashlee Norene Andrews.

a tireless advocate for her son's educational growth; today he is a successful computer engineer. Nina told me she doesn't need an image of Kālī to feel close to the divine mother because she is, after all, the universe itself. At the same time, Nina believes that Kālī was especially present at her shrine that morning twenty years earlier. In light of this, when she is scared or faced with a major challenge, she sits before her shrine and, in her words, "dump(s) everything at (Kālī's) feet."

In his study of Marian devotion, Robert Orsi suggests that immigrant communities frequently construct religious networks that "establish connections between heaven and earth that stretch as well between one environment and another and among families, friends, teachers, and others around the world in their new homes and in the ones they left" (2007: 3). Nina's shrine exemplifies this religious work. The Durgā and Kālī images in particular visualize both transnational and metaphysical networks between Nina, her family, and beloved deities and as a consequence help her to feel connected to everyone within this network. Nina said much of this to me explicitly. First, she suggested, perhaps not surprisingly, that her shrine helped bridge the geographical gaps between herself and her family in Kolkata and Australia, saying, "Even though I am far away from Kolkata family and Sydney, I don't feel alone. I feel connected to my family, and I feel that the connection is not a spatial thing. It is a heart thing." Later, when she reflected upon her curation of the items in her shrine, she significantly suggested that the familial relationships that inform her deity images augment the divine presence and blessing that she feels they provide, saying, "I feel like (these deity images) have come into my life for a reason. Well-wishers—my mom, my dad, my grandparents—they have given me these things, so I associate God's blessings with them too." In saying so, she not only demonstrates precisely the kind of networks between people and divine beings that Orsi describes, but, significant for our understanding of *bhakti*, demonstrates the interconnected nature of participation with divinity and participation with family. Her shrine image provides her life-sustaining connections with Kālī, and this connection with Kālī is augmented and matched by her connection with her family members.

Conclusion

Throughout my research in the United States, I have asked women to consider the differences between their self-made home shrines and Chicago's public temples. Most women told me that they feel they better express love and experience intimate connections with divinity at their own home shrines. In the temples in Chicago, as in most temples in India, public ritual is mediated by trained, usually male, brahmin priests, and the massive deity forms are to be approached carefully and with awe. In contrast, at home, where women can be the primary ritualists, shrine-makers can build up and maintain intimate, familial relationships with their shrine's particular divine embodiments. This allows them to experience greater intimacy and, therefore, a higher quality *bhakti* in the traditional sense of the word. As I have demonstrated throughout this chapter, maintaining, gazing, and worshipping at their self-made shrines also allow women to participate with subjects beyond particular divinities. At home, a woman like Shushmita can incorporate images of beloved ancestors and family heirlooms that help her invoke, take blessings from, and maintain connections with her ancestors. A woman like Subrata can perform the rituals she watched her maternal predecessors perform with the very deity images her ancestors had performed, helping her to both maintain relationships with her ancestors and participate in family traditions. A woman like Nina can carefully curate items within her shrine that visualize and strengthen the relational networks between herself, her faraway family, and her beloved deities.

These utilities of and preference for the home shrine are significant for a number of reasons. For one, the unique capacities of the home shrine to connect Bengali American women to family, tradition, and ethno-religious identity highlight the particular importance that home shrine image-making can have for immigrant communities. Indeed, one function of my research is to make visible and value immigrant women's domestic religious labor and the work it accomplishes for immigrant women, their families, and their ethno-religious communities. At present, the amount of scholarship devoted to exploring Hindu women's domestic religious labor in the United States is simply not proportional to the importance of this labor for women and their ethno-religious communities. As I have demonstrated throughout this chapter, my findings are also significant because they encourage the expansion of our scholarly conceptions of *bhakti* and its visuality to reflect the desires particular to Hindu immigrant communities and the visual forms these communities utilize to fulfill these desires. The practitioner and context-specific nature of *bhakti* means that what *bhakti* means for one practitioner may not "count" as *bhakti* for another and that one *bhakti* visuality may accomplish the goals of *bhakti* for one person but not another. Indeed, it is possible that this chapter has explicated meanings and images of *bhakti* that contradict or disturb what other *bhakti* practitioners or traditions explored in this collection envision as *bhakti* and its visuality. It can be hard to hear a *bhakta* like Kabīr in Sita's reflection that her shrine is valuable because it helps her connect to worldly strappings like family or tradition. However, as the other contributors in this book are also likely to show, expansions, contradictions, and adaptations are nothing new to *bhakti* and its visuality.

Notes

1 Here I adopt Joyce Flueckiger's argument that Hindu interpretations of the nature of the physical image of the divine posit that the deity image is either a representation or an embodiment of the deity (Flueckiger 2015: 78). While Flueckiger is speaking specifically about deity images, these are helpful categories to think about the nature of the shrine as well.

2 This discussion draws substantially from Robert Orsi's argument that religion is a network of relationships between heaven and earth, and that devotional media provide points of encounter not only between people and their sacred figures but also between people (Orsi 2007: 49).

3 It is worth noting that aside from a few important contributions (Sahney 2016; Mazumdar and Mazumdar 2003; Saunders 2019; Gunn 2018) scholars specializing in Hinduism in North America have largely ignored the traditions of home worship. Scholars of Hinduism working in the United States have focused largely upon public temple communities, aptly showing how the temple gains importance for immigrants in the United States as a location to synthesize, institutionalize, and transmit Hindu traditions (Dempsey 2006; Eck 2001; Narayanan 2006). My research demonstrates that for some immigrant Hindu communities, the home gains its own significance in the diaspora as a space for immigrant communities to connect to family and familial traditions in the United States.

4 In the course of my research, I witnessed shifts in the BAGC community as older members retired and new immigrants took on roles of leadership and participation. As one woman put it to me, "There are new (non-upper caste) names on the roll call." I hope to continue research with these new families.

5 In 2017, a new temple sponsored largely by a single Bengali family was inaugurated. The temple houses a number of *mūrti*s of deities that are of particular significance to Bengalis, with Kālī Ma at the temple's center. Significantly, the temple is called the Chicago Kali Bari, which translates as Chicago Kālī home. The founders derive this name from Ramakrishna's discourse, but it also recognizes how they envisioned the temple like a home because, for Bengalis, the home is where you worship.

6 Women explained these gendered divisions of space and labor as having always been, but historian Partha Chatterjee (1993) and ethnographer Henrike Donner

(2008) have aptly demonstrated that these divisions became especially cemented among the middle class in Kolkata during the colonial era. During this time, middle-class Bengali men took on positions in colonial administration and adopted British cultural norms outside the home. In response to men's movement into the British "world," middle-class Bengali women's roles and realms became more acutely defined in terms of the "home."

7 As with every Hindu tradition, variety in home shrine image-making abounds, and there are limits to the female-centered nature of this tradition. I interviewed a handful of women in Kolkata and the United States who did not have a home shrine. I also encountered a small handful of families in India and the United States, where male family members had shown greater interest in *pūjā* and were the primary home shrine caretaker and ritualist.

8 I met with Shushmita's swami and discussed my ethnography. He was kind and generous with his time, but ultimately espoused this very interpretation and critique of *pūjā*.

9 See, for example, Figure 2.4. Subrata has constructed an impressive ancestral bookshelf to the left of her central shrine.

References

Chatterjee, P. (1993), *The Nation and Its Fragments: Colonial and Postcolonial Histories*, Princeton: Princeton University Press.

Davis, R. (2002), "Introduction: A Brief History of Religions in India," in Donald Lopez (ed.) *Religions of Asia in Practice*, 3–50, Princeton: Princeton University Press.

Dempsey, Corinne (2006), *The Goddess Lives in Upstate New York: Breaking Convention and Making Home at a North American Hindu Temple*, Oxford: Oxford University Press.

Donner, H. (2008), *Domestic Goddesses: Maternity, Globalization and Middle-Class Identity in Contemporary India*, Burlington: Ashgate Publishing Company.

Eck, D. L. (1998), *Darśan: Seeing the Divine Image in India*, 3rd ed., New York: Columbia University Press.

Eck, D. L. (2001), *A New Religious America: How a "Christian Country" Has Now Become the World's Most Religiously Diverse Nation*, 1st ed., San Francisco: Harper San Francisco.

Flueckiger, J. (2015), *Everyday Hinduism*, Hoboken: Wiley-Blackwell.

Ghosh, P. (1995), "Household Rituals and Women's Domains," in M. W. Meister (ed.), *Cooking for the Gods: The Art of Home Ritual in Bengal*, 21–35, Newark: The Newark Museum.

Gunn, J. (2018), "Ganesha and the Chocolate Almonds: Ritual Innovation and Efficacy in Diaspora," in A. Allocco and B. Pennington (eds.), *Ritual Innovation: Strategic Interventions in South Asian Religion*, 214–59, Albany: SUNY Press.

Holt, A., and K. Pechilis (2019), "Contemporary Images of Hindu *Bhakti*: Identity and Visuality," *The Journal of Hindu Studies* 12 (2): 129–41.

Jhala, J. (2000), "Pūjā, Pūjāri and Prabhu: Religious Worship in the Hindu Home," *Visual Anthropology* 13 (2): 103–28.

Mazumdar, S., and S. Mazumdar (2003), "Creating the Sacred: Altars in the Hindu American Home," in J. Iwamura and P. Spickard (eds.), *Revealing the Sacred in Asian and Pacific America*, 142–57, New York: Routledge.

Morgan, D. (1998), *Visual Piety: A History and Theory of Popular Religious Images*, Berkeley: University of California Press.

Narayanan, V. (2006), "Hinduism in Pittsburgh: Creating the South Indian 'Hindu' Experience in the United States," in J. S. Hawley and V. Narayanan (eds.), *The Life of Hinduism*, 231–48, Berkeley: University of California Press.

Orsi, R. (2007), *Between Heaven and Earth: The Religious Worlds People Make and the Scholars Who Study Them*, Princeton: Princeton University Press.

Pechilis, K. (2019), "Bhakti's Visualities of Connection in the Arts Today," *The Journal of Hindu Studies* 12 (2): 142–67.

Pintchman, T. (2016), "Introduction," in T. Pintchman and C. Dempsey (eds.), *Sacred Matters: Material Religion in South Asian Traditions*, 1–14, Albany: SUNY Press.

Prentiss, K. P. (1999), *The Embodiment of Bhakti*, Oxford: Oxford University Press.

Sahney, P. (2016), "*Darśan*, Decoration, and Transnational Hindu Homes in the United States," *Asian Ethnology* 75 (2): 279–302.

Saunders, J. (2019), *Imagining Religious Communities: Transnational Hindus and the Narrative Performances*, Oxford: Oxford University Press.

Turner, K. (1999), *Beautiful Necessity: The Art and Meaning of Women's Altars*, New York: Thames and Hudson.

3

Merchant Patronage and Royal Hanumāns

A Modern Devotional Visuality

R. Jeremy Saul

The nationwide intensification of Vaiṣṇava devotion within the last thirty or so years has increased demand for temples dedicated to Hanumān, the representative of Rāma and preeminent Vaiṣṇava provider of miracles.[1] This is all the more evident in northern Rajasthan, the ancestral homeland of the famously Vaiṣṇava merchant-industrialists known as Marwaris, comprising Agrawals, Maheswaris, Oswal Jains, and some brahmins, who generally now live in cities throughout India. In this chapter, I suggest that Marwari patronage centered on this region has subsidized a materialization of devotion—*bhakti*—in a new idiom of upscale imagery and architecture suited to Marwari aspirations for a modernity of miraculous prosperity and wellbeing. Alluding to this new visual culture, a priest at the sumptuous merchant-established temple of Icchāpūrṇ ("wish-fulfilling") Bālājī (a local name for Hanumān) in Rajasthan commented to me that there are three kinds of Hanumān images. There is *vīr* Hanumān, the god as an active hero; second, *dās* Hanumān, the god in devotion to Rāma; and third, *rājā kā rūp*—royal Hanumān, in which he presides as a monarch dispensing moral guidance (Figure 3.1). Among these, the priest considered the first two to be traditional, while royal Hanumān is new and possibly unique to Icchāpūrṇ Bālājī. However, I propose to retheorize this third type to cover a much broader range of merchant-funded, opulent Hanumāns as Bālājī, which came to the fore in the 1990s and constitute a new vision of devotion.

Devotees visiting shrines commonly say that miracle deities are needed now more than ever, since we live in the cosmological era known as the Kali Yuga, typically equated with "modernity." The Kali Yuga is a degenerate time, predetermining humanity to immoral behavior and suffering. However, certain deities that are especially accessible to humanity, notably Hanumān, offer

Figure 3.1 Bālājī, Icchāpūrṇ Bālājī temple, Sardar Shahar. Photograph R. Jeremy Saul.

practical guidance for us to live in a way that is morally upright, even as we aspire to prosperity in line with modern life. As any devotee knows, in the epic *Rāmāyaṇa*, Rāma granted Hanumān the boon that he will always stay close to humanity to serve the faithful through good and bad times. And so, merchants, although fully committed to getting ahead in the world, also recognize that the worship of Hanumān, as represented in imagery, is necessary as an antidote to this troubled existence. Hence, as we will see, Marwaris, the dominant class of patrons in northern Rajasthan, and indeed much of India, bring a mercantile sensibility to creating temples and images for Hanumān, the bestower of miracles.

In this chapter, I will consider four Bālājī temples in Rajasthan to discuss how Marwari patronage has materially transformed the visuality of devotion in that region in the last thirty-plus years. Each Bālājī represents a different narrative of Marwari involvement. The first two Bālājīs to be discussed are the most renowned manifestations of Hanumān in northwestern India. They are *svayambhū* or naturally occurring, divinely self-revealed aniconic images from old times on which rough depictions of the deities have been painted. One is in the village of Salasar in northern Rajasthan, and the second is in the village of Mehandipur, farther to the east in that state. Salasar Bālājī more or less corresponds to a *dās* manifestation, while Mehandipur Bālājī is *vīr* in nature, as these deities perform miracles in ways that are perceived to match those characterizations. Marwaris had become prominent patrons of the Salasar temple by the end of the 1980s and subsequently modified this temple in a more sumptuous direction as testimony of their prosperity from faith in the deity. I suggest that this material transformation anticipates, or leads to, the development of royal Hanumān in the following decade. Prior to this transformation, most Marwaris already felt reverence for their ancestral land, including its shrines, but Vaiṣṇava, or specifically Hanumān-focused patronage, was low key at most. Meanwhile, Marwaris have been relatively quiet in Mehandipur, apparently because it lies outside their ancestral area, hence it makes no claim to any aspect of Marwari identity. So, in the later twentieth century, these two temples exemplified opposite extremes of Marwari visual engagement.

Although Mehandipur in its own right tells us much less about Marwaris, this site is useful to keep in mind because the Marwari-promoted rush of pilgrimage to Salasar in the 1990s hastened the construction or upgrading of not only Salasar-like Bālājī temples in that region but also temples following the model of Mehandipur, even though Mehandipur itself remained somewhat distant from Marwari devotional activity at that time. Moving forward, then, I will be discussing two temples in northern Rajasthan that are derivative of the first two—one, in the city of Ratangarh, follows the devotional style of Mehandipur, and another, Icchāpūrṇ Bālājī, follows Salasar. Icchāpūrṇ Bālājī exemplifies a Marwari aesthetic of devotion in its most luxurious form. Most of the temples discussed are not new: the Salasar and Ratangarh temples will demonstrate how Marwari patronage significantly modified long-standing religious establishments. There are of course many other temples in the area too, but I have selected the four temples described earlier as the best-known examples for discussing the impact that Marwari patronage made in developing a visual expression of *bhakti*.

Localizing Hanumān as Bālājī

All manifestations of Hanumān discussed in this chapter are commonly called Bālājī, a name that until recent decades was heard only in northern Rajasthan (notwithstanding Tirupati Bālājī of Andhra Pradesh, a very different deity). This name is explained as meaning "dear child," and some locals suggest that it was formerly also used to demonstrate devotion for other village gods as well, not just Hanumān. If so, perhaps the subsequent Marwari patronage of Bālājī amounted to an appropriation of the term to specify only Rāma/Hanumān-centered Vaiṣṇava. The name "Bālājī" in reference to Hanumān first appeared in writing in the late 1970s, when a brahmin in Salasar published a study about Hanumān in regional devotional songs (Kaushik 1979). Around 1990, this name started to come into vogue as a designation for numerous newly formed Marwari devotional organizations dedicated to Hanumān in cities around India, and so the name "Bālājī" became better known among Marwaris.

By the mid-1990s, Marwari merchants were financing new temples in the name of Bālājī in northern Rajasthan and more recently even in cities where they currently live. The name as a symbol of rustic Rajasthani life seems to have appealed to Marwari nostalgia, but there is no evidence that it was known in Marwari society until recent decades. The upshot of this is that pan-Indian Hanumān had been redesignated in terms that appeal to Marwari society. Nowadays, it is hard to find even one Hanumān-oriented Marwari group or devotional event anywhere in India that does not elevate one of Rajasthan's local Bālājīs as their preferred representation of Hanumān. Meanwhile, back in Rajasthan, Marwari patronage of Bālājī has provided facilities for pilgrims, such as rest houses and free roadside food during festival times. This funding has supercharged devotional life in Rajasthan by attracting large-scale public interest in the prosperous temples that Marwaris acclaim for miracles.

Alluding to this Hanumān-centered transformation in shrine-deity devotion, Ann Gold has used the term "Vaishnavization" to describe the recent suppression of village-style animal sacrifice and alcohol offerings in Rajasthan in favor of Vaiṣṇava vegetarian rituals (Gold 2008). To this, we can add two other developments of Vaishnavization: the widespread establishment of cow sanctuaries and of course Rāma-centered devotion (and often for Kṛṣṇa, his fellow *avatāra*), as championed by Hanumān. Gold notes that in some instances, goddess images have even been replaced with Hanumān, underlining that devotion for Hanumān/Bālājī is in the vanguard of Vaishnavization (Gold 2008: 176, fn. 24). As privileged patrons collaborating with priests, Marwaris have actively supported these changes.

The case of Agroha, a Marwari-associated site on the Rajasthan-Haryana border, illustrates both the Vaiṣṇava turn and its restatement in Rajasthan-centric Marwari piety, paralleling the Marwari interpretation of Hanumān as Bālājī. Bharatendu Harischandra, the famous colonial-era Marwari of Varanasi, had imagined Agroha as the site of a legendary ancient kingdom ruled by Agrasen, the ancestor of all Agrawal Marwari clans (Babb 2004: 185–215). Not much happened at the site identified with this legend until Marwari-funded construction commenced in the mid-1980s on a splendid white marble temple for Lakṣmī, the goddess of prosperity and consort of Viṣṇu (Babb 2004: 197). Lakṣmī had long been revered in finance-centered Marwari life, but I suggest that this construction also marked a first-time effort to localize the pan-Indian Vaiṣṇava goddess in a shrine specific to the Agrawal Marwari homeland. Further emphasizing this Vaiṣṇava direction, a few years later a colossal Hanumān image was set up near Lakṣmī's temple.

The material expression of Marwari Vaiṣṇava culture in Rajasthan is the most recent iteration in an ongoing historical pattern of Marwari preoccupation with that region. Anne Hardgrove has observed that merchants were moving away from northern Rajasthan's trade towns for business opportunities since colonial times, making Kolkata and certain other cities centers of a diasporic Marwari society (Hardgrove 2004). Marwaris fancied their dignified, prosperous, and magnanimous Rajasthani heritage as a model for their tradition of philanthropy, which arguably counteracted their notorious reputation among urban host communities (such as Bengalis) as miserly usurers. By the early twentieth century, emulating Rajput royal aesthetics as a representation of Rajasthan, Marwaris were channeling their wealth into building splendid mansions in their ancestral villages, which Marwari men would only infrequently inhabit, since their occupations kept them in distant cities (Hardgrove 2004: 91–126). I would theorize these mansions as an early harbinger of a Rajasthan-based Marwari aesthetic seen today in the form of opulent temples for Bālājī and certain other miracle deities.

At the same time, from the 1980s on, we see a nationwide ramping up of the public discourse of faith in Rāma, including among Marwaris, as a symbol of classical Hindu values. Rāma's ancient society is thus advocated as a solution for the Kali Yuga's ills. One manifestation of this thinking has been the Ram Janmabhumi movement, the politicized effort to demolish the Babri mosque in Ayodhya so as to rebuild a Rāma temple that had allegedly been destroyed by Mughal rulers on the same spot centuries before.[2] The early public actions of that movement in the 1980s, culminating in the mosque's destruction in late 1992, roughly correspond to the trajectory of rising Marwari public devotion for Hanumān/Bālājī, as seen in the advent of their Bālājī organizations (since the 1980s) and construction of Bālājī temples (since the 1990s).

The Visuality of Divine Agency

A key premise of this chapter is that obtaining miracles through divine intervention has become the core ideology of practice for most pilgrims coming to Bālājī sites. Conversations with devotees easily turn to miracles from Bālājī or other deities, such as turning around failing businesses, saving people from accidents, enabling passing exams, aiding in finding a suitable spouse, and so on. Entering into a devotional relationship with Bālājī through imagery may bring to mind Alfred Gell's theorization of an "anthropology of art," in which material representations of divinity are studied as social beings interacting with humans (1998: x). Certainly, scholars of Indic religions, such as Christopher Fuller, have acknowledged an ontological continuity between deities and humans, making Gell's extension of human life to objects seem theoretically persuasive in the Indic context (Fuller 1992: 3–4). Gell additionally speaks of hierarchies of agency comprising humans and divine objects, with each side potentially manipulating the other. For example, patrons agentively summon divine power through priest-mediated ritual activities to obtain miracles (1998: 28–50). Or, from the other side, the deity chooses to bestow miracles according to its judgment of the devotee, with the image serving as an "index" (in Gell's words) for the deity. We can say, then, that inasmuch as Marwaris are notable patrons of religious sites, they potentially become agents in shaping the way a deity is represented to the public. This will be evident in discerning a Marwari Vaiṣṇava aesthetic in this chapter.

Philip Lutgendorf's many studies relating to Hanumān are quite instructive for understanding this god's imagery. He discusses, for example, the increasing popularity of commissioning white marble divine imagery from Jaipur (with its upscale aesthetic) and the recent proliferation of five-headed Pañcamukhī

Hanumān images, which he associates with a modern mingling of Vaiṣṇava and Śaiva practices (2001: 276; 2002: 88, fn. 10). In this chapter, we certainly do encounter Marwari-funded marble images and Pañcamukhī Hanumān too. But I would take Lutgendorf's idea about the five-headed Hanumān a step further to say that this image materializes a common Marwari desire for obtaining continuous upward prosperity, with the mindset that five heads can accomplish more than one. The Marwari promotion of miracle-conducive forms of Bālājī is a manifestation of the upscale Vaiṣṇava mindset that I have theorized. We see this mindset of prosperity in other ways too; mercantile devotional groups like to say that each year their events get bigger as a reflection of the deity's ability to provide greater wealth, resulting in larger donations to support their activities. I would say that this ethic is commensurate with "royal Hanumān" as a category of imagery that materializes the promise of prosperity.

Given the recentness of Bālājī in Marwari devotion, it is also worth considering if, or how, the visual nature of *bhakti* in our era can be "modern." Sumathi Ramaswamy contemplates whether theories about visuality as a marker of international modernity could apply to the recent Indian setting as well (2003: xiii–xiv). In particular, she considers visuality as making "social realities." If we apply this question to Bālājī, about whom merchants promote discourses of miracles to justify their patronage, I would contend that visuality is indeed important to this variety of devotion. After all, patrons commonly fund temples in gratitude for a miracle, so we could surely make the case that such outcomes originate in a visual experience of the deity, even if just through the worshipped image. But is this "modern"? Plausibly yes, I would say. In a mercantile worldview, the material quality of the image is not just surface decoration but rather a testimony of the deity's efficacy in bringing about a donor's prosperity. We could argue that this approach has acquired new significance in the era of India's post-1991 economic liberalization, with its promotion of individualistic aspiration (requiring miracles through faith). In this sense, the visual experience of Bālājī that I am discussing in this chapter is a "modern" act, responding to new socioeconomic conditions.

Visuality in Marwari Devotion

In this section, I will consider the historical background of Salasar and the evidence of its material transformation from the early 1990s on, which exemplifies a Marwari Vaiṣṇava aesthetic of devotion. No formal history of Salasar has ever been written, but all locals can readily recite its foundation story. As Lawrence Babb has noted in his discussion of premodern Marwari-Rajput

Figure 3.2 Poster of Bālājī, Salasar. Photograph R. Jeremy Saul.

relations, a block of stone hailed as Bālājī was discovered by a farmer tilling his field in 1754 CE (2004: 37–40). A Rajput chieftain took control of the image, which divinely willed that the oxcart carrying it away should stop on the spot where the temple now stands. For most of Bālājī's history, the image was housed in a modest cell under a *khejḍī* tree.[3] The slab of stone is said to have had a relief depicting Hanumān carrying Rāma and Lakṣmana on his shoulders, but since it has always been covered in *sindūr*—red paste used in worship—nobody alive today knows for sure. The image has, in effect, been reshaped to conform to the priests' preferred narrative of the deity (Figure 3.2).

As Salasar's hereditary brahmin priests say, Bālājī granted a boon to an ascetic named Mohan Das, of the same lineage as them, decreeing that the ascetic's bearded visage would henceforth be painted on the stone (over the *sindūr*) instead of Hanumān's own face to represent the god, as is still the case. Moreover, the god said that the ascetic's sister's children, of the Dadhich brahmin clan, would be permanently granted the privilege to ritually mediate Bālājī to the devotional public. So, the story of Bālājī's image upholds a socioeconomic hierarchy. And since Marwaris venerate Bālājī as a protector that many of their ancestors had ostensibly worshipped, this materialization of the god ensures that the Dadhich priests will always be responsible for serving the god's Marwari patrons.

But the Marwaris' prominent role in this relationship has meant that they, too, potentially exercise agency in creating the form of this god. As early as 1936, a donation plaque from a merchant of Kolkata indicates that the site was known to Marwaris, although it was still of rather small caliber in those days, judging from the residual early structure of the temple. By comparison, the temple of Rānī Satī in the same region, already a favored Marwari Rajasthani lineage goddess in those days, was bestowed an impressively large, ornate rest house for pilgrims in 1933, indicating that Bālājī's Vaiṣṇava identity had not yet reached such popularity. Furthermore, in 1973, a single photograph of Salasar Bālājī in a large volume on Marwari clans of Kolkata suggests that the Salasar temple had fairly plain walls, which is quite different from its current sumptuous state (Kaushik 1973). A Rajasthani-language feature film, *Vārī Jāūṅ Sālāsar Bālājī*, apparently financed by Jain Marwaris and produced in 1990, similarly depicts the temple as having nondescript walls. The narrative of the film promoted the deity's miracles, warning that disasters await families who neglect to maintain their relation to this god. The temple's sparse setting was to radically change in the ensuing decade.

Rāma and Hanumān's ascent in Indian society in the 1980s seemingly reverberated in material enhancements in Salasar's temple during the 1990s. Visual splendor from patronage substantiated Bālājī's reputation for great miracles, since donations are a measure of the efficacy of a deity. The underlying semi-aniconic image of Bālājī remained the same, but everything around it was transformed. For instance, due to the escalation of pilgrimage in the early 1990s with the rise of devotion to Hanumān in Indian public life, priests told me, it was deemed necessary to make a circumambulation passageway around the back of the main image. If the film mentioned earlier gives an accurate depiction, we can see that prior to this time devotees had circumambulated a small shrine set up in front of the main image in the middle of the temple rather than in back. However, the potential rear circumambulation passageway was blocked by a *khejḍī* tree growing behind the deity's inner cell. Fortuitously, by Bālājī's own will, it is said, the tree thereupon fell down, making the rear passageway possible.

In the following years, the mid-to-late 1990s, the new circumambulation passageway was completely covered in silver plaques depicting Vaiṣṇava deities, and even with duplicate reliefs of Salasar Bālājī himself, often listing the names of donors. The donor inscriptions on those plaques frequently specify two addresses—one in this part of Rajasthan and one in a city farther away, which perfectly describes the pattern of Marwari dual geographical allegiance that we saw in the absentee construction of mansions in colonial days. Additional silver plaques and various paintings soon covered the entire inner temple, much of it later recovered in gold, in gratitude for miracles. The inside of the temple had thereby been transformed into a visual testimony of prosperity among a particularly privileged segment of the devotional population, largely Marwaris.

I suggest that this transformation points to the development of royal Hanumān, which likewise testifies to Marwari prosperity from piety.

At the same time, new references to Rāma became visible. The phrase "*jai śrī rām*" was prominently inscribed on the wall just above Bālājī's head. A garland with pendants each inscribed with the word "*rām*" was draped around Bālājī's neck, and a single large pendant reading "*śrī rām*" was also added. Further, a medallion was placed on Bālājī's chest, showing Hanumān opening his own chest to reveal Rāma and Sītā in his heart. This motif echoes a popular scene in poster art that has been greatly disseminated in this age of Vaiṣṇava devotion. In the 1973 photograph mentioned earlier, none of these Rāma-oriented elements are evident. Therefore, it appears that by or during the 1990s the temple was more explicitly drawn into the pan-Indian worship of Rāma that anchors Hanumān's place in canonical Hinduism. Additionally, a modest crown had already been placed on the image by 1973, but it has since been replaced by a much larger, more splendid crown that comes closer to what we see in Icchāpūrṇ Bālājī. Further afield, in 1998 Marwari patronage provided Salasar with a cow sanctuary—now the largest in Rajasthan, and later two separate Rāma temples, as well as a colossal outdoor Hanumān. These developments parallel the Vaiṣṇava visual culture that has been spreading across northern India.

If Bālājī Were Not Marwari

It is worth briefly considering what was happening in Mehandipur at the same time, if only to illustrate that without overt Marwari patronage this Bālājī had a divergent material history (Figure 3.3).[4] The fundamental difference between Salasar Bālājī and Mehandipur Bālājī is that the former is regarded as having a long relationship with Marwari society due to his location in their ancestral land, while the latter is found in a tribal region that had never been inhabited by Marwaris and so has no such connection. In reality, though, some Marwaris, afflicted with the troubles of modern urban life as much as anyone, were no doubt coming to Mehandipur too, but without the ancestral connection there was no pride accrued in being publicly recognized as patrons. And so, in the temple itself, there are no donation plaques to be seen. In recent years, after 2000, Mehandipur Bālājī's reputation for miracles has started to win more followers in the Marwari community, but, even so, Salasar Bālājī remains the one most associated with Marwaris in public perception.

As for measuring the material development of devotion in Mehandipur, many families of afflicted individuals freed of possession have set up small altars on an adjacent hillside where exorcised spirits can be kept forevermore under the watch

Figure 3.3 Poster of Bālājī, Mehandipur. Photograph R. Jeremy Saul.

of Bālājī. These families have typically inscribed biographical information, similar to what would be seen in a donation plaque. Virtually all of these inscriptions state that they have come from cities in the area of Haryana, Delhi, and Uttar Pradesh immediately to the north—never from more distant places, such as Kolkata, thus comprising a somewhat different devotional demography. But, as in Salasar, pan-Indian Vaiṣṇava piety has been felt in some ways. For instance, in 1989, a new temple that enshrined opulent white marble Rāma and Sītā images was built directly facing Mehandipur Bālājī's own temple, asserting Rāma's canonical authority over Hanumān. More recently, a colossal outdoor Hanumān statue was erected nearby in the same town, likely with merchant funding. We can interpret this image, like numerous giant Hanumān images constructed across northern India in recent years, as testimony to the conviction that this god represents resurgent Hinduism (Lutgendorf 2007: 3–10). Similarly, a colossal Hanumān image in Salasar was completed around 2016 with Marwari funding.

While Salasar was bustling with Marwaris, Mehandipur Bālājī entered Marwari awareness as a contrastive reference point—Salasar's darker "other"—represented by charismatic gurus providing miracles for followers through occult or "tantric" methods (Lutgendorf 2007: 262–70). This is the perception also voiced by Salasar's priests, who disparage such esoteric practices as an affront to their own scripturally authorized livelihood. Nonetheless, the majority of visitors to Mehandipur itself, not to mention Mehandipur-oriented Bālājī shrines established in northern Rajasthan, are simply attracted by the promise of divine boons, implicit in the deity's famous exorcistic powers, even though most devotees do not personally require such extreme treatment. By contrast, Salasar's priests say that it is impossible for a spirit possessing a visitor to even enter their own temple; it would temporarily depart when that person comes into Salasar and then reinhabit the visitor later on. Consequently, a need for occult Hanumān services has arisen in Marwari-centered northern Rajasthan that the exorcism- eschewing priests of Salasar cannot address. Mehandipur-like temples in the region of Salasar have thus found opportunities to supplementarily serve the Marwari devotional public.

Bālājī as a Marwari Occult Deity

Although the Marwari presence in Mehandipur has been relatively quiet, in the mid-1990s Marwaris became quite prominent patrons of Mehandipur-like establishments in northern Rajasthan. The key point is that these places were part of the Marwari ancestral domain, hence of potential interest to Marwaris as patrons. One such Mehandipur-oriented Bālājī temple, which had been founded decades earlier, was, as we have seen in Salasar, subsequently modified in line with Marwari patronage that elevated Bālājī's ritual significance. Currently known as the Ghata Mehandipur Bālājī temple, it is run by a family of brahmin gurus of the Joshi lineage in the old market city of Ratangarh, somewhat north of Salasar. I call them "gurus" because this word is often used in Hindi for charismatics who oversee occult treatment for afflicted devotees, as opposed to hired priests (different from Salasar's hereditary priests), who merely carry out routine rituals. As the Ratangarh temple solidified its Marwari clientele, especially from Kolkata, in conjunction with Salasar's rising pilgrimage traffic, these gurus were able to establish several branch temples in other locations, with Marwari funding. The long-standing Ratangarh temple itself was too hemmed in by neighboring buildings to expand.

The Joshi gurus claim the charismatic power to facilitate miracles in the name of Bālājī through an ancestor who they say went to Mehandipur in the middle of the nineteenth century. There, he performed *tapasyā* or austerities for Bālājī for many years before returning to Ratangarh. Due to this man's austerities, Mehandipur Bālājī granted him the boon that his lineage would be infused with the god's *śakti* or divine power for seven generations, endowing them with the ability to miraculously treat devotees' troubles. The current gurus are of the fifth generation. Notwithstanding this story, there is no evidence of any religious activity in Mehandipur until the 1970s, so this may be an apocryphal account to attract current-day devotional interest. Nonetheless, the story illustrates how gurus can enhance their ritual authority by attributing their powers to an already-famous site. Indeed, the gurus state that the *jyot* or sacred ritual flame burning in the Ratangarh temple was brought from Mehandipur; therefore, this site embodies the divine power of Mehandipur Bālājī. Moreover, the gurus have instituted a ritual protocol, reminiscent of Mehandipur-oriented mediums, that involves long sessions of chanting, albeit with less overt exorcism.

The Bālājī image of the present-day Ratangarh temple is said to have been brought from Mehandipur by the ancestral guru that had performed *tapasyā* (Figure 3.4). This crowned image has a semi-aniconic form on which a face has been delineated, suggesting that it may be of some antiquity. It also has a very large mustache, which is reminiscent of generic village Bhairavas, a very common type in Rajasthan. Bhairava, like this Bālājī, would typically have a mustache but not a beard. Similar to Salasar Bālājī, a pendant inscribed "*rām*" has been added to the image. As in Salasar, with the escalation of Marwari patronage, this image has not really been transformed in its own right, but the surrounding space has.

Figure 3.4 Bālājī, Ghata Mehandipur Bālājī temple, Ratangarh. Photograph R. Jeremy Saul.

Residents in the neighborhood of the Ratangarh temple concur that even before the current temple was constructed in 1905, it had existed since 1854 as a collection of several small shrines primarily dedicated to Kṛṣṇa and Rādhā and collectively known as the Govind temple. The early dedication to Kṛṣṇa, who is now seen in this temple as a generic-looking small image, seems consistent with a generalized colonial-era Marwari devotional preference for Kṛṣṇa. Surviving paintings in old merchant mansions in the region, and even the oldest known wall paintings in the complex of Salasar Bālājī's own temple (from around 1920), suggest that Kṛṣṇa, typically shown in scenes from puranic scriptures, such as dancing with cowherd girls, was a favorite subject for merchants. And insofar as the Joshis' temple was located in the heart of the market district, they served a Marwari clientele, as is still the case.

When the present building was built in 1905, it remained a Kṛṣṇa temple. The Bālājī image, if it had existed at that time, only served an adjunct role and so it was at some point placed against one of the side walls, along with some other deities and pictures of the revered gurus of the lineage. But apparently due to the increase in pilgrimage to Salasar Bālājī from the northern, Haryana-Delhi side in the early 1990s, which often passed through Ratangarh, the gurus astutely renamed the temple after Balaji and made some structural modifications. Reflecting this rising acclaim for Hanumān/Bālājī as a primary deity of miracles, visitors desired to circumambulate the god's image in the Ratangarh temple, which was impossible to do while he only served as a supplementary figure propped up on the side. The shrine for Kṛṣṇa did have a small circumambulation passage behind the image, but there was not sufficient room to add Bālājī alongside Kṛṣṇa. It was a predicament of shifting ritual priorities similar to what Salasar's priests faced at the same time, with their own lack of a circumambulation passageway.

Resolving this situation, the Joshi gurus took a rather unconventional approach. They erected a floor-to-ceiling wall blocking the entrance to the temple except for a narrow alcove at each end, thereby obstructing those coming up the steps from the street from seeing Kṛṣṇa. The gurus then moved Bālājī's image to face the inner side of the temple from a niche situated in that new wall, thereby putting his back toward the street-side entrance. I have never seen such a deployment of imagery in any other Hindu temple, inasmuch as having all deities facing the entrance, or at least looking on from the sides, is the typical arrangement. With this modification, visitors could henceforth circle the interior of the entire temple space, passing through the two side-alcoves at the entrance, to circumambulate Bālājī's image. Bālājī had evidently been elevated to be the main deity (an enhanced status seen in temples throughout northern Rajasthan at this time), while Kṛṣṇa, remaining in his original spot, had seemingly lost some of his former preeminence. In keeping with this promotion of Bālājī, in around 2000 the gurus set up an additional room on the roof where devotees in rotating shifts have been continuously reciting Tulsidas's *Rāmcaritmānas* (the Hindi version of the *Rāmāyaṇa*), invoking Hanumān's name to generate additional divine power for this site.

In this altered arrangement, in which Kṛṣṇa and Bālājī face each other from opposite sides of the temple, there is still, of course, *āratī* or public worship several times a day. This activity is considerably more elaborate here than in Salasar Bālājī's temple, because of the need in the Ratangarh temple to invoke Bālājī's presence, not to mention other deities, to facilitate occult miracles, not just normative wishes for boons. Each time there is *āratī*, all devotees first face Bālājī, with men in front and women behind, and when that session is complete everyone turns to repeat the routine facing Kṛṣṇa, this time with women in front. Perhaps this gendered arrangement is meant to accommodate Hanumān's masculine ascetic demeanor, which dictates aloofness from women, while Kṛṣṇa, the romantic god, would be more receptive to having women in front, closer to him.

Marwari Patronage of Temple Networks

Marwari visitors from cities around the country have been eager to take a major role in financing the Ghata Mehandipur Bālājī temple's continued development in gratitude for (or anticipation of) miracles. With this in mind, the gurus have established three new branch temples to channel that patronage, each with a ritual protocol similar to the original temple in Ratangarh. The fourth-generation guru in Ratangarh, who died around 2008, had five sons, and three of them were delegated to each lead one of the new temples, while two remained at the Ratangarh temple. The location of these new temples shows that the Joshi gurus were strategically aiming for proximity to preexisting networks of Marwari devotion. And, we could also say that the merchant patrons, who had formed financial trusts under the authority of the gurus, chose these new sites according to their ancestral interest in that region.

The first of Ratangarh's spinoff temples, Kajla Dham, was established around 1994, very close to Agroha, the up-and-coming center of Agrawal Marwari ancestral piety near the Haryana-Rajasthan state line. A second temple, Chaudhriwas Dham, initiated around 1996, was set up on the road just south of Hisar, the main city of southern Haryana, through which many devotees coming from Delhi and elsewhere pass on the way to Ratangarh and then Salasar. And a third Bālājī temple was established in Kolkata, the ultimate center of Marwari society and business. All of these new temples had been set up at a time when, as we have seen, Marwari funding was materially transforming Salasar, and pilgrimage for Bālājī and other miracle deities was on the rise. Marwari patronage was thus the key to the coalescence of a regional network of devotional sites.

At the two sites mentioned in the Haryana-Rajasthan area, which I have visited various times, the way in which this vision of Bālājī temples was initially materialized was to set up very small Bālājī shrines as place markers. When funding had been confirmed, by around 1993 to 1995, construction got underway on a medium-sized temple for each site, dedicated to a *jhāṇḍevālā* or "flag-bearing" Bālājī. This seems very suitable, since it is common for pilgrims coming to Salasar to carry a red flag bearing Hanumān's image to symbolize a wish made that was miraculously granted. For that matter, the scene of Hanumān carrying the red flag of *dharma* has been used to exhort the public to activism for the Rāma temple in Ayodhya, as seen in Hindu nationalist poster art.

Marwaris seeking to thank Bālājī for financial success have been giving increasingly extravagant donations, which led to the construction of grand new Bālājī temples at Kajla Dham and Chaudhriwas Dham by 1998. Visually immaculate white marble was used for these new temples and their imagery. At the new Chaudhriwas Dham temple, a Pañcamukhī Bālājī was installed as the main image, in line with the perception that this deity has superior efficacy, thereby also serving as a statement of the miraculous prosperity of the benefactor. Small two-dimensional images of Mehandipur Bālājī and Salasar Bālājī were installed on each side of the main image, signifying that this temple would offer all the capacities of those famous Bālājīs.

Kajla Dham's new temple honors Hanumān in his familiar mountain-bearing pose. It is a splendid rendition of a northern Indian-style temple, anticipating the glorious new devotional era envisioned in models of the future Rāma temple in Ayodhya that are now ubiquitous in social media. Interestingly, though, the gurus at both Kajla Dham and Chaudhriwas Dham prefer to continue conducting virtually all of their public ritual work at the adjacent medium-sized temples that date from the mid-1990s. It seems that wealthy benefactors are so eager to finance magnificent new edifices that they have outpaced actual ritual need. But utility aside, these temples are designed to broadcast the expectation of continuous upward prosperity—always a concern for those engaged in the uncertainties of the business world.

Making a New Salasar Bālājī

The history of Bālājī temples in this chapter demonstrates a trend toward increasingly upscale devotion in accord with the dominant sensibility of Marwari merchants. We see a culmination of this process in Icchāpūrṇ Bālājī, the royal Hanumān (see Figure 3.1). This deity was originally conceived as an alternative, grander version of Salasar Bālājī, and the temple itself is located along one of the roads leading south toward Salasar. However, the appearance of Icchāpūrṇ Bālājī's image is quite different from the Bālājī that we see in Salasar. Icchāpūrṇ Bālājī's image is markedly anthropomorphic and is larger than human size, signaling an aesthetic of towering grandeur unlike most traditional Hanumān images, including the comparatively miniscule Salasar Bālājī. In this sense, the Icchāpūrṇ Bālājī image points to the now ubiquitous trend of erecting colossal outdoor Hanumān statues. Made of marble commissioned from Jaipur, the Icchāpūrṇ Bālājī image is seated on a throne like a king, hence it broadcasts both moral authority and material prosperity. Bālājī's prominent crown confirms his regality. Most Hanumāns from any date do indeed have crowns, but this one has more of an air of actual kingliness because of his anthropomorphism.

Various stories have circulated about the site's benefactor Mulchand Malu, who died a few years back in his eighties. His life narrative enhances the miraculous claims made on behalf of the temple and its deity. Mulchand was an industrialist whose ancestors had lived in the vicinity of Sardar Shahar, a small city north of Salasar. And he was a Jain of the Terāpanthī sect and was from the Oswal clan, like many Jains in this part of Rajasthan. Terāpanthī Jains traditionally disavow image-worship and miracles in favor of an ideal of ascetic salvation, but, in my observation, they are nowadays essentially identical to Hindu Marwaris in their pursuit of deity-mediated prosperity. On the face of it, the stringent canonical Jain denial of miracles would seem to be at a severe disadvantage in this era of economic liberalization, globalized consumerism, and seeking divine shortcuts to good fortune. Thus, other than revering their own ancestral deities, such as the Oswal goddess, in recent decades Terāpanthī Jains have easily transitioned to more emphatic Vaiṣṇava devotion, like other Marwaris.

It is said that Mulchand had been living a profligate lifestyle, but then, inspired by the public turn to Hanumān in the early to mid-1990s, he had a dream in which the god came to him in the resplendent form of Icchāpūrṇ Bālājī, as now represented in the temple. Impressed by this vision, upon awakening Mulchand held a *laṅgoṭiyā* over his head—the characteristic masculine loincloth worn by Hanumān and wrestlers who emulate his ascetic disposition—and vowed that he would henceforth pursue a pious life in dedication to Bālājī. He thereupon set up a financial trust with the aim of building the largest Hanumān temple in the world within seven years. At the same time, he earned a positive public reputation by sponsoring food and lodging for pilgrims coming on the road to Salasar.

Mulchand also became known as Salasar's greatest benefactor, and so, in keeping with his vow after the dream, he proposed to the priests there that his trust would fund a reconstruction of their temple. But the priests, already comfortable in their traditional setting, rebuffed his intention. Mulchand then resolved to build his own splendid version of Bālājī's temple on an empty plot of land adjoining his family property near Sardar Shahar. When the new temple was completed in 2005, after more than five years, Mulchand sponsored a grand opening, which generated local enthusiasm for this Bālājī-of-Fulfilled-Miracles. Building on Salasar's reputation, the inauguration of the temple entailed bringing a sacred flame from Salasar's temple to serve Icchāpūrṇ Bālājī. Amid the performances and processions, the opening day of the temple presented to the public a huge 11,000-kilogram *laḍḍū*, a consecrated sweet normally given to devotees in Hindu temples as small bite-sized pieces. The message was clear: this new temple would offer miracles of the highest efficacy, perhaps even surpassing Salasar. The magnitude of the *laḍḍū* exemplified the Marwari aim of assured upward prosperity; and as generally understood, the greater the offering, the greater the ensuing miracles as well.

The Visuality of Icchāpūrṇ Bālājī

Royal Icchāpūrṇ Bālājī's sovereignty seemingly extends over the canonical Hindu gods represented in his temple. Adjacent to his grand figure are much smaller, standardized marble representations of Rādhā-Kṛṣṇa, Śiva-Śakti, Rāma Darbār (including Hanumān in his standard form), and even Mohan Das, the famous ascetic who was the first devotee of Salasar Bālājī. Indeed, relief images of Salasar Bālājī himself appear as decorative motifs near the innermost cell of the temple and in the large adjacent circumambulation passage. It is evident that Icchāpūrṇ Bālājī is not just a *vīr* fighter for the gods, nor only their *dās* devotee, but in a sense their ruler by virtue of the fact that by Rāma's ancient boon, he is best suited of all to save humanity in this perilous Kali Yuga. So, he is deservedly depicted as a royal figure.

Two additional features inside the Icchāpūrṇ Bālājī temple merit extra attention, as they visually support the promise of miracles for the public. First,

Figure 3.5 The monkey construction foreman, Icchāpūrṇ Bālājī temple, Sardar Shahar. Photograph R. Jeremy Saul.

at the left of the entryway to the circumambulation passage, we see a naturalistic marble image of a monkey (Figure 3.5). This image is said to represent an actual monkey that showed up on the first day of constructing the Icchāpūrṇ Bālājī temple in 1999 and that monkey assumed the role of construction foreman until the temple was finished. The monkey is now widely understood to have been a manifestation of Hanumān himself. Each day, the monkey insisted on examining all construction materials brought to the site, and if he was not satisfied then he would stop the workmen from going further until they had made the needed corrections. If they had made any other errors in their work by the end of the day, the monkey would come during the night and dismantle their work. He also physically beat workmen who did not obey his instructions. Clearly, this temple had gained Hanumān's personal endorsement, so it was primed for miracles.

In 2005, the temple was nearly complete except for an immensely heavy lotus-shaped stone pinnacle to be lifted by crane to the top of the temple's main tower. The crane collapsed under the pinnacle's weight, but the monkey foreman came to the rescue. Taking the pinnacle in one hand, the monkey effortlessly lifted it to the top of the temple, to the amazement of all. In this feat, he reenacted the famous passage in the *Rāmāyaṇa* when Hanumān flew through the air to Lanka carrying a Himalayan mountain on which medicinal herbs were growing, so as to heal Rāma's brother Lakṣmana after he had been wounded in battle. Following this miraculous precedent at the Icchāpūrṇ Bālājī temple, it seems no surprise that numerous devotees have been saying that this Bālājī has bestowed miracles on them, too. As for the monkey, he disappeared from the temple after its completion but was later spotted swinging on rooftops above Sardar Shahar until he grabbed an electrical wire and was electrocuted, falling dead to the ground (a common occurrence in India, as I have witnessed). He was thereupon accorded a *samādhi* (memorial) where he had died, now served by a full-time priest. To this day that site has been a source of miracles too. A second story is visually referenced by a statue of the god Kubera, to the right of the exit of the circumambulation passage (Figure 3.6). This deity is not common in modern temples, but he was of special significance to the benefactor. On the face of it, the god's role as "accountant" for the gods, being skilled at making money, could explain Mulchand's allegiance. Additionally, according to Icchāpūrṇ Bālājī's priests, at a time when young Mulchand had not yet found his direction in life, he became a follower of the chief ascetic of a well-known Śiva temple near Sardar Shahar. Seeing that Mulchand had a habit of spitting, the ascetic advised that he go into the business of chewing tobacco and similar kinds of oral products (which commonly induce spitting). He did so, eventually expanding to DVDs of devotional songs, hotels, and even an airline. Nowadays, all his diverse products are sold under the same brand name, "Kubera." So, like the characterization of

Figure 3.6 Kubera, Icchāpūrṇ Bālājī temple, Sardar Shahar. Photograph R. Jeremy Saul.

Icchāpūrṇ Bālājī as a royal deity, the use of Kubera seems aimed at broadcasting the benefactor's divinely endorsed capacity for attracting wealth.

Kubera was a half-brother of Rāvaṇa, the demonic king in the *Rāmāyaṇa*, and so by extension, according to Icchāpūrṇ Bālājī's priests, as a *yakṣa* (nature spirit) or ogre-like figure, he had some unspecified "bad" habits too, alongside his skills in finance. Even Tirupati Bālājī in southern India, today India's greatest deity of miracles—a manifestation of Viṣṇu (not Hanumān, despite the similar name) and consort of Lakṣmī, the goddess of prosperity, who is much revered by Marwaris—supposedly owed clever Kubera money. In other words, Kubera fit the image of a Marwari financier and should be admired.

However, a deeper meaning of this story may be that Mulchand, a bit like Kubera, started off as a wayward character, but he ultimately found his devotional calling in an era of Vaiṣṇava piety. And, like Kubera—indeed, like Marwaris everywhere (as reputed in popular culture)—he knew how to profit from life experiences. In this dual concern—being good at finance but also seeking acceptance in society as a reformed, now pious person at heart (through embracing Bālājī), we are reminded of the core Marwari condition that is resolved in embracing Rajasthan and its village deities. As noted earlier, Rajasthan rhetorically served as a redemption for Marwaris' necessary engagement with unseemly urban modernity. In that line of thinking, royal Hanumān visualizes the patron's attainment of a prosperous life that is, in the end, also morally respectable and dedicated to a divine power.

Conclusion

This chapter started with the argument that *bhakti* as a visual practice significantly changed in a more overtly Vaiṣṇava direction from around 1990 on in northern Rajasthan, although it was already nascent in the preceding decade. This transformation was primarily driven by an upswing in Marwari patronage in the construction and upgrading of Hanumān temples in this region. Due to nostalgic ancestral associations, this part of Rajasthan had already been receiving Marwari attention during colonial times in the construction of Rajput-like grand mansions, demonstrating that these merchants valued this heritage, despite having moved to distant cities. But a modification in this pattern can be discerned by 1990, when Marwaris were more emphatically embracing Rāma and Hanumān devotion. This manifested in Marwari patronage of religious establishments with an interest in generating miracles of prosperity and other boons. This agenda of construction helped to develop a visual aesthetic of Marwari Vaiṣṇava devotion geared to achieving perpetual prosperity.

In discerning this new visual culture, this chapter has considered several sites. We initially saw the transformation of Salasar Bālājī's temple from a relatively quiet place to a magnet for lavish Marwari patronage, while Mehandipur Bālājī moved along a very different path, with less Marwari involvement, because of its reputation for occult miracles discouraged in Salasar. By the mid-1990s, the general perception of Marwaris' skills in business, and their prominent sponsorship of Salasar's visitor facilities, had boosted a regional culture of devotion for Salasar Bālājī. This spurred the establishment of numerous new or enhanced Bālājī temples along the routes leading to Salasar. The material expression of *bhakti* for Bālājī at these new sites, exemplified by Icchāpūrṇ Bālājī, placed importance on images as signifiers of anticipated miracles of prosperity and wellbeing. It is in this setting, I have argued, that we see the flourishing of a visual culture centered on Bālājī and miracles, which ultimately produced royal Hanumān. This enhanced vision of Bālājī as a savior in this era, the Kali Yuga, places him on an especially high plane in the world, thus in a sense transcending the old binary of *vīr* and *dās* Hanumān.

This chapter has also shown that in India's post-liberalization economy, financial elites with their greater resources have played a key role as initiators of an upscale visuality of *bhakti*, normalized in the broader population as local deities with reputations for miracles. Looking at these visually splendid images and accompanying architecture, popular conviction among devotees is that elites, with their inside track as moneyed patrons, know where to find efficacious deities of prosperity and so they conceivably lead the way. With that in mind, I recall Ramaswamy's contention that visuality is an aspect of modernity. I suggest that in contemporary Hanumān-centric devotional visuality, we can see a kind of "Hindu modernity," whereby images indexing both deity and patron (recalling Gell's formulation) are needed for us to attain our personal goals.

Notes

1 This research was initially funded by a one-year Fulbright-Hays fellowship in India, supplemented by several short visits and archival research funded by the College of Religious Studies, Mahidol University, and at my own expense.

2 Scholarship on this movement is too ubiquitous for me to cite a single source here. Devotees at shrines do not routinely link the Rāma temple movement to Hanumān temples in Rajasthan, but they certainly see Hanumān as leading the way to a restoration of Rāma's ancient moral polity.

3 This kind of tree is nowadays the official tree of the state of Rajasthan and symbolic of the state's cultural heritage.

4 Numerous studies have been carried out on Mehandipur Bālājī, although my brief discussion is based on my own fieldwork. Lutgendorf (2007: 262–70) gives the most distinctive treatment of Mehandipur, inasmuch as he frames it as illustrating a kind of modern Tantra.

References

Babb, L. (2004), *Alchemies of Violence: Myths of Identity and the Life of Trade in Western India*, London: Sage Publications.

Fuller, C. (1992), *The Camphor Flame: Popular Hinduism and Society in India*, Princeton: Princeton University Press.

Gell, A. (1998), *Art and Agency: An Anthropological Study*, New York: Oxford University Press.

Gold, A. G. (2008), "Deep Beauty: Rajasthani Goddess Shrines Above and Below the Surface," *International Journal of Hindu Studies* 12 (2): 153–79.

Hardgrove, A. (2004), *Community and Public Culture: The Marwaris in Calcutta*, New York: Oxford University Press.

Kaushik, J. (1973), *Maiṅ Apne Mārvāḍī Samāj ko Pyār Kartā Hūṅ*, 4, Calcutta: Janwani Printers and Publishers.

Kaushik, S. (1979), *Śri Sālāsar Hanumānjī*, Calcutta: Shri Champalal Dugad.

Lutgendorf, P. (2001), "Five Heads and No Tale: Hanuman and the Popularization of Tantra," *International Journal of Hindu Studies* 5 (3 December): 269–96.

Lutgendorf, P. (2002), "Evolving a Monkey: Hanuman, Poster Art, and Postcolonial Anxiety," *Contributions to Indian Sociology* 36 (1–2): 71–112.

Lutgendorf, P. (2007), *Hanuman's Tale: The Messages of a Divine Monkey*, New York: Oxford University Press.

Ramaswamy, S. (2003), "Introduction," in Sumathi Ramaswamy (ed.), *Beyond Appearances?: Visual Practices and Ideologies in Modern India*, xiii–xxix, London: Sage Publications.

Vārī Jāūṅ Sālāsar Bālājī (1990), Music director: Rajkamal. Producer: Bajrang Films Ltd.

4

Evolving Material Authority

Devotion, History, and the Svāminārāyaṇa Museum

Shruti Patel

Introduction

The Svāminārāyaṇa *sampradāya*, or community, formed in western India's region of present-day Gujarat during the early nineteenth century, where a variety of Hindu and Islamic practices were active. Sahajānanda Svāmī was the founder and leader of the *bhakti*, or devotional, community with a popular following. He was revered as an elite figure, a teacher, and many followers regarded him as a deity and some even as the Supreme God, Puruṣottam. Alongside oral and written texts, visuality was key to bolstering his multifaceted personality. It established the founder as an object of veneration in the region through various representations of himself and of other deities that referenced Sahajānanda as divinity, through sculpture, paintings, sketches, and prints.[1] Significantly, Sahajānanda installed *mūrti*s (sacred images) in the early Svāminārāyaṇa *mandir*s (temples) of various deities that might have been intended to correspond with the founder's proclaimed divine status, though not without inconsistency, complexity, and caution (Williams 2001: 71–82). Overall, the emphasis on *saguṇa bhakti* (conceiving the divine with attributes) and insistence on a *sākār* interpretation (divinity having a distinct and definite form) made visuality integral in the Vaiṣṇava *sampradāya* for comprehending the divine and approaching worship (*Vacanāmṛta* Kāryāṇī 8; *Vacanāmṛta* Gaḍhaḍā I.45). I would further argue that the visuality of *bhakti* practically constituted the community as it aided *sampradāya* establishment in western India, and of which some came to be preserved and collected in archives like that of the Shree Swaminarayan Museum in Ahmedabad, Gujarat.

The construction of the *sampradāya* was an energetic pursuit. Early leadership and followers enthusiastically generated cultural markers and initiatives to create a new institution, with the production of Svāminārāyaṇa literature, music, architecture, paintings, as well as rituals, doctrine, and associated vocabulary and practices. Its results were a distinctive, robust and recognizable identity. As I have claimed elsewhere, this was an "elastic" creation. The new formation selectively drew on earlier, familiar *bhakti* modes and tropes already well-established in the region, like that of the Vaiṣṇava Puṣṭi Mārga, while simultaneously stretching toward its own distinct ideas and systems (Patel 2017: 53). Such efforts earned public attention. Various local populations were drawn to Sahajānanda's personality, message, and initiatives, and eventually became loyal adherents. Critically, in the early nineteenth century the performance of affective worship, but also the performance of functional, logistical activities which could strengthen the *sampradāya*, defined *bhakti*. This established a framework in which individual spiritual pursuit and collective development were congruent (Patel 2017: 60–3).

From the vantage point of visuality and devotion, the essay specifically explores how non-textual, physical constructs of space, objects, and image—what I refer to as "materiality" in the essay—mediated *bhakti* as dual pursuits of personal practice and community organization. Materiality represented something beyond solely the visual effects of sanctification deserving worship; they were also effects of the past that generated institutional power. At the outset I will establish a historical framework for the visual mode, to then trace materiality's conditions and relationship to *bhakti* after two centuries. This reading reveals the passionate yet unobvious ways materiality is used for institutional sustenance today. A survey of nineteenth-century materiality's orientation and production, distribution and afterlife, makes vividly apparent that its appeal rests on a powerful value it explicitly embodies and implicitly expresses—the intertwined notion of devotion and history.

Material Visions in the Nineteenth Century

The Svāminārāyaṇa *sampradāya* embraced a hybridized devotional and historical mode of *bhakti*. Such braiding emerged out of the community's larger epistemological and philosophical commitments to appreciate the elements of divinity and non-divinity (humanity), and matters of the otherworld and earthly concerns. Fundamentally, this indicated a capacious view of time and space, and related elements. As demonstrated in my larger work, this was a deeply held sensibility that integrated devotional and historical arts. While conceptually creative, it was also materially productive. The hybridized mode produced defining community practices that were generative for establishing Sahajānanda's layered personality "define his character" as community founder, an object of worship, and with divine status. Ultimately, this time-space-sensitive outlook and steadfast attention on Sahajānanda produced an incredible archive in the nineteenth century of materiality, in addition to written and oral forms (Patel *forthcoming* b). *Bhakti* was interpreted expansively.

Visuality was at the core of offering a deified form of adoration to Sahajānanda. Thus, while visual depictions of or implicit references to Sahajānanda conformed to traditional forms of *mūrti*s, novel formulations were also created, like the "portrait-*mūrti*s" that art historian Ankur Desai compellingly introduces in this volume. Consider the following. In the earliest years the *sampradāya* was developing and stabilizing, local populations were just being introduced to Sahajānanda. They were still learning about the founder, his views, and perhaps participating in some of the *sampradāya*'s regular public initiatives. That is, the founder and community's reputation, growth, and power were in the nascent stages of development, which occurred as a responsive and relational process (Patel *forthcoming* a). People's firmer commitments as devotees would have been rooted in exposure to the founder's charismatic personality (Schreiner 2001). Positive, interactive and immediate experiences of Sahajānanda, as opposed to the abstract concerns of doctrine or rules, more likely drew ordinary populations to the *sampradāya*, subsequently exposing them to its ideas through engagement in regional activities. And for some, this would have further compelled their loyalty as followers. In this process, visuality and related materiality were one of the most compelling means for direct social engagement.

The draw to Sahajānanda's company and the interactive activities he inspired translated into a culture of enjoying Sahajānanda maximally. He was celebrated. The appreciative ethos that centered on him for adulation as well as for his being a source of popular leadership was, at the most empirical and arguably most accessible level, trained toward a deep attention on Sahajānanda's corporeal form, among other aspects. For instance, the initial generation of *sampradāya* ascetics expressed in literary compositions a common theme and enthusiastic perspective of fully knowing and capturing the founder physically, and also socially. We overwhelmingly observe this in an account highly popular with his devotees, the *Svābhāvika Ceṣṭā*, a poetic composition reciting Sahajānanda's mannerisms, major and minor tendencies, daily lifestyle, and personality traits

(*Kīrtanmuktāvalī*). However, this all-consuming interest emerged at its greatest intensity, by virtue of spirit and sheer volume, in the form of visual accounting, or notes of imagery. Visual records, outside of written accounts, minutely observed Sahajānanda's being. His body such as his nails, teeth and hair, his personal effects like clothing and handkerchief, were especially noted, along with concern for objects that he had physical contact with, such as his seat. Similarly, any space, built architecture, natural environments, and large landscapes that the founder once visited or inhabited, like a home or a room, were all incorporated into a formula for adoration and observation of Sahajānanda. Given the visual sensitivity and cherishing of him in the *sampradāya*, which led to the total documentation of him, it appears to have also been necessary to keep a similar, close relationship with his contemporaneous space, objects, and people, those who were perceived as being physically enfolded in Sahajānanda's engaging presence.

Visual habits that witnessed, remarked on, and appreciated the charismatic founder's qualities, movements, peculiarities, behavior, and activities do not entirely capture the *bhakti* model. Non-animate elements mattered. Those in direct or close physical proximity to Sahajānanda were deemed to embody and reflect him, thereby physically extending his presence. This was based on the idea that Sahajānanda regularly propagated: the empirical realm was altered upon having contact with divinity. An association could mutate physical matter by provoking it to become *nirguṇa* or be marked by no characteristics or flaws (*Vacanāmṛta* Kāryāṇī 8). Hence, this materiality was noted, marked, collected, and preserved, but also classified as *prasādī* (divinely graced or sanctified)—byproducts of a dual logic of recording and cherishing Sahajānanda. Sanctified space was termed *prasādīnī jagyā* and sanctified object as *prasādīnī vastu*. In sum, the sensibility combined of devotion and history that sustained a culture of profound affection for and observation of Sahajānanda produced an immense material archive of him, the early *sampradāya* in his lifetime, and everyday aspects of western India. Nineteenth-century *bhakti* had a historically oriented perception colored by an enchanted lens.

Prasādi was not solely the physical effect of Sahajānanda's personage, but also a generative means of devotion. How? Materiality was a catalyst to recover the past. This principle and practice I characterize as a kind of mnemonic chain reaction.[2] Adherents would adore and worship Sahajānanda, partaking in an experience of his physical extension, or materiality, through sensory perception. The beholder would engage these sanctified elements by doing *darśan* (devoutly viewing, exchange of sacred sight), touching them if it was sandalwood paste, enjoying their scent if the materiality was a flower or perfume, and eating it if it were food. These acts flooded the senses with the divine, making the consumer a model devotee or one who best took advantage of their human body as per Sahajānanda (*Vacanāmṛta* Gaḍhaḍā II.48). In essence, through the act individuals would have accessed an aspect of Sahajānanda himself. Furthermore and in turn, the somatic engagement would conjure a memory of Sahajānanda. As a result, a deep fondness for Sahajānanda would be rekindled having recalled a certain historical experience with him, ideally stemming from the specific materiality. For instance, when sensorily engaging with a wooden cup once used by the founder, an individual's memory would be prompted to recall the instance when Sahajānanda paid a visit to their home and drank water from the particular cup. Sahajānanda encouraged the view that simply absorbing divinity through the senses would purify one's inner life, enabling an unending recollection of him as the Divine (*Vacanāmṛta* Gaḍhaḍā I.18.)

Critically, the *smṛtī* (recollection) of one's various experiences with Sahajānanda and others within the community was believed to be powerfully redemptive at the end of one's life—in some sense, cutting through one's personal deficiencies (*Vacanāmṛta* Gaḍhaḍā I.3.). The past was a soteriological passport. Combining visual emphasis with a distinctive historiographic-inflected practice put empirical materiality and human sensorium at the forefront of the *sampradāya*. Accordingly, this strength was utilized for enhancing individual piety, as just outlined, and, second, for building institutional strength.

Distributive Materiality and Institutionalization

Throughout his life in western India, Sahajānanda distributed his personal effects such as clothing, jewels, and shoes, which would come to be known as *prasādīnī vastu* in the community. He presented people with items leaving them behind so others might remember him. Significant is that the prescription of materiality as sanctified, or at the very least as especially valuable, seems to have been upheld from the very start. Beyond discussions in early nineteenth-century texts, this understanding of object, space, and image as records of him remains prevalent in the *sampradāya* today.[3] People in western India collected and preserved the empirical elements as prized possessions over generations.[4] But beyond its soteriological import, their geographically wide dissemination in the region supported the transformation of a budding community into an institution. In other words, the role of materiality was at once personal and theological, broader and infrastructural—aims not at odds with one another in the nineteenth-century formulation of *bhakti*.

By living a life of regular contact with people and continuous activity in the region, Sahajānanda had abundant opportunity to be sociable and distribute his belongings and images as well as elements like food (*thāḷ*), flowers, and garlands, and allow people to physically engage with him through acts like touching, embracing, and honorably anointing him with sandalwood paste (Prasādānand Svāmī 1880: 76). For the purposes of spreading the *sampradāya*, Sahajānanda and his ascetics invested considerable energy traveling, sharing their ideas, and spending time with people even outside of western India (*Bhaktacintamaṇī* 50.18-19, 50.22-24). Deep and active social engagement was at the crux of their efforts. Counseling his ascetics, Sahajānanda emphasized that rather than retreat from the disturbances of everyday life to better focus on one's individual practice of meditation and worship, it was mundane activity in the world to serve the institution that was *bhakti* (*Vacanāmṛta* Vadtāl 17; *Vacanāmṛta* Gaḍhaḍā 1.31). This model compelled an outgoing orientation.

Historical patterns consistently reveal the innumerable and extensive points of social contact that served as natural opportunities for Sahajānanda and his ascetics to develop relations with people to distribute materiality, or produce it, by being physically present and conducting activities that encouraged vigorous beliefs and practices around material culture. Sahajānanda's own frequent circulation was constituted by meeting and staying with different audiences, well-wishers and committed devotees, in different areas and seasons, and even by staying mobile across the region to circumvent antagonistic forces and troubles (Akhaṇḍānand Svāmī 2002: 1.40.20–3, 1.40.28; Adbhutānand Svāmī 2010: 72–4). It appears that he spent a vast amount of time with non-elite populations, in rural spaces, amongst those with more humble means, while also holding some engagements in urban centers.[5] In addition to intensive travels, the founder and his ascetics regularly organized festivals along the lines laid down in the Puṣṭi Mārga tradition, as well as for other celebratory occasions and ceremonies, from small to large scale, collecting as many as tens of thousands of people over a number of days to celebrate and disseminate teachings (Williams 2001: 27; Śatānandamuni 1831: 4.55.2).

Taken together, the practice of distributive materiality appears to have played a role in the *sampradāya*'s institutionalization in several ways. For one, dispersing and denoting materiality would introduce, stimulate, and help distinguish the *sampradāya*'s identity in the region—a context where other religious communities with overlapping identities had long existed, like the aforementioned Puṣṭi Mārga. Over time, the distributive practice would prime a more sympathetic and amenable population for the still-expanding community while motivating some to commit substantial efforts for this very expansion. Sahajānanda shared items informally—on a whim, to show favor, or to shower affection—given to a select few or to many people. On account of Sahajānanda's robust travels and that of the ascetics, the habit of distributing materiality would be a very apt means to sustain the aim of *sampradāya* spread. The intensive practice of classifying regional space and object anew, undoubtedly, would have been a powerful ambassadorship. Effectively, Sahajānanda's personality was made mobile vis-à-vis distributive materiality. Wherever he traveled or recipients resided, materiality was the founder's signature and that of his attendant ideas.

It is quite likely that his very association with certain physical things sparked new meaning and value-making for otherwise common items. Materiality would be an effective tool to forge new social connections and deepen existing relationships. The act of distribution itself would set positive terms with strangers as it would indicate the source's friendliness; specifically, presenting a memento of oneself would imply affective interests to the recipient. Dissemination of the founder's belongings would also project him as a figure of esteemed rank and likely, as magnanimous. In comparison, it would not have been likely that a leading figure, say the sovereign of a princely state, would extensively interact, let alone personally share gifts, with ordinary subjects. Ultimately, materiality exemplified the charged emotional integration of Sahajānanda with other people. This quality of interaction is not minor. The mode of materiality would have been an extremely effective technology to communicate with nonliterate populations. Direct, inclusive, and broad, the tool would relate to vast segments of society, fostering grassroots level affection for Sahajānanda and the *sampradāya*. And if one acquired materiality associated with an honorable figure, this enriched position could foster pride and, perhaps, social capital. Sahajānanda's regional popularity would have certainly increased under this pattern. As a consequence, distributive materiality helped voluntarily and intimately draw people to the teacher. Importantly, the connective tissue formed from such a relationship must have been arguably different than the formal and more restrictive networks of caste, kinship, and economics that placed people into obligatory contact with one other in this era.

Of note is the way that the informal world of distributive materiality genuinely would have intimately linked people to the charismatic founder. Popular distribution could facilitate agency and social equality, common themes of *bhakti*. Possessing materiality could remove ordinary people from having to face social, intellectual, and spiritual intermediaries—like an ascetic or elite figure—who were otherwise key for accessing community resources, philosophy, doctrine, and texts. By deliberately extending accessible, inviting terms for relations, Sahajānanda would have been attractive to marginalized populations. A relatively direct expression of warmth offered through treasured materiality would have encouraged some degree of following from those who otherwise experienced a more disenfranchised existence in the region. Altogether, the distribution, reception, circulation, and great valuation of materiality among people who were well-wishers, laity, and mobile ascetics reinforced regard and care for/from the community founder and codified an attitude of preserving cherished elements.

Non-textual tools, which might not be well highlighted or recognized as part of canonized literature, should not be dismissed in the process of religious institutionalization. The mechanism of distributive materiality brought a valuable mix of features together that was unlike other medias used to regularize and propagate the *sampradāya*. As physical elements, they were visible, recognizable, and relatively permanent markers that could publicly signal a specific identity. Their spatial dissemination could relatively swiftly and with ease mark space with considerable reach, from interiors to cities, intimate domestic sites to public areas, and cotton fields to city gardens. Imaginatively and practically, this conception of materiality as object, space, and image would traverse Gujarat's diverse geography and inherently sustain itself in challenging ecological terrains—whether hinterlands, villages, deserts, or forests in Kathiawar and Kutch, or in cities like Bhuj and Ahmedabad.[6]

Additionally, materiality would generate goodwill in an uninterrupted relationship with people. Non-animate expression was advantageous. In areas more antagonistic to the founder, the quiet physical form would inconspicuously symbolize Sahajānanda's personality for local supporters long after his departure. Finally, the medium's mobility was beneficial in the process of institutional expansion on the ground in a way that surpassed geopolitics in the nineteenth century. Material elements were separately located. Unconnected, they were easily dispersed amongst discrete territories of western India—an area highly splintered into innumerable neighboring and often conflicting princely states with overlapping sovereignties of transregional powers of the Marathas and the East India Company—yet cumulatively, materiality built a shared conceptual community and affirmed a functional network zigzagging throughout the region.

Objects alone did not affirm Sahajānanda's multidimensional status. Space was another aspect. The very territory Sahajānanda visited—land, property, structures, natural or constructed—were all understood as material anchors. Like the objects, sanctified space or *prasādīnī jagyā* was a site with which the founder was believed to have had physical contact, and thus, notable. Unsurprisingly, the founder covered a significant amount of geography and specific sites with his active lifestyle and travel. Not all of these locations are explicitly marked today, though very many are. Stone umbrellas (Figure 4.1) as well as signboards, plaques, structures, images, and quite often an area's local residents (usually elderly)—who are sometimes themselves the descendants of the families who met with Sahajānanda—demarcate the significance of these sites. Marked spaces are homes and estates of nineteenth-century well-wishers and devotees. Wherever Sahajānanda resided, rested, ate, spoke, prayed, taught, tied his horse, celebrated festivities, met with local residents, or simply frequented became sites of wonder and recordkeeping.

Homes are just one domain. A foundational culture that stressed terms of affection and archiving yielded extraordinary output. Beyond an immediate residence where the founder visited, other *prasādī* spaces usually extend into

Figure 4.1 Stone umbrella (*chatrī*) with sculpted footprints (*caraṇārvinda*) of Sahajānanda mark a sanctified space (*prasādīnī jagyā*). Shree Swaminarayan Mandir, Vadtal, Gujarat, mid-nineteenth century.

neighboring and public areas of a given village or town. Locations where Sahajānanda was understood to have simply moved about and acted, such as fed people meals, labored in construction, competitively swam, raced horses, danced, enjoyed swings, held a meeting, fell ill, ate a late-night meal, rode an elephant in a public procession, or drafted a scripture, were all recognized as relevant sites. Today this materiality is in the form of architecture of city/ town gates, shops, housing clusters, streets, town squares, buildings, farms, sheds, water wells, gardens, and so on, which can sometimes be well-preserved, deteriorating, or no longer in its original form.

Natural terrain and formations became materiality of value too. These are sites devotees believe Sahajānanda bathed, spoke, walked, and meditated, amongst other activities, which trees, large stones, fields, and bodies of water naturally mark. Moreover, in addition to spaces defined by the ground, walls, and natural elements, objects within these areas were also considered worthy. Today such materiality is mainly preserved in families. These commonly consist of domestic elements like a seat for bathing and eating, plates, bowls and pots, beds, blankets, and quilts. Other such objects used by Sahajānanda reflect everyday life, like a buttermilk churner (*chāśnu valoḍṇu*), large wooden chests, a metal ring outside a home to tie a horse, and elements of an earlier era of agrarian life such as grain storage bins (*koṭī*).

Materiality was the physical narrativization of a history of human relationships. Whether Sahajānanda directly gifted an item to someone or it was incidentally incurred during his visit, or a traveling ascetic shared it with them, or it was inherited in a family over generations, all these parties universally placed great worth on the empirical due to its physical contact with Sahajānanda, which effectively brought them together as a collective. Furthermore, if a committed adherent owned materiality, then their experience with the founder was not complete with the end of the said social contact; instead, materiality reflected and extended Sahajānanda's personage, albeit an enchanted one. In sum, materiality expressed a hybridized compulsion of recording and adoring the founder and his context, which in turn fulfilled aims of personal piety and institutionalization.

At the most fundamental level, materiality acted as empirical notes on a known historical figure. Arguably, it represented a record of an experience understood to have been had or an event known to have occurred according to some people in the nineteenth century. Knowledge architecture rooted in enchanted and empirical accounting untiringly pursued broad and minute documentation. It recorded space from farm to street, objects from clothing to rosaries, as key records because of their relation to Sahajānanda's distinctly perceived personality—all while being firmly located in nineteenth-century India. All-consuming affection, or *bhakti*, was not the antithesis of historical arts or institution building at this period in time. It was the catalyst.

Unwritten Archives in the Twenty-First Century

Materiality's significance has endured over two centuries as a source of identity and devotion for the Svāminārāyaṇa *sampradāya*. By continuing to embody hybridized devotional and historical characteristics, materiality today evokes further appeal: the idea of authenticity. Objects, spaces, and images possess the clout of veracity as records of Sahajānanda Svāmī and the early *sampradāya* in the larger tradition, beyond their sanctified value. Such temporal credibility marks the mode of materiality with virtue in a way that is unlike written records in the community. Ultimately, without Sahajānanda's contemporary presence, materiality's significance as an archive of the past is now even further amplified.

Contemporary materiality is priceless. It remains intensely sought-after by individuals and different branches of the now larger and diversified Svāminārāyaṇa tradition. At its core, the practice of retaining materiality is for worship and holding records of the past. Today, these precious sources yield several types of values for private owners besides soteriological benefit. Materiality for some is understood as memorabilia of a popular and respected regional figure, while certain owners emphasize that it is a rare relic of the nineteenth century. It is also a source of social prestige as evidence of Sahajānanda's relationship with one's ancestors, and finally, it is valued as an element of divinity.[7]

A considerable number of *prasādī* objects (and some images) are found in the ownership of ascetics and families primarily in India, although some can be found in unexpected sites like the suburbs of London and Atlantic City in the United States, having relocated with their owners. Such parties have taken care to preserve materiality in their respective family or ascetic lineages over at least seven to eight generations since their origination or since they have received it at some other point through means like purchase or trade. At an institutional level, materiality is housed in temple archives in western India (Gujarat and Maharashtra) as well as in Uttar Pradesh (Sahajānanda's birthplace)—all sites belonging to the most established seats of the *sampradāya*. At its founding, Sahajānanda configured the community into two *gādī*s or "seats" for the ease of administration: the northern seat of Narnārayaṇ Dev Gādī, the seat popularly known as the Ahmedabad Gādī, and the southern seat of Lakṣmīnārayaṇ Dev

Gādī, commonly referred to as Vadtal Gādī. They were socially and culturally akin, theologically consistent, and bound together but divided for pragmatic purposes. Each seat was designated a territory that spanned India from Dwarka to Calcutta and essentially divided the country into north and south (Dave: 284). While still upholding identical structures and systems, a separate preceptor or an Ācārya, was assigned to lead each Gādī's spiritual and organizational charge (Śatānandamuni 1831: 4.40.26–4.40.29).

Both Gādī collections are wide-ranging. Overlapping somewhat with the range of objects found in private possession, at an institutional level, the Gādīs' temples hold greater quantities and more rare objects. The range includes simple and elaborate forms of furnishings from beds (*khāṭlo*), blankets, embroidered cushions, decorative backgrounds (*picchvāī*), seats (*pātlo*), and fans (*pankho*) to utensils made of different materials like brass, silver, wood, and clay, and various types of nutcrackers, spoons, plates, and water pots (*pāṇī no loṭo*). Importantly, materiality in temples can often include Sahajānanda's corporeal remains of teeth, nail and hair clippings, and ashes. Various rosaries (*tulsīnī māḷā* and *berkho*) and different pairs of footwear (*mojaḍī* and *cākhḍī*) are part of the founder's preserved personal articles (Figure 4.2 bottom). Carts (*gādu*) and related aspects of transport,

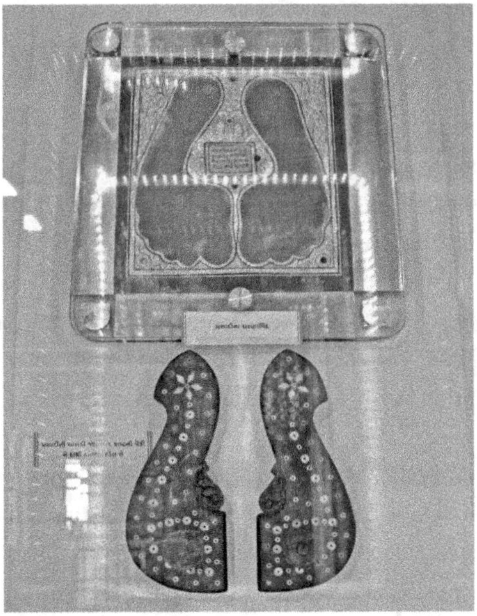

Figure 4.2 Printed footprints (*caraṇārvinda*) and sandals of Sahajānanda are examples of sanctified objects (*prasādīnī vastu*). Shree Swaminarayan Mandir, Vadi Vadodara (Baroda), Gujarat, early nineteenth century. Photograph: Ankur Desai.

swings (*hindoḷā*), and canopies are some of the collections' larger features. As opposed to the simpler materiality found in rural homes, sartorial elements here show more sophistication. These are rich, ornate clothing as well as rural dress (*jāmo*, *khes*, and *keḍiyuṃ*), handkerchiefs, shawls, and various types of turbans (*pāgh*) as well as elaborate crowns, but also gold and precious-stone jewelry such as earrings, armlets (*bājubandh*), and necklaces. Other physical elements believed to have been in Sahajānanda's proximity include items such as cymbals, *sārangī*, and various musical instruments used by early ascetics.

One of the most valued forms of materiality today are *caraṇārvinda* (footprints) made with vermillion on cloth (Figure 4.2 top). Impressions attributed to Sahajānanda were distributed by him and perhaps his ascetics. Prints mainly fall into two styles. Some show distinct signs on each foot, sixteen symbols in total, interpreted as auspicious indicators of Sahajānanda's divinity in the *sampradāya*, while other prints are solid. The observable near-uniformity of the prints' compositions indicates the industrious efforts on the part of early leaders. Today, they are revered as a close representation and extension of Sahajānanda's physical being, somewhat akin to corporeal remains.

Dedicated buildings near the respective temples of the two headquarter campuses of Ahmedabad Gādī and Vadtal Gādī hold the materiality. While Ahmedabad is the former capital of Gujarat, Vadtal, located in the lush agrarian economy of Kheda in central Gujarat is a small town whose main claim in the region is its respected position as a historical Svāmināráyaṇa center. The buildings that display materiality in both locations are called "Akshar Bhuvan" (Figures 4.3 and 4.4). The Akshar Bhuvans do not house the full extent of their collections.

Additional *prasādī* is kept in more secluded areas of the two campuses, such as the *sabhā maṇḍap*, an area of ascetic *āsans* or ceremonial seats, which mark where the initial generation of ascetics in the nineteenth century would have counseled devotees; it is from these prominent ascetics that key collectives and their lineages (*sādhu maṇḍaḷs*) formed and continue today. Finally, the private holdings of the Ācāryas at their family residences maintain considerable materiality.

Materiality at the Akshar Bhuvans is for storage and *darśan*. It is securely and visibly preserved in glass cabinets behind barred window-like openings with assigned ascetics for caretaking (Figure 4.4). Some objects are packed in what seems to be wooden boxes or small spaces on the wall enclosed by framed windows, while a few appear to be in some type of plastic wrap. Individual elements are combined in smaller groups for display and in several instances nestled closely, squeezing the myriad of objects together to fit into storage. The holdings are displayed at eye level

Figure 4.3 Exterior view of Akshar Bhuvan, which was created to house and display Sahajānanda's materiality (*prasādī*). Shree Swaminarayan Mandir, Vadtal, Gujarat, late nineteenth century. Photograph: Ankur Desai.

Figure 4.4 Interior view of the display and storage of Sahajānanda's *prasādī* (sacred objects and images). Akshar Bhuvan, Shree Swaminarayan Mandir, Vadtal, Gujarat, late nineteenth century. Photograph: Ankur Desai.

and higher. For this reason, and because viewing must take place from a distance of approximately five to ten feet away through bars, the visibility of details can be challenging. Some devotees strain to discern the holdings while others can be observed to be content to pass by with quick, expedient glances in their routine on campus. Additionally, the walls, between and above the storage, display images of Sahajānanda, created in various mediums, along with framed paintings of detailed scenes depicting the teacher and devotees in the nineteenth century. While the two structures are unique and their collections are recognized in the *sampradāya*, the display is not limited to Gādī headquarters. Other temples in the network of the northern and southern Gādīs also hold key collections. For instance, the temple in Jetalpur, a town about 20 kilometers away from Ahmedabad that Sahajānanda frequented, preserves and showcases materiality in the form of objects, images, and specially marked spaces in the town.

The same can be said for other nineteenth-century temples. Among them, Kathiawar's Gadhada (Bhavnagar area) and Salangpur (Sarangpur) as well as Muli (Surendranagar area) hold major collections that are varied and rare. While not all objects are displayed for view, materiality is more diversely displayed here than in the arrangements at Ahmedabad and Vadtal. Objects are not always found behind glass or bars, but at times, set out in a room on the floor, behind ropes. For instance, in Gadhada, which was his residential base for many years of Sahajānanda's life, objects and space are presented at once; notable items are placed in the dwelling areas and rooms of the *darbār* (estate) (Figure 4.5).

Female ascetics, moving about, closely monitor such key areas of Gadhada to ensure the security of these objects. Beyond such prominent temples, there are many modest *mandir*s inconspicuously located in villages with similar configurations, where the materiality of objects, images, and marked local space reflect specific events and accounts of Sahajānanda and others. Today, materiality is authoritative. Ultimately and unanimously across the contemporary tradition, materiality is fundamentally associated with the nineteenth-century figure of Sahajānanda Svāmī, profiled as founder, teacher, and object of worship.

One outstanding factor common to all collections is careful guardianship. It reveals the intense degree to which material elements are coveted and fragile. For instance, some individuals hesitate to show materiality from personal collections to strangers (such as scholars), while others show them with eagerness and pride. Some encourage touching the objects with bare hands, while others request observers to maintain a distance so as to not threaten the item physically

Figure 4.5 Courtyard and neem tree on estate (*darbār*) of Dada Kachar, devotee and patron of Sahajānanda. Another example of a sanctified space (*prasādīnī jagyā*). Shree Swaminarayan Mandir (Gopinathji Dev), Gadhada, Gujarat, early nineteenth century. Photograph: Ankur Desai.

or in terms of perceived impurity. Commonly, the items are kept apart in a secure case, box, or some equivalent and handled with varying degrees of care. One senses high vigilance in the form of physical security and bureaucracy on campus temples, whether for concerns related to the prevalence of illicit art and antiquity trading in India today or otherwise. Throughout, materiality is at a distance from observers and variously safeguarded.

The protected storage in Vadtal and Ahmedabad, for instance, cannot be easily opened for closer viewing whether for devotees or the curious scholar. Apparently, this is not a matter of gaining permission from local guardians or temple authorities but requires more extensive authorization. The complexity of permission, along with a series of other dynamics, reveals a delicate form of checks and balances created between diverse patrons of the community. Views differ on the subject of materiality's preservation. Parties invested in this subject have at various stages included select lay devotees, elected and appointed ascetics, and temple management like chief administrators (*kārbhāri*). For instance, Vadtal Gādī has cited legal restrictions that impede opening material archives extensively without the physical presence of all relevant parties, despite influential voices from individual groups like the Trustee Board and the Satsang

Mahasabha. In essence, a larger history of complex and intersecting debates that thread theology, authority, leadership, and property together, manifests in various aspects of a single temple or a Gādī, and at times, between the different branches of the expanded *sampradāya* today. The topic of materiality provides a natural site for these differences to play out.

For instance, in Vadtal, despite the highly visible and public nature of materiality's display on campus, different parties see the fate of Akshar Bhuvan in contrary ways. For nearly a decade, influential groups within the Gādī have debated over the construction of a building conceptualized and designated as a "museum." The argument for its creation has rested on the opinion that such a space would better display and preserve *prasādī*. This idea came on the heels of having seen similar arrangements take place among their northern counterparts, Ahmedabad and Bhuj, where large "museum" spaces were created for materiality once housed in traditional temple archives.

Trust is a pressure point. Despite the availability of land for such construction on the Gādī's properties in Vadtal, the project remained at an impasse for years because of the passionate concerns of various parties. What if, in the process of transferring the materiality from its present location to the new building, less than a mile away, materiality was stolen? Though materiality might be compressed and less clearly visible in Akshar Bhuvan, has it not still remained preserved sitting there for decades? Despite relatively reasonable countermeasures—namely, its safety would be ensured by transferring the objects and images with key witnesses present, objects would be moved one at a time allowing the transfer to occur slowly and in the daytime for public visibility—negotiation and a clear path forward has been difficult for years. No mechanisms for security or common assurance had gained enough of the confidence of all parties to launch the project beyond conception. Only very recently was there agreement for the construction of a museum space on the banks of Vadtal's Gomti River, now substantially underway.[8] The configuration of unwritten archives with their considerable value in the twenty-first century further elevates materiality's position in the larger Svāmīnārāyaṇa tradition, allowing for the construction of such large archival buildings to be desired and attainable.

The Swaminarayan Museum

The Ahmedabad Gādī, which self-identifies as the "Original Shree Swami narayan Sampradaya," inaugurated the Shree Swaminarayan Museum in

Figure 4.6 Exterior view of the "Shree Swaminarayan Museum," Ahmedabad, Gujarat, 2011. Courtesy of Vinit Vyas.

Ahmedabad, Gujarat, in 2011 (Figure 4.6). His Holiness Moṭā Mahārāj Śrī (as he is affectionately known to his followers), the former Ācārya of the Gādī and a seventh-generation descendant of Sahajānanda Svāmī, conceived the museum. He retired early from formal leadership, transferring authority to his son Ācārya Koślendraprasādjī, to fully concentrate on this novel project. Of key note, devotees recognize the Ācārya and his larger family lineage descending from Sahajānanda Svāmī as unwaveringly divine. Materiality kept in the main temples of the Gādī is technically the property of the Ācārya's family or the Dharmakuḷ. The museum was formulated on this basis, namely the shifting of a considerable amount of his personal inheritance, including objects large and small, manuscripts, letters, and paintings to premises well outside Akshar Bhuvan, the temple complex, and the family's private residence.

Moṭā Mahārāj Śrī took extensive measures to gather materiality from the private possession of Svāminārāyaṇa devotees. He requested such families to donate nineteenth-century objects and images to the museum for better preservation and the opportunity to present them to broader audiences. Several reasons spurred this. The retired Ācārya recounts that over the years during his travels and visits with devotees, he would find materiality in less-than-fortunate conditions. It was also his sense that in some of these settings, religious commitments were less vibrant than in earlier generations, causing materiality to be cared for inappropriately. In a particularly distressing instance, Moṭā Mahārāj Śrī learned that a set of Sahajānanda's auspicious footprints had been torn in half. The legacy was split between two brothers who were each keen to have his share of the family inheritance. Further, the state of institutionally-held materiality drew concern. Museum administrators shared that though many temples in the Gādī's network had fantastic holdings they did not always adequately conserve them. The future of all of this materiality worried Moṭā Mahārāj Śrī, and he long nurtured the idea of gathering it together for safety in one place. In the process he faced a challenging proposition due to the geographically wide dispersal and circulation of objects and images over the past two centuries.

According to museum administrators, H. H. Moṭā Mahārāj Śrī's wish to urgently conserve belongings attributed to Bhagavāna Śrī Svāminārāyaṇa (Sahajānanda Svāmī) and provide a more public orientation for them drove him to create the Shree Swaminarayan Museum. The administrators pursued preservation in consultation with professional conservationists, developing a system of processing, documenting, and cataloging materiality, and dedicated an on-site conservation space for continued work. The museum's website reiterates H. H. Moṭā Mahārāj Śrī's goal of inclusivity in its desire "to project exhibits to the common masses and preserve them for further study."[9]

An energetic consolidation effort produced a voluminous collection, numbering a few thousand items for the museum. This unique possession over a great quantity of materiality, coupled with the materiality's prized historical-devotional value, highlighted and further reinforced the Ahmedabad Gādī in the eyes of devotees. As one studious and pious devotee who frequents the museum commented in Gujarati, "This is the real matter." His statement implies that what the Gādī represents on the basis of possessed materiality, and the voluminous materiality itself, is synonymous with the reality of the tradition, as opposed to the many other branches that have arisen in the contemporary tradition.

Genealogy also adds unusually special value. The ancestry of Ācāryas as prime patron, guardian, and inheritor of materiality stresses a key historical thread itself: "Dharmavanśī Ācārya," or Ācāryas descended from the Dharmakuḷ, exemplify Sahajānanda Svāmī's two-century-old family lineage, and thus critically, he singularly represents the administrative lineage, the spiritual lineage, and ultimate divinity through his particular position and genealogy. This is a formula for exponential authority. In terms of the Ahmedabad Gādī, the feature of historical integrity authenticates their entitlement to being the "Original"—the formal identifier they reinforce officially and publicly. Effectively, it can be strongly inferred that the Gādī wishes to entirely differentiate itself from all other branches, which it perceives to be historically, and thus spiritually, derivative. History has become a sign of virtue.

No branch in regard to materiality is comparable to the two foundational Gādīs. Indeed, the Gādīs possess the overwhelming majority of institutional culture from its point of origination. For instance, Bocāsaṇvāsī Śrī Akṣar Puruṣottam Svāminārāyaṇ Sansthā, a branch known by the acronym BAPS, adheres to a particular philosophical stance; in the process of forming and upholding its specific view, the group was compelled to separate and depart from the Vadtal Gādī in 1907.[10] But in this regard it also resigned two aspects as it separated from Vadtal Gādī: an affiliation with Ācāryas, or Sahajānanda Svāmī's lineage, and second, organizational access to materiality. Rather this branch now prioritizes a different kind of genealogical grammar—the lived virtue of its divinely revered spiritual and administrative lineage of ascetics, as opposed to nineteenth-century historical enchantment. This is not to say BAPS is entirely without materiality, but in this capacity, it stresses the personal effects, space, and imagery related to the spiritual lineage of its own teachers (gurus) beginning in 1907.

While the museum is certainly an initiative dedicated to materiality's preservation as it has been communicated by representatives, its conception and execution also hint at aims to invigorate and make deep claims to the past. The museum documents and archives sacred materiality while distinctively foregrounding a historic lens more so than a devotional one. As one moves through the museum's halls, the exhibits present materiality with general regional and historic accounts effectively situating *sampradāya* pasts along with narratives of the British Empire as well as the history and culture of the city of Ahmedabad. A corresponding position is noticeable on the website. It discerns the museum's intent and attentive audiences from that of temples' material collections and visitors, underscoring that in the latter context: "People who pass by them have no historical information about these items."[11] The museum today braids together the work of adoration and recordkeeping that continues from the early community, but with a pivotal adjustment. Upon entry into the museum, a welcome video, including H. H. Moṭā Mahārāj Śrī and the current Ācārya, greets visitors. Remarkably, in a mix of Gujarati and English, the collection of materiality is depicted as possessing "vibrations." The "vibrations" that Swaminarayan Bhagwan possessed did not end with his physical departure, but rather, today the objects embody his "vibrations" and these can even be felt, the current Ācārya explains to visitors. In addition, the museum's website states that this physical space "invigorates thoroughly in the presence of His own artifacts."[12] Here, I would note, a sharp distinction about and emphasis on the past is being made. First, classifying traditional *prasādī* as an "artifact" instantly conjures the past, readily designating the said object as a site of historical interest and even of social science investigation. Critically, then, the inanimate element is relinked to the impulse of enchantment, where the artifact is said to exude Sahajānanda's personality. I would suggest that the unprecedented label of "artifact" and dichotomously framed (and then reframed) depiction of materiality are profoundly revealing: they disclose that contemporary desires for broader audiences and secular perceptions now inflect foundational nineteenth-century narratives.

The museum's exhibits, displays, explanatory text, organization, activities, and the expressed desires of its creative team reveal varied lines of rationalization. For instance, the intent to address audiences beyond Svāminārāyaṇa devotees is evident. Throughout the museum, accompanying text in the language of Gujarati and English frames the objects. These descriptions are composed for visitors, whether or not they are acquainted with the given account or tradition, or whether they are local visitors or Indians living abroad. Museum administrators have sought varied audiences. As a museum administrator communicated to me, courting visitors from diverse walks of life like journalists and artists was part of their early interest; visitor comments penned in the guest book also affirmed this broader audience. Unlike temple settings, materiality in the museum is displayed in LED-lit glass cases, spaciously accommodated therein or on the floor and accessible for a clear view. Select objects are contextualized with adjacently placed paintings. These visuals were specially commissioned to illustrate the object as it was known to be part of an event with Sahajānanda. Overall, the museum's self-presentation reveals multiple kinds of gestures: it aims to orient, inform, and promote appreciation of *sampradāya*-specific materiality, whether for committed adherents, the unfamiliar, or otherwise.

The Shree Swaminarayan Museum vigorously identifies as a "museum" with "no exception," using the criterion established by the International Council of Museums (ICOM). It references "Statutes, Article 2, Paragraph 1, 'A museum is typically a non-profit making, permanent institution in the service of society and of its development, open to the public, which acquires, conserves, researches, communicates and exhibits, for purposes of study, education and enjoyment, the tangible and intangible evidence of people and their environment.'"[13] One reason Moṭā Mahārāj Śrī cites for utilizing the English term "museum" rather than Akshar Bhuvan or some other name for the site is the early *sampradāya*'s relations and engagement with the British. Both parties not only came into the region together, he notes, but it was the British who first provided Sahajānanda with the land for the initial temple.

The second reason Moṭā Mahārāj Śrī gives for the title of "museum" is its striking uniqueness. He points out that while similar materiality might be found among temples, ascetics, and devotees across the *sampradāya*, the museum's collection is unprecedented. It has on public display "*amūlya*" or priceless, one-of-a-kind objects, stemming only from Moṭā Mahārāj Śrī's family inheritance; such exceptional objects include Sahajānanda's silver toothpick. This compels the descriptor of "museum." But perhaps most terrifically, evident by Moṭā Mahārāj Śrī's enthusiasm, is the collection's highlight which has been kept "exclusive" and not reproduced; the museum claims to possess the only known handwritten signature of Sahajānanda anywhere, evident in a legal document signed by Sahajānanda to issue power of attorney on his behalf, sprinkled with English phrases, signed by three witnesses, and notarized by a British official. The legal document is dated in the Common Era and not in the Hindu calendar format of Sāmvat year, as was the norm for the founder's letters and other writings. Moṭā Mahārāj Śrī especially notes that this is unlike many of the other letters that Sahajānanda composed and had his ascetics transcribe; instead, it is written entirely in his own hand and is consistent with the handwriting of the signature.[14] Materiality, put simply, hews closely to signs of authenticity and authority for the Gādī.

A museum is not an obvious building choice in the *sampradāya*. Conceptually speaking, why develop a museum aesthetic as opposed to a temple? Or why not another traditional style of architecture that correlates with the Gādī's visual vocabulary, or a style prevalent in the umbrella tradition, or even in the region like a *darbār*?[15] Museum representatives noted that they sought a presentation mode which did not compete with the main attraction, the materiality (see Figure 4.6). Admittedly, the architecture's spare, minimalist sensibility and unadorned white walls do produce that effect. But it was also implied that there was a wish to have a space and aesthetic apart from the familiar temple and other Indic modes. The Gādī's renowned Narnārayaṇ Dev temple, the first one built in the *sampradāya* by Sahajānanda Svāmī in 1822, is located in the area of Kalupur within the congested, bustling older section of Ahmedabad. The museum, itself pristine and quiet, was constructed in 2011 in Naranpura, a more spacious and affluent neighborhood in the newer side of Ahmedabad.

But the draw of having a "museum" as an exceptional aspect of the building's name, and as a unique visual and conceptual mode, comes into clearer focus when we recall that museum representatives hoped to attract broader attention. While not announced, administrators implied that they sought varied urban audiences from schools to journalists, academics to artists, parties who might not ever visit the temple in Kalupur. Thus, it is highly probable that the museum format was elected to translate community-specific ideas as more accessible content, but further, I would argue, the concept of a "museum" would be attractive because of the widely acceptable framework that it conjures: secularism. Ultimately, a museum displays public authorization in a way a temple likely does not—historically.[16]

And yet, devotion is at the crux of this materiality, signaling the museum's active combination of "religion" and "history." As per the museum's website, "The Swaminarayan religion is only a 230-year old institution. Thus, projecting the museum for historical purposes will not do justice to the concept."[17] In actuality, many visitors view and understand the museum as a site of devotion. Objects are available and visible for worship, and such visitors can be observed reverentially offering their respects to the displays. To better attend to such an audience—both local and from the Indian diaspora—the museum has introduced special formats of worship; quite popular is an initiative where followers may sponsor and participate in ceremonial practices of *havan* and *abhiṣeka* in the central hall. Despite the illustrious temples and their environments in the area, many visit, view, and participate in the museum as a space of worship and marvel. Thus, the museum site allows the Ahmedabad Gādī to uphold multiple purposes, audiences, and strengths in the twenty-first century, secular and devotional.

Conclusion

In sum, the Ahmedabad branch's authority is generated with different audiences from its possession of a tremendous volume of prized soteriological and *bhakti*-oriented objects, prominent display of such rare objects, self-presentation from a framework of regional history, and the novel use of a museum format in the *sampradāya*. In fact, relocation of materiality from cloistered temples and residences to their far-reaching presentation style, in some sense, has facilitated one branch's collection to stand in as a significant representation of the entire tradition for general public audiences. Compounded and circuitous in its claims, the museum allows the Ahmedabad Gādī to achieve distinction on its strength of the past and subtly signal a complex kind of authority internal and external to the Svāminārāyaṇa tradition, at once and together. Devotional virtue, archival production and preservation, charisma, affection, self-knowledge, habits of recollection, and community strength were well-configured conjointly in the Svāmināráyaṇa tradition. These emotional and intellectual features that made materiality so valuable for community institutionalization in the nineteenth century also make it so in the twenty-first century, but of added interest is its distinct authoritative ability to sustain branches in contemporary circumstances.

Notes

1 For a detailed and excellent history of early imagery, see Ankur Desai's chapter in this volume.

2 This understanding is built on conversations with senior, learned devotees of Ahmedabad Gādī, Ahmedabad, 2011–12.

3 See http://www.swaminarayanmuseum.com/history.html (accessed June 26, 2022).

4 My observations and analysis of materiality, historically and in the present day, mainly rest on extensive fieldwork conducted in 2008, 2011, 2015 in rural areas and cities of present-day Gujarat, across private family, neighborhoods, public sites, and temples. It was undertaken both independently and with the generous assistance of several *sampradāya* branches: BAPS, Ahmedabad Gādī, Vadtal Gādī, Kundaldham, Bhuj Mandir (Narnārayaṇ Dev), and Gadhada Mandir (Gopinātjī Dev).

5 The founder's occasional and formal engagements with officials in cities, outside common rural-dwelling populations, are evidenced by items he left behind and held privately today. For instance, the rich turban Sahajānanda wore and gifted to the Parsi police officer, Ardeshar Kotwal, who received the founder in Surat in 1825 is still preserved by his descendants.

6 Over the last decade, an increasing number of branches and individuals have made efforts to document such sites and publish booklets, guides, and videos.

7 These reflect the general categories of responses provided by materiality owners across the diverse settings and social backgrounds I encountered. For some, multiple categories were relevant, while for others, only one or two of these values mattered.

8 For more information, see https://english.gujaratexclusive.in/vadtal-museum-on-lord-shri-hari/ (accessed June 26, 2022).

9 See http://www.swaminarayanmuseum.com/purpose.html (accessed June 26, 2022).

10 For instance, for a history of how conflicting views and tensions between branches of the two Gādīs and the younger BAPS branch influenced BAPS temple construction projects, see Kim (2012: 363–6).

11 For more information, see http://www.swaminarayanmuseum.com/purpose.html (accessed June 26, 2022).
12 See http://www.swaminarayanmuseum.com/highlights.html (accessed December 4 2022).
13 See http://www.swaminarayanmuseum.com/purpose.html (accessed June 26, 2022).
14 See https://www.youtube.com/watch?v=qKqNyj9-CO0 (accessed June 26, 2022). Similarly, the BAPS branch has noted in the last few decades that it has the "only existing letter handwritten" by the founder. A replica of the letter is displayed in Gandhinagar, Gujarat, while the original is reportedly under safe preservation. For more information, see http://www.swaminarayan.org/lordswaminarayan/holyrelics/theoneandonly.htm (accessed June 26, 2022).
15 This was raised by devotees who participated in the creative process for designing the site.
16 Here, I partly follow Elaine Oliphant's assessment of how Catholic materiality in France is equated with secularism and also understood to correspond with the history and culture of the region. While it is the privilege of "banality" of Catholicism in French public space that generates such equivalents for Catholic materiality, it is also the privilege of uniqueness that locates *bhakti* materiality in a specially circumscribed Indian space—a museum, which then draws materiality closer to notions of secularism and the history and culture of the region (Oliphant 2021: 3–6).
17 See http://www.swaminarayanmuseum.com/purpose.html (accessed June 26, 2022).

References

Adbhutānand Svāmī, S. Ś. (2010), *Sadguru Śrī Adbhutānand Śvāmīnī Mūdguru*, Kungur: Tīrthdhām Kundaldham tathā Śrī Svāmīnārāyaṇ Mandir Kārelībāg-Vaḍodarā.

Akhaṇḍānand Svāmī (2002), *Śrīakhaṇḍānandvarṇiviracita Bhaktiśāstra Śrīharicaritra*, ed. and trans. Shastri Gnanprakashdas, Gandhinagar: Shrisvaminarayan Sahitya Prakashan Mandir Gurukul (Sector 23).

Dave, J. M. (1997), "Reappraisal of the 'Lekh,'" in R. N. Mehta, D. Chandra, M. R. Trivedi, and B. Ganorkar (eds.), *New Dimensions of Indology*, 284–95, Delhi: Bharatiya Vidya Prakashan.

Kim, H. H. (2012), "The BAPS Swaminarayan Temple Organisation and Its Publics," in J. Zavos, P. Kanungo, D. S. Reddy, M. Warrier, and R. B. Williams (eds.) *Public Hinduisms*, 417–39, New Delhi: Sage Publications.

Kīrtanmuktāvalī (2003), Amdāvād: Svāminārāyaṇa Akśarapīt Publishing Institute.

Niṣkuḷānand Svāmī, V. Ś. S. Ś. (2010 [c.1831]), *Bhaktacintāmatp*, Kuakta: Tīrthdhām Kuṇḍaḷdhām tathā Śrī Svāmīnārāyaṇ Mandir Kārelībāg-Vadodarā.

Oliphant, E. (2021), *The Privilege of Being Banal: Art, Secularism, and Catholicism in Paris*, Chicago: University of Chicago Press.

Patel, S. (May 1, 2017), "Beyond the Lens of Reform: Religious Culture in Modern Gujarat," *The Journal of Hindu Studies* 10 (1): 47–85.

Patel, S. (forthcoming a), "Networks of Power in the Nineteenth Century: The Sampradaya, Princely States and Company Rule," Unpublished paper.

Patel, S. (forthcoming b), "The Play of History: The Swaminarayan Religious Community in Modern India," Unpublished manuscript.

Prasādānand Svāmī, S. Ś. (1880), *Śrīsvāmīnārāyaṇ Vicaraṇlīlāmṛt*, Kuīsvā: Tīrthdhām Kuṇḍaḷdhām tathā Śrī Svāmīnārāyaṇ Mandir, Kārelībāg-Vaḍodarā.

Śatānandamuni, S. Ś. (1981 [*c.* 1831]), *Satsaandamunitp: Granth*, trans. Sadguru Śastrī Śrī Śvetvaikunthdāsjī. Bhāg 1–2, Jetpur: Śrī SvāmīnārāyaŚrī Śvetvaikunt.

Schreiner, P. (2001), "Institutionalization of Charisma: The Case of Sahajānanda," in V. Dalmia, A. Malinar, and M. Christof (eds.), *Charisma and Canon: Essays on the Religious History of the Indian Subcontinent*, 155–70, New York: Oxford University Press.

Śrī Svāmīnārāyaṇ Bhagvān (2010), *Vacanāmṛt, Śrī Svāmīnārāyaṇ Bhagvānī Paravānī, Vacanāmṛt*, Kuṇḍaḷ: Tīrthdhām Kuṇḍaḷdhām tathā Śrī Svāmīnārāyaṇ Mandir Kārelībāg-Varoḍarā.

Williams, R. B. (2001), *An Introduction to Swaminarayan Hinduism*, New York: Cambridge University Press.

Part II

Mirroring and Immaterializing Portraits

5

Kabīr in Indo-Muslim Visual and Literary Culture

Murad Khan Mumtaz

Introduction

Verse: What a crazy world
where people worship a piece of stone
no one worships the millstone at home
yet they eat what is ground from it.

Seeing the millstones turn, Kabīr weeps.
Commentary: Kabīr's son was Kamāl Das, both "kabīr" and "kamāl" are Arabic words that are not found in any local languages. There is a great debate around Kabīr being a Hindu or a Muslim. The themes show that he is describing the Oneness of God [tawḥīd]

Verse: Between the two stones no one survived intact
Commentary: So Kabīr's son answered by saying that you have stopped at the wrong spiritual station. Your thought has stopped at that state which is not the state of Essence but the state of the Qualities. So Kabīr asked what is the right station?

Verse: Everyone says millstone, millstone
no one says axle
He who attaches himself to the axle
not even a hair of his is injured

Commentary: It is pure evidence that those seeds that manage to find the center close to the axle don't get ground, so for him who grasps the Oneness of God [tawḥīd], there is no question of his being discarded.

At this statement Kabīr Das was shaken. He understood, and said:
Verse: Kabīr is only half a devotee
while Kamāl is the complete devotee
It is good this burden is off my head![1]

These verses describe a much-loved twenty-first-century *qawwālī* performance by Pakistani singer Munshi Raziuddin and his sons.[2] The words are attributed to Kabīr, the fifteenth-century poet who remains a central voice in *nirguṇa bhakti*, the Indic non-dualist devotional tradition. Like most *qawwāls*, Raziuddin was a Muslim and a Chishtī *sufi*.[3] How is it that for him and for so many *sufis*, Kabīr's verses remain relevant? Raziuddin's commentary that is scattered through his *qawwālī* performance gives us insights into how Muslims not only have identified with devotional ideals shared among Indic spiritualities but have also used these voices to define themselves. The *qawwālī*'s refrain is: "It is good that my pot is broken, I don't have to go fill water, this burden is off my head!" For the oral tradition of Kabīr and many Indic *sufi* poets, the image of the village woman fulfilling her daily chore of collecting water from the well stands for the straight-and-narrow path of prescribed religious practice. While such practice is an important stepping stone toward union with the Divine, union occurs only when pietistic constraints are shattered. Continuing with this theme, in the next verse from the *qawwālī* Kabīr proclaims:

> It is good that my rosary is broken
> I am relieved from singing praises of Rām
>
> The wooden rosary says
> "O, why do you turn me?
> Turn the beads of the mind
> and see how in an instant you will find union."
>
> I don't count the rosary
> I don't repeat Rām's name,
> My Rām repeats my name
> The mind finds contentment O Kabīr!

At this point Raziuddin interjects with his own commentary, where he elaborates on Kabīr's verse by using a Quranic utterance where God says, "Remember Me and I will remember you" (2:152). He goes on to further interpret Kabīr through an Islamic/*sufi* lens when he relates how the famous Chishtī saint Bābā Farīd Ganj Shakar (d. 1266) from Pakpattan remembered God to such an extent, invoking "Allah Allah" so profusely, that God Himself cried out "O Farīd, O Farīd," leading to the common practice of his devotees calling loudly upon his name as they enter his shrine to this day.[4]

Munshi Raziuddin's *qawwālī* is one late iteration in a centuries-old tradition of Muslim engagement with Kabīr devotion. The *qawwālī* touches upon questions that are central to my chapter. Why do Muslim communities—in particular *sufi* communities—care so much about Kabīr? What is the importance of the elusive figure of his son Kamāl? Since this chapter is a first step toward understanding Kabīr's role in the transcultural dialogue between the commonly assumed notion of *bhakti* as a solely Hindu practice and *sufi* devotional expressions, I single out some of the earliest documentation, primarily from the sixteenth and seventeenth centuries. By focusing on this literary and visual evidence, I discuss how one of the most important devotional poets of Hindustan was imagined and understood within the framework of Indo-Muslim culture. By collating images of Kabīr with contemporaneous literary accounts of the saint-poet produced by Muslim authors for Muslim audiences, the chapter addresses two major lacunae in Kabīr studies: first, the fact that scholars have primarily viewed Kabīr through the lens of Devanāgarī sources, without giving the parallel stream of literary material written in the Persian/Urdu script the same level of importance; and second, the lack of scholarly attention given to depictions of Kabīr as found in north Indian schools of miniature painting. This oversight is a curious one given that Kabīr and his son Kamāl were important subjects in seventeenth and eighteenth-century painting (Figure 5.1).

By combining visual and literary analyses, this chapter provides a methodology that can be used for studying other histories and expressions of *bhakti* as well, potentially shedding new light on important mystics and their spiritual legacies across the interwoven fabric of devotional communities in Hindustan. Additionally, the chapter also suggests a way forward in the study of *bhakti* by including voices from other local religious and spiritual traditions that were inextricably linked to this history. In this chapter, for instance, I have shown how nuanced Kabīr's reception was for early modern Muslims. Artworks made for Muslim patrons highlight Kabīr's importance as a mystic but frame him as a non-Muslim, while some of the most important hagiographical literature embraces him as a *sufi*. On the other hand, the presence of his son Kamāl in Indo-Muslim texts and images appears to provide a more cohesive link between Indic and Persianate devotional cultures.

One author whose work has helped me frame my own arguments—not only for the study of Kabīr in a Muslim context but also for understanding Indo-Islamic expression in general—is the late religious studies scholar Shahab Ahmad, who provides a methodical way of considering Islamic art and culture and its relation to the sacred. Ahmad explains that the underlying goal of Islamic philosophical and speculative thought—much of which has been the driving engine behind the multiform creative expressions in Muslim history—has been to seek knowledge and ultimately, union with God/Truth-Reality (*ḥaqīqa*). Muslim philosophers, *sufi*s, and legal scholars all agree that Revelation links the

Figure 5.1 *Kabīr and Kamāl*, from the *St. Petersburg Album*, *c.* 1680, Institute of Oriental Manuscripts, Russian Academy of Sciences (MS.E-14, fol. 68r).

divine and the human, and is the means for people to actively seek knowledge of the Truth. Ahmad divides Revelation into three facets. The scripture, which he labels as the "text" is one limited expression of Revelation given to Muslims in the Arabic language. The "Pre-text" is the timeless, original message of Truth, of which the "text" is just one particular articulation. The "Con-Text" is the lived, historical engagement with it and through it, as seen in the arts, philosophy, and metaphysics, and includes both "proscriptive" and "explorative" historical unfolding. "Con-Text is that whole lexicon of meanings that is the product and outcome of previous hermeneutical engagements with Revelation which are already present in the context of a given time and place *as Islam*" (Ahmad 2015: 435). Such a perspective that expands our understanding of Islam to embrace cultural variance and difference discards syncretism as a useful means of inquiry. As Ahmad explains, "we are now able to move beyond the lens of 'syncretism' to a more capacious understanding. We have seen repeatedly that the idea that the Truth of Pre-Text exists beyond the Text has enabled Muslims routinely to find Pre-Textual meaning in extra-Textual form" (Ahmad 2015: 435). It is thus, I argue, that an explorative inquiry into other religious traditions—such as that made by artists, musicians, *sufi*s, and Mughal elites in their engagement with the figure of Kabīr and his words—can be understood, paradoxical as it may seem, as a truly Islamic and "Islamizing" pursuit for Truth-Reality.

In this chapter, after a brief historiographical overview, I begin by introducing some early visual and textual records—mostly from the late sixteenth century to the first half of the seventeenth century—that feature Kabīr, attempting to contextualize them from the perspective of those who wrote and commissioned them. The second half of the chapter examines the visual legacy of Kabīr and Kamāl more extensively, and also includes a discussion of artworks from the eighteenth century.

Kabīr and His Historiographical Legacy: A Brief Analysis

Kabīr was a beloved devotional figure in the writing and art of seventeenth and eighteenth-century Muslim nobility, and he has been valorized in Indian popular culture through the medium of ghazals, *bhajans*, and *qawwālī*s sung across the subcontinent. He is an important representative of a widespread form of mystical expression unique to Hindustan that coalesces *sufi* and Yogic, Hindu, and Muslim practices and conceptualizations of devotion. Kabīr himself resisted being categorized as either "Muslim" or "Hindu," yet both groups revere him in popular culture to this day. Although his own life and beliefs are shrouded in mystery, his verses have continued to be widely popular among diverse religious communities. In recent times, social activists have repurposed his words to speak out against caste-based discrimination and other forms of injustice in modern and contemporary India (Hess 2015: 359–98).

In the disciplines of comparative literature and religious studies, Kabīr's life, words, and enduring legacy have been examined at length. Scholars and translators have painstakingly surveyed both oral and textual traditions to identify and map Kabīr's verses. Others have shown Kabīr's legacy in the various branches of the Kabīr Panth. These and many other surveys have enriched our understanding of Kabīr, his poetry, and his pivotal role in shaping various religious communities (Bangha 2019: 126–8). And yet, a vast reserve of Indo-Persian sources remains surprisingly underexplored. Scholars mention Rizvi's thorough account as sourced from Persian hagiographical literature (1978: 411–13) but seldom engage with the sources he cites directly. Vaudeville, in her seminal biographical introduction of Kabīr, primarily uses Hindi sources and refers to Persian records only in passing (Vaudeville 1993: 48–51), giving "a confused and distorted version of the concepts surrounding" technical terms used by the original authors (Rizvi 1978: 411). Surprisingly, even studies aiming to highlight Kabīr's presence in Muslim literature fail to engage with early modern texts written in Persian (Gaefke 2002: 157–64).

In Hindustan, *sants*, *bhaktas*, yogis, and *sufis* journeyed far and wide, spreading and sharing their songs of devotion across the subcontinent, a territory that is today a divided landscape. The political scission separating the modern nations of India and Pakistan over the last seven decades has led to divisive historiographical trends that frustrate holistic approaches to studying the devotional cultures of northern Hindustan. The history of Hindustan is increasingly viewed through a lens in which the subcontinent is conflated with a postcolonial, post-Partition, modern India. From a cultural and linguistic perspective, Hindi and Sanskrit come to represent India and Hinduism, while Urdu is seen as representing all things Muslim and Pakistani. In this shrinking matrix, sources written in Persian/Urdu scripts, as well as the subcontinent's Persianate literary and devotional cultures, slip through the cracks. In addition to Rizvi's contribution, another scholar who touches upon early modern Muslim engagement with Kabīr and his followers—albeit very briefly—is Supriya Gandhi (2020: 170–1). In the field of art history, the presence of Kabīr and Kamāl, a recurring theme among artworks made for Muslim audiences between circa 1650 and 1800, has never been examined thematically. This oversight, of both the visual and textual record, has led scholars to assume that Kabīr's "reception amongst Muslims was rather modest . . . and he was not discussed by Muslims as a poet until the twentieth century" (Bangha 2019: 128). However, when we examine these two distinct forms of primary sources together, a different picture of Kabīr's reception among early modern Muslim circles begins to emerge. In this survey, I develop avenues touched upon by both Rizvi and Gandhi. Rather than providing an exhaustive list of every reference that includes the presence of Kabīr, I discuss a selection of key sources that have helped me contextualize Kabīr, his visual legacy, and his poetry for a Muslim audience.

Early Sources

No serious attempt to understand Kabīr and his son Kamāl from within the language and epistemology of Indo-Muslim spirituality is possible without considering the multivalent figure of Prince Dārā Shikoh. As the heir apparent to the Mughal throne, he was a prolific patron of painting and an author of devotional poetry, metaphysical treatises, and two important hagiographies.

Most importantly, he was a practicing mystic initiated into a *sufi* order, and this affiliation directly informed both his patronage and his writing.

A uniquely ambitious painting from the collection of the Victoria and Albert Museum—made in the last decade of Emperor Shah Jahan's reign for Dārā Shikoh—attempts to capture the multidimensional devotional landscape of mid-seventeenth-century Mughal India (Gadon 1986: 153–7; Gandhi 2020: 199–201). The composition consists of an odd patchwork of scenes stitched together into a large single painting showing a gathering—or gatherings—of ascetics (Figure 5.2). Keeping true to Indic pictorial conventions, the vertical page is divided into distinct horizontal registers, each containing particular groups and activities. Taken as a whole, the scene appears to represent the *'urs*, or death anniversary, of the most popular Muslim saint in India, Mu'īn al-Dīn Chishtī, at his shrine in Ajmer. The various vignettes in the painting show mystics from different eras and communities congregating in one timeless space. Echoing the idea of a Mughal-era plinth base found in mosque and shrine architecture, the arches in the lowermost register of the painting act as both niches and subtle haloes for a row of twelve non-Muslim sages who represent distinct strains of Indic spirituality. The group is a who's-who of the spiritual personalities who increasingly captivated Dārā Shikoh throughout the 1650s (Figure 5.3). This

Figure 5.2 *Gathering of Ascetics*, c. 1655, Victoria and Albert Museum (IS.94-1965). © Victoria and Albert Museum, London.

Figure 5.3 *Gathering of Ascetics* (detail), *c.* 1655, Victoria and Albert Museum (IS.94-1965). © Victoria and Albert Museum, London.

row includes Kabīr—bare-chested and wearing a cap with a peacock feather—along with his son Kamāl Das, shown as an adolescent wearing a patched cloak. The row also includes other *nirguṇa*, or non-dualist, ascetics such as the Śaivite, Gorakhnath, and the Vedāntin, Jadrup, who were central in intercultural exchanges between Indic and Persianate devotional cultures. Since at least the fifteenth century, Muslim thinkers labeled non-dualists by the Arabic/Persian term *muvaḥḥidān*, or monists (singular: *muvaḥḥid*). Prince Dārā Shikoh's was only one voice in this long lineage. In his writings, Dārā described them as those "who have attained perfection, who have reached the extremities of ascetic practice, comprehension and understanding, and the utmost levels of mystical experience, God-seeking and gravity" (Gandhi 2020: 188). It is safe to assume that the Victoria and Albert painting was made for Dārā Shikoh as it shows his own spiritual guide, Mullā Shāh, at the top-center in the middle of a large group of *sufis*. From that we can conclude that the lowermost row of Indic saints represents the very group of monotheists (*muvaḥḥidān*) that the prince considered at par with the greatest Muslim gnostics.

Around the same time as the V&A *Gathering of Ascetics*, Dārā Shikoh compiled a collection of ecstatic utterances of saints titled *Ḥasanāt ul-ʿārifīn* (Excellent Words of the Gnostics). Near the end of the book there is a short chapter dedicated to Kabīr. This section provides a narrative framework for understanding aspects of the idiosyncratic V&A painting. Completed sometime between 1652 and 1654 (Gandhi 2020: 164), this volume is a retort addressed to "the dastardly, the low-minded, the bland ones of dry piety who, owing to their shortsightedness, are always quick to hurl a hundred castigations and accusations of heresy" (Shikoh 1973: 2). The growing dissent among some elite religious scholars against Dārā for his increasingly strong views on the unity of religions prompted him to compile the *Ḥasanāt ul-ʿārifīn*, which includes utterances gathered from Quranic verses, Hadith literature, and the exclamations of Muslim and Hindu ascetics, whom Dārā describes as "monists" and "gnostics" (*muvaḥḥidān* and *ʿārifīn*). In fact, this book acts as a bridge between Dārā's previously *sufi*-centric outlook and his growing love for monist Indic thought (Gandhi 2014: 71). *Ḥasanāt* participates in a long-lived Persianate literary tradition of quoting and commenting on *koan*-like paradoxical statements called *shaṭḥiyāt*, meant to assist the spiritual traveler in overcoming the limitations of mind and logic. Similar in spirit to the *ulat-bānsī* of Kabīr, these upside-down sayings were often associated with radical, antinomian *sufi* groups linked to the Malāmatī and Qalandarī orders. The principal intention of *Ḥasanāt* was to situate these radical utterances within the fold of Islamic spirituality, tracing them back to themes found in the Quran and Hadith. Dārā Shikoh's innovation in this genre was to include voices from outside Islamic mysticism as a means to interpret Quranic truth-claims, which is why he uses a specifically *sufi* vocabulary in order to characterize Kabīr and his legacy through an Islamic lens. For example, he has no problem describing Kabīr's Hindu master, Rāmānand, as a *faqīr* "of a Hindu order." He also defines Kabīr's *bhakti* spiritual order as a *ṭarīqa*, the Arabic word for a *sufi* brotherhood, and identifies Kabīr as a knower of *tawḥīd*, the Arabic term to describe the Oneness of God, which is the ultimate aim of all *sufis*.[5] The fact that four centuries later Raziuddin *qawwāl* uses the same term, *tawḥīd*, to describe Kabīr's philosophy speaks of the astonishing continuity of transmission in Indo-Muslim devotional circles.

In his book the prince includes utterances from contemporary *sufis*, including his own guides. These are followed by sayings from Indic saints including Kabīr, Jadrup, and Swami Lāl Dās, all of whom are also present in the V&A painting. In both *Ḥasanāt ul-ʿārifīn* and the painting, *sufis* are privileged through their sheer number and the space that they occupy. However, the monist group is presented in a contemplative and dignified manner, perhaps suggesting their foundational role for the larger Indic spiritual community.

Acknowledging Kabīr as representing a legitimate path outside the limits of Islam is already present in an earlier text from the sixteenth century. It comes from the very first compilation of the lives of Indo-Muslim saints completed in 1590/1, by ʿAbd al-Ḥaqq Muḥaddith-i Dehlavī, and titled *Akhbār-ul akhyār* (Accounts of the Virtuous Ones). Dehlavī, a Chishtī *sufi*, was also one of the great Hadith scholars of his time. The Mughal court patronized him and his work widely circulated in the seventeenth century. Dehlavī himself came from a prominent Muslim family of *sufis* from Delhi, who were also scholars of great repute. They represented mainstream Indo-Muslim society, one that was shaped by Islamic spirituality and orthopraxy. In the final chapter of his book, speaking of his grandfather, Dehlavī notes that he would spend entire nights reciting verses of mystic poets. Evidently, Kabīr was also part of his repertoire. One day Dehlavī's uncle as a child asked his father—Dehlavī's grandfather—about "this Kabīr who is famous for his verses that are sung, was he a

Muslim or an infidel?" Dehlavī's grandfather, confounding his son, replied "he was a *muvaḥḥid*." His young son asked, "isn't a *muvaḥḥid* neither a *kāfir* nor a Muslim?" He answered, "it is difficult to understand the meaning of this, [soon] you will understand." Dehlavī's grandfather passed away in 1522 CE (Dehlavi 2005: 599).

This conversation between Dehlavī's grandfather and uncle would have taken place sometime in the second decade of the sixteenth century, maybe around 1515, just a few years before his demise. This would make it among the earlier known anecdotes of Kabīr—definitely the earliest in Persian. There has been considerable debate among scholars regarding Kabīr's dates, but David Lorenzen has convincingly shown that he was active in the second half of the fifteenth century, possibly into the second decade of the sixteenth century (Lorenzen 1991: 9–18). Dehlavī's account appears to corroborate that. It confirms that Kabīr's fame spread rapidly across northern India through the oral tradition of singing perhaps even during the tail end of his own lifetime and that already by this time *sufis* sang or recited his Hindi verses as part of their devotional repertoire. As I discuss later, sixteenth-century *sufi* poets also referenced him in their own compositions, occasionally responding to his verses.

Kabīr and Early Sufi Literature

When we place Kabīr's verses in conversation with Indic *sufi* poetry from the sixteenth and early seventeenth century, we realize that Kabīr was part of a larger group of mystics that participated in a shared metaphorical and literary idiom. For instance, the Punjabi saint from the Qādirī order, Haji Muhammad Naushā (1552–1654), who wrote in Hindi and Punjabi, uses a poetic language now more commonly associated with Kabīr. One poem, which echoes this shared language, is on the concept of the Truth of Certainty (*ḥaq al-yaqīn*), which is considered to be the highest spiritual station among *sufi* practitioners:

> The breath of life plays inside the puppet of five elements (*pānch tatt kā putlā*)
> Listen Naushā, Rām Guru says; who am I, who are you?
>
> The puppet of five elements, you and I come and go (*avāgavan*)
> I've seen the unmanifest become manifest, you-me a delusion who else!
>
> I've seen the unmanifest become manifest, so what is idolatry [*kufr*] what is Islam?
> Listen Naushā, Rām Guru says; what are these names, Hindu and Turk?
>
> I've seen the unmanifest become manifest, in this is there idolatry or Islam?
> Rām Guru! Hindu and Turk are both names of illusion
>
> If all that happens is in illusion, then where are Truth and Certainty?

Truth and Certainty are *nirvāṇa* (*nirbān*), so says the humble Naushā.
(Nosha 1975: 185)

In this poem *ḥaq* and *yaqīn* (Truth and Certainty) are akin to Kabīr's use of *sat*, the Sanskrit term for ultimate Truth. Or perhaps we can pair these *sufi* terms with another favorite word that Kabīr uses to describe that ineffable state that a practitioner experiences once he or she has transcended duality: *sahaj* (Dharwadker 2008: 90, 286; Sethi 1984: 257)? That state is similar to the ease or comfort that Munshi Raziuddin's *qawwālī* evokes when Kabīr says, "My Rām is the one who invokes me, and I find contentment (*vishrām*) O Kabīr!" For Naushā, this state of *nirvāṇa* or extinction of ego lies beyond illusory distinctions between idolator and Muslim, Turk and Hindu, a refrain also found in Kabīr. In another poem Naushā says, "Hindu and Turk are one, only illusion has made them two" (Nosha 1975: 296). Anyone even slightly familiar with Kabīr will recognize several other resonances with his poetry, not least in the use of Rām as an archetypal guru or as a liberating *mantra*. Furthermore, for Kabīr as with Naushā, the vital breath is key for attaining enlightenment, the rest of the body with its five senses is in the domain of contingency (Hess 2002: 69, 70).

One Hindi poem, written in the Persianate *masnavī* form, shows Naushā's great respect for Kabīr. He includes the poet-saint in a long list of ascetics and *avatāras*—Muslim, Sikh, and Hindu—who, by sacrificing their egos, attained to the highest station of Truth-Reality (*ḥaq*). "When he [the pure hearted] sacrifices his head, he attains the great secret (*sirr*) . . . just as . . . the weaver, Bhagat Kabīr; found Truth when he desired the Truth" (Nosha 1975: 299).

Another Naushā poem is composed entirely as a call and response based on two Kabīr couplets. It shows how widespread Kabīr's poetry was in north India by the end of the sixteenth century, so much so that a *sufi* could hold a poetic dialogue with Kabīr, interpreting his words through the lens of Islamic mysticism. Naushā's first response is to a *dohā* that urges the seeker to leave the way of the yogis and seek the Truth within:

Kabīr: If you desire the essence of Love (*prem rasa*)
don't follow the yogi's way
make the mind a mirror
see that in this

In his response, Naushā presents the same idea but with a *sufi* twist:

Naushā: If you desire the essence of Love
set up the shop of he who sells nothing (*darveshī*)
your guide makes your mind a mirror

makes that appear in this

Kabīr's couplet urges the seeker to turn inward, rather than following the way of the yogis, often seen as wandering renunciants. The onus is on the seeker. Naushā subtly changes the emphasis and says that rather than relying on yourself, become a dervish—one who is spiritually poor—and rely on a true guide. Naushā is expressing a typical *sufi* belief that proclaims that too much self-reliance can lead to egoism, whereas complete trust in God and the guide is a simpler way toward the Truth.

Next, Naushā responds to a couplet based on a popular Kabīrian theme sung by both *qawwāl*s and folk singers to this day (Virani 2016: 64). The Raziuddin performance also includes these verses (7:11 minutes):

Kabīr: walking within limits; human
walking beyond limits; *pīr*
dropping both limits and no-limits
those are called *faqīr*

Everyone stays in limits
no one goes into the limitless
only Kabīr is left standing
in the field of the limitless

Naushā: None walked within limits
none walked beyond limits
people came into the world to pronounce the Name
only a few accomplished that

Walked within limits, so what?
Walked in the limitless, so what?
What was lost by walking in limits?
What harm was caused by walking in no-limits?

Those in limits and those in no-limits are both deluded
only the *faqīr* is not deluded
Naushā is his own disciple
his own guide (*pīr*)

There's no harm within limits
no harm in no-limits
Walk within limits or in the limitless
just don't become forgetful

He [the Lord] is the limit and the limitless
there is none other than He
The limit and the limitless
all is in Him

The limit and the limitless are two only in name
there is none but the One
Whether you walk within limits or in the limitless
there will be no second

The limited make claims (*da'wā*) the unlimited make claims
only the *faqīr* makes no claims
The lover makes no claims
he is a stranger to himself.

(Nosha 1975: 259–60)[6]

Naushā appears to be having an intoxicating dialogue with a fellow knower of Truth. In fact, Kabīr is in agreement with Naushā when he says, "dropping both limits and no-limits those are called *faqīr*." The other *dohā* seems to accept a difference between the spheres of limits and the unlimited, and that becomes a pretext for Naushā to take this theme a step further, prizing out other facets. In his response, Naushā is expressing a widespread *sufi* belief in the Unity of Being (*waḥdat-al-wujūd*), which states that while all creation is suffused by the presence of God—or Truth-Reality—and is thus paradoxically a limited manifestation of the limitless, Truth-Reality itself is beyond any description or duality. The only person who can access that reality is the one who is utterly poor, the *faqīr*, who is synonymous with the dervish.

Surprisingly, in at least one stream of the Indo-Muslim reception of Kabīr, the debate over his spiritual station is a running theme that continues right into the twenty-first century, as seen in the *qawwālī* performance quoted at the beginning of this chapter. In the *qawwālī*, Munshi Raziuddin interjects to explain how Kabīr's son, Kamāl, reproaches his father for having stopped at the station of Qualities (*ṣifāt*) rather than the station of God's Essence (*ẕāt*). Quranically, God's qualities are contained within His ninety-nine names and symbolize the highest ontological realm of creation. Above that is the station of Beyond-Being, where only God's Absolute Essence persists, with no other associate (Chittick 1989: 16). When Kabīr asks for the right station, Kamāl replies, "Everyone says millstone, millstone but no one says axle. He who attaches himself to the axle, not even a hair of his is injured."[7] Raziuddin's commentary explains that the axle stands for the Oneness of God. In this anecdote, it is Kamāl, Kabīr's son, who is the complete devotee (*bhagat*). Kabīr calls himself a half-*bhagat*, ending the poem by stating, "It is good this burden is off my head!"

The well-known hagiographical account by the *sufi* 'Abd al-Raḥmān Chishtī (d. 1683), given in his *Mir'āt ul-asrār* (Mirror of Secrets, 1654), also hints at Kamāl's spiritual superiority over his father (Rizvi 1978: 412–13). The author explains that "Sheikh Kamāl was Sheikh Kabīr Malāmatī's son and received his training from him. His method was also *malāmatī*. In fact, he was even more audacious than his father" (Chishtī 1775: 1230–1). By the late medieval and early modern periods Malāmatī *sufis* were usually attached to other *sufi* orders but kept their affiliations hidden. While mainstream *sufis* "wore particular clothes, organized various orders, and assumed all sorts of titles," the Malāmatīs, seeking anonymity, went to great lengths to hide their spiritual stations and affiliations.[8] It is thus, Chishtī claims, that both father and son were secretively part of the Suhrawardī *sufi* order, but owing to their *malāmatī* disposition, kept their *sufi* affiliations hidden. Most importantly, Chishtī points out that Kamāl was even more antinomian—and therefore a worthier *malāmatī*—than his father. It is as if Chishtī uses Kamāl as an anthropomorphic representation of *sufi* voices critiquing Kabīr's metaphysical concepts. The fact that it is his son who "completes" Kabīr also shows that these critiques were not serious ones. The overall respect for the poet-saint far outweighs these debates.

At least one stream of Indo-Persian devotional literature followed Chishtī in embracing Kabīr as a hidden *sufi*. The Aurangzeb-period hagiographer and *sufi* from Kasur, Sheikh 'Abdullāh Kheshgī, in his *Ma'ārij ul-wilāyat* (Summits of Sanctity, 1666), follows Chishtī in stating that Kabīr was a disciple of the Suhrawardī guide and fellow weaver Sheikh Taqī, but chose the *malāmatī* way for himself, "in order to remain unknown" (Rizvi 1978: 413). The same essential assertion carries into Muftī Ghulām Sarwar Lahorī's nineteenth-century hagiographical tome *Khazīnat ul-aṣfiyā'*, or the "Treasury of the Saints," from 1863 (Lahori 2001: 385).

No account prior to Chishtī's *Mir'āt ul-asrār*—including Dārā Shikoh's *Ḥasanāt ul-'ārifīn*—mentions Kabīr's son Kamāl. Nor do these earlier sources point to Kabīr's *sufi* affiliations. For instance, Dārā Shikoh learned about Kabīr from the *bairāgī* ascetic Bābā Lāl Das, whom he visited on several occasions to ask about Indic philosophy. In his conversation with Dārā Shikoh, as given in *Ḥasanāt*, Bābā Lāl suggests that he knew Kabīr personally and that he learned from him directly. This is of course impossible since a century and a half separated Kabīr's final years and Bābā Lāl's conversation with Dārā Shikoh. It is likelier that Bābā Lāl Das was in Kabīr's spiritual order and might even have been initiated by a direct disciple of the great poet-saint. Yet, despite this clearly non-*sufi* lineage, the prince does suggest Kabīr's knowledge of Quranic principles:

> As an explanation of the [Quranic] verse "travel in the land" [Quran, 29:20],[9] Kabīr has said that God told us to travel in order to witness the wonders of the earth, and this [tradition] is adopted by the perfect gnostics. The foolish scholars (*'ālim*), on hearing this exegesis went to Kabīr to accuse him. They asked for the meaning of this verse, "in what way does one travel on earth?" Kabīr got up from where he had been sitting and left, and after an hour came back from where he had gone and said, "this is how one should travel."
>
> (Shikoh 1973: 54)

Furthermore, Kabīr's *malāmatī*, or self-anonymizing perspective, is also evident in Lāl Das's account:

> He [Kabīr] has also said that a person must, out of humility, become like gravel. But what use is that? Gravel hurts the feet of the traveler. Instead, a person must become dust on the path, so that he will not cause feet to be hurt. But if he is dust, what use is that? Dust sits on the heads and faces of travelers. A person must become like water. And what is the use of that, since water can turn hot or cold? A person must not show indignation towards anything. Instead, a person must become like God. If he becomes like God, what is the use, since everything comes from God? Instead, a person (*bandah*) must become a servant (*bandah*), so that nothing comes from him.

Another account of this period written in Persian, the *Dabistān-i maẕāhib* (*School of Creeds*, *c.* 1653), includes anecdotes from Kabīr's life, many of which are also found in Hindi texts (Lorenzen 1991: 49). Even though this ethnographic study on various seventeenth-century religious groups was composed by a Zoroastrian passing off as a Shia Muslim, his Persianate lens interpreted Kabīr and his biography through the language of Sufism (Ali 1999: 365–73). This includes the popular anecdote narrating how Kabīr tricked his guru, Rāmānand, into initiating him:

> Kabīr the weaver, who is one of the most well-known *muvaḥḥidān* of India, was a *bairāgī*. It is said that at the time of guide-seeking, Kabīr went to both Hindu and Muslim sages. What he was looking for he couldn't find. Eventually someone advised him to go to the enlightened *pīr*, Rāmānand Brahman, the one who never takes Muslims for followers. Thus, since Kabīr knew that Rāmānand

would never speak to a weaver (*jaulāhā*, a lowly Muslim caste), he dug a hole on the road and hid himself in it. In the evening, when Rāmānand was on his way to the riverbank to ritually purify himself (*ghusl*), he arrived near the hole that Kabīr had dug. Kabīr emerged from his hole and grabbed Rāmānand's feet. Since Rāmānand Brahmin, through Truth-witnessing (*ḥaq-bīnī*), always had his mind fixed on Rām—which is a name for the transcendental lord (*īzad-i mutta'āl*)—he spontaneously shouted "Rām!" As soon as Kabīr heard the name of Rām from Rāmānand's tongue, he let go of his feet, and made this name his daily invocation. He kept invoking (*ẕikr*) "Rām, Rām," just like Rāmānand, until his eyes saw nothing but Rām. And after that he started giving his famous commentaries on the Unity of Being (*waḥdat-al-wujūd*), which only the searchers of truth (*muḥaqqiqān*) can speak of.

People asked Rāmānand: There is a weaver in this town who claims to be your disciple, but how is this possible if you haven't even looked at someone from the weaver caste before, the most lowly of people? Rāmānand asked that Kabīr be brought to him. They brought Kabīr, and his eyes fell on Rāmānand, and he started uttering "Rām Rām." Rāmānand also said "Rām Rām," and enveloped Kabīr in a tight embrace. Everyone present was dumbfounded, and wanted to know the reason for this special attention given to Kabīr. Rāmānand replied, "the Brahmin of this age is Kabīr, who truly understands *Brahman*—which is the Essence of Truth (*ẕāt-i ḥaq*)."

Later Sources

Most early Indo-Muslim sources for Kabīr—from circa 1590 to 1666—are textual, while later ones are predominantly visual. The V&A painting made for Dārā Shikoh stands out as an exception, as it includes perhaps one of the first painted portraits of Kabīr and his son Kamāl. There is one earlier Jahangir period artwork, a *nīm qalam* (half-tinted drawing) dateable to circa 1610, from the Cleveland Museum of Art, that is titled in the museum's online catalogue as *Kabir and His Two Followers on a Terrace* (Figure 5.4).[10] The figure in the artwork, who is clearly a mystic of some kind, sits on a raised, reed-matted platform under the shade of a tree. But is it really meant to be a portrait of Kabīr? The stooped posture, lanky figure with attenuated limbs, and square cap all point to similarities with the V&A portrait. However, in popular history, Kabīr is thought to have been illiterate. In the Cleveland drawing he is reading from a book.

Additionally, the other two figures in the scene, one holding a *tasbīḥ* (a Muslim rosary), the other making his ablution by running his fingers between the toes of

Figure 5.4 *An ascetic with two disciples*, *c.* 1610, Cleveland Museum of Art (2013.326.a). Creative Commons Public Domain, CCO 1.0 Universal.

his feet, are clearly Muslim. If this truly is a portrait of Kabīr, then the painting would be an early instance of showing Kabīr in dialogue with Muslim religious groups or perhaps showing him with two Muslim disciples. Unfortunately, there are no markers in the artwork linking the portrait to Kabīr. Unless we discover an inscription or another similar artwork that points to the figure's identity, it is impossible to definitively label it as his portrait.

This is why, when mapping the visual legacy of Kabīr as patronized by the Persianate elite in miniature painting, we must begin with the V&A painting. Having examined two streams of literary reception—one that situates Kabīr squarely in the *bhakti* tradition and the other that adds a *sufi* layer to it—it is safe to conclude that Kabīr's visualization in artworks is closely connected to how Dehlavī, Dārā Shikoh, and the author of the *Dabistān-i maẕāhib* viewed and situated Kabīr in the larger world of Indic mysticism. None of them describe him as a hidden *sufi*. By including Kabīr with other Indic mystics, the painting acknowledges the validity of their spiritual paths. But by placing the group at the base of the large symbolic platform that acts as a stage for showcasing Islamic spirituality, the composition associates them to a parallel tradition outside the pale of Islam proper.

The presence of Kamāl complicates this neat division between the two strains of Indo-Persian reception of Kabīr. In Hindi texts his historiographical significance is contested (Lorenzen 1991: 18–19). What is his role in the V&A painting and in subsequent artworks that reference it? Can we analyze the painted figure of Kamāl through Chishtī's hagiographic account—one that remains relevant to this day in the form of *qawwālī*—that claims that Kamāl perfected the teachings of his father? The increasing importance of Kamāl Das in paintings made for early modern Muslim patrons suggests that in the latter half of the seventeenth century, the two strains interwove.

Beginning with the V&A *Gathering of Ascetics*, Kamāl is often shown wearing a cap and a patched cloak, trappings associated with Muslim antinomian groups in the Indic region, such as the Malāmatīs and the Qalandars (Figure 5.3). The black cord that loops around his left shoulder is an intriguing piece of gear shared with members of the larger Indic community of monists, including both Muslim antinomians and individuals from other denominations.[11] Since Malāmatīs, Qalandars, Kabīr-*panthīs*, *Gorakh-nāthīs*, and Sikhs consciously distanced themselves from mainstream Hinduism and Islam, they scoffed at caste distinctions, attitudes of piety, and the rigidity of social hierarchies. Is it possible then that the black thread they wore on top of their garments is a symbolic inversion of the sacred thread (*jāneu*) worn by upper-caste Hindu men? A wry sign of the rejection of conventional hierarchies?

The V&A *Gathering of Mystics* became the model for depicting Kabīr and Kamāl, particularly in a composition that became a standard for centuries to come. One folio from the *St. Petersburg Album* is a late seventeenth-century example of this convention, showing Kabīr weaving on his pit loom (Figure 5.1). Next to him is the demure-looking Kamāl Das. Two young noblemen are visiting the father and son who sit outside their humble hut on a riverbank under the shade of a large tree. The way the visitors' *jāma*s tie under the left arm suggests that they are both Hindus (Akimushkin 1996: 63). Behind the green hillock, in the distance, is a city, perhaps the sacred town of Kashi, present-day Varanasi. Given that Kabīr's portrait is similar in its posture, iconography, and scale as the V&A painting, it is probable that the artist of the *St. Petersburg* folio possessed a tracing or copy of the original. The only difference is the right arm that now extends out to hold a shuttle and his legs that dangle into the pit. Kamāl's portrait diverges slightly from the original. Rather than looking away from his father, he now faces straight ahead, eyes downcast. He still wears the *jāneu*-like cord and also has his hands folded in front of him, but his facial features are more delicate. His garb is also different.

Figure 5.5 *Kamāl Das*, c. 1720, Freer Gallery of Art, Smithsonian Institution, Washington, D.C.: Purchase—Charles Lang Freer Endowment (F1936.14).

Intriguingly, in the *St. Petersburg* painting his father retains the Vaiṣṇava *tilak* on his forehead from the original, but Kamāl no longer dons the sectarian mark.

Another painting from the early to mid-eighteenth century—with a later addition of a multicolored bush in the foreground—follows exactly the same composition but has Kamāl Das without his father (Figure 5.5). Next to him is a Dārā Shikoh-esque prince shown in strict profile as a beardless youth.

In my forthcoming monograph on images of Muslim devotion in Indian painting, I discuss how, after Dārā Shikoh's patronage, the image of the beardless youth—a symbol of Divine beauty in Persianate culture—became synonymous with the Mughal heir apparent. Subsequent artworks from the seventeenth and eighteenth centuries that depicted Muslim youths visiting ascetics were based on earlier portraits of Dārā Shikoh. Given the historical gap, Dārā Shikoh could not have met with Kamāl Das. Instead, his presence signifies the growing interest that Muslim nobility had with Indic monist thought at this time. The eighteenth and nineteenth centuries were also a period when the myth of Dārā Shikoh as an exemplar prince-mystic scholar was spreading across Hindustan (Gandhi 2020: 249–54). In this artwork Kamāl's figure is iconographically closer to the *St. Petersburg* example, rather than the V&A original, although the patched cloak does reference the earlier artwork. Following earlier models, he is shown in a three-quarter profile, but he now sits on a tiger skin that establishes his eminence as a mystic, since usually individuals with a high spiritual rank are shown seated on lion or tiger skins. Instead of Hindu nobles, two musicians are shown entertaining the prince and the mystic. As with the prince, the *jāma* of the drum player ties under the right arm, suggesting that Kamāl Das's company in this artwork is Muslim.

By the second half of the eighteenth century, the iconographic and compositional convention of depicting Kabīr and Kamāl had begun to spread across regions, and artists began to gradually localize the language initially established in Mughal centers. One painting, likely from circa 1760, is a simpler version of the otherwise familiar composition showing Kabīr at his loom, accompanied by his son (Figure 5.6). The fact that this later artwork is a mixture of all the paintings discussed earlier shows the extent to which images traveled among northern Indian workshops. Although the style still follows a Mughal aesthetic, the overall handling of the landscape and rendering of the figures is broader. Additionally, Kamāl is now shown in a strict profile. In general, Hindustani schools of painting have always preferred the profile. The three-quarter face was introduced via Persian painting and popularized by the Mughals. Depicting Kamāl Das in a style more familiar to a regional artist shows a gradual distancing from Mughal influence and the subtle localization of this theme. Curiously, both Kabīr and Kamāl are now shown with their original Vaiṣṇava marks.

Figure 5.6 *Kabīr tending his loom*, *c.* 1760, Art Gallery of New South Wales (113.1986). Bequest of Mr. J. Kitto 1986. Photo: AGNSW, Christopher Snee.

Figure 5.7 *A gathering of holy men of different faiths*, c. 1770, by Mīr Kalan Khan, Metropolitan Museum of Art (2009.318). Creative Commons Public Domain, CCO 1.0 Universal.

The subtly changing iconography of the perennially youthful Kamāl over a period of a century and a half suggests that his identity for Indian audiences was never fixed. Perhaps for some Muslim connoisseurs he represented a link between Indic and Persianate devotional cultures. It must have been a deliberate artistic choice to show Kamāl as a beardless youth, evoking Persianate literary and visual ideals in which the handsome adolescent manifests God's beauty. In other cases, the sectarian marks firmly locate him within Hindu tradition.

The overall emphasis on Kabīr and Kamāl also suggests that by the late-seventeenth and eighteenth centuries, Kabīr's path had come to denote Indic monotheism in the popular Muslim imagination. A painting from around 1770, made by the court artist Mīr Kalan Khan for the Nawab of Lucknow, repurposes the saints from the lower register of the V&A painting to create a completely new composition that puts the two figures front and center (Figure 5.7). The pale tints in the background with hues of gold evoke a gathering at dusk. The group is shown sitting outside a hut, whose gaping entrance forms a dark halo around Kabīr. The only other figure placed in front of the hut is Kamāl. Already, in the V&A composition, Kabīr is given a prominent position among the ranks of ascetics, but in Kalan Khan's reconfiguration, he is shown leading a *satsaṅga*, a devotional musical gathering, surrounded by what are now his followers. The other saints who were originally awarded individual status, each with their own label, now quietly slip into anonymous types.

According to the interpretations of the early modern biographer Chishtī and the modern-day *qawwāl* Raziuddin, Kabīr's path finds its perfection in the figure of the youthful, and therefore virginal and virtuous, Kamāl, who then becomes a mirror reflecting Kabīr's own inner state. It is no coincidence that the Arabic word *kamāl* literally means "perfection" and hints at the *sufi* ideal of the perfected human being, the *insān al-kāmil*. In Hindi and Urdu, the word also denotes something miraculous. By extension, going by the visual and literary record, it is likely that Kamāl became a didactic tool in service of Indic Sufism as a paragon of the perfect devotee.

Conclusion

In the eighteenth and nineteenth centuries, Hindu and Sikh patrons also prolonged Kabīr's visual legacy that was first initiated in Muslim centers. One late eighteenth or early nineteenth-century painting from Jaipur, which shows Kabīr accompanied by three other saints—Ravidās, Nāmdev, and Pīpā, all of whom also feature in the V&A painting—distantly echoes its original source.[12] It is clear that the artist had no direct awareness of the mid-seventeenth-century Mughal work made for Dārā and must have modeled his figure of Kabīr on later examples. The other three saints bear no resemblance to the V&A painting.

Another artwork, a preparatory drawing from nineteenth-century Punjab, shows Kabīr again at his pit loom, but on this occasion facing his wife Loī, shown spinning wool (Figure 5.8). Since the drawing was most

Figure 5.8 *Kabīr with his wife Loī*, c. 1830, British Museum (1926,0301,0.3). © The Trustees of the British Museum.

likely made from a tracing, the figure of Kabīr is flipped when compared to earlier examples. In all later artworks, even those that move considerably away from the Mughal style, Kabīr is shown bare-chested, with a square cap and peacock feather. This basic iconography has seeped into everyday Indian imagination down to modern times as can be seen by government-issued stamps and popular posters.[13]

Focusing on the reception and interpretation of poet-saints such as Kabīr and Kamāl provides us a window into the world of patrons and practitioners of Indic Sufism who assimilated and performed elements of *bhakti* traditions in the early modern period. This reception was by no means limited to the elite sphere. Visual and literary representations of Kabīr and his son Kamāl in Indo-Persianate culture raise important questions about the evolving negotiations between *sufi* thought and *bhakti* devotion under Muslim patronage, and the latter's role in the development of an Indic *sufi* imagination.

As an interdisciplinary foray into the legacy of Kabīr for a Muslim audience, this chapter considers visual and textual evidence simultaneously. It is only the first step toward understanding Kabīr's role in the intricate fabric of Indic and Persianate cultural exchange, and as a first step, I leave this chapter with more questions than concrete answers. It is my hope that by presenting first-time translations of some key passages from the Persianate and *sufi* worlds, and by discussing central artworks that had not been considered in this light previously, we may begin to understand how Islamic devotional culture positioned one of the most important devotional poets of Hindustan. Perhaps, as more Indo-Persianate material is uncovered, scholars can even begin to fill important gaps in Kabīr's own biography and poetry.

It is clear from the sources I have presented that there was a centuries-long robust dialogue between Indic *sufi* and *bhakti* traditions. Today, in a postcolonial context, this dialogue has become rare, particularly in scholarship. As a step toward reviving this conversation, I end this chapter with a sequence of Kabīr *dohās* that Prahlad Singh Tipanya, the great Kabīr singer from Malwa, often opens his *bhajans* with. It reverberates beautifully with Raziuddin's *qawwālī* in which the mill features prominently:

> Human life is like a bubble
> It will disappear as suddenly as a star at sunrise
> The mill of time grinds for many days and nights
> Formlessness (*aguṇa*) and Form (*saguṇa*) are the two slabs crushing all souls
> Those who wander between these two are quickly ground
> Cleave to the axle and you will remain untouched!

Notes

1 These are excerpts from a live *qawwālī* performance by Munshi Raziuddin, early 2000s. See https://www.youtube.com/watch?v=Rjnorsnabm8 (accessed March 15, 2021). For another discussion of this *qawwālī*, see Pauwels (2010: 8).

2 I am extremely grateful to Linda Hess and Christine Marrewa-Karwoski for their comments and edits for an earlier version of this chapter, and for their suggestions for translating Kabīr and Naushā's poetry.

3 In order to keep consistent with the spelling of "*bhakti*," I have preferred to write Sufi with lower case and with italics, "*sufi*."

4 This theme recalls a well-known Hadith, or saying, of the Prophet Muhammad, in which God spoke on the tongue of the Messenger uttering, "My servant draws not near to Me with anything more loved by Me than the religious duties I have enjoined

upon him, and My servant continues to draw near to Me with supererogatory works so that I shall love him. When I love him, I am his hearing with which he hears, his seeing with which he sees, his hand with which he strikes and his foot with which he walks." See Ibrahim and Johnson-Davies (1980), number 25.

5 For translated passages of Kabīr's chapter in Dārā Shikoh's book, see Gandhi (2020: 170–1); and Rizvi (1978: 411–12).

6 For an alternate translation, see Rizvi (1978: 438–9).

7 Parts of Kabīr's verses from this *qawwālī* are scattered across several Hindi poems of Kabīr. For an example from the *Bijak*, see Hess (2002: 104), *sakhi* 129.

8 https://www.britannica.com/topic/Malamatiyah (accessed March 15, 2021).

9 The complete verse reads, "Travel in the land and see how He originated creation, then Allah bringeth forth the later growth. Lo! Allah is Able to do all things" (*Quran*, 29:20).

10 https://www.clevelandart.org/art/2013.326.a (accessed March 12, 2021).

11 For an example of an antinomian mystic in Indian painting, see Victoria and Albert Museum (D-1197.1903).

12 The artwork is in the National Museum New Delhi. To view the image, see https://commons.wikimedia.org/wiki/File:Saint_Kabir_with_Namdeva,_Raidas_and_Pipaji._Jaipur,_early_19century,_National_Museum_New_Delhi_(2).jpg (accessed April 20, 2021).

13 For an image of the stamp, see http://www.indianpost.com/viewstamp.php/ Paper/All%20over%20five%20pointed%20multiple%20star%20watermark%20paper/KABIR (accessed April 20, 2021).

References

Ahmad, S. (2015), *What Is Islam? The Importance of Being Islamic*, Princeton: Princeton University Press.

Akimushkin, O. F. (1996), *The St. Petersburg Muraqqa': Album of Indian and Persian Miniatures of the 16th–18th Centuries and Specimens of Persian Calligraphy of 'Imād Al-Ḥ'Imād*, Lugano: Arch Foundation.

Ali, M. (1999), "Pursuing an Elusive Seeker of Universal Truth: The Identity and Environment of the Author of the *Dabistān-i-Mazāhib*," *Journal of the Royal Asiatic Society* 9 (3): 365–73.

Bangha, I. (2019), "Shifts in Kabīr Contexts and Texts from Mughal to Modern Times," in M. Burger and N. Cattoni (eds.), *Early Modern India: Literatures and Images, Texts and Languages*, 125–72, Heidelberg: CrossAsia-eBooks.

Chishtī, A. (1775), *Mir'āt al-Asrār*, British Library, Or. Mss. 216.

Chittick, W. (1989), *The Sufi Path of Knowledge: Ibn al-'Arabi's Metaphysics of Imagination*, Albany: State University of New York Press.

Dehlavi, A. (2005), *Akhbār-ul akhyār fī asrār ul-abrār*, ed. A. A. Khan, Tehran: Danishgah-i Tihran.

Dharwadker, V. (2008), *The Weaver's Songs*, Delhi: Penguin India.
Gadon, E. (1986), "Dara Shikuh's Mystical Vision of Hindu-Muslim Synthesis," in R. Skelton, A. Topsfield, S. Stronge, and R. Crill (eds.), *Facets of Indian Art*, 153–7, London: Victoria and Albert Museum.
Gaefke, P. (2002), "Kabīr in Literature by and for Muslims," in M. Horstmann (ed.), *Images of Kabīr*, 157–64, New Delhi: Manohar.
Gandhi, S. (2014), "The Prince and the Muvahhid: Dārā Shikoh and Mughal Engagements with Vedānta," in V. Dalmia and M. Faruqui (eds.), *Religious Interactions in Mughal India*, 65–101, New Delhi: Oxford University Press.
Gandhi, S. (2020), *The Emperor Who Never Was: Dara Shukoh in Mughal India*, Cambridge, MA: The Belknap Press of Harvard University Press.
Hess, L. (2015), *Bodies of Song: Kabir Oral Traditions and Performative Worlds in Northern India*, New York: Oxford University Press.
Hess, L., and S. Śukadeva (2002), *The Bijak of Kabir*, Oxford: Oxford University Press.
Ibrahim, E., and D. Johnson-Davies (1980), *Forty Hadith Qudsi*, Aldahieh: Revival of Islamic Heritage Society.
Lahori, S. (2001), *Khazinat ul-asfiya'*, Urdu trans. Iqbal Ahmad Faruqi, Lahore: Maktaba-I Nabaviyyah.
Lorenzen, D. (1991), *Kabir Legends and Ananta-Das's Kabir Parachai*, Albany: State University of New York Press.
Nosha, S. H. M. (1975), *Intikhab-e-Ganj Shareef*, Lahore: Darul Muarrikheen.
Pauwels, H. (2010), "'The Woman Waylaid at the Well' or Paṇaghaṭa-Līlā: An Indian Folk Theme Appropriated in Myth and Movies," *Asian Ethnology* 69 (1): 1–33.
Rizvi, S. A. A. (1978), *A History of Sufism in India*, New Delhi: Munshiram Manoharlal.
Sethi, V. (1984), *Kabir: The Weaver of God's Name*, Amritsar: Radha Soami Satsang Beas.
Shikoh, D. (1973), *Ḥasanāt ul-ʿārifī*, ed. Makhdum Rahin, Terhan: Muʾassasah-i Ta:// exampleIntishārāt-i Vīsman.
Vaudeville, Charlotte. (1997 [1993]), *A Weaver Named Kabir: Selected Verses with a Detailed Biographical and Historical Introduction*. Delhi: Oxford University Press.
Virani, V. (2016), "Find the True Country: Devotional Music and the Self in India's National Culture," PhD diss., University of California, Los Angeles.

6

The Devotional Role of Paintings and Photographs in the Puṣṭi Mārga

Shandip Saha

This essay proposes to look at the material role of paintings and photographs in the Vallabha *sampradāya*, a particular Vaiṣṇava community, whose beliefs are built around the teachings of the sixteenth-century philosopher Vallabha or Vallabhācārya (1479–1531). It is also called the "Path of Grace," or Puṣṭi Mārga, because of Vallabha's insistence on living a householder life grounded in a full reliance on Kṛṣṇa's grace (*puṣṭi*). Vallabha's male descendants, known as *mahārājas*, spearheaded the community's migration in the late seventeenth century from northern to western India, where they largely remain to this day.[1] In western India, the *mahārājas* established a network of temples throughout the region with the help of the Rajput nobility and the wealthy Gujarati mercantile (*baniyā*) community, which continue to constitute the majority of the community's present-day devotee base. The most important of these temples has been in Nathdwara, Rajasthan. Nathdwara is home to Śrīnāthjī. This is a black stone image of the child Kṛṣṇa which is believed to represent how Kṛṣṇa looked as he held Govardhan hill on his left hand to protect the residents of his earthly home of Braj from the torrential rains of the god, Indra. This image is the central image of adoration within the Puṣṭi Mārga because the community believes the image miraculously manifested itself to none other than Vallabhācārya himself.

The *mahārājas* of the Puṣṭi Mārga were also instrumental in nurturing the community's luxurious temple rituals known as *sevā*. One usually associates *sevā* with the performance of rituals toward metal images of the child Kṛṣṇa known as *svarūpas*, but the veneration of paintings, drawings, and photographs—collectively known in the Puṣṭi Mārga as *citrajī*s—has also played a central role in the religion of the community. The performance of *sevā* to *citrajī*s and their sculptural counterparts has acted for both *mahārājas* and devotees alike as the means to transcend their material surroundings and enter into a divine realm with Kṛṣṇa's continual presence. In non-ritual contexts, however, *citrajīs* have also been used by devotees and their gurus to visually express their personal devotion to Kṛṣṇa while at the same time affirming their worldly pursuits of prestige, honor, and authority. This essay will argue that even though the role of *citrajīs* has been central to the rituals of the Puṣṭi Mārga as a means of creating a deeply personal relationship with Kṛṣṇa, they also visually express a theme that has continually shaped the history of the community: the tension between the realms of the material worldly (*laukika*) and the spiritual, transmundane, or non-worldly (*alaukika*).

Visually Engaging Kṛṣṇa: The Logic of *Svarūpa Sevā* in the Puṣṭi Mārga

The foundation of ritual worship in the Puṣṭi Mārga has been Vallabha's assertion that there is ultimately no difference between the material world and Kṛṣṇa himself. Kṛṣṇa, according to the Vallabha *sampradāya*, is conceived as the embodiment of truth, bliss, and consciousness who manifests himself through the creation of the material world and the souls who inhabit it. Individuals (*jīvas*) are partial manifestations of Kṛṣṇa who are ignorant of this truth because their perception of bliss is obscured. Vallabha, however, asserts that through the regular practice of devotion, one may achieve what is called *sarvātmabhāva*. This refers to the mental state in which the distinctions between the realms of the spiritual and the worldly are erased, and the individual comes to the realization that the world and everything in it is a manifestation of Kṛṣṇa's own form.

Within this philosophical framework, the Vallabhite perspective on sculptural and pictorial representations of the sacred is rather distinctive within Hinduism. Three-dimensional sculptural images (*mūrtis*) of deities within Hinduism are the likenesses of the divine that must be subject to the traditional Hindu consecration ritual known as *prāṇapratiṣṭhā* before it can be considered worthy of worship (*pūjā*). In the Puṣṭi Mārga, however, there is no distinction to be made between the material world and Kṛṣṇa himself. Thus, in the Puṣṭi Mārga, images of Kṛṣṇa are treated as living deities and are called *svarūpas* because the images are considered to be Kṛṣṇa's own divine form. A similar logic applies to pictorial representations of Kṛṣṇa in the Puṣṭi Mārga. In general, pictorial representations (*citras*) of Hindu deities may be honored in public temples and home shrines, but pictorial representations are not subject to the same guidelines concerning ritual bathing or clothing as their sculptural counterparts (Taylor 2005: 201–2). Consequently, they are not accorded the same level of importance as temple *mūrtis*. In the case of the Puṣṭi Mārga, Kṛṣṇa can be concretely experienced in the material world so that a pictorial representation of Kṛṣṇa is not considered to be a mere likeness produced by human hands. It is the pictorial equivalent of a *svarūpa* and is viewed as a living manifestation of Kṛṣṇa himself. When a pictorial representation (*citra*) of Kṛṣṇa—be it a painting, drawing, or photograph—is viewed as a living deity in the Puṣṭi Mārga, it becomes known as a *citrajī* to distinguish it from the more traditional sculptural *svarūpa*. The ritual worship of a *svarūpa* and a *citrajī* in the Puṣṭi Mārga is known as *svarūpa sevā* and *citra sevā* respectively.

In the Puṣṭi Mārga, *sevā* refers to the expression of *bhakti* through the performance of selfless service to Kṛṣṇa. Members of the Puṣṭi Mārga view traditional Hindu temple worship (*pūjā*) as being done strictly out of spiritual and material self-interest. Furthermore, the rules and regulations (*maryāda*) that govern the performance of *pūjā* ultimately inhibit the spontaneous expression of love toward God. *Sevā*, as it is stressed within the Puṣṭi Mārga, is not about attempting to secure a specific favour from Kṛṣṇa, be it spiritual or material. The practice of *sevā* is understood as the spontaneous expression of the devotee's love for Kṛṣṇa and the desire to put the happiness of the *svarūpa* before one's own personal desires (Bennett 1993: 69–75). Being preoccupied with worldly concerns and desires will only serve to render one's devotion to Kṛṣṇa ineffectual and will be unconducive to the cultivation of *bhāva*.

Bhāva refers to the devotional state of mind which is adopted by the devotee during performance of *sevā* to deepen the devotee's relationship with Kṛṣṇa. In the Puṣṭi Mārga, emphasis has been placed upon *vātsalya bhāva* or the emulation of motherly tenderness and affection that Kṛṣṇa's mother, Yaśodā, is said to have showered upon her son. Devotees will perform *sevā* to a *svarūpa* or *citrajī* of Kṛṣṇa by bathing and feeding it, dressing it appropriately depending on the weather, and even play games and engage in conversations with the image. Thus, the more the image becomes the object of the devotee's feelings of love and tenderness, the more it begins to assume its own personality until at some point the devotee realizes that—like the rest of the material world—the image is none other than a full manifestation of Kṛṣṇa himself (Bennett 1993: 90–3, 97). It is at this point that the ritual space in which devotees perform *sevā* becomes the land of Braj, where they can fully participate in Kṛṣṇa's pastimes.

The Veneration of Images in the Puṣṭi Mārga: A Historical Perspective

While *svarūpa sevā* can be traced back to Vallabha's lifetime, it is more difficult to ascertain when the practice of *citra sevā* started within the Puṣṭi Mārga. The earliest references to the practice are in a sixteenth-century Sanskrit text called *Sādhana Dīpikā* attributed to Vallabha's eldest son, Gopīnāth (1512–42). In verses 82 and 86 of the text, Gopīnāth endorses *citra sevā* (Śārmā 2010: 81–2) alongside *svarūpa sevā* as does Vallabha's grandson, Gokulnāth (1551–1640), in a collection of verses known as the "Twenty-Four Nectarian Utterances of Gokulnāth" (*Gokulnāthjī ke Caubīs Vacanāmṛta*). In these verses, one can find *citra sevā* being listed as a suitable form of *sevā* along with *svarūpa sevā* and the veneration of relics such as the clothes (*vastra sevā*) or handwriting (*hastākṣar sevā*) of Vallabha and his descendants (Gokulnāth 1996: 62).[2] It does seem fairly clear, however, that the practice of *citra sevā* was popular by the eighteenth century. The important eighteenth-century Vallabhite hagiographical text, known as the *Do Sau Bāvan Vaiṣṇavan kī Vārtā*, details the famous story of Raskhān, who is a Muslim who falls in love with the young son of a mercantile devotee of the Puṣṭi Mārga. In order to divert Raskhān's interest from his son, the merchant shows Raskhān a small painting of Śrīnāthjī that the merchant has hidden in his turban. Once Raskhān looks at the painting, his love for the young boy is transformed into a single-minded love for Kṛṣṇa that Raskhān expresses through devotional poetry (Harirāy 1992: 341–7).[3] The story of Raskhān shows that by the eighteenth-century *citra sevā* was popular within the Puṣṭi Mārga, not only for its efficacy in cultivating devotion to Kṛṣṇa but also because it served as a more viable alternative for the mobile mercantile (*baniyā*) patrons of the Puṣṭi Mārga who may have found it difficult to carry small metal images of Kṛṣṇa on their travels.

The veneration of *citrajīs* also seems to have been commonplace among the Rajput nobility who had taken initiation into the Puṣṭi Mārga when the community migrated from Braj to Rajasthan at the end of the seventeenth century. Mahārāṇa Rūp Singh of Kishangarh, for example, is said to have acquired, in the mid-seventeenth century, a painting of Vallabha for which Vallabha himself is said to have posed. The painting was then revered as a living manifestation of Kṛṣṇa and its worship continues to the present day in Kishangarh (Taylor 2005: 210–11). One sees a similar pattern in the Rajput state of Jhalawar that was established in the early decades of the nineteenth century. In order to cement the royal family's links with the influential *mahārājas* of Nathdwara, the walls of the Jhalawar royal palace—known as the Garh Mahal—were painted with images of important Puṣṭi Mārga *svarūpas* and the images of the Nathdwara *mahārājas*. While some of these images were in the public spaces of the palace, others also could be found painted on the walls of the palace's private apartments where the images could be privately venerated as *citrajīs* (Nardi 2020: 91–5). The royal kingdom of Kota also may have followed this practice. There is pictorial evidence indicating that the current practice of privately conducting *citra sevā* within the precincts of the Kota royal palace dates back to the eighteenth century (Taylor 2005: 211–12).

Figure 6.1 The Gopāṣṭamī festival being celebrated in the late nineteenth century by the Nathdwara *mahārāja*, Govardhanlāl (left), using a *citrajī* of Śrīnāthjī, which is placed upon an altar. Unknown artist. Opaque watercolour and gold paint on cotton 61.2 × 49.4 cm (image) 62.8 × 51.4 cm (sheet). The National Gallery of Victoria Collection, Melbourne.

The still current and more public practice in Kota of displaying a *citrajī* of Śrīnāthjī on a throne alongside the family *svarūpa* named Brijnāthjī seems to follow this pattern and is meant to denote Kṛṣṇa as the true living ruler of Kota. *Citra sevā* became such an important part of Puṣṭi Mārga religious life that even the Nathdwara *mahārājas* promoted the practice for large outdoor festivals with a *citrajī* of Śrīnāthjī that served as a substitute for the actual Śrīnāthjī *svarūpa* (Figure 6.1).

The use of a *citrajī* as a substitute for Śrīnāthjī still continues into the present day. In certain temples in Mumbai, for example, one can find life-size *citrajī*s of Śrīnāthjī that are worshipped on a daily basis. In temples that have served as former homes to the original Śrīnāthjī *svarūpa*, simple paintings of Śrīnāthjī are now used as the objects of *citra sevā*. This is what one finds in the case of the first Śrīnāthjī temple established in Braj by Vallabhācārya as well as in temples found in Ghasiyar and Udaipur, both of which are in Rajasthan and housed the original Śrīnāthjī *svarūpa* temporarily in the nineteenth century.[4] More commonly, however, one can find *citrajī*s of Śrīnāthjī in the home shrines of devotees (Figure 6.2), who perform their *sevā* according to ritual manuals (*praṇālī*s) or by looking toward websites like Pushtishangar.com. This website and other similar websites specialize in selling clothing and other accessories needed to perform *citra sevā*. In the case of Pushtishangar.com, the site provides links to detailed and very elaborate videos on YouTube about how to adorn both a *svarūpa* and a *citrajī*.[5]

Figure 6.2 A home shrine in London, England, with the *citrajī*s of Śrīnāthjī (right) and the river goddess Yamunajī (left), whose waters flow along the banks of Kṛṣṇa's childhood home of Gokul. Courtesy Bhagwat Shah, www.pushti-marg.net.

Performing *Citra Sevā* in Domestic Contexts

The instructional videos provided by such websites raise an important question about *citra sevā* and its relationship to *svarūpa sevā*. Traditional *svarūpa sevā* as performed in public shrines is an extremely elaborate affair structured around eight viewings (*darśan*s) of the deity throughout the day in which food, music, art, and clothing are carefully coordinated to help devotees make the transition from the realm of the material to Kṛṣṇa's spiritual realm. Those who are responsible for performing *sevā*, however, not only carry out the responsibility of maintaining the *bhāva* for all who are present, but they also carry out the responsibility of caring for Kṛṣṇa himself in the same way that Yaśodā did. Great care is taken to ensure that no discomfort will come to Kṛṣṇa over the course of each *darśan*. During the *maṅgala* or morning *darśan*, the *svarūpa* is kept locked behind closed doors. This is done to avoid Kṛṣṇa being startled by devotees desiring to see him or to prevent Kṛṣṇa from running out the door to play with his companions. In the *sṛṅgār darśan*, a mirror is held up in front of the *svarūpa* so he may approve the clothes in which he has been dressed. The *rājbhog darśan* includes keeping Kṛṣṇa's flute, the staff he uses to herd his cows, and a small ball for his amusement in front of the *svarūpa*. The same care is also accorded to the *svarūpa* during festival celebrations. The coming of spring is welcomed by adorning the *svarūpa* in white clothing that has been tinged with different types of colored powder in reference to the springtime festival of *Holī*, while the coming of the monsoons is marked by dressing the *svarūpa* in green to signify the transformation of the countryside into a lush color of green (Ambalal 1987: 21–36, Bennett 1993: 104–14, Saha 2014: 143–5).

There are differences in the ritual guidelines between *citra sevā* and *svarūpa sevā*. A picture can only become a *citrajī* only after it has been offered food that was first offered to an already established *svarūpa*. Once this is accomplished, the picture becomes a *citrajī* and is considered to be suitable for the performance of *sevā*. Additionally, a *citrajī* is not ritually bathed but wiped down gently with a lightly dampened cloth, and a *citrajī* cannot be adorned with fitted clothing that one uses for a *svarūpa*. The clothing, instead, is applied using beeswax or another form of adhesive that can stick easily to the glass protecting the *citrajī*. Otherwise, a *citrajī* is expected to be cared for in the same way as a *svarūpa*. A *citrajī* will be wrapped in fabric to keep Kṛṣṇa from being cold in the winter months, or it will be adorned with the same degree of elaborateness as a *svarūpa* on festival occasions. *Citra sevā* overall tends to be more simple than traditional *svarūpa sevā*. Currently, *citra sevā* is performed in the temples that temporarily housed the Śrīnāthjī *svarūpa* with the offering of a garland or a shawl. In the case of outdoor processions, the current practice among *mahārājas* is to adorn a *citrajī* with a simple garland. It is not surprising, then, that *citra sevā* is favored by devotees in their private shrines. It allows devotees to perform an abbreviated form of *sevā* that is more suitable for their busy worldly lives and does not require the large manpower and financial resources required for the elaborate *sevā* performed in public temples.

Does this mean that *citra sevā* is somehow a lesser form of *sevā*? Gokulnāth leaves one with the impression that *svarūpa* and *citra sevā* are equal in status, though he is silent about whether the two require the same amount of ritual involvement. Gopīnāth, however, says the opposite. He states in *Sādhana Dīpikā* that *citra sevā* is an acceptable alternative for those who neither have the time or the inclination to engage in *svarūpa sevā*, which implies that while *citra sevā* is of value, traditional *svarūpa sevā* is far more desirable. The *sevā praṇālī*s tend to be silent on this question, perhaps because the superiority of one form of *sevā* over the other is rather irrelevant. In the Puṣṭi Mārga, it is not the type of *sevā* or the degree of elaborateness with which it is performed that ultimately matters. It is the sincerity, regularity, and purity of emotion with which *sevā* is done that is of the utmost importance. The *citrajī*, when served with diligence and proper devotion, is much more than a mere picture. It is Kṛṣṇa's living being and serves as the primary entry point into a spiritual realm where devotees can feel his presence.

Paintings and Photographs in the Puṣṭi Mārga

Another important aspect of visual culture within the Puṣṭi Mārga is the art of painting which began after the community migrated from Braj to Rajasthan in the late seventeenth century to seek the patronage of Rajput rulers. Between 1670 and 1672, the rulers of Rajput kingdoms such as Jaipur, Bundi, Bikaner, and Kota began to offer refuge to various Puṣṭi Mārga images that were once housed in Braj with the temple for the Śrīnāthjī *svarūpa* being established in 1672 in Nathdwara within the kingdom of Mewar. The Nathdwara *mahārājas*—like their counterparts in other Rajput states—were annually given donations of lands by their royal patrons and their temple lands were designated as estates over which the *mahārājas* exerted full administrative and economic control. The *mahārājas* thus straddled both the realms of the spiritual, non-worldly and the worldly. In the realm of the sacred, the *mahārājas* were spiritual leaders whose authority to bestow divine grace upon individuals at the time of their initiation made them—in the eyes of their devotees—quasi-divine manifestations of Kṛṣṇa (Bennett 1993: 58–63). On the other hand, in the material realm of the worldly, the *mahārājas* were high-ranking members of the Rajput nobility who immersed themselves in the daily administration of their estates and pursued secular activities ranging from horseback riding to being power brokers in regional politics. Thus, it is not surprising that the *mahārājas* became important patrons of the arts who encouraged poets, musicians, and artists to come to their temples to help enhance the *sevā* performed to Kṛṣṇa.

There is no historical evidence to indicate that the formal patronage of artists by the Puṣṭi Mārga *mahārājas* predated their migration to Rajasthan, and it is generally assumed that the practice began in the eighteenth century under the patronage of the Nathdwara *mahārājas* (Ambalal 2015: 26–7; Śarmā 2008: 68–71). The earliest examples of paintings from Nathdwara depict *sevā* being performed either to the Śrīnāthjī *svarūpa* at festival times or to other smaller *svarūpas* who are shown being rocked back and forth with loving adoration by a particular *mahārāja*. These early paintings that are described by art historian Amit Ambalal as being rather "folksy" in nature would mature over time as artists from Nathdwara became increasingly influenced by the painting styles from the neighboring Rajput kingdoms of Kishangarh and Kota (Ambalal 1987: 63–8 and 2015: 26–33). By the nineteenth century, the mixture of these different styles of Rajput art gave shape to a distinct style of painting known as the Nathdwara school, which was characterized by highly stylized images of the Śrīnāthjī *svarūpa*, idealized landscapes, and human figures whose most noticeable feature were the large almond-shaped eyes so prominently associated with the Kishangarh school of painting.

The Nathdwara school would reach its apogee under the *mahārāja* Govardhanlāl (1862–1934), who assumed the Nathdwara throne at a time when the reputation of the Puṣṭi Mārga was severely damaged. The lavish lifestyles of the *mahārājas* opened the community up to critiques of sexual immorality and religious heterodoxy from disaffected devotees, Hindu reformers, and British Orientalists. The 1862 Maharaja Libel Case involving the *mahārāja* Jadunāth of Surat and the former devotee Karsandas Mulji (Haberman 1993; Shodhan 2001) only served to reinforce these negative stereotypes about the Puṣṭi Mārga in the public imagination and was made even worse by the continual criticisms of the Puṣṭi Mārga by Dayānanda Sarasvatī (1824–83) of the Ārya Samāj (Jordens 1998: 140–59) and a mysterious figure named Svāmī Blākaṭānanda, who made the sensational charge that the Śrīnāthjī *svarūpa* was not an image of Kṛṣṇa but a deity found in tantric Hinduism known as a *bhairava* (Saha 2020). These events were paralleled by the unfortunate circumstances under which Govardhanlāl assumed the Nathdwara throne. Govardhanlāl's father, Giridhar (1843–1903), was forcibly exiled from Nathdwara by the British and the Mewar royal court after he attempted to unsuccessfully establish Nathdwara as an independent Rajput state (Saha 2007: 276–8). This, in turn, triggered a very public and protracted legal battle between father and son for control of Nathdwara estates that ended in 1903 with Giridhar's death (Saha 2007: 279–84). These controversies, however, would plunge devotees into a crisis of faith as they found themselves questioning for the first time the extent to which their spiritual teachers were quasi-divine figures or merely flawed human beings (Saha 2007: 278–9).

Govardhanlāl was determined to restore the image of the Puṣṭi Mārga by turning Nathdwara into an important center for arts and religious learning. He had a deep love for the arts and made great efforts to attract poets, musicians, and painters to Nathdwara in the service of Śrīnāthjī. Govardhanlāl commissioned an illustrated manuscript of the *Bhāgavata Purāṇa* that took thirty-five years to complete, and he became the patron to master painters such as Champalal Hiralal Gaur (1875–1930), Sukhdev Krishandas Gaur (1825–1925), and Ghasiram Sharma (1869–1931). These painters and their contemporaries painted not only for Govardhanlāl and the Nathdwara temple but also for wealthy devotees from urban areas like Bombay who insisted on the incorporation of European paintings into the works they commissioned. The result was the evolution of the Nathdwara school into a curious hybrid of Indian and European painting styles. Kṛṣṇa's pastimes in Braj were depicted against a backdrop that resembled the English countryside, and Kṛṣṇa and Rādhā were sometimes depicted in buildings that resembled the interior of Victorian mansions (Ambalal 1987: 82 and 2015: 34). This change in style was also influenced by European realist painting and the newly emerging technology of photography both of which tried to capture a precise, accurate, and objective representation of reality (Ambalal 2015: 34; Nardi 2020: 94–6 and 2019: 35–9). In certain works, painters staged their subjects using the same type of props and poses that photographers used in their studios and, in some cases, the portraits of individuals were painted to look like they were photographs. Thus, the portraits as well as paintings of *sevā* from Govardhanlāl's reign were markedly different from their predecessors as artists adopted this new style of painting—sometimes known as the photographic style or photo-realistic style—to achieve a greater sense of realism in their work.

Paintings and Photographs as Documents of Legitimation

The Nathdwara *mahārāja*s were well-known for commissioning elaborate paintings of nature scenes or the Braj countryside to be used as backdrops (*pichavāi*s) for the purpose of heightening the aesthetic experience of *sevā* for the devotee.[6] The *mahārāja*s, however, increasingly used paintings to underline their dual status as noblemen and spiritual leaders. This could be accomplished by painting multiple pictures of a single *mahārāja* in both ritual and non-ritual contexts. This is the case with paintings that concern the *mahārāja* Daujī II (1797–1826). One can find paintings of him carrying a spear while on horseback or riding atop an elephant in a procession. In other paintings, he devoutly performs very elaborate *sevā*s to Śrīnāthjī for which he was renowned.[7] Other approaches that painters used to capture the dual nature of the *mahārāja*s was to use particular conventions borrowed from Mughal and Rajput paintings to emphasize the divine right of royalty to rule over their subjects. In the formal portraits of the *mahārāja*s and their heirs, they are frequently depicted as noblemen or kings with halos around them to underline their status as religious leaders. One painting goes a step further by depicting Govardhanlāl with his young children dressed as Kṛṣṇa as if to emphasize that Govardhanlāl's semidivine status will be transferred to the future heirs of the Nathdwara estates.[8] In other examples, the religious and secular authority of the *mahārāja*s was captured on a large and lavish scale. A painting depicting a young Govardhanlāl touring the Nathdwara estates with his father, Giridhar, during *Vijayadaśmī* shows both figures atop elephants and surrounded by a multitude of attendants, palanquins, and a small contingent of soldiers that included British troops whose duty was to protect the Nathdwara estates. The halos around both father and son underline their claims to divinity and also suggest that it was from this divine authority that they derived their secular authority to rule Nathdwara.[9]

When the controversies surrounding the *mahārāja*s began to erode their divine authority, *mahārāja*s both within and outside Nathdwara began to adopt the technology of photography to strengthen ties with their devotees. Photography became popular in Nathdwara in the mid-nineteenth century in order to meet the growing demand for pilgrims wanting souvenir photos commemorating their pilgrimage to see Śrīnāthjī. It is estimated that by the mid-nineteenth century, there were about forty photography studios in Nathdwara alone, and even Ghasiram and his contemporaries stored photographic equipment in their studios to meet the demands of pilgrims. Painters in Nathdwara also saw in photography an opportunity for greater creative expression. *Mahārāja*s could pose for studios

Figure 6.3 A photograph of the popular *mahārāja* Devakīnandanācārya (1859–1903) of Kamvan from *Svarūpa Darśan*. © British Library Board (Shelfmark number: 14154 .de.8, pg. 74).

Figure 6.4 A painting of Devakīnandanācārya inspired by the photograph in *Svarūpa Darśan*. Unknown artist, early twentieth century. The Amit Ambalal Collection, Ahmedabad.

in photographs and the negatives would then be used as the basis to produce more detailed and embellished paintings of the *mahārājas* at a later date (Ruia 2017: 8–12). The photographs would also serve as the basis for pictures as well as miniature holy cards that could be reproduced on a mass level and then sold in the marketplaces around Nathdwara for use as *citrajīs* in personal shrines.[10] The use of photography as a means to encourage personal devotion to the *mahārājas* became so popular that a compilation of photographic *citrajīs* of *mahārājas* across western India would be published in 1923 with the intent of making the visual argument that the *mahārājas* were indeed living manifestations of Kṛṣṇa. The book was simply titled *Svarūpa Darśan* (Figures 6.3 and 6.4).[11]

Manoratha Paintings: Incorporating the Self into *Bhakti*

Puṣṭi Mārga paintings and photographs, however, did not function purely as objects of veneration. Paintings were commissioned by the *mahārājas* since the establishment of Nathdwara to record the daily *sevā* rituals in the temple, but paintings also were used to record a more significant venerative act known as the *manoratha*.[12] A *manoratha* refers to a long, cherished desire or dream of a *mahārāja* or devotee to perform *sevā* to Śrīnāthjī or another important Puṣṭi Mārga *svarūpa* in a way that reflects the individual's own personal relationship with the image.

Manoratha paintings are usually divided into two categories; the first are known as traditional-style *manorathas* (Nardi 2019: 24–9). These were commissioned by the *mahārājas* themselves or their royal patrons and tended to be liturgically focused in nature because they depicted the *mahārājas*, their families, and their royal patrons fulfilling a *manoratha* to Śrīnāthjī. This type of *manoratha* could have depicted the desire of a *mahārāja* to see Śrīnāthjī adorned in particular clothing for a particular *darśan* or to simply do an elaborate *sevā* for an important family occasion such as the birth of a child. In some cases, paintings were meant to celebrate the prowess of a *mahārāja* in organizing a special *sevā* on the most elaborate scale possible. This is illustrated in a painting capturing the 1908 event (Figure 6.5), when Govardhanlāl performed an extremely elaborate *sevā* to the Śrīnāthjī image and four Vallabha *sampradāya svarūpas* highly revered within the community for their association with Vallabha's son, Viṭṭhalnāth (1515–88). This festival was meant to recreate the splendor associated with a very similar and legendary *sevā* that was performed in 1822 by Daujī II, but the 1908 event was also carried out as part of Govardhanlāl's efforts to rehabilitate the image of a scandal-plagued

Figure 6.5 *Festival of the Five Svarūpas*. Ghasiram Hardev Sharma, *c*. 1908. Opaque watercolour and gold on paper, 56.6 × 40.5 cm. The Anil Relia Collection, Ahmedabad.

Puṣṭi Mārga. The painting commemorating the 1908 *sevā* depicts Govardhanlāl and the Udaipur king Fateh Singh (r. 1884–1930) adoring the five *svarūpa*s with other *mahārāja*s and temple attendants. It functioned as both an expression of Govardhanlāl's devotion to Śrīnāthjī and a visual call for religious unity within his fractured community.

The second type of *manorathas* are known as popular-style *manorathas* because these paintings were commissioned by the larger body of devotees who came on pilgrimage to Nathdwara. They became quite popular among devotees in the early decades of the twentieth century and were also known as mixed-media *manorathas* due to their combining of traditional painting and photography into one. Photographs of individual participants were taken in a studio against a plain cloth backdrop and once the photograph was developed, the face of the devotees were cut and pasted onto a sketch which would show the Śrīnāthjī *svarūpa* at the center. Once the photographic portraits were glued to the sketch, the work was then finished by painting over the images (Nardi 2019: 35–51). This became a popular option with pilgrims who came to Nathdwara for many reasons. For pilgrims who did not have the luxury of spending a lengthy period of time to pose for a painter, the mixed medium *manoratha* allowed for a faster and more cost-effective way to produce a *manoratha* painting. Mixed *manoratha* paintings also allowed patrons greater freedom to customize their paintings. They could experiment with different types of outfits and poses or choose the backdrops against which they would like to be shown. Since the photographs of the participants were taken individually, they further could be arranged in the painting according to gender and hierarchy (Nardi 2019: 42–4). For devotees, however, who could not afford such elaborate arrangements, the best option was to be photographed in a photographer's studio with a simple painting of Śrīnāthjī that would later function as a *citrajī* in their homes.

Popular *manoratha* paintings and photographs functioned as souvenirs for devotees to commemorate their trip to Nathdwara. It is important to remember that access to the Śrīnāthjī image was quite limited for devotees. Devotees were not permitted to come into close contact with the image and given how crowded the *darśan* room could become, devotees could sometimes have only a momentary glimpse of the *svarūpa* before being hurried out of the room. In this context, *manoratha* photographs and paintings fulfilled the longing of devotees to have close contact with Śrīnāthjī in what they considered to be the most ideal of settings. This could mean being photographed next to a *citrajī* of Śrīnāthjī in an open courtyard against a backdrop of clouds and lush vegetation or it could mean being depicted with one's family members in a quasi-Victorian setting adoring Śrīnāthjī and Vallabhācārya (Figures 6.6 and 6.7). The desire to serve Kṛṣṇa, however, was not only regulated to small, intimate settings. This is certainly the case in a 1915 *manoratha* painting that was commissioned by a wealthy Gujarati patron named Mantubāi (Nardi 2019: 27–8). The painting commemorates the fulfillment of Mantubāi's desire to serve another image of Kṛṣṇa named Navanītapriyajī that was also housed in the Nathdwara temple. Mantubāi covered all the expenses

Figure 6.6 Group photograph with devotees next to a *pichvāi* of Śrīnāthjī. Narendra Kumar Paliwal, *c.* 1950s. Gelatin silver print, 24.8 × 30.5 cm. The Anil Relia Collection, Ahmedabad.

for the *sevā* during the festival of *Sāṁjhī* that was officiated by none other than Govardhanlāl and his son Dāmodarlāl (1897–1936).

Figures 6.6 and 6.7 are indicative of how popular *manoratha*s were an expression of middle and upper-class mercantile social values. The *baniyā* community was attracted to the Puṣṭi Mārga because Vallabha's message emphasized the compatibility between *bhakti* and the pursuit of one's worldly duties. Merchants did not have to abandon their worldly responsibilities but, instead, could continue with their pursuit of wealth as long as it was channeled toward cultivating a single-minded devotion to Kṛṣṇa (Saha 2007: 304, 307). For members of the *baniyā* community, this form of devotion was expressed primarily in two ways. The first way was to use their wealth for the regular performance of *sevā* at home or making pilgrimages to important Vallabha *sampradāya* shrines. The second way was to engage in acts of religious patronage that could range from financially supporting the *mahārāja*s and their families to sponsoring an elaborate *sevā* on special occasions such as a *mahārāja*'s birthday or an important religious festival.[13] The fulfillment of these obligations was viewed by devotees as being societally beneficial and also essential to maintaining and increasing one's prestige and honor in society. In the case of women, the protection of family honor became their primary responsibility in the aftermath

Figure 6.7 *Manoratha of Śrīnāthjī*. Artist Khubiram and Sons, *c.* 1950s. Cut-and-pasted gelatin silver prints, opaque watercolour and gold on paper, 50 × 60 cm. The Anil Relia Collection, Ahmedabad.

of the Maharaja Libel Case and the other sexual and legal scandals that befell the Puṣṭi Mārga in the nineteenth century. In order to prevent even the appearance of impropriety, women were increasingly encouraged to consign their religious activities to the domestic sphere and to severely restrict their activities in public shrines (Sharma 2017: 98–9). When viewed within this larger historical context the popular *manoratha* images represented by Figures 6.6 and 6.7 can be viewed as visual statements of individuals declaring their commitment to upholding and fulfilling the core values of their *baniyā dharma*: the belief that the pursuit of *bhakti* is central to both societal and personal betterment.

Conclusion

These visual expressions of devotion are important historical tools for reconstructing the ritual and institutional history of the Vallabha *sampradāya* and by looking at these images and following their evolutionary development, it shows how they uniquely and continually are shaped by the intersection between the realm of the worldly (*laukika*) and the spiritual, non-worldly (*alaukika*).

Citrajīs can be viewed on one level as a simple pictorial representation of Kṛṣṇa, but to the Puṣṭi Mārga devotee, regular *citra sevā* is actually an invitation to participate in the spiritual realm of Kṛṣṇa's pastimes. In the case of the popular *manorathas*, the images function as visual expression of both devotion and a commitment to the social values valued by Puṣṭi Mārga devotees. The sense of ambiguity that one sees in *citrajīs* and the *manoratha* images is particularly strong in the photographic and painted depictions of the *mahārājas*, where they are seen posing as both royal noblemen and spiritual leaders. In this context, these images are powerful visual reminders of the central question that concerned Puṣṭi Mārga Vaiṣṇavas from the mid-nineteenth century onward: the degree to which their *mahārājas* were to be considered divine or human.

On another level, Puṣṭi Mārga visual culture also invites a scholarly reconsideration into the visual and devotional significance of typical material objects in Hindu ritual. It has been suggested in some scholarship that the introduction of prints and photographs into Hindu religious practice during the nineteenth century had the effect of displacing the traditional three-dimensional use of sculpture as living objects of devotion and with it the place of brahmins as the mediators between the individual and the divine (Jain 2012: 184–5). This is not the case with the Puṣṭi Mārga. The veneration of two-dimensional and three-dimensional representations has existed as parallel practices in the Puṣṭi Mārga since the sixteenth century and offered devotees multiple means by which they could enter into a direct and intimate devotional relationship with Kṛṣṇa. This did not displace the authority of the *mahārājas*. Paintings and photographs in the nineteenth century were used to strengthen their authority during a time of deep crisis for the Puṣṭi Mārga and to reinforce the religious and social conservatism that shaped the identities of the *baniyās* who made up the community. Nonetheless, the use of pictorial representations in the Puṣṭi Mārga should first and foremost be viewed as important tools for understanding—even if they can be highly staged and idealized in nature—the devotional aspirations of both *mahārājas* and their devotees and how these aspirations have contributed to the continued vitality of *sevā* and the religious arts within the Puṣṭi Mārga over the centuries.

Notes

1 For institutional histories of the Puṣṭi Mārga, see Mītal (1968), Saha (2004), Saha (2007), Śāstrī (1939).

2 See utterance number twelve for Gokulnāth's brief mention of *citra sevā*.

3 The main sources for tracing the history of the Puṣṭi Mārga come from the body of hagiographical literature redacted between the sixteenth and eighteenth centuries, known as the *vārtā* literature. These texts are generally attributed to Gokulnāth and Gokulnāth's nephew, Harirāy (1590?–1715). One of the earliest and probably the most reliable of these texts is the seventeenth century *Caurāsī Vaiṣṇavan kī Vārtā* which deals with the lives of Vallabha and his eighty-four most exemplary disciples. The *Do Sau Bāvan Vaiṣṇavan kī Vārtā* deals with the life of Vallabha's youngest son Viṭṭhalnāth (1515–85) and his 252 disciples. For extended considerations concerning the dating, the historicity, and the theological vision of the *vārtā* literature, see Bachrach (2020), Saha (2006), and Ṭanḍan (1960).

4 The Nathdwara temple was sacked by the Marathas in 1802. The Śrīnāthjī image was first removed to Udaipur before being relocated to a small village sheltered by hills known as Ghasiyar. The image remained there for five years before being returned to Nathdwara.

5 *Sevā praṇālī*s are published privately by devotees under the guidance of a particular *mahārāja* or by individuals who do daily *sevā* in a particular temple. These manuals provide broad guidelines for *sevā* and give a certain amount of latitude for individuals to use their own individual creativity when performing *sevā*. For some examples, see Parikh (n.d) and Śivjī (1931). There are many websites that supply devotees with the material necessary to perform *sevā* for both *citrajī*s and *svarūpa*s such as Pushtishangar.com, Nandanshringar.com, and Pushtishringar.com. For instructional videos from Pushtishangar.com, see, for example, https://youtu.be/e6PgsCbcrCE or https://youtu.be/yRuz8ATS9zI (accessed March 24, 2022).

6 The development of *pichvāi*s has been well documented by art historians studying the Puṣṭi Mārga. For examples of studies, see Krishna (2015), Krishna and Talwar (2007), and Lazaro (2005).

7 For examples of these images, see Ambalal (1987: 65) and Ghose (2015: 80–8, cats. 15–17 and 147–8, cats. 82–4).

8 See the painting dated to around 1890 entitled *Sitting along with His Children against Large Bolster* in Relia (2013: 34).

9 See Relia (2013: 16).

10 Govardhanlāl was highly revered during his lifetime and is still highly regarded by devotees today for ushering in what has been called the "Golden Age of Nathdwara." His portraits were produced in various sizes and were by far one of the most popular images that was circulated in Nathdwara during the late nineteenth century. For examples of these images, see Relia (2013: 40) and Ruia (2017: 43–4, cats. 21–2).

11 The *mahārāja* in Figures 6.3 and 6.4 was the Kamvan-based Devakīnandanācārya (1859–1903), who was extremely popular among devotees in Bombay. His photograph in *Svarūpa Darśan* would serve as the inspiration for countless

paintings and pictures found in both sectarian and controversial literature from the nineteenth century. For the photograph in *Svarūpa Darśan*, see Desai (1923: 74). For other photographs of Devakīnandanācārya, see Ruia (2017: 46–7, cats. 22–3).

12 For the ranges of themes found in *manoratha* images, see Nardi (2019), Krishna and Talwar (2021), Relia (2013), and Ruia (2017).

13 For an account of the patronage practices of one Puṣṭi Mārga family, see Shah (2015).

References

Ambalal, A. (1987), *Krishna as Shrinathji*, Ahmedabad: Mapin Publishing.

Ambalal, A. (2015), "The *Tilkayats* as Patrons: History and Painting in Nathdwara," in M. Ghose (ed.), *Gates of the Lord: The Tradition of Krishna Paintings*, 26–35, Chicago: Art Institute of Chicago.

Bachrach, E. (2020), *In the Service of Krishna: Illustrating the Lives of Eighty-Four Vaishnavas from a 1702 Manuscript*, Ahmedabad: Mapin Publishing.

Bennett, P. (1993), *The Path of Grace: Social Organization and Temple Worship in a Vaishnava Sect*, Delhi: Hindustan Publishing Corporation.

Desāi, L. C. (1923), *Svarūpa Darśan*, Ahmedabad: Lallubhāi Chaganlāl Desāi.

Ghose, M., ed. (2015), *Gates of the Lord: The Tradition of Krishna Paintings*, Chicago: Art Institute of Chicago.

Gokulnāth (1996), "Śrī Gokulnāthjī ke Caubīs Vacanāmṛta," in B. P. Devapura (ed.), *Gosvāmi Gokulnāth Smṛti-Granth*, 57–73, Nathdwara: Nāthdvāra Sāhitya Maṇḍal.

Haberman, D. (1993), "On Trial: The Love of the Sixteen Thousand Gopees," *History of Religions*, 33 (1): 44–70.

Harirāy (1992), *Do Sau Bāvan Vaiṣṇavan kī Vārtā*, vol. 3, Indore: Vaiṣṇav Mitr Maṇḍal.

Jain, K. (2012), "Mass Reproduction and the Art of the Bazaar," in V. Dalmia and R. Sadana (eds.), *The Cambridge Companion to Modern Indian Culture*, 184–205, Cambridge: Cambridge University Press.

Jordens, J. T. F (1998), "Dayananda and Karsondas Mulji: Their Condemnation of Vallabhacharyas," in J. T. F. Jordens, *Dayananda Sarasvati: Essays on His Life and Ideas*, 140–62, Delhi: Manohar Publications.

Krishna, K. (2015), "Pichvais: Narrative Textiles and Their Origins," in M. Ghose (ed.), *Gates of the Lord: The Tradition of Krishna Paintings*, 36–41, Chicago: Art Institute of Chicago.

Krishna, K., and K. Talwar (2007), *In Adoration of Krishna: Pichhwais of Shrinathji*, Bombay: Garden Silk Mills Limited.

Krishna, K., and K. Talwar (2021), *Nathdwara Paintings from the Anil Relia Collection*, New Delhi: Niyogi Books.

Lazaro, D. P. (2005), *Materials Methods and Symbolism in the Pichhavai Painting of Rajasthan*, Ahmedabad: Mapin Publishing.

Mītal, P. (1968), *Brajastha Ballabha sampradāya kā itihāsa*, Mathura: Sāhitya Saṃsthān.

Nardi, I. (2019), *Portraits of Devotion: Popular Manorath Paintings in the Collection of Anil Relia*, Ahmedabad: Mapin Publishing.

Nardi, I. (2020), "Portraiture and Politics: Royal and Devotional Allegiances in the Paintings of the Garh Mahal," *South Asian Studies* 36 (1): 88–101.

Parkih, J. (n.d), *Srīnāth Sevā Rasodadhi*, Ahmedabad: Pārul Prakāśan.

Relia, A. (2013), *The Indian Portrait II—Sacred Journey of Tilkayat Govardhanlal (1862–1934) Nathdwara*, Ahmedabad: Archer House.

Ruia, A. (2017), *Nathdwara: Photography as Propaganda*. Available online: https://www.academia.edu/37148479/Nathdwara_Photography_as_Propaganda.

Saha, S. (2004), "Creating a Community of Grace: A History of the Puṣṭi Mārga in Northern and Western India (1493–1905)," PhD diss., University of Ottawa, Ottawa.

Saha, S. (2006), "A community of Grace: The Social and Theological World of the Puṣṭi Mārga," *Bulletin of the School of Oriental and African Studies* 69 (2): 225–42.

Saha, S. (2007a), "The Movement of Bhakti along a North-West Axis: Tracing the History of the Puṣṭimārg between the Sixteenth and Nineteenth Centuries," *International Journal of Hindu Studies* 11 (3): 299–318.

Saha, S. (2007b), "The Darbār, the British, and the Runaway Mahārāja: Religion and Politics in Western India," *South Asia Research* 27 (3): 271–91.

Saha, S. (2014), "Kṛṣṇa Devotion in Western India," in P. Pratap Kumar (ed.), *Contemporary Hinduism*, 138–47, London: Routledge.

Saha, S. (2020), "From Vaiṣṇavas to Hindus: The Redefinition of the Vallabha Sampraday in the Late Nineteenth and Early Twentieth Centuries," *International Journal of Indic Religions* 2 (3). Available online: https://digitalcommons.shawnee.edu/indicreligions/vol2/iss3/3

Shah, A. (2015), "Devotion and Patronage: The Story of a Pushtimarg Family," in M. Ghose (ed.), *Gates of the Lord: The Tradition of Krishna Paintings*, 42–53, Chicago: Art Institute of Chicago.

Śarmā, C. (2008), *Nāthdvārīya Citrakalā aur Citrakār*, Nathdwara: Ciranjīvlāl Śarmā.

Śarmā, G. (2010), *Śrī Vallabh Cintan: Śrī Vallabhnandan, Gopīnāth Prabhucaran*, Indore: Śri Vallabh Prakaśan Nyās.

Śāstrī, K. (1939), *Kānkarolī kā Itihās*, Kankaroli: Śrīvidyā-Vibhāg.

Sharma, S. (2017), "Middle-Class Modernities and the Reproduction of Sectarian Identity among Puṣṭimārg Vaiṣṇavas in the Bombay Presidency," *The Journal of Hindu Studies* 10 (1): 86–111.

Shodhan, A. (2001), *A Question of Community: Religious Groups and Colonial Law*, Calcutta: Samya.

Śivjī, R. (1931), *Vallabhpuṣṭiprakāś*, Bombay: Khemrāj Śrīkṛṣṇadās.

Ṭaṇḍan, H. (1960), *Vārtā Sāhitya. (Ek Bṛhat Adhyayan)*, Aligarh: Bhārat Prakāśan Mandir.

Taylor, W. (2005), "Agency and Affectivity of Paintings: The Lives of *Chitrajis* in Hindu Ritual Contexts," *Material Religion* 1 (2): 198–227.

Websites

www.nandanshringar.com
www.pushtishangar.com
www.pushtishringar.com
www.pushti-marg.net

7

The Iconic Sūrdās

John Stratton Hawley

Suppose you are searching for an image of the great Brajbhasha poet Sūrdās—Sūr for short—what do you do? You google him, of course, and if you had done that from 2019 through most of 2021, you would have been gazing at a screen divided in two. On the left you would have seen the Wikipedia article about Sūrdās—lots of text—while on the right you had the chance to see how the poet looked. Some half-dozen images appeared, but two were dominant. I cannot show you the first of these because of Bloomsbury Academic's interpretation of international copyright regulations, so I must ask you to go to the internet yourself. Type in "Surdas," click on the "images" box at the top, scroll down a bit, and there you'll see "Sant Soordas," an image from a website called "India! Her Glorious Spiritual Heritage!!" (https://spiritual-heritage-of-india.blogspot.com/2018/10/sant-soordas.html). Sūr is seated by a riverbank wearing a red cap. His head inclines gently downward and one arm crooks across his chest.

This is the first of the two images that were dominant from 2019 to 2021. Not surprisingly, others have also posted this image to the internet, and the range of its appeal was evidently so great that it jumped the line separating Hindus from Muslims: this same Sūrdās can be called a Sufi (https://sufinama.org/poets/surdas/). There is a third important permutation, as well. This we see on a stamp that was issued by the Government of India's Department of Post in 1952 as part of a series depicting celebrated poets of northern India. This version, finally, I can reproduce, since it is regarded for copyright purposes as inhabiting the public domain (Figure 7.1). Because it is a stamp, the color has disappeared, and we only see the head and upper torso, but otherwise the image is unchanged. The poet is evidently lost in contemplation.

Elsewhere, though, his mood can change, as we immediately see in the second Sūrdās image that dominates the internet (Figure 7.2). Luckily I can reproduce this one straightaway, since I own a copy of the lithograph it projects. Produced

Figure 7.1 Commemorative four-anna postage stamp issued by the Government of India on October 1, 1952, with Sūrdās's name written in Devanāgarī letters beneath the dates ascribed to him, 1479–1586. Ministry of Communications, Government of India, 1952. A commemorative postage stamp on Saints and Poets: Surdas 1479–1586; India Postage Stamps; 1 October; https://postagestamps.gov.in/Stamps_List.aspx; Government Open Data License GODL. Accessed at Wikimedia Commons, https://commons.wikimedia.org/wiki/File:Surdas.jpg. In the internet image to which this stamp most closely corresponds, the dates have been altered to 1478–1583.

in 1953 or 1954, it's roughly contemporary with the postage-stamp image we just saw, but everything else has changed. Now the poet faces right, not left; now his demeanor is jubilant; and this time he is not alone. The youthful Kṛṣṇa has joined him, the very god of whom he sings.[1]

These two images of Sūrdās—Figure 7.2 and a full-frame, full-color version of Figure 7.1—popped up as equals on the internet until August 15, 2021, but on that day Google changed the format. Figure 7.2 evidently surfed the internet's tide of change more expertly than Figure 7.1. Contemplative silence gets drowned out in an ever-noisier world.

And what about the poet's own time, the sixteenth century? What images of Sūrdās circulated then? Disappointingly, nothing visual has survived, but we do have generous records of songs that bore his oral signature. The first dated manuscript containing some of them appeared in Fatehpur in northeastern Rajasthan in 1582, and in about 1660 the poet made his visual debut. This

Figure 7.2 Sūrdās painted in oil by Kalicharan Verma in 1953–4; published by India Picture Palace, Chandni Chowk, Delhi, which went out of business in 2000 or immediately thereabouts. Author's collection, thanks to a gift by Lynn Marie Ate. An image of this painting appeared in a one-click Google search from 2019 to 2021.

happened at Udaipur, and by the time we get to 1730 in the same city we find so many paintings of Sūrdās poems that 150 or so are extant today. In all of these save three the poet himself appears, watching the action of the poems he is understood to have created. Usually, it is easy to recognize this visual Sūrdās: one painting prepares you for the next. Thus, both in our own time and 300 years earlier we encounter a healthy roster of images of Sūr, deeply interconnected. But do they reveal a shared sense of an iconic Sūrdās? Only a closer look will tell.

Let's begin to ask this question by returning to the modern day—the several steps of our Google search. In the first image we saw, where no musical instrument was present, we thought we saw a middle-aged man lost in contemplation. This may be so, but perhaps his downward gaze signals something else: as everyone nowadays assumes, Sūr is blind.[2] Indeed this emerges as the indispensable baseline of his iconicity, both in our own time and as close as we can come to his own. In its internet analogues our postage-stamp Sūrdās takes on color, as we have seen. He usually wears a *dhotī* that is white and has a long strip of cloth draped over his left shoulder—white with a vibrant red stripe. To his head is fitted a tight red cap of the sort that appears with some regularity in the art of the Puṣṭimārg (Path of Fulfilment) or Vallabha *sampradāya*—followers of the early sixteenth-century theologian Vallabha or Vallabhācārya (Bachrach 2020:

119; Ghose 2015: 87). You glimpse a long necklace of *tulsī* beads, attesting to his Vaiṣṇava identity, and you could perhaps be forgiven for wondering whether one of these *tulsī* strands might actually be a *yajñopavīt*, the sacred thread that signifies "twice-born" initiation. In Vallabhite circles, indeed, Sūrdās is thought of as being brahmin. One final thing: he holds a piece of cloth, as if to wipe his brow. Or perhaps this last item was added to justify the sharp bend of Sūr's elbow, which amplifies the humility suggested by his downward-pointed nose. Here is a man lost in thought, just as he has lost his sight.[3]

This image, but without the sacred thread, is well known to readers of the scholarly literature on Sūrdās. It appears, for example, on the cover of books by Prabhudayāl Mītal (1957, 1982), Deśrājsiṃh Bhāṭī (1977), and Krishna P. Bahadur (1999)—sometimes reversed, as in the case of the two Mītal books. In the "Sant Soordas" internet version the poet's name appears at the top of the image and his impressive life span, 1478–1583 CE, is written across the bottom. If one turns to the text of the Wikipedia entry, one discovers that these dates are "uncertain," and in truth they are entirely fictitious, but they give the scene a definitive, encyclopedia-like flavor.

Most significant, however, may be the possible Vallabhite ambience, consonant with the Wikipedia text. Although the saint's forehead bears no sectarian *tilak*, his modesty could be interpreted as suggesting that he acknowledges a position lesser than that of his guru. In the course of the seventeenth century, indeed, the fledgling *sampradāya* went to some lengths to claim this already famous *bhakti* poet as their own. On the basis of the available historical and textual evidence I find it hard to believe that there actually was such a disciple-guru relationship between Sūrdās and Vallabha (Hawley 2018: 19–23). Yet to see his humility here—and that rather distinctive cap—might seem to prove me wrong. Seeing is believing and has been so for a very long time.

In the second dominant Google image these vague sectarian shadings disappear; the child Kṛṣṇa wears a Vaiṣṇava *tilak*, but it is not specifically Vallabhite (Figure 7.2). We are surely intended to imagine ourselves in a sixteenth-century scene, but one of the signs used to mark its distance from the present has an even more classical feel—classic in the Mediterranean sense. There are parrots and vines, both suggesting an Indian ambience, but what about the flower pot we see embedded in the wall to the far right? It hardly reminds us of anything native to Braj, where both the poet and his god are understood to have spent so much time. A Roman villa seems more likely.

Where did this image come from? Nothing in the painting itself gives a hint: there is no title and no reference to either the artist or the manufacturer. But

Figure 7.3 Sūrdās sings to Kṛṣṇa. Painted in water colors by Indra A. Sharma, 13½" × 17". Mumbai: S. S. Brijbasi & Sons, *c.* 1965–6. Author's collection.

since I had a different and seemingly older version of this image in my own collection (Figure 7.3)—I bought it in the 1970s—I thought I knew the answer: Figure 7.2 must be a later adaptation of Figure 7.3, which shows us a portrait of Sūrdās that was published by S. S. Brijbasi & Sons from their office on Mirza Street in Mumbai, in the mid-1960s.[4] Printed at the Brijbasi offices in Mathura, it circulated widely throughout the northern part of India in the medium of poster art and could be seen as well in the south and abroad.

Here too we see the aged Sūrdās, and Kṛṣṇa is again rapt in attention. He has the same peacock crown (*mor mukuṭ*), and some of the flora are also familiar. They gather in the background as they do in the internet example. This time, however, the stone wall of Figure 7.2 vanishes into a picket fence. This too is an item you're scarcely apt to see in the Braj countryside—New England would be a better bet—yet in a certain way it might fit Mumbai, where this scene was actually painted. Could one have encountered such a fence among the painted backdrops to be found in a photographer's studio in that great city, not just in the late nineteenth or early twentieth century but even later? Quite possibly. A *nāgara*-style temple in the distance marks the scene as definitively Indian, but it too has a rather stage-set feel. Indeed, the artist who fashioned this scene was living and working in Mumbai. His name is Indra Sharma, as we can see in the lower left-hand corner, and he went on to become one of India's most celebrated devotional painters. Sharma trained in Nathdvara, a major center of Vallabhite culture, and then in Mumbai itself. His association with Brijbasi & Sons was long-lasting (Bae and Sharma 2001: 21–4; Pinney 2004: 92–104; Davis 2012: 169–99).

Sūrdās is far less gaunt here than he was in the internet version of this same scene (Figure 7.2). The child Kṛṣṇa too seems better fed; even his nimbus is more substantial. And the flower pot? It's gone—replaced by the pillar we find at the left extremity of this Mumbai counterpart, Roman in style and enlivened by a burst of pink blossoms. This pillar lends a certain classical dignity to the Sūrdās scene, just as a portrait photographer of the time (or a portrait painter such as Sharma himself) might have wished to do for his clients. Then comes the most obvious contrast. The whole scene is backward; it's a mirror image of what our Google search first revealed. Pillar, poet, deity—everything is flipped. Which image came first, then, and who was responsible for the flipping? Indeed, was anyone responsible, or did this transformation result from some mechanical glitch endemic to Walter Benjamin's "age of mechanical reproduction" (Benjamin 1935, trans. 1968)?

At first I thought ISKCON, the International Society for Krishna Consciousness founded in New York in 1965, might have played a role in mediating between these two images. Where Kṛṣṇa appears on the internet, ISKCON is often behind the scenes, projecting the "neo-Vedic" art it developed in a stream of publication projects issued from its Los Angeles-based Bhaktivedanta Book Trust in the course of the 1970s. Indeed, there is an ISKCON variant on this image that actually predates the Bhaktivedanta Book Trust. It's a pen and ink sketch done by the Texas-born artist Govinda dasi in the late 1960s, when the movement was still based in New York (Figure 7.4).[5] Clearly, Govinda dasi had Indra Sharma's image before her. Tellingly, however, she omitted the picket fence, which must have seemed strange to someone living at that time on the eastern seaboard of the United States: How could it anchor a classic Indian scene? She replaced it with a horizontal pillar and an *āmalaka* finial, evidently hoping these would be seen as remnants of some ancient, ruined Braj temple. Ruins have a history of their own in the Romantic imagination.

But could this ISKCON version have led the way to the internet image we know as Figure 7.2? The transition is hard to imagine. How could ISKCON's rouged, rounded depictions of the faces of Kṛṣṇa and his companions anticipate the Kṛṣṇa we see in Figure 7.2? There Kṛṣṇa's face seems more intense, less

Figure 7.4 Sūrdās sings to Kṛṣṇa. Pen and ink, Govinda dasi, 1967. Courtesy of Govinda dasi. This image may be viewed at http://www.govindadasi.com/more-artwork.html.

patterned, and his hair is coifed in a distinctive way: it has a cord (*laṭkan* or *lūm*) that matches the one that decorates his flute.

As it turns out, I had the sequence wrong. Figure 7.2 actually preceded Figure 7.3 and its ISKCON version. Murari Lal Garg of Noida, the senior figure at Brijbasi Art Press (one of two firms descended from the original Brijbasi & Sons) and the greatest living expert on its history, has identified the artist responsible for Figure 7.2 as Kalicharan Verma, who worked from his native Jhansi at the southern border of the Braj region. He learned the trade by apprenticing himself as a boy to Rup Kishore Kapoor, whose Chitrashala atelier was located in Kanpur, later Dehradun. Kalicharan painted this Sūrdās image at some point in the years just before 1956–7, when Garg, traveling with his father on a business trip, met the artist in person.[6] It was Brijbasi that had printed Kalicharan's image—as a chromolithograph from its press in Mathura, probably in 1953 or 1954—but the publisher of record was India Picture Palace of Chandni Chowk, Delhi. The name and address of India Picture Palace appear in the lower left-hand corner of the original print. That too is visible on the internet, but in 2019–21, at least, it took some sleuthing to get there.[7]

How then to explain the fact that Brijbasi later issued its own version of this scene and commissioned Indra Sharma to do the work? That was as a result of Kalicharan's success. People loved the way the child sits rapt before the aged poet, said Mr. Garg, so Brijbasi wondered if Indra Sharma could produce a new variant on the theme, something that would sell all over again. Sharma did just that, exercising his own creativity, and one measure of that creativity was his decision to reverse the positions of poet and god. Thereby he clearly preserved the integrity of Kalicharan's original painting, separating it from his own "copy," yet taking Kalicharan's creativity as the stimulus for his own. The roster of changes we have noticed was thus anything but mechanical, though as it happens the technology of reproduction had now changed. By the time Indra Sharma produced his version, Brijbasi had shifted from lithographs to an offset process. The Mumbai office commissioned the painting, but the work of reproduction happened at Mathura, the city to which Mr. Garg's family ancestrally "belonged," as the Hindi phrase has it. They were Brajbasis indeed, residents of Braj, though they spelled the term "Brijbasi," as so many did.[8]

Taking all this into account we see that in the present day the "iconic Sūrdās" of our title is actually not a single icon but a set of two—Figures 7.1 and 7.2 with various adjustments—and the latter of these has spawned a distinctive third (Figure 7.3). A similar roster of variants lies behind Figure 7.1—the postage stamp is part of this lineage—and amid them once again we find the mirror twist: book covers displayed this image both recto and verso.[9] The Kalicharan image was even more productive. It served, for example, as the visual basis of an episode of the television series *Upaniṣad Gangā*, released by India's public Doordarshan TV service in 2012.[10] Icons are too powerful to be hemmed in by a single medium.

If we turn once again to the sixteenth and seventeenth centuries for a comparison, we find quite a very different scene. There too we meet a range of representations of Sūrdās, but few of them are visual. They register Sūr's fame and creativity, but they do not show us how he looked. This comes as no surprise. We lack visual images for any vernacular *bhakti* poet other than Maulānā Dāud before the middle of the seventeenth century; if others existed, time has since erased them. But there is another difficulty, even in the visual realm. We have no biography for Sūrdās that dates to the sixteenth century; such accounts emerge only in the following century, and they diverge from one another when they do.

Yet despite this element of contradiction, there was always at least a hint of the poet's blindness, even though it is impossible to establish that trait on the basis of the early poems themselves.

Dated manuscripts show that Sūr was a widely renowned poet even in the sixteenth century. We have already noticed that the first extant dated manuscript of poetry attributed to Sūrdās comes from Fatehpur, some 100 miles north of Jaipur, in 1582 (V.S. 1639). That anthology, in turn, brought forward two preexisting models. It embedded those earlier anthologies, one of which also included other poets than Sūr, without altering their order or numbering. The Fatehpur scribe seems to have copied what he saw, perhaps adding other poems he also knew. This gives us 239 Sūr poems from Fatehpur, some appearing more than once. When we combine these with other poems that can be shown to have circulated in the same period under Sūr's name, we can be sure that at least 434 poems deserve to be dated to the latter half of the sixteenth century.[11] The poet may well have been alive at that time.

Who was this Sūrdās? The poet who is revealed to us in these early manuscripts stands at some distance from the Sūrdās whom we have been observing in the twentieth and twenty-first centuries. First and foremost, he seems hardly to have been defined by his relationship to the child Kṛṣṇa. To be sure, a certain number of child-Kṛṣṇa (*bāl kṛṣṇa*) poems appear in this early group of Sūrdās poems, but they are by no means the most numerous genre. They form only one element in the output of a much more complex and variegated poet. We do not know whether a single person actually composed all the poems that appeared under Sūr's name in this early period: the oral signature associated with a poet could also be embraced by others (Hawley 1988). But there is enough consistency of style and poetic energy to make it seem that one great poet could have been responsible for most. This poet's interests and aptitudes were far more diverse than what we might expect from any of the images we have so far seen. He composed lyrics in the first-person *vinaya* (modest, petitionary) genre; he depicted scenes from both great epics, the *Rāmāyaṇa* and *Mahābhārata*; and he found time to address hymns to the Yamunā and the Gaṅgā. To be sure, he also composed many compositions about and to Kṛṣṇa, but these are most often poems of absence and longing (*viraha*)—far from the amiable child we have come to expect.

So how did it come to pass that the poet of the child—the *vātsalya* poet—came to emerge as the iconic Sūrdās for our times?[12] I do not claim to know exactly, but I believe I can point to the earliest known moment when a collection of child-Kṛṣṇa compositions first came to symbolize the full range of Sūr's poetry.

This transformation occurred in the first decade of the eighteenth century, and it happened at a specific place: Udaipur, the capital city of the kingdom of Mewar. There we encounter a collection of Sūrdās poems that applies to itself the capacious name *Sūrsāgar* (Sur's Ocean) yet consists entirely of child-Kṛṣṇa poems. In fact, there are two such manuscripts. One, which Kenneth Bryant and I have designated U2, contains only text, no images, and is dated to V.S. 1763 (1706 CE)—170 lyrics in all (Bryant and Hawley 2015: xlvii). The other might seem more modest—only 50 poems in all—but actually there's nothing modest about this manuscript at all. Each poem is accompanied by a sumptuous illustration, making it the first illustrated *Sūrsāgar* of which I am aware. In the second half of the seventeenth century, a few individual poems attributed to Sūr had been given visual form at Udaipur—again this apparently happened only there—but this is the first time we get a complete set. This *Sūrsāgar*, seemingly produced during the reign of Maharana Amar Singh II (1698–1720), was evidently intended to be experienced not as a random cluster of individual moments but as a sequential, narrative whole. Earlier collections of Sūrdās poems sometimes sorted child-Kṛṣṇa poems and others so that they would form a meaningful sequence, but none of these anthologies was illustrated. The new visual dimension adds something conclusive: we can actually see the child grow from painting to painting.

This collection of images proclaims its identity outright. The term *Sūrsāgar* appears at the top of the very first page (Figure 7.5). Oddly, the title is actually rendered as *śūrsāgar*—some sort of scribal peculiarity—and it is followed by the syllable *li*, which probably stands for *likhitam*, meaning "written" or "inscribed." But *śūrsāgar* or not, *Sūrsāgar* is meant. Once this collective title has been given, we proceed to the first poem, whose *rāga* is assigned before the text of the poem appears: *rāg sārang*. Yet the general title is not forgotten: it appears again in the middle of the manuscript, as a part of the inscription of poem 22, and we find it once more at the very end (poem 50). The scribe wants us to know (and probably the artist does too) that it's a *Sūrsāgar* we're experiencing here. These childhood poems were perhaps understood as the purest, most innocent waters of that ocean.

Neither this nor the unillustrated U2 was the first collection of poems to be called *Sūrsāgar*. That honor belongs to a manuscript bearing the date V.S. 1697 (1640 CE); Bryant and I call it U1. It was compiled at Ghanora, very likely the town of that name that lies about a hundred miles south of Udaipur. This Ghanora manuscript was impressive in its size—792 *pads* (rhymed lyrics), although the scribe seems to have counted 812. Among extant dated manuscripts it was the largest collection of Sūrdās poetry in its time; it was subsequently brought to

Figure 7.5 Bowing in praise before the Lord's sacred feet. Illustration to "I bow in praise before your lotus feet," *vaṁdũ caraṇ saroj tumhāre* (compare Nāgarīpracāriṇī Sabhā 94). #1 in the Amar Singh *Sūrsāgar*. *Rāg sāraṅg*. India, Rajasthan, *c.* 1700. Ink, opaque watercolor, and gold on paper, 36.9 × 24.7 cm. Edwin Binney 3rd Collection, The San Diego Museum of Art, 1990.610. For a zoom-able version, see http://collection.sdmart.org/Obj5705?sid=14040&x=25800.

Udaipur and added to the royal Mewar collection. We do not know exactly when this happened, but it is possible that the artist and scribe who created our fifty-page illustrated *Sūrsāgar* saw or had at least heard of this earlier manuscript. In any case, they repeated its title. By the time they did so, the term *Sūrsāgar* had also been adopted in two other large collections of Sūr's poetry, but this happened elsewhere; they would have had no reason to know.[13] The important thing is that the term *Sūrsāgar* was evidently in familiar use in Udaipur by the beginning of the eighteenth century when this illustrated manuscript was prepared.

Just when did this happen? No date is given on any of its extant pages, front or back, but we can be relatively sure that these emerged around the turn of the eighteenth century.[14] This is so because of the style and specific imagery, both of which connect it to the court of Amar Singh II. Let us therefore call it, in an informal way, the Amar Singh *Sūrsāgar*.[15] We know how Amar Singh looked. We see him in his regnal years in a clearly datable (*c.* 1707–8) painting now to be found in the Metropolitan Museum of Art in New York (Hawley 2018: 240, Fig. 7.16). There he sports a noteworthy mustache, and this element of facial decoration evidently became all the rage during the period in which he ruled. Luckily for us, from a dating point of view, it seems to have gone out of fashion when he died. This same handlebar mustache can be seen throughout the Amar Singh *Sūrsāgar* (Hawley 2018: 238, 248, 273, 277, 282, 301). It appears, for example, on page 19 (Hawley 2018: 282), where it has been transferred from the court of Amar Singh to that of Kṛṣṇa's foster-father Nanda. Nanda is depicted as being old enough to wear a white beard, but the three younger men who surround him sport exactly the "Amar Singh" mustache.

This is not the world's first *Sūrsāgar*, as we have seen, but it has the honor of being the world's first extant <u>illustrated</u> *Sūrsāgar*. Nor does its distinction stop there. Each of the pages from this manuscript that have survived to public view—twenty-nine of the original fifty—contains an image of the poet himself. As I have said, there were a number of earlier depictions of Sūrdās in the Mewar style—I count eight. Some of them represented the same poetic vignettes (Hawley 2018: 213–18, 224–33, Figs. 7.5, 7.9, 7.11–12), but none of them formed part of an illustrated set. This means that the Amar Singh *Sūrsāgar* was the first to generate a truly stable image of the poet despite the change of narrative scene. Here Sūr is distinctly recognizable as the same person and no page fails to display his image. In this way, we could say, he functions as an icon.

We have already seen the opening page of this remarkable manuscript (Figure 7.5). Now it is time to meet its closing counterpart—page 50. To my knowledge this painting has not been displayed publicly since it formed part of an exhibition in Minneapolis in 1969, and its present whereabouts are unknown, so I am only able to refer to a black-and-white photograph of the page on which it appeared in the catalogue of the Minneapolis exhibit (Hawley 2019: 27). Even so it will be plain that these first and last pages were constructed, so to speak, as bookends that would frame the manuscript as a whole. At the top of each we see the upraised foot of *trivikrama* (triple-victory) Kṛṣṇa/Viṣṇu prominent—first pointing right and therefore "into" the manuscript that is to follow; then at the conclusion pointing left, as if to mark out what has transpired on the intervening pages. This representation of the three-world-conquering Kṛṣṇa/Viṣṇu became quite standard in Mewar.

Here it is used as a dramatic way to frame his earthly childhood, which appears in the middle register. Both in the poem and in its illustration, we are intended to see that what all the gods and sages always longed for—a vision of the transcendent Lord, the ultimate truth—is fully manifest not at the extremities of human experience, not as a product of well-developed spiritual or bodily discipline but first and foremost at home, in the space of common intimacy. With respect to Kṛṣṇa, therefore, this world-shattering level of attainment was available first and foremost to his mother Yaśodā—or to be precise, his foster-mother.

The feet tell the story eloquently, both in this last poem and in the first, and it is no surprise that this should be so. More than any other part of the body, feet are closely associated with hierarchy and status, just as they are with the gradient that connects the outside to the inner realms, the unclean to the clean. One removes one's footwear upon entering a Hindu temple or house, leaving behind the dust of the outside world. Foot-washing may also be involved. Similarly, to depict one's own relatively profane or lesser status in the presence of a person of greater honor—or indeed a deity—one places one's head at that person's feet. The first poem in the Amar Singh *Sūrsāgar* (Hawley 2018: 252; 2019: 24) dramatically enters this realm (Figure 7.5):

I bow in praise before your lotus feet—
Lovely as the blossoms of a pink water lily,
    beguiling, bearing the sixteen marks of beauty.
Those peerless feet—the wealth of eternal Śiva,
    breast to which the daughter of the ocean ever clings;
Those peerless feet—their touch made pure the River of the Gods,
    the very sight of whose waters cuts away the weight of sin;
Those peerless feet—by merely touching a stone
    they freed the sage's wife whose body that stone had become;
Those peerless feet—in their compassion to Prahlād
    they rescued him from the terror of having an enemy father;
Those peerless feet—they caused the women of Braj

to give up body and soul, forgetting husbands, sons, and homes;
Those peerless feet—through Vrindavan they themselves wandered,
settling on the cobra's head, killing countless foes.
Those peerless feet—they approached the Kauravas' house
and made themselves messengers, saving the fate of us all.
These peerless feet—these joyful feet, says Sūr—
let them steal away our pain, our threefold suffering.

This poem contains what is for the Amar Singh *Sūrsāgar* an uncharacteristically broad array of episodes (Hawley 2018: 248, Fig. 7.21, and 294–303). We do have childhood *līlās* (episodes, sports, *gestes*) such as the moment where Kṛṣṇa pries apart the beaks of the heron demon that Kamsa has sent against him or the time when he dances on the head of Kāliya the snake, but the range is much wider. We see the dramatic moment when Viṣṇu as Narasiṃha comes to the rescue of his youthful devotee Prahlād, and we see how Kṛṣṇa joins the assembly of the Pāṇḍava brothers just before the great Bhārata war begins. There are other episodes too. Each of those vignettes is introduced from the perspective of the feet of Kṛṣṇa/Viṣṇu. "Those peerless feet"—*e pad padam*, as the poem says in verse after verse—are the devotee's point of access. Hence that is where the poet himself is poised as the painter gives visual life to the text. Sūrdās is shown offering his obeisances to the feet of Rādhā and Kṛṣṇa (or Lakṣmī and Viṣṇu, if you prefer) even if the feet themselves are invisible beneath their lower garments. We can already see on the manuscript's first page that Sūrdās is an icon of *bhakti*.

For the artist of the Amar Singh *Sūrsāgar* this is an unusual depiction of the poet. Rather than being placed in a distinct space of his own, he enters the central arena of the poem; he is directly attentive to the divinities who appear before him. He is thus made to be an actor in the visual poem, as befits his first-person representation in the oral or written version. There his personal name appears at the end—in his signature (*bhaṇitā*) or seal (*chāp*)—but his first-person identity is announced at the very outset. Hence it is appropriate for him to appear at the upper left, the typical point of beginning for the "reading" of a visual image, just as it is the point of beginning for a text written in Devanāgarī, as this one is. His presence is iconic. It will be repeated more or less as such on every successive page—normally in one of the bottom corners, unlike here. We note the poet's hat with its peacock feather, suggesting Kṛṣṇa. We note his orange or saffron *dhotī*—elsewhere the color may range to a purer yellow. We note his array of *tulsī* beads. His *dupattā* is exceptional—it appears only here, a gesture to the royal scene—but even so, being diaphanous, it is not allowed to obscure the torso below, bare above the waist. This is a standard feature of what we will see on each succeeding page.

We note that he has a bit of a beard, a five-o'clock shadow, something for which modern images of Sūrdās leave us unprepared. This is no reference to the time of day, of course, but could it hint at the fact that it is not always easy for a blind person to stay clean-shaven? Or perhaps this suggestion of a beard is meant to group our great Brajbhasha poet with a broad range of other saintly males—pointedly, both Hindus and Muslims? His cap also seems to strike a capacious note: again, both Muslims and Hindus wear such attire. Finally, we have the poet's blindness, which was clearly a matter of shared perception by the time this image was made. The idea of Sūr's being blind from birth—a Vallabhite perception, to be sure, but shared by many others—is one that never emerges from his own poetry. In fact, if we judge by the dated manuscripts that give us a view of how Sūrdās seemed in his own time, there is no clear reference to physical blindness at all (Hawley 2018: 22–36). Yet we clearly see that by the beginning of the eighteenth century in Udaipur Sūrdās was considered distinctively and indisputably blind. That is the major key to the meaning of his icon. Absent mortal sight, he nonetheless sees what so many of us are blind to—the divine presence that infuses our very midst.

Page 11 of the Amar Singh manuscript displays this very clearly (Hawley 2018: 291; 2019: 35). Here the poet "watches" the infant Kṛṣṇa walk, which makes him figuratively one of the Braj women—Yaśodā supporting Kṛṣṇa from behind, other women eager to receive him up front. It is hardly incidental that Sūr is shown here as a musician, even if not the sort we typically see on the internet. His instrument at Mewar is not the one-stringed *ektār* or the pair of clackers (*khaḍtāl*) we associate with wandering mendicant singers. Rather, he is at home in a group setting; one can even think of him as being at court, as these impressive buildings may suggest. The sound he produces with his little hand-cymbals (*manjīrā*, *majīrā*) is the sort that would typically be heard in an ensemble, as so often when *bhajan*s are communally sung. In the images we have seen from Mewar, of course, Sūr accompanies his own voice—the voice that produces the poem coming to life on the page. But his *manjīrā*s also anticipate an ensemble, a *satsaṅga*, even if we viewers are the ones who must provide it. Indeed, this is just the invitation Sūr issues. We are meant to join the world being painted and sung—to recognize that we are a part of it already. The poet's mouth is always closed; ours are meant to open.

We see all these same features again in the painting that appears at the end of the manuscript (page 50). The theme is once again the feet, hence this closing poem functions as the second bookend (Hawley 2018: 254; 2019: 28):

Hari—how I love, love my little Mādhav.
He clambers over a threshold and tumbles, tumbles,
    but grasps with his lotus-petal palm and crawls on.

He has come to Yaśodā on account of love
  and placed his feet upon this earth, the ground—
The feet that he used to outwit King Bali,
  the feet from which the Ganges flowed
    as the merest sweat from beneath the toenails,
The feet whose visage captivated Brahmā and the gods,
  generating millions of moons and suns:
Those feet, says Sūrdās, inspired me to offer,
  offer,
    offer up my all.

Once again the message conveyed by the motif of the feet is clear. We have a pointed contrast between the most remote realm and the most accessible. Compare the foot at the top—the one that vaults the three registers of the entire universe—to the one that appears at the center of the painting. The former shows us the steps that Vāmana, the dwarf-Viṣṇu, asked King Bali to grant him in the *trivikrama* story—and the shocking cosmic results they soon achieved. That foot breaks through to heaven and is the recipient of offerings from Brahmā, on behalf of the gods. As for the latter—the feet in the middle of the painting—they belong to a child who manages to vault but a single tiny step. It leads up to the house in which he was raised. This is Kṛṣṇa learning to walk, and he needs his mommy's hand to be able to execute that challenging next step. This time it is she who leans toward him, not the gods. The contrast between gods and mother, heavens and home, comes out even more clearly in the painting than it does in the poem it portrays. Once again the poet makes his offering, just as he does in the first poem in the set, but this time he does so not in the first verse but in the last. The person who designed the Amar Singh *Sūrsāgar* thus gives us a beginning's beginning to start with and an ending's ending to finish. As for the poet who makes this mental bow, he is granted a little pavilion of his own, appropriate to the status of his signature in the poem: it occupies its own space while nonetheless participating in the whole. This, along with the pose, appears frequently throughout the sequence.

On every page of the set—at least the pages that are extant—this iconic Sūrdās appears, always looking pretty much the same. On page 4, for example (Hawley 2018: 273), he sings of how all the neighbors gathered to celebrate the birth of a son—a divine son, though they could scarcely know. We see Sūr in the lower left-hand corner. The poet is shown on every other page as well, though his position may vary according to the theme. He is there not just to record his oral signature but to teach us the kind of vision we all ought to have. His poetry is the lens that makes it possible for us to see the divine childhood. We typically speak of this as an inner vision—something we have to cultivate within. But here that affirmation is turned inside out. The poet, as he sings, sees beyond what he sees. The painter shows us the reality that is actually there in the world that surrounds us—often very close, at domestic range. If only we had the eyes to see! If only we could become blind enough to the world that we could see what lies at its core! Having the poetry painted helps us do so.

Why did this revolutionary affirmation about transcendent childhood get pictured in Udaipur around 1700? The fact is striking. Of the several Sūrdās paintings that clearly preceded the Amar Singh *Sūrsāgar* explosion, only one depicts Kṛṣṇa as a child (Hawley 2018: 212), so why do we have this dramatic narrowing to the ambience of childhood in the time of Amar Singh? Molly Aitken has made the intriguing suggestion that it may have had to do with women—the women of the Mewar palace scene. Perhaps our Amar Singh *Sūrsāgar* was especially intended to be performed in the *zanana*, that special area cordoned off from the rest of the palace complex. This may have been so—certainly there are plenty of women in these paintings—but I haven't yet been able to identify any architectural feature that bears the unique mark of Udaipur's Zanana Mahal. The general Udaipur palace, yes: the *jharokhā* window with the triple spires at the upper left of the Manohar painting is a good example. But not the Zanana Mahal as such.

An alternate hypothesis about why we encounter a sudden fascination with the child Kṛṣṇa in the Amar Singh *Sūrsāgar* would surely bring in the Puṣṭimārg—the Vallabha *sampradāya*, in other words. The Vallabhites received patronage from the Maharana of Mewar as they settled into nearby Kankarauli in 1671 and into the town that would later be called Nathdvara in 1672. The leaders of the Puṣṭimārg and the deities they served became beneficiaries of royal support, and this patronage intensified in later years. It was hardly exclusive, but it was real. Yet so far as I can see, there is nothing specifically Puṣṭimārgī about the Amar Singh *Sūrsāgar*, despite the fact that Vallabhites' sensibilities were also drawn to the mood of *vātsalya*, the special bond that exists between parent and child.

There is nothing to suggest that the classic Mewar Sūrdās bears the Vallabhite brand. Three paintings that do show a recognizably Vallabhite influence come on the scene at Udaipur only later, somewhat after Amar Singh's reign: the distinctive mustache has disappeared. These three paintings are recognizable as a group not only because of their focus on and depiction of Mount Govardhan, where the Puṣṭimārg's principal image was initially to be found in Braj, but because they illustrate poems bearing the "seals" of two specifically Vallabhite poets—Caturbhujdās and Chītsvāmī. Along with them

Figure 7.6 "They worship Mt. Govardhan with great liberality." Illustration to *govardhan pūjat param udār* (no *Paramānand-Sāgar* designation). *Rāg sārang*. Government Museum, Udaipur, numbering unknown, *c*. 1720.

we see a more senior poet, Paramānanddās, whom the Vallabhites also claimed as their own but after his own time; this is what they did for Sūrdās. These three paintings, taken as a group, show that there was indeed a time in Mewar when the Vallabhite impress was felt, but it didn't happen in the reign of Amar Singh, and apparently when it did occur it had a limited effect. Figure 7.6 shows the Paramānanddās example.

It is safe to say, then, that we see no Vallabhite influence on the patterning of Sūrdās at Udaipur. Udaipur's Sūrdās, like the poet himself, was not sectarian in this way. His orbit and influence were evidently much broader. A devotee of Kṛṣṇa he surely was, but a devotee of Vallabhācārya—no.

If this Udaipur Sūrdās had a distinguishing feature, it was not his sectarian affiliation but something else. The Amar Singh *Sūrsāgar* shows him as a poet of the court—a court musician. He hovers around the palace of Nanda and Yaśodā, and one cannot help thinking of Udaipur's own palaces when he does. He may have his own little pavilion, but a palace of this type is never far away. In that way the Mewar Surdas stands apart from the ambience of a temple—the environment to which the Vallabhite account of Sūrdās's life was eager to attach him. This becomes clear in the Sūrdās chapter of the *Caurāsī Vaiṣṇavan kī Vārtā* (Lives of 84 Vaishnavas), a Vallabhite text whose earliest manuscript seems to date to 1640 (V.S. 1697; see Hawley 2018: 7). The main temple to which reference is made there is indeed a specifically Vallabhite temple: the temple to Kṛṣṇa atop Mount Govardhan. But except for the Puṣṭimārg-influenced Paramānanddās painting we have just seen, where a temple appears in the vicinity of the mountain, the Govardhan depicted at Udaipur is in no way a temple but the mountain itself. And except in the three-painting Puṣṭimārgī group, it is always held aloft by the young Kṛṣṇa (e.g., Hawley 2018: 240–2, Figs. 7.17–18). The internet's meditative "Vallabhite" Sūr is even farther away from the Udaipur scene. He apparently developed on a track of his own.

The iconic Sūrdās who emerged in the late seventeenth century at the court of Mewar and assumed definitive form in the period of Amar Singh was not a sectarian figure (Figure 7.7). Nor was he attached to a temple mode. If anything, he has a touch of the courtly, but the air he breathes is freer than that. It reaches

Figure 7.7 Sūrdās, as he appears in the lower left-hand corner of the painting illustrating "Muralī has cast her spell on Krishna, our lad," *muralī mohe kuṅvar kanhāī* (Nāgarīpracāriṇi Sabhā 1272). *Rāg sārang*. Government Museum, Udaipur, 1097/26:27.

beyond the walls of royal buildings as if to encompass the somewhat humbler backgrounds of the artists who worked in the royal ateliers. He has a musical sensibility, to be sure, but not the solitary type symbolized by the single-stringed *ektār* we know so well from the Kalicharan Verma and Indra Sharma images; he doesn't perform in the forest. At Udaipur, Sūr's music seems to be envisioned instead as a thing to be shared with a group—the music of *bhajan* or *satsaṅga.* There's nothing solitary about those *manjīrās.* Were it not for his blindness, in fact, we'd be seeing in this Sūr a rather ordinary guy—middle-aged and neither portly nor spare. One of us. He's set apart, of course, given his own little pavilion so as not to disturb the scene that surrounds his mesmerizing Lord,

Figure 7.8 "Peacocks have mounted whatever peak they can." Illustration to *sīṣanī saṣaranī caḍ ṭer suṇāyo* (compare Bryant 226, *Nāgarīpracāriṇi Sabhā* 3946), *c.* 1660, 27.3 × 20.9 cm. Private collection, photograph © Christie's Images Ltd. 2012.

yet he connects to those of us who watch with him and sing along. He's the musician in us all, wanting to sing to God. The Sūrdās of Kalicharan Verma and Indra Sharma does that directly: the child Kṛṣṇa takes his seat directly across from his *ektār* and his open mouth. That was the genius that captivated so many modern viewers. Here, by contrast, we see the song, the whole poem. The poet emerges only within that frame—at its edge (Figure 7.8).

Doesn't he look familiar (Figure 1, https://spiritual-heritage-of-india.blogspot.com/2018/10/sant-soordas.html)? There's that elaborate string of *tulsī* beads, that red cap (though of a different shape), the left-facing profile, the positioning of his arms and legs. There are differences too, of course. The *dhotī* is yellow, not white, and the back arm rests not on the ground but on an ascetic's stick (*yogaḍaṇda*). Still, look at the other arm: it seems so convincingly the same. In a way better, in fact. The position of the poet's right hand is now justified by the fact that he fondles some *tulsī* beads. Somehow this Sūrdās, painted in Mewar in the mid-seventeenth century, has spawned an image of himself in the mid-twentieth century. The scene he surveys is not a childhood scene. Rather, it depicts the ravages of the monsoon when one's lover—one's Kṛṣṇa—is gone and one has to face that intimate time alone. The mood is sad, reflective, even threatened. No wonder the poet seems lost in contemplation.

This was before Sūr became the archetypal *vātsalya* poet; it's closer to the early corpus of Sūr's poetry as a whole. How did this image leap over the child-Kṛṣṇa poet and land in the twentieth century? That I cannot say. Perhaps an icon is owed a bit of mystery.

Notes

1 On the vagaries of copyright law and their utter contrast to traditional Indian practice in regard to the field we are surveying, see Hawley (forthcoming). For a certain period of time in 2019 and 2020, a third option joined the archetypes represented by Figures 7.1 and 7.2. There one saw Sūrdās accompanied by two figures in Mughal dress—the Mughal emperor Akbar and his favorite musician Tānsen and labelled "Hindu Saint-Poet Sant Surdas." This was a Sūr who seemed to belong to history, yet the difficulty was that this historical Sūr was actually not Sūrdās but Tānsen's reputed musical guru, Haridās. Some eager internet adept had made a mistake—or posted there one that came before.

2 Probably not, however, in historical fact. Though blindness may have overtaken him late in life, there is no clear evidence of it in poems that circulated in Sūr's name in the sixteenth century (Hawley 2018: 3–36).

3 The exact source for this particular image, including the written information it bears, is as yet unknown, but it is patterned very closely after an image that seems first to appear in a print context on the cover of and inside Prabhudayāl Mītal's *Sūr-Sārāvalī* (1957); that, in turn, seems to reproduce a painting that is archived in museum-style white-ink letters on the painting itself. The number involved—4.14/51—suggests it was acquired in 1948 (further, see Hawley forthcoming).

4 On these points I had discussion with Richard H. Davis (email communication January 8, 2021), M. L. Garg (interview with Sushant Bharti on August 3 and 14, 2021), and N. Sharma (email communication January 7, 2021).

5 This image is available at http://www.govindadasi.com/more-artwork.html and in Govinda dasi's *Srila Prabhupada, the Classical Art Master*, p. 78, at http://www.govindadasi.com/. I am grateful to Priyasakhi Barchi for calling this image to my attention (Barchi 2017).

6 For this information and what follows, I am deeply indebted to M. L. Garg, and as well to Sushant Bharti, who interviewed him on my behalf at the Brijbasi offices in Noida on August 3 and 14, 2021. On Kalicharan's arrival in Kanpur as a boy about twelve years old, son of a blacksmith, see Pinney 2004: 131. Brijbasi & Sons acquired some ten to twelve of Kalicharan's paintings in the course of the 1950s. It was at least in part to locate and acquire paintings such as these that M. L. Garg's father undertook the trip in which Garg himself participated as a teenage boy.

7 https://imcradiodotnet.wordpress.com/2010/11/16/raga-cds-of-the-months-1110-kalpita-sangita-compositions-in-indian-classics/, which is listed as having been posted to the internet by Eljay Arem of IMC OnAir on November 16, 2010. I am grateful to Karen Pechilis for directing me to this website (email communication July 15, 2021). Further, see Hawley (forthcoming).

8 Garg, interview with Sushant Bharti, August 14, 2021.

9 For details, see Hawley (forthcoming).

10 The motif of Sūr singing to the child Kṛṣṇa is the visual frame for episode 19 of *Upaniṣad Gangā*, concerning the first eight of the "classic" sixteen life-cycle rituals (*ṣodaśa saṃskāra*; Dwivedi 2012). At minute 37.42 one sees a "live" version of the Kalicharan image: https://www.youtube.com/watch?v=jG3Q9hCeMco. The frame story is provided by the tale of Sūrdās's meeting Vallabhācārya and being initiated by him. This is now interpreted as a divine response to the fact that being blind, Sūr's parents did not judge him capable of receiving the sacred thread in a normal *upanāyaṇa* ceremony in the course of his own youth. I am indebted to Sushant Bharti (2021) for making the connection between Kalicharan's image and Chandra Prakash Dwivedi's Doordarshan script.

11 In the edition prepared by Kenneth Bryant and published in Bryant and Hawley (2015), 433 poems appear. An additional one was inadvertently omitted.

12 The term *vātsalya*, frequently associated with Sūrdās both in scholarly and in popular literature, designates the emotions that arise in relationships between parents and children, paradigmatically between a mother and a son and more often from the parent's side than from the child's.

13 These are the manuscripts Kenneth Bryant and I have denoted J4, written in 1650 (V.S. 1706) at Chatsu, near what would be Jaipur, and A1, whose location is unspecified but whose date is given as V.S. 1743 (1686 CE). See Bryant and Hawley (2015: xliv–xlviii).

14 It is regrettable that the current whereabouts of the manuscript's final page (50) is not known. We therefore have no record of its verso side. It is conceivable, though not likely, that the patron's name and the manuscript's date may have been recorded there.

15 I have followed this practice in the revised and enlarged edition of *Sūrdās: Poet, Singer, Saint*, Chapter 7.

References

Bachrach, E. (2020), *In the Service of Krishna: Illustrating the Lives of Eighty-Four Vaishnavas from a 1702 Manuscript*, Ahmedabad: Mapin Publishing.

Bae, J. C., and I. Sharma (2001), *In a World of Gods and Goddesses: The Mystic Art of Indra Sharma*, San Rafael: Mandala.

Bahadur, K. P. (1999), *The Poems of Sūradāsa*, Delhi: Abhinav Publications.

Barchi, P. (2017), "Neo-Vedic Krishna: Fusion of Tradition and Innovation," Unpublished paper, Barnard College/Columbia University.

Benjamin, W. (1968), "The Work of Art in the Age of Mechanical Reproduction," in *Illuminations*, trans. H. Zohn, 219–54, New York: Harcourt, Brace & World. Originally "Das Kunstwerk im Zeitalter seiner technischen Reproduzierbarkeit," 1935.

Bharti, S. (2021), Zoom communication, August 16.

Bhāṭī, D. (1977), *Sūrdās aur unkā Sāhitya*, 2nd ed., Agra: Vinod Pustak Mandir.

Bryant, K. E., and J. S. Hawley (2015), *Sur's Ocean: Poems from the Early Tradition*, Cambridge, MA: Harvard University Press.

Davis, R. H. (2012), *Gods in Print: Masterpieces of India's Mythological Art*, San Rafael: Mandala Publishing.

Dwivedi, C. (2012), *Upaniṣad Gangā*, episode 19, part 1: ṣodaśa saṃskāra, "The 16 Milestones," Delhi: Doordarshan.

Ghose, M. (2015), *Gates of the Lord: The Tradition of Krishna Paintings*, Chicago: Art Institute of Chicago, distributed by Yale University Press.

Hawley, J. S. (1988), "Author and Authority in the *Bhakti* Poetry of North India," *The Journal of Asian Studies* 47 (2): 269–90.

Hawley, J. S. (2018), *Sūrdās: Poet, Singer, Saint*, revised and enlarged ed., Delhi: Primus Books.

Hawley, J. S. (2019), "When Blindness Makes for Sight," in M. Burger and N. Cattoni (eds.), *Early Modern India: Literatures and Images, Texts and Languages*, 19–38, Heidelberg: CrossAsia-eBooks.

Hawley, J. S. (forthcoming), "Poetic Selfhood and the Copyright Raj," in M. Horstmann, H. Nagasaki, K. Okita, and H. Pauwels (eds.), *Proceedings of the 14th International Conference on Early Modern Literatures of North India*, Heidelberg: CrossAsia.

Mītal, P. (1957), *Sūr-Sārāvalī*, Mathura: Agravāl Press.

Mītal, P. (1982), *Sūrsāgar-Setu*, Mathura: Sāhitya Sansthān.

Pinney, C. (2004), *Photos of the Gods: The Printed Image and Political Struggle in India*, Delhi: Oxford University Press.

8

The Visual Multiplicity and Materiality of Guru Nityānanda's Portraits

Amy-Ruth Holt

A small Hindu temple opened in Columbus (Delaware), Ohio, in 2007 called the "Nithyananda Vedic Temple." It was dedicated to the guru Paramahaṃsa Nityānanda from Bangalore (Bidadi), India, who had recently won worldwide recognition for his courses in Life Bliss Meditation and Nithya Yoga in southern India and abroad. During my initial tour of the temple (a remodeled country home), the local Indian manager proudly explained to me how Nityānanda (literally "Eternal Bliss")[1] had finalized the carving of the faces of the black stone sculptures in worship here and had come to the temple on April 14, 2007, shortly before my visit, to inaugurate them. I noticed at this time that many of these god sculptures had the same distinctive oval face and square jawline as Nityānanda, possibly suggesting they were meant to be divine self-portraits of the guru (Figure 8.1). While no one at the temple was able to confirm my suspicions of Nityānanda's hidden identity in these sculptures, additional verification came with the names of the main deities being labelled as "Anandeshwara-Anandeshwari," "Ananda Ganesh," and "Ananda Murugan." These names, like those taken by his initiated devotees, purposefully draw a connection to that of the guru's own name. More than a decade later, another avenue for uncovering the identity of these god sculptures arises with Nityānanda's online videos called "Oneness Capsules." In these videos, he demonstrates his visual and material connection to these figures by dressing as deities and blessing viewers with shooting *maṇḍala* diagrams and puffs of sparkling glitter that appear to originate from his form.

Historically, the well-noted multiplicity of the visual image has the ability to encapsulate all the various symbolic dimensions between the individual and the divine in Indic art (Huntington 1992; Kaimal 1994; Rabe 1997; Copeman and Ikagame 2012: 38; Willis 2014). Scholars of modernity have noted that the visual dominates in the current era, often conferring evidence for spirituality beyond the literary tradition to include the modern mediums of film, television, and

Figure 8.1 Ānandeśvara-Ānandeśvarī (Śiva and Pārvatī as Nityānanda), Nithyananda Vedic Temple, Columbus (Delaware), Ohio. Photograph Amy-Ruth Holt.

the internet (Benjamin 1968; Levin 1993; Ramaswamy 2003; Meyer 2009; Holt and Pechilis 2019). In this regard, Nityānanda specifically has taken advantage of the power of contemporary visual culture to promote his own particular form of guru *bhakti*. Following in the guru scholarship of Jacob Copeman and Aya Ikegame, who define "guru-ship" as "conceptual modelling tools for other forms of social phenomena" (2012: 1), I would say that Nityānanda uses his visually focused brand of guru *bhakti* as a tool to blend the boundaries between materiality and immateriality. He accomplishes this through his prevalent use of his own image in various forms—from temple sculptures, guru "cut-outs," tantric diagrams, and yogic meditations to his numerous internet broadcasts—that proactively rematerialize his visual form over and over again as evidence of his (and potentially everyone's) divine immateriality in all things.

Portraits of royal and historical figures as gods and goddesses may have a very long history in Indian art, but the methodology for identifying such images largely has been contingent upon the finding of written inscriptions in conjunction with these images due to their frequent generic appearance, where often the distinction between the images of deities and humans is very slight, if at all (Coomaraswamy 1939; Dehejia 1998; Willis 2014). For example, the popular Chola queen Sembiyan Mahādevī's possible portrait sculpture, now housed in the Freer Gallery of Art in Washington, D.C., shows a goddess-like standing female figure that mainly is considered as a portrait of her from the finding of later inscriptions stating that such portraits were made of her as a goddess for local festivals (Dehejia 1990 and 1998; Balasubrahmanyam 1971: 182). Portraits of important royal devotees or saints also may take on part of the iconography of a god such as in the case of the Chola king Rājarāja I, who wore the dreadlocks of the god Śiva as shown in his painted portraits at Thanjavur along with his Chidambaram guru, Karuvūr Tēvar; while bronze images of the Nāyaṉmār saint Sambandar show him in the well-known dancing posture of the child-god Kṛṣṇa to possibly reference his youth and sung poetry (Dehejia 1998: 42–50). Due to the similarity between divinities and human likenesses, images of Sambandar, as Vidya Dehejia further notes, often are mistaken for images of Kṛṣṇa in Indic collections. Nityānanda's unusual appearance as divinities at his U.S. temples suggests a similar blurring or hidden nature to his appearance typical of the use of *śleṣa* or visual metaphors that are used to explain the multiple meanings found within a singular work of art (Huntington 1992; Kaimal 1994; Rabe 1997).

In my discussions and interactions with devotees at U.S. Nityānanda temples, I discovered that most devotees do not recognize Nityānanda's temple god sculptures as approximating his likeness, even though Nityānanda himself claims to be a living, incarnated God. Often devotees describe his divine essence or "cosmic energy" as working through and filling up the temple images of gods, rather than the sculptures being reflective of his external physical attributes (Nithyananda 2007a: 8). Such statements echo the common adage of the Sanskrit treatise on art of Śukrācārya's *Śukranītiśāra* that "praises the making of deities and condemns the portrayal of human likenesses as 'not heaven leading'" (Coomaraswamy 1939: 74; Kaimal 1995: 10). Another obstacle for the identification of these god images as guru portraits is that there does not exist in either Tamil or Sanskrit a term for portraiture (Kaimal 1999: 60), and certainly not for self-portraiture, since traditionally artists were anonymous craftsmen whose authorship was rarely noted. Regardless of these linguistic obstacles, my study into Nityānanda's portrayal of himself as Hindu divinities suggests there is a visual primacy in his contemporary devotion similar to that uncovered in the Svāminārāyaṇa and Puṣṭi Mārga traditions discussed in this volume. While Nityānanda devotees were uncertain about the exact appearance of their temple deities, their common responses on the significance of the shared immateriality or cosmic energy between all things and the guru were actually a wayward affirmative answer in itself that became clearer to me over time.

The Foundations of Nityānanda's Immateriality

To begin with, Nityānanda did not invent his philosophy of materiality all on his own. As in other Hindu traditions, the creation of new ideologies often is based upon older religious traditions that take on an "aggregated" or a "neo-traditionalist" form, and Nityānanda's philosophy is no different in this regard (Singer 1972; Weiss 2005; Bate 2009; Flueckiger 2015; Holt and Pechilis 2019). His belief system, while claiming to be the true Vedic tradition like other known guru traditions today (*Sarvajnapeetha* 4), builds heavily upon medieval Śaiva Siddhānta temple culture and its frequent overlap with the later non-dualist philosophy of Advaita Vedānta (Copeman and Akegame 2012: 17; Burchett 2019: 41–57). For instance, at the Naṭarāja temple in Chidambaram today there appears a seamless blending of Śaiva duality and Vedānta non-dualism with the five main deities of the *cit sābha* (main temple), representative of the fivefold division of the tantric Sadāśiva (Supreme Śiva), being worshipped as equivalent to the famous *Cidambara Rahaśya*, a Śrī Chakra-based diagram of the all-inclusive cosmos (Holt 2007). Nityānanda, in a similar manner, often redefines dualist terminology as non-dualist. He gives a non-dualist interpretation for the Śaiva Siddhānta term of the *jīvan mukta*, or the evolved person, as one who is "living enlightenment" while simultaneously using the term *śakti*,

Figure 8.2 Portrait *mūlvar* or "main deity" of Nityānanda (left) with Mt. Meru (center) and goddess Ānandeśvarī *vigraha* (right), Nithyananda Vedic Temple, Columbus (Delaware), Ohio. Photograph Amy-Ruth Holt.

commonly referred to as "cosmic energy," to explain the unity of the gods and all living things (Nithyananda 2006: 150). This extension of non-dualism onto traditionally dual imagery continues at his temples today with the installation of the Mt. Meru image, a three-dimensional *yantra* diagram, as the divine union of all the individual god sculptures present in the temple (Figure 8.2).

One of Nityānanda's most telling influences for his non-dualist beliefs are those associated with his appreciation and understanding of temple imagery from his hometown of Tiruvannamalai, Tamil Nadu, where the famous ninth–sixteenth century Śiva Aruṇāchaleśvara temple is found along with the *maṭha* of guru Ramaṇa Maharṣi. Today the spread of Advaita Vedānta outside India is thought to be largely the result of guru Ramaṇa Maharṣi's influence (Forsthoefel 2005: 51). Nityānanda's emphasis on temple imagery and practice in his philosophy reflects a large part of Ramaṇa Maharṣi's discourse, where Maharṣi told stories involving the agency of temple images to move and act miraculously. Hearing of one such occasion involving the elephant-headed deity Gaṇeśa, as described in his biography, the child Nityānanda took it upon himself to fast until his own image of this deity ate his food offering (Nithyananda 2006: 45–7 and 2007b: 88–90). Later on, Nityānanda went to study at the Ramaṇa Maharṣi *maṭha* with a later disciple of Maharṣi's, Aṉṉāmalai Svāmīkal, before becoming a wandering *sannyāsī* at the tender age of seventeen (Nithyananda 2007b: 171–84). Now Maharṣi's understanding of temple imagery is reflected in

Table 8.1. Nityānanda's Life Bliss Mediation

Chakras	Bodily Location	Emotion	Deity
Mūlādhāra chakra	Spine base	Sexual desire	Gaṇeśa
Svādhiṣṭhāna chakra	Lower torso	Fear	Murugaṉ
Maṇipūraka chakra	Navel	Worry	Sūrya
Anāhata chakra	Heart	Love	Viṣṇu Veṅkaṭeśvara
Viśuddhī chakra	Throat	Jealousy	Lakṣmī-Ambal
Ājñā chakra	Third-eye	Ego	Śiva Ānandeśvara
Sahasrāra chakra	Top of head	Gratitude	Guru-Dakṣiṇāmūrti

Nityānanda's philosophy of how deity images are the materializations of the divine that are filled with the immaterial cosmic energy of the guru during their installation or *prāṇapratiṣṭhā* (Nithyananda 2007c: 8–9; *Sarvajnapeetha* 6).[2]

In order to become an "enlightened-living person," or what he calls a *jīvan mukta*, Nityānanda says that the individual must practice his Life Bliss Meditation to remove all the "*saṃsāras* or *engrams*—memories that have engraved themselves upon us which compel us to behave in negative ways" (Nithyananda 2011b: 87). He describes the immaterial, subtle yogic body as having seven *chakra* points (or energy centers) from the base of the spine to the top of the head (*mūlādhāra* at the spine base, *svādhiṣṭhāna* at the lower torso, *maṇipūraka* at the navel, *anāhata* at the heart, *viśuddhī* at the throat, *ājñā* at the third-eye, and *sahasrāra* at the top of head) that are opened with the release of particular emotions (sexual desire, fear, worry, love, jealousy, ego, and gratitude respectively), which block the movement of cosmic energy as *kuṇḍalinī śakti* in the body (Table 8.1; Nithayananda 2008b). When each is opened, the individual unites with the deity that resides over each *chakra*. Gaṇeśa is at the spine base, Murugaṉ is at the lower torso, Sūrya is at the navel, Viṣṇu Veṅkaṭeśvara is at the heart, the goddess Lakṣmī-Ambal is at the throat, Śiva Ānandeśvara is at the third-eye, and guru Nityānanda or Śiva Dakṣiṇāmūrti is at the top of head, as the place where the individual reaches enlightenment.

To some extent, Nityānanda's temple images and their accompanying *pūjā*s are organized to allow the worship of each deity to occur in the same order they are represented in the *chakra*s of the practitioner, although not all Nityānanda temples have each of these deities so exceptions are made. For instance, the Ohio Nityānanda temple has no image of Sūrya (usually found within the *navagraha*s or nine planets) so the volunteer-priest goes outside to offer the *prasāda* to the sun; and instead of a singular image of Viṣṇu Veṅkaṭeśvara, the temple holds a separate chamber called by devotees as the "Viṣṇu Room" with images of Rāma, Kṛṣṇa, their attendants and consorts, and a central image of the guru Śirdi Sai Baba

Figure 8.3 Viṣṇu Room with Śirdi Sai Baba (center), Kṛṣṇa and Rādhā (right), Rāma, Sītā, Lakṣmana, and small Hanumān (left) in the Nithyananda Vedic Temple, Columbus (Delaware), Ohio. Photograph Amy-Ruth Holt.

(Figure 8.3). When a certain deity's *pūjā* is performed, the volunteer-priest may point out the *chakra* point associated with that deity and instruct devotees to focus on its emotional and spiritual release.[3] Nityānanda also encourages his followers to prepare their bodies for the alchemic changes of enlightenment by practicing his Nithya Yoga, which traditionally involves 108 *āsana*s that are to be practiced with accompanying *mantra*s and visualized deities before a copper plate of a Śrī Chakra placed at the top of their yoga mat (Nithyananda 2008d; *Sarvajnapeetha* 20–1).[4]

Nityānanda's *jīvan mukti* derives from the traditional understanding of the tantric *siddha* as "the living person who has attained life's final goal" of enlightenment and may demonstrate a variety of psychic powers (Gold 1995: 232–3; Babb 1987: 181). The history of religion scholar Patton Burchett (2019: 29–64) notes that orthodox Tantra tradition and *siddhi* magic have frequently gone together. Itinerant *siddha yogi*s offered healing and other magical feats of entertainment to the villages they passed through in ways that were beneficial to locals and were a recognized part of the tradition that added legitimacy to orthodox practice as significant "social acts" (Davis 1998: 9–11). *Siddha yogi*s like Nityānanda commonly envision all worldly materiality as reflective of "concentrated spiritual energy" like that found in their own bodies that they have learned to control (Gold 1995: 233; Williamson 2010: 158). Nityānanda's tantric abilities include a seated, hopping-like levitation during his *satsaṅgas*, where his vision (*darśan*) starts a rhythmic pulsating in the body of the devotee, causing them to periodically rise up off the ground (Nithyananda 2011b: 41, 59).[5] Other practices of his include teaching women how to have painless childbirths, healing, object transmigration, alchemy, metallurgy, and attempts to use cosmic energy to power aircraft, submarines, and batteries (Nithyananda 2008c; *Sarvajnapeetha* 22–3, 27). Similar to other modern *siddha* traditions, Nityānanda claims that these events are not miracles but the result of an ancient yoga-inflected science no longer understood (Nithyananda 2006: 196). This understanding of *siddha* abilities and the yogic body—dependent upon Nityānanda's immaterial divine-being—also applies to his materialized art forms and onscreen persona.

A Self-Materializing Divinity: God Sculptures and Guru Portraits

One of Nityānanda's earliest *siddha*-like abilities was his creative manifestation of divine images. At a young age, while other children played with toys and dolls, Nityānanda started making his own images of temple deities from the clay left behind by the Gaṇeśa *pūjā* potters each year (Nithyananda 2007b: 92). He sculpted five small deities, Gaṇeśa, Pārvatī, Lakṣmī (Ambal), Mt. Meru, and the *liṅga* on a *yoni* pedestal, as well as a number of other *pūjā* items and tiny decorative attributes for the deities that he carried with him everywhere (Nithyananda 2007a: 8).[6] When he was twelve years old, Nityānanda had a golden vision of the goddess Pārvatī from the Aruṇāchaleśvara temple at Tiruvannamalai that caused him to run home and carve the complicated design of the Śrī Chakra on a small copper sheet with a nail, completely astonishing people with his sudden mastery of its difficult form (Nithyananda 2007a: 9). He also sculpted the goddess Parāśakti in soapstone (Nithyananda 2007a: 7), and he was described in these creative moments as having energy and power far beyond his years (Nithyananda 2007b: 92). Now his followers see his finalizing of the faces of the divinities at his Ohio temple as a continuation of his divine artistic talents first discovered in his childhood.

Nityānanda's implied self-portraiture as deities at Ohio must be contextualized with his meditational-based understanding of non-duality. While the art historian Padma Kaimal (1995: 8) has demonstrated from early Tamil inscriptions on portrait images that the "sculptural representation is equated with the Self [*ātman*, or individual soul] of the subject" as a type of direct manifestation of the individual into art,[7] Nityānanda explains this melding of the individual self and the divine in art, by asking, "the idol before you is cast in the same form as yours, and yet it is divine, what does that say about you? . . . Creation itself is a creator" (Nithyananda 2011a: 84 and 2006: 51). By recognizing the same immaterial cosmic energy in temple deities as in the individual self, Nityānanda understands his sculptures as images of himself and the divine that collapse the presumed distinction of the artist and the divine object (*ātman* and *Brahman*) or what the tantric scholar Heinrich Zimmer saw as "the perceiver and perceived" (1989: 27).[8] Divine universality, or multiplicity, as it is conveyed through art, aptly converges all of these categories for Nityānanda's self-portraits into one materialized form.

Another means by which Nityānanda expresses his non-duality with his god-temple images is through the concept of visual agency or where objects are given the ability to act on others (Gell 1998). Devotees commonly tell stories about certain miraculous moments when they believed that Nityānanda himself was working directly through these images. One such story at the Los Angeles (Montclaire) Nityānanda temple tells of how the six-foot tall stone *mūrti* of Viṣṇu Veṅkaṭeśvara was brought through the very low double doors of a remodeled theater room. Witnesses claim that as they were carrying the massive sculpture it became clear that the sculpture would not fit through the doorway of the sanctum. Nityānanda was asked to intervene by telephone, and he instructed the devotees to chant his name. Doing this, the devotees were astonished to find that the sculpture shrank and the doorway got bigger, allowing the sculpture to be brought into the room. From such stories, it became evident to me that devotees recognize Nityānanda's god sculptures as extensions of himself and his immaterial cosmic energy that have the power to act as his divine self. Even when these are images made by outside artisans or not commonly seen as looking like him, devotees still cite stories of these temple images as demonstrations of Nityānanda's power.

All of Nityānanda's temples in India and abroad have a large central black stone *mūrti* known as Ānandeśvara-Ānandeśvarī or "Bliss Lord and Bliss Goddess" of the god Śiva with the goddess Pārvatī, lovingly seated on his lap (see Figure 8.1). The first image of this kind was installed at Nityānanda's ashram temple in Bangalore on January 1, 2007, to coincide with the guru's birthday, and the Ohio temple's image was ritually installed by the guru a few months later, becoming the first of his diaspora temples. According to Nityānanda, the posture of the goddess seated on Śiva's lap represents the scene when Śiva instructs Pārvatī in the *Vijñāna Bhairava Tantra* that includes a number of specific *tantra*s based around the union of Śiva and the goddess (Nithyananda 2007c: 11–12). Throughout northern India and parts of southern India, it is common to find depictions of the goddess Lakṣmī seated on the lap of Viṣṇu (or their incarnations) such as at Bhadrachalam, Telangana, and an example of a similar posture with Śiva and Pārvatī is found at Ellora, Maharashtra, from the late eighth century that shows them as a sacred *mithuna* or loving couple (Huntington 1985: 348).[9] A form of Śiva alike in concept to Nityānanda's Ānandeśvara-Ānandeśvarī is Śiva Ardhanārīśvara ("Half-Woman Lord"), whose body contains the goddess on his left side (Kramrisch 1981: 199–206).

In the Nityānanda temple program, Ānandeśvara-Ānandeśvarī (or Śiva Ānandeśvara) represents the center of the cosmos also known as the *bindu* in the center of tantric *maṇḍalas* or the *ājñā chakra* found on the forehead between the eyes (see Table 8.1). Nityānanda describes its unique dual-gender identity, in the following way:

> An important truth we need to understand is that a man is not 100% man and a woman is not 100% woman. A man is 51% man and 49% woman. Similarly, a woman is 51% woman and 49% man. To experience fulfillment, we need to be able to accept and express both the masculine and feminine aspects of our nature. (Nithyananda 2008b: 41)

If the Ānandeśvara-Ānandeśvarī image is meant to be a dual male and female portrait of Nityānanda, as I believe it is, its iconography further goes to show Nityānanda as the progenitor of his entire system of meditation and serial self-materialization. Nityānanda encourages his devotees to envision this same divine form within themselves through his Life Bliss Meditation, and all the black stone *mūrtis* in the Ohio temple of which Nityānanda appears similar to and is said to have carved the faces represent different chakra-bound deities from his meditation practice.

In addition to this main image of Śiva and Pārvatī, Nityānanda's U.S. temples contain a variety of images that differ between locales based upon the preference of donor-devotees and the availability of imagery for particular temples. Many U.S. devotees were actually devotees of other specific gods or gurus that have now been brought into the diaspora Nityānanda temple as evidenced by the unusual Viṣṇu Room at the Ohio temple (see Figure 8.3). Even though the donor of the Ohio temple was originally a devotee of the guru Śirdi Sai Baba—the marble-like images found in her Viṣṇu Room being gifts from Nityānanda made in northern India—today, she claims, "Whatever god or guru I see, now I only see Nityānanda. He is everywhere." Since many of Nityānanda's devotees are of Tamil origin, deities such as Murugaṉ with his two wives from the *aṛupaṭai vēṭu*s (six battleground shrines) in Tamil Nadu (Figure 8.4), Mīnāṭcī, the "fish-eyed" goddess from Madurai, and Viṣṇu Veṅkaṭeśvara (who is also known as "Bālājī") from Tirupati, Andhra Pradesh, are often central figures in Nityānanda temples.

Figure 8.4 Murugaṉ and his two wives, Nithyananda Vedic Temple, Columbus (Delaware). Photograph Amy-Ruth Holt.

The image of Lakṣmī in the San Jose Nityānanda temple also appears in the form of the southern saint Āṇṭāḷ with her characteristic hairstyle that falls to the side,[10] and the Mīnāṭcī image here has the special honor of being carved completely by Nityānanda himself. These traditional black stone *mūrti*s of popular Tamil gods reflect not only Nityānanda's appearance and meditational practices associated with certain *chakra*s but also the past worship traditions of a number of his followers that he has brought under the umbrella of his divine form.

Other than the stone *mūrti*s of Nityānanda temples, there exist actual guru portraits of Nityānanda that are worshipped with these images of the gods and goddesses.[11] The most common manner in which gurus are adored is through the use of "cut-outs" or printed images of the guru taken from photographs that are blown up to life-size and backed with cardboard to stand upright. At Ohio, this type of guru image with a decorated guru seat and golden *pādukā*s (sandals) placed before it is set to the right of the main sanctum *mūrti*s to allow the worship of the gods and the guru conjointly—with the guru's image representing the highest *chakra* point of the body, *sahasrāra*, worshipped at the end of most *pūjā*s (Figure 8.5). The conflation of guru and god in this iconographic program, however, is best revealed through the *vigraha*, or smaller offering-image, of Śiva Ānandeśvara, seated in front of the main central

Figure 8.5 "Cut-out" of Guru Paramahaṃsa Nityānanda, Nithyananda Vedic Temple, Columbus (Delaware), Ohio. Photograph Amy-Ruth Holt.

mūrti. It appears as a standing bronze portrait of the guru Nityānanda dressed in a maroon turban and *dhoti*. It is known as the *mūlvar* or "main deity," which should be telling enough to its identity, and it stands to the left of the smaller goddess image of Ānandeśvarī's *vigraha* (see Figure 8.2). As a worshipped pair, these bronze *vigrahas* reveal Nityānanda as the hidden inner character within the large sculpted image of Śiva and Pārvatī behind them. When viewed from the audience hall, the large "cut-out" portrait of Nityānanda beside the stone image of Śiva Ānandeśvara-Ānandeśvarī, each of nearly identical size, suggests that these two figures are meant to be merged within the mind of the devotee as the same divinity.

In addition to these central images, stone *mūrtis* of Śiva Dakṣiṇāmūrti are worshipped as Nityānanda in his Los Angeles (Montclair), San Jose (Milpitas), and Bangalore (Bidadi) temples. This association comes from his Life Bliss Meditation, where Śiva Dakṣiṇāmūrti or the guru Nityānanda represents the highest *chakra* point in the body (see Table 8.1). Images of Śiva Dakṣiṇāmūrti are often accompanied by smaller *vigraha* portraits of Nityānanda (or *mūlvar* images) to demonstrate this association. Nityānanda specially references Śiva Dakṣiṇāmūrti, the sage form of Śiva in the southern direction, as a model *jīvan mukti* or *siddha* for himself and his devotees to emulate, making Śiva Dakṣiṇāmūrti a favored image of worship at Nityānanda temples (Nithyananda 2007c: 18–19; Elgood 1999: 49–50). Typically portrayed as a young ascetic seated cross-legged under a banyan tree with long matted hair or a turban, Nityānanda's own images and biography describe his enlightenment story in the manner of this southern image of Śiva (Nithyananda 2007c: 16–19 and 2007b: 123–32). Even now when bronze portrait sculptures of Nityānanda have been made available like those at his Bangalore and San Jose temples, these commissioned guru portraits still follow the basic iconography of Śiva Dakṣiṇāmūrti in their dress, turban, and cross-legged seated posture, and they are normally placed beside older images of Śiva Dakṣiṇāmūrti.[12]

Nityānanda's setup of deities in his U.S. temples has a distinct iconography that illustrates the flow of cosmic energy between the immaterial and material worlds. It includes materialized *saguṇa* deities (with qualities), images depicting the abstract symbolism of the *nirguṇa* or the formless immaterial divine (without qualities), and aniconic images that fall in between these two poles. While most devotees focus their attention on the large figural *mūrtis*, there exists in the main sanctum of the Ohio temple four different kinds of visuals. First are the large stone *mūrtis* and the second are their smaller *vigraha* versions, where both of these represent *pratimās* (likenesses) of the deities that are identified

Table 8.2 The Nityānanda Pañca Bhūta Temples in the United States

U.S. Temple Site	Element	Deity or Imagery	India Location
Columbus, Ohio	Water	Three water sources	Prayag, Himalayas
Los Angeles, California	Fire	Śiva Dakṣiṇāmūrti Guru portrait	Tiruvannamalai, Tamil Nadu
Houston, Texas	Air	Śiva Liṅga	Kalahasti, Andhra Pradesh
San Jose, California	Earth	Mīnāṭcī	Madurai, Tamil Nadu
Seattle, Washington	Ether	Śiva Naṭarāja	Chidambaram, Tamil Nadu

by the commonly represented characteristics and attributes of the individual gods and goddesses (Zimmer 1989: 29–31). Beyond these *pratimā*s, toward a level of greater abstraction, is the image of the *liṅga* placed in front of Ānandeśvara-Ānandeśvarī. In Tamil Śaiva temples, the aniconic *liṅga* is traditionally the main image in worship found in the central sanctum, and its placement in front of Ānandeśvara-Ānandeśvarī suggests a return to this temple scheme in part. Like the image of Ānandeśvara-Ānandeśvarī, the *liṅga*, set on a *yoni* pedestal (a sign of the goddess), represents the union of Śiva and Śakti as the cosmic divine but in a more symbolic manner (Kramrisch 1981: 241–9; Zimmer 1989: 30).

The *liṅga* with *yoni* pedestal at Ohio is abstracted further to represent the immaterial world by a smaller three-dimensional *yantra*, or geometrical design of the cosmos, referred to as Mt. Meru that receives the main offerings of Śiva and the goddess instead of the *liṅga* or *pratimā*s in Nityānanda temples (shown in center of Figure 8.2). It is said that Nityānanda created this image from a three-dimensional *yantra* of the goddess at Tiruvannamalai, most likely a Śrī Chakra like that used in his Nithya Yoga (Nithyananda 2007c: 26). As in Nityānanda's Life Bliss Meditation, the Mt. Meru *yantra* is composed of seven levels to represent the seven *chakra*s of the body and the seven gods they are ruled by found in the larger temple program. Placed at the center of the temple, it is this *nirguṇa* symbol of Mt. Meru that radiates outward the immaterial cosmic energy of the guru into the surrounding deities, temple, and devotees.

Nityānanda additionally envisions the entirety of his temples spread throughout the world as satellites that continue to disperse his immaterial cosmic energy and symbolize the fivefold bodily division of Śiva, and himself, as the supreme Sadāśiva (Table 8.2; *Sarvajnapeetha* 6; Davis 1991: 50). Specifically, there are five major temples in the U.S. that he has designated as the *pañca-bhūta*s (five elements) of Sadāśiva. The Los Angeles (Montclair), California, temple is fire; the Columbus (Delaware), Ohio, temple is water; the Houston, Texas, temple is air; the Seattle,

Washington, temple is ether; and the San Jose (Miliptas), California, temple is earth. Each of these temples in the U.S. also mirrors an important Śaiva site; Los Angeles is Nityānanda's home temple of Aruṇāchaleśvara in Tiruvannamalai, Tamil Nadu; Columbus is the sacred Prayag Rivers of the Himalayas; Houston is the Śiva Śrīkalahasti temple in Kalahasti, Andhra Pradesh; Seattle is the Naṭarāja temple in Chidambaram, Tamil Nadu; and San Jose is the Mīnāṭcī temple in Madurai, Tamil Nadu. Each of these temples also have specific imagery to reference their corresponding site and element as listed in Table 8.2. For example, the Columbus, Ohio, temple is located on the confluence of a river, creek, and underground spring that Nityānanda claims are the three sacred rivers of Prayag in the Himalayas. These attributions, extending from the yogic body of Nityānanda, actively manifest him in all materiality from the smallest microbe to the larger macro region.

Onscreen Materiality: Modern Media Gurus and Devotee Imagery

A more recent means to uncover the identity of Nityānanda as his god sculptures at Ohio is through his use of contemporary medias. As it has been explained in various previous studies, the advent of television and the internet has further changed how gurus like Nityānanda can visually demonstrate their immateriality on a global scale (Copemand and Ikegame 2012; Froystad 2012; Lundby 2013). While certainly the words used by gurus fill these platforms, it is often their outwardly intimate appearance in online videos and "live" internet broadcasts that hold the greatest interest for devotees. Due to their popular devotion from fans, celebrity figures in film and politics in India are frequently depicted as popular Hindu deities that merge the social and sacred by way of the media (Holt 2019). Gurus, having a similar celebrity-like appeal, make up another common focus of the Indian media (Copeman and Ikegame 2012; Froystad 2012). Given this importance placed on the media, in the years since I first visited the Ohio Nityānanda temple in 2007, Nityānanda has considerably expanded his presence on the internet in a vast and pervasive manner, including satellite Nithyananda TV, his main website Nithyananda.org, his frequent use of two-way internet broadcasting, a number of individual devotee podcasts, music videos, and yoga tutorials as well as a large social media following on multiple platforms, and literally hundreds of video programs and recorded *satsaṅgas*.

From a very early age, Nityānanda recognized the power of modern media imagery to directly influence people in a personal manner. Even though it was very difficult to come by cameras in India during Nityānanda's childhood, his yoga teacher, Raghupati Yogi, hired a professional photographer to take pictures of Nityānanda in various meditational poses. Raghupati even wrote on the back of one photo, "The whole world will thank me one day for these photographs!" (Nithyananda 2007b: 100; for images, see Nithyananda 2007a: 7, 14). Nityānanda also remembers the first time he saw a movie, a horror film, and the feeling that "fear was trying to get into him," which caused him to immediately leave the theater (Nithyananda 2007b: 112). From these instances, Nityānanda came to recognize how mediated images increased his popularity and directly influenced his viewing audience. For the onscreen image, he claims: "When we watch television or a movie, the frames per second played through them are so high that they directly penetrate our consciousness," infusing that mood into us and shaping our character without our knowing (Nithyananda 2007b: 113).

With this power of modern medias, Nityānanda encourages his followers to watch him on television, on the computer, or if possible in person, for *ānanda darśan*, a "blissfully seeing," where simply "gazing at the master" is seen as an initiation into "living enlightenment" or *jīvan mukta*-hood (Nithyananda 2009: 419–23 and 2008a: 161). Blissfully seeing is another means for instilling cosmic energy into the devotee similar to meditation or the rites of installation for a temple image. Since *darśan* is typically understood as an exchange of sight between god and devotee (Eck 1998), devotees frequently claim that Nityānanda enjoys watching them as well so that nearly everything that happens in the Nityānanda diaspora temple is broadcasted on the internet and/or photographed by devotees to be posted on their social media platforms for his appreciation and viewing. The "live" *satsaṅga* is the most important for devotees; for at this time, Nityānanda can see them through the computer screen and often calls out the various diaspora temples or even the names of individual devotees that are currently watching online to their great delight. The onscreen image does not appear to hinder the conveyance of Nityānanda's cosmic energy; in fact, some devotees would say it increases it. Through the large numbers of people who are thought to witness these "live" occasions, Nityānanda is said to become energized by their viewing of him, which in turn intensifies his overall *siddha* power that he shares with viewers (White 2009: 66; Copeman and Akegame 2012: 14–15).

From my extensive viewing of these online *satsaṅga*s, I noticed that devotees within the filmed audience would often fall into fits of ecstasy (and even levitation) during times when Nityānanda would pause between thoughts, sometimes gazing widely at the audience, as if he was not really present. In early *satsaṅga* video recordings, he would sometimes laugh these moments off as a result of his nerves, but later on, these moments seem to have become codified as times when he periodically fell into *samādhi* (Nityānanda's "living enlightenment") and viewed the world from his third-eye or *ājñā chakra* (Nithyananda 2011b: 9). It is my belief that it was his devotees' attempts to capture these intense visual moments of Nityānanda's *samādhi* that led to the development of what is now called the Oneness Capsule.[13] These short online videos invoke the three "*m*'s" of tantric practice: *mudrā* (hand gestures), *mantra* (sacred syllables), and *maṇḍala* (sacred diagrams). In these videos, Nityānanda, appearing most often as Śiva with his tiger-skin dress and golden trident in a temple or heaven-like setting, begins to perform undefined *mudrā*s, believed to be spreading his immaterial cosmic energy that sometimes appears on the screen in front of him in outlined cinematic effect as *maṇḍala*s or sparkling puffs of powder. While Nityānanda gazes intently and directly at the camera, Śiva *mantra*s, or *bhajan*s (holy songs) often with the inclusion of his own name, repeat on an endless loop in the background. Devotees claim that the extensive watching of these short films fills them with the cosmic energy of the guru that heals any mental or physical problem. Sometimes devotees even use these videos while healing or performing miraculous actions, and the onscreen *maṇḍala*s may refer to the Śrī Chakra or the three-dimensional Mt. Meru of the temple sanctum, but many are of unknown or secret origin. These Oneness Capsules make *darśan* of the guru into an action for the *siddha* evolution of the devotee through the tantric imagery of Nityānanda as an onscreen materialized divinity.

This act of Nityānanda dressing as various Hindu deities in his Oneness Capsules illustrates a case of ritual embodiment or onscreen materialization, commonly associated with possession and other ritual theater traditions in India. To paraphrase the work of Catherine Bell (1992), in such cases, the act of ritualizing a person causes them to attain a ritual body that is automatically equivalent to the divine form the performer invokes. The Hindu deities Nityānanda chooses to embody in these videos are often taken from his temple sculptures, namely Śiva, Murugaṉ, and variations on the combined image of Śiva and the goddess, also called Ardhanārīśvara (or the "Half-Woman Lord"). In the particularly interesting Oneness Capsule #126, he performs a marriage ritual for the goddess Mīnāṭcī and Śiva Sundareśvara, commonly celebrated at the Mīnāṭcī temple in Madurai, Tamil Nadu.[14] After adorning his bronze image of Mīnāṭcī, he puts her golden crown on his head and takes up her silver staff. Seated on his golden throne with her crown and staff, Nityānanda gazes intently at the camera while *bhajan*s continue in the background for the remainder of the video. With this ritual action, he presents himself as the tantric unity of Śiva and Śakti within his own ritual body like the temple *mūrti* of Ānandeśvara-Ānandeśvarī or Ardhanārīśvara. But, unlike his temple sculptures, that claim a level of possible secrecy in the duality of their identity as Nityānanda, the onscreen ritualization of Nityānanda's image fully conflates his ritual body with that of his main temple deity, causing an immediate visual identification between his divine image and the temple image. Other Oneness Capsules involving Nityānanda's singular appearance as Śiva or Murugaṉ imply this same formula of materialized unity between himself and his temple *mūrti*s.

The onscreen materialization or multiplicity of his divine image, seen in his Oneness Capsule videos, continues with the imagery of Nityānanda's devotees, who frequently appear in online videos with him. This especially concerns those residing at his ashram as *sannyāsī*s, who typically dress in the same manner as Nityānanda, which includes long, extensive dreadlocks, large *rudrākṣa* bead necklaces, saffron-colored attire, and sometimes saffron-colored turbans. Devotees recognize this particular dress code as a sign of their renunciation much like Nityānanda's own living enlightenment and his emulation of Śiva Dakṣiṇāmūrti. A unique side-effect of Nityānanda devotion, according to devotees I spoke with, is the common belief that, like their guru, they appear more "youthful and attractive" by having an outward "glow" and an inner sense of happiness. Historically, these qualities of the guru are associated with *teja*s, or "splendor," which may be gained through the acts of mediation, penance, and yoga that allow for the accumulation of heat (*tapas*) in the immaterial subtle-body that outwardly appears on the material physical body as marks of beauty (Flood 1996: 63; Mahony 1997: 227).

In addition to having an outward appearance like the guru, devotees of all ages may demonstrate iconic *siddha* powers like transmutation, levitation, transmigration, alchemy, blind reading, and advanced yoga abilities that may be posted and viewed online. Nityānanda sometimes names certain advanced students to be teachers in his place at his ashram, and in his videos, due to their achievement of these divine abilities. A group of advanced children dressed like Nityānanda are often shown online for their special powers.[15] In a similar manner, the donor-manager of the Nityānanda temple in Ohio told me that she was once called a "goddess" by one of her students based upon her knowledge of Life Bliss Meditation. These onscreen living examples of the "perfect devotee," or Nityānanda's *jīvan muktis* (whose enlightenment derives from their imitation of him) affirm the continuing dispersion of Nityānanda's rematerializing and mediated divine form (Cutler 1984; Jacob 1997; Holt 2019).

Concluding Rituals: Between Materiality and Immateriality

While tantric images are often defined as tools for meditation and ritual practice, especially those of abstract *yantras* and *maṇḍalas*, Nityānanda's sculptural *pratimās* (likenesses) found at his Ohio temple actually support his Life Bliss Meditation by appearing to have his likeness and that of Hindu deities (Zimmer 1989; Mookerjee 1985; Vatsyayan 1997; Rawson 2010). The purpose for this multiplicity, or *śleṣa*, of Nityānanda's imagery arises from his doctrine of immaterial cosmic energy found in both the human body and the outside world that unites all living beings, as well as the individual Self (*ātman*) and the Divine (*Brahman*). As an artist, Nityānanda takes this concept of non-duality farther with the merging of the "creator" with that of his "creation" as a self-portrait. Many examples of Hindu imagery throughout India and its visual history contain levels of visual multiplicity, and certainly Nityānanda is not the first to recognize this function of imagery, but he is, to the best of my knowledge, the first to have developed it into the core doctrine of his guru *bhakti* through the use of both traditional and modern onscreen portraiture. Such a finding may additionally suggest that the failure to identify the significance of guru portraiture as deities in India's past may result from the literary and spiritual pronouncements against its clear identification and its hidden nature—reflective of some of the devotee responses in this study—rather than its nonexistence.[16]

The unusual dominance of the visual in Nityānanda's guru *bhakti* becomes even more apparent when viewed from the perspective of ritual practice, where the devotee is instructed to envision themselves in the form of the guru. Before the start of any *pūjā* (worship), the devotee makes the following declaration:

1. Cosmic energy exists,
2. Nithyananda and these temple images are the embodiment and representation of that cosmic imagery,
3. Whatever I offer during this *puja* to Nithyananda and these images will reach the cosmic source directly, and
4. The truth of "*sohamasmi*" is that when I worship "I am him."

(*Sri Guru Puja Sadashiva Puja* 28–9)

Figure 8.6 Portrait of Guru Paramahaṃsa Nityānanda with *Tat Tvam Asi* (*You Are That*) hung over the sanctum, Nithyananda Vedic Temple, Columbus (Delaware), Ohio. Photograph Amy-Ruth Holt.

Through this four-part declaration, devotees define themselves, the temple god images, and the guru as one in the same. In essence, the devotee's ritual declaration is a verbal variation of the divine visual multiplicity described in Nityānanda's temple sculpture and online videos, but now turned to the individual's self-materialization of the divine. Nityānanda informs his devotees of this fact through the popular statement: "my mission is not to prove my divinity, it is to prove *your* divinity" (Nithyananda 2007a: 6). Along the same lines, a painted portrait of Nityānanda with the popular Vedānta phrase, "*Tat Tvam Asi* (*You Are That*)," placed directly over the main sanctum defines the devotee's worship at the Nityānanda temple as visually multiple, since the main temple deity is commonly depicted over the temple doorway (Figure 8.6). As in the tantric image, the worship of Nityānanda's divine image allows devotees to uncover the inner cosmic divine within themselves through his guru *bhakti*. A final step in Nityananda's Life Bliss Meditation then involves the viewing of oneself in a mirror. At the Columbus temple, this mirror was coincidently placed across from the sanctum "cut-out" of Nityānanda, which caused the devotee's reflection to literally appear within that of the guru's. Similar to the message of the painting above the sanctum, this ritual use of the mirror allows the devotee to access their immaterial connection to the divine guru through the material visual image.

The use of visual multiplicity as a tool for spiritual materialization brings the entirety of Nityānanda's practice into focus. From the *siddha* belief in cosmic energy that can be visualized through meditation and their corresponding *chakra*-bound deities, these same deities materialize externally in the temple's sculpture to become extensions of the guru. Belief in the agency of these images comes from Nityānanda's childhood home of Tiruvannamalai, where he studied at guru Ramaṇa Maharṣi's *maṭha* and frequented the Aruṇāchaleśvara temple. The multiple images used in Nityānanda temples reflect Nityānanda's devotees' backgrounds and his identity as a fully enlightened, self-materialized *jīvan mukti* that is united with the cosmos, androgynous, and Śiva Dakṣiṇāmūrti or a model *siddha yogi*. Additional online images of himself and his like-appearing devotees rematerialize and ritualize him in the same manner as his divine temple portraits. Nityānanda's divine visual multiplicity brings his image into the individual body of his devotees and outward into his temple sculpture and guru temples, creating a constant fluidity between the material and immaterial worlds, and establishing for himself a powerfully visual brand of guru *bhakti*.

Notes

1 The defining of these terms is how Nityānanda (often written in English as "Nithyananda") has explained them (Nithyananda 2007b: 25). In 2019, Nityānanda moved from his Bangalore (Bidadi) ashram to an island east of Ecuador that he owns called Kailasa.

2 Information gathered from devotee interviews carried out at the Columbus Nithyananda Vedic Temple from June to October 2019. A video of Nityānanda performing a deity installation is available online at https://youtu.be/DD3rl53DPf0 (accessed March 24, 2022).

3 A unique aspect of Nityānanda temples is that there is no actual head priest; instead, initiated male and female volunteers take turns doing the main weekend *Śiva pūjā* or nightly *pāda pūjā* based upon their own availability.

4 I also witnessed this after attending a yoga class on International Yoga Day at the Nithyananda Vedic Temple, Columbus, Ohio in 2019. Nityānanda claims to have rediscovered 1,008 more *āsana* postures soon to be released. See https://www.youtube.com/watch?time_continue=2564&v=tXO4pWY2l_I (accessed March 24, 2022).

5 Devotees often comment upon entering Nityānanda temples in the U.S. that they feel vibrations inside these buildings or when viewing the guru on television or when performing magical feats themselves such as rolling coconuts with their

minds. To see examples of levitation, see https://youtu.be/5QTKTY 1LNs4 (accessed March 24, 2022).

6 These images were found at his ashram in Bangalore (Nithyananda 2007a), but they may have been moved since his move to Kailasa.

7 Bracketed text and definition of "Self" added by author.

8 This practice is very much reflective of the creation of clay images of Gaṇeśa for Gaṇeśa *pūjā* that once worshipped are destroyed, and this practice was discussed by practitioners at the Ohio temple.

9 Early Pallava images of Śiva and Pārvatī seated together on Mount Kailasa are also found, such as at the Kailaśanātha temple in Kanchipuram. But, in Tamil iconography, this Śiva-Śakti image is never found as the main image of worship in traditional Śiva temples; instead, this position is almost always taken by the *liṅga*.

10 This hairstyle is a notable feature of the *bhakti* saint Āṇṭāḷ, who is also seen as an incarnation of the goddess Lakṣmi due to her devotion to Viṣṇu in Tamil Nadu. The Lakṣmī figure at the Nityānanda temple ashram in Bangalore was also referred to as Ambal (Nithyananda 2007c: 25).

11 The first temple to have a bronze guru sculpture of Nityānanda was his temple ashram in Bangalore in 2008. Today, a similar bronze guru portrait sculpture exists at the San Jose temple along with a Dakṣiṇāmūrti stone image that originally was found in front of the sacred *bilva* tree in Bangalore.

12 According to devotees, Los Angeles and Columbus temples are both planning to replace their main portrait image of Nityānanda (the "cut-out" at Columbus and Śiva Dakṣiṇāmūrti sculpture at Los Angeles) with bronze portrait sculptures (like that now found at San Jose) when they are made available to them.

13 Some of his Oneness Capsules also emphasize his cosmic energy reaching the devotees as they appear to levitate and shake with the effects of this energy transfer.

14 To see this Oneness Capsule #126 of Śiva and Mīnāṭcī's wedding ritual performed by Nityānanda and his devotees, go to https://www.youtube.com/watch?v=P _zqHZ4WRro (accessed March 24, 2022).

15 These devotees can be seen online at https://youtu.be/P_zqHZ4WRro (accessed March 24, 2022).

16 For additional examples of portraiture in India, see Coomaraswamy (1939), Kamal (1994, 1995, and 1999), and Dehejia (1998). Nityānanda believes that all Hindu temples in India are the result of gurus installing their divine cosmic energy in a place. Although there is no evidence for this in the case of most temples, certainly gurus or saints do have temples made in their honor, and some temples do have special sites dedicated to or associated with religious figures, who might have visited these sites at some time performing miracles and writing devotional hymns.

References

Babb, L. (1987), "Satya Sai Baba's Saintly Play," in J. S. Hawley (ed.), *Saints and Virtues*, 168–86, Berkeley: University of California Press.

Balasubrahmanyam, S. R. (1971), *Early Chola Temples: Parantaka I to Rajarja I (AD 907–985)*, New Delhi: Orient Longmen.

Bate, B. (2009), *Tamil Oratory and the Dravidian Aesthetic: Democratic Practice in South India*, New York: Columbia University Press.

Bell, C. (1992), *Ritual Theory, Ritual Practice*, Oxford: Oxford University Press.

Benjamin, W. (1968), "The Work of Art in the Age of Mechanical Reproduction," in H. Arendt (ed.), *Illuminations*, 217–51, New York: Schoken Books.

Burchett, P. (2019), *A Genealogy of Devotion: Bhakti, Tantra, Yoga, and Sufism in North India*, New York: Columbia University Press.

Coomaraswamy, A. (1939), "The Traditional Conception of Ideal Portraiture," *Journal of the Indian Society of Oriental Art* 7: 74–82.

Copeman, J., and A. Ikegame (2012), "The Multifarious Guru: An Introduction," in J. Copeman and A. Ikegame (eds.), *The Guru in South Asia: New Interdisciplinary Perspectives*, 1–46, London: Routledge.

Cutler, J. (1984), "The Devotee's Experience of the Sacred Tamil Hymns," *History of Religions* 24 (2): 91–112.

Davis, R. (1991), *Ritual in an Oscillating Universe*, Princeton: Princeton University Press.

Davis, R., ed. (1998), *Images, Miracles and Authority in Asian Religious Traditions*, Oxford: Westview Press.

Dehejia, V. (1990), *Art of the Imperial Cholas*, New York: Columbia University Press.

Dehejia, V. (1998), "The Very Idea of a Portrait," *Ars Orientalis*, 75th Anniversary of the Freer Gallery of Art, 28: 40–8.

Eck, D. (1998), *Darsan: Seeing the Divine Image in Image*, New York: Columbia University Press.

Elgood, H. (1999), *Hinduism and the Religious Arts*, London: Cassell.

Flood, G. (1996), *An Introduction to Hinduism*, London: Cambridge University Press.

Flueckiger, J. B. (2015), *Everyday Hinduism*, Oxford: Wiley Blackwell.

Forsthoefel, T. (2005), "Weaving the Inward Thread to Awakening: The Perennial Appeal of Ramana Maharshi," in T. Forsthoefel and C. A. Humes (eds.), *Gurus in America*, 37–54, New York: State University of New York Press.

Froystad, K. (2012), "The Mediated Guru: Simplicity, Instantaneity, and Change in Middle-Class Religious Seeking," in J. Copeman and A. Ikegame (eds.), *The Guru in South Asia: New Interdisciplinary Perspectives*, 181–201, London: Routledge.

Gell, A. (1998), *Art and Agency: An Anthropological Theory*, Oxford: Clarendon Press.

Gold, D. (1995), "Guru's Body, Guru's Abode," in J. M. Law (ed.), *Religious Reflections on the Human Body*, 230–50, Bloomington: Indiana University Press.

Holt, A. R. (2007), "Shiva's Divine Play: Art and Literature at a Hindu Temple," PhD diss., The Ohio State University, Columbus.

Holt, A. R. (2019), "Symbols of Political Participation: Jayalalitha's Fan Imagery in Tamil Nadu," *Journal of Hindu Studies* 12 (2): 242–69.

Holt, A. R., and K. Pechilis (2019), "Contemporary Images of Hindu Bhakti: Identity and Visuality," *Journal of Hindu Studies* 12 (2): 124–41.

Huntington, S. (1985), *Art of Ancient India: Hindu, Buddhist, Jain*, New York: Weatherhill.

Huntington, S. (1992), "Aniconism and the Multivalence of Emblems: Another Look," *Ars Orientalis* 22: 111–56.

Jacob, P. (1997), "From Co-Star to Deity: Popular Representations of Jayalalitha Jayaram," in V. Dehejia (ed.), *Representing the Body: Gender Issues in Indian Art*, 140–65, New Delhi: The Book Review Literary Tradition and Kali for Women.

Kaimal, P. (1994), "Playful Ambiguity and Political Authority in the Large Relief at Mamallapuram," *Ars Orientalis* 24: 1–27.

Kaimal, P. (1995), "Passionate Bodies: Constructions of the Self in South Indian Portraits," *Archives of Asian Art* 48: 6–16.

Kaimal, P. (1999), "The Problem of Portraiture in South India, Circa 870–970 A.D.," *Artibus Asiae* 9 (1/2): 59–133.

Kramrisch, S. (1981), *The Presence of Śiva*, Princeton: Princeton University Press.

Levin, D. M. (1993), *Modernity and the Hegemony of Vision*, Berkeley: University of California Press.

Lundby, K., ed. (2013), *Religion Across Media: From Early Antiquity to Late Modernity*, New York: Peter Lang.

Mahony, W. (1997), "The Guru-Disciple Relationship: The Context for Transformation," in D. R. Brooks, S. Durgananda et al., *Meditation Revolution: A History and Theology of the Siddha Yoga Tradition*, 223–76, New York: Agama Press.

Meyer, B., ed. (2009), *Aesthetic Formations: Media, Religion, and the Senses*, New York: Palgrave Macmillian.

Mookerjee, A. (1985), *Ritual Art of India*, Rochester: Inner Traditions.

Nithyananda, P. (2006), *You Are No Sinner!* Bangalore: Life Bliss Foundation.

Nithyananda, P. (2007a), *His Name Is Nithyananda*, Bangalore: Nithyananda Vedic Sciences University Press.

Nithyananda, P. (2007b), *Nithyananda (Glimpses from the Biography of Paramahamsa Nithyananda)*, vol. 1, Bangalore: Life Bliss Foundation and Adwit Limited.

Nithyananda, P. (2007c), *Sri Anandeshwara Temple & The Healing Tree*, Bangalore: Nithyananda Vedic Sciences University Press.

Nithyananda, P. (2008a), *Rising in Love with the Master: The Greatest Love Affair*, Bangalore: Nithyananda Vedic Sciences University Press.

Nithyananda, P. (2008b), *Instant Tools for Blissful Living: Exercises, Practices and Meditations*, Bangalore: Life Bliss Foundation.

Nithyananda, P. (2008c), *You Can Heal: Nithya Spiritual Healing*, Bangalore: Life Bliss Foundation.

Nithyananda, P. (2008d), *Nithya Yoga: The Ultimate Practice for Body, Mind and Being*, Bangalore: Nithyananda Vedic Sciences University Press and Aditya Printers.

Nithyananda, P. (2009), *Living Enlightenment (Gospel of Paramahamsa Nithyananda)*, Abridged ed., Bangalore: Life Bliss Foundation and Aditya Books.

Nithyananda, P. (2011a), *Open the Door . . . Let the Breeze In! Tools for Joyful Living*, Bangalore: eNPublishers.

Nithyananda, P. (2011b), *2012 Truth: Not Just Prophecy*, Bangalore: eNPublishers.

Nithyananda, P. (n.d.a), *Sarvajnapeetha: The All-Knowing Spiritual Seat*, Bangalore: Nithyananda Dhyanapeetha Charitable Trust.

Nithyananda, P. (n.d.b), *Sri Guru Puja Sri Sadashiva Puja*, Bangalore: Nithyananda Dhyanapeetha Charitable Trust.

Rabe, M. (1997), "The Mamallapuram Prasasti: A Panegyric in Figure," *Artibus Asiae* 57 (3/4): 189–241.

Ramaswamy, S. (2003), "Introduction," in S. Ramaswamy (ed.), *Beyond Appearances? Visual Practices and Ideologies in Modern India*, xiii–xxix, New Delhi: Sage Publications.

Rawson, P. (2010), *The Art of Tantra*, London: Thames & Hudson.

Singer, M. (1972), *When a Great Tradition Modernizes: An Anthropological Approach to Indian Civilization*, New York: Praeger Publishers.

Vatsyayan, K. (1997), *The Square and the Circle of the Indian Arts*, Delhi: Abhinav Publications.

Weiss, R. (2005), "The Global Guru: Sai Baba and the Miracle of the Modern," *New Zealand Journal of Asian Studies* 7 (2): 5–19.

White, D. (2009), *Sinister Yogis*, Chicago: University of Chicago Press.

Williamson, L. (2010), *Transcendent in America: Hindu-Inspired Meditation Movements as New Religion*, New York: New York University Press.

Willis, M. (2014), *The Archaeology of Hindu Ritual: Temples and the Establishment of the Gods*, New York: Cambridge University Press.

Zimmer, H. (1989), *Artistic Form and Yoga in the Sacred Images of India*, Delhi: Oxford University Press.

9

Darśan in Twelve Ways

Portraying the Divine in Early Svāminārāyaṇa Art

Ankur Desai

Introduction

In March of 1816, Sahajānanda Svāmī (1781–1830), founder of the Svāminārāyaṇa *sampradāya* (tradition), gathered with his devotees in the town of Vadtal, Gujarat, to celebrate the annual *puṣpadolotsava* (flower-swing festival). As sprays of colored powder clouded the air, Sahajānanda ascended a twelve-sided wooden swing suspended between two mango trees. Ornamented with gold flowers, the sparkling construction swayed as he sat in its center. He was enrobed in silks and jeweled ornaments. According to textual accounts, the festival culminated in a miraculous event where Sahajānanda's form multiplied into twelve parts, appearing in diverse moods at each window of the swing. Devotees and *sādhus* (ordained renunciants) partook in the *darśan* (auspicious sight) of these forms, showering each expansion with garlands, before the forms ultimately merged back with the original figure in the center (*Śrīharilīlāmṛtam* III.7.59). This incident, among others transmitted in the hagiographic corpus of the Svāminārāyaṇa *sampradāya*, highlights the importance of Sahajānanda's bodily form as it occupies the nucleus of the tradition's theological and ritual world. Manifesting in a variety of media, from architecture to painting, the artistic output of the *sampradāya* in many ways engaged with long-familiar art forms established in western India. At the same time, however, these emergent works also addressed the Svāminārāyaṇa community's own historical and philosophical identity in complex ways, prompting the formation of highly distinct sacred imagery.

This essay advances the analysis of an understudied group of early nineteenth-century works that centrally feature Sahajānanda Svāmī, who was regarded by sectarian followers as the manifestation of a deity on earth. In the scope of this analysis, consideration is given to three categories produced during Sahajānanda's lifetime: literary images, two-dimensional artworks, and sculpture. By examining this range, I reveal how the *sādhus* and devotee-artists of the community strategically utilized an array of aesthetic tropes and artistic styles in order to craft innovative portrayals that fully acknowledged Sahajānanda's historicity as a figure situated in nineteenth-century Gujarat, as well as his identity as an omnipotent being according to the *sampradāya*'s religious constructs. Namely, how the *sampradāya* managed to fashion images of its founder at the crossroads of historical observation and notions of the ideal, divine body long established in Indic aesthetics.[1] In turn, I propose that early images of Sahajānanda Svāmī were shaped by, and ultimately embody, what historian Shruti Patel refers to as a flexible form of *bhakti*, or a devotional model that did not pit the limitations of worldly or historical existence against the realm of divine possibility, but rather aided in their coalescence (Patel 2017: 50–70). While previous examinations of Indic devotional visuality have forwarded the binary frames of *laukika* (worldly) and *alaukika* (non-worldly or transmundane) as a means to evaluate aesthetic traditions and works of art, I show how early Svāminārāyaṇa imagery—itself a product of Sahajānanda's teachings—synthesized these categories to form an alternative understanding of what constitutes divine form.

In this regard, my inquiry of these artworks is expressly underpinned by Patel's foundational study, *The Play of History: The Swaminarayan Religious Community in Modern India*, which examines the Svāminārāyaṇa *sampradāya*'s institutional formation. Patel cogently advances how the political, social, and cultural elements of early nineteenth-century Gujarat significantly shaped the community's expression of devotion and regard for its founder (*forthcoming* b). Patel specifically notes that from a sectarian viewpoint the historicity of Sahajānanda along with the temporal components of colonial Gujarat, inclusive of spatial and material realities, were entirely divinized by his life and presence. In other words, Sahajānanda's historical or *laukika* existence was thoroughly understood as *alaukika*, and that *bhakti* toward Sahajānanda could be accessed and realized through historical particulars of the time, including the *sampradāya*'s material and aesthetic culture (Patel 2017: 82).[2] Through visual and iconographic analysis, I demonstrate how the crimping of this binary between terrestrial and divine is evidenced in the conceptualization, production, and resultant forms of early artistic works that centrally depict Sahajānanda. I further suggest that the symbiotic relationship between the production and reception of his image effectively blurred the boundaries between two known figural genres in Indic art, namely historical portraiture and embodied sacred images, or *mūrti*s (Kaimal

1995: 6).[3] As such, although images of Sahajānanda are venerated within the community simply as *mūrtis*, I propose the alternative categorization of divine portraits or "portrait-*mūrtis*."

The Foundations of Svāminārāyaṇa Imagery

The historiographic record of the Svāminārāyaṇa *sampradāya* places its founding in Gujarat in the year 1801 by the religious leader Sahajānanda Svāmī, who was known to his followers as Bhagavāna ("Lord") Svāminārāyaṇa. It is not the focus of this essay to relay the development and nuances of Svāminārāyaṇa philosophy, but it is sufficient to say that the *sampradāya*'s doctrine, although distinct, was in many ways informed by the theistic aspects of the Vedānta tradition (Paramtattvadas 2017: 12). Taking cues from this broader philosophical spectrum, Sahajānanda strongly promoted the veneration of Vaiṣṇava divinities such as Kṛṣṇa, as well as the belief in a two-armed embodied godhead known as Parabrahman Pūrṇa Puruṣottama Nārāyaṇa with whom Sahajānanda fully identified (Williams 2001: 73; Paramtattvadas 2017: 121–5).

The moment when a consistent iconographic pattern emerged within the *sampradāya* is not clearly understood, but textual sources strongly suggest that materializing a sacred visual system was an early priority during the community's initial formation. The creation of an iconographic framework not only fulfilled the need for a visual extension of the *sampradāya*'s theological belief in a formed godhead but also unified the Svāminārāyaṇa network through the shared ritual of devotional image veneration. Consequently, by 1820 the *sampradāya*'s visual output largely focused on the construction of temples and large-scale sculpted images drafted from stone and metal. In addition to providing the community with exclusive spaces for its core practice of image veneration, the founding of permanent structures ensured the *sampradāya*'s status as a prominent religious institution in nineteenth-century Gujarati society. Understanding the significance of establishing sacred sites as a means to concentrate and perpetuate the life of the community, Sahajānanda himself inaugurated six large-scale stone temples across Gujarat in the period between 1822 and 1828 (Williams 2001: 29; Patel 2017: 65).

Due to the Vaiṣṇava orientation of the community, the veneration of divinity pairs particular to that broader tradition was initially prioritized, resulting in the subsequent consecration of specific images within the early group of sectarian temples (Packert 2016: 245). Even though scholarly consensus affirms that temple construction in the community commenced only after 1820, it is probable that a type of iconographic order was developed prior, possibly starting between 1805 and 1810, or just a few years immediately ensuing the *sampradāya*'s establishment in 1801. Evidence for attributing the beginnings of a uniform pattern of Svāminārāyaṇa iconography to the first decade of the nineteenth century is based on early textual references to specific deities preferred for veneration. The very first Svāminārāyaṇa scripture, *Yamadaṇḍa* (1804), mentions the invocation and adoration of such figures as Nara-Nārāyaṇa and Rādhā-Kṛṣṇa, deity pairs that would later become the tangible focus of ritual veneration in the *sampradāya*'s future temples (Niṣkuḷānanda [1804] 2010: 192–4). Out of the *Yamadaṇḍa*'s 1,100 verses, several explicitly invoke Sahajānanda by his birth name Ghanaśyāma, but also by names associated with other deities (Williams 2001: 17). In verses six and eighty, for example, Sahajānanda is referred to as Badarikāiśa, or "Lord of Badarikā," and Badarīpati, or "Master of Badarikā," in reference to the abode of the deities Nara-Nārāyaṇa (Niṣkuḷānanda [1804] 2010: 6–7, 12). Similar to the *Yamadaṇḍa*, other passages in the *Vacanāmṛta*—the Svāminārāyaṇa community's most important scripture—also describe divinities regarded by Sahajānanda and how devotees were encouraged to venerate them. In one sermon, Sahajānanda explicitly commands of devotees: "One should meditate on Shri Krishna Bhagwān together with Rādhikā" (*Vacanāmṛta* Gaḍhaḍā I.5).[4] In another passage Sahajānanda describes the divine pair Nara-Nārāyaṇa as residing "within my [Sahajānanda's] heart" (*Vacanāmṛta* Gaḍhaḍā I.18). Despite the fact that the first of these extracts are dated between 1819 and 1821, the repeated references to specific deities within Sahajānanda's discourses suggest that they were important to his philosophical system at an earlier date, anticipating their eventual positioning at the core of the *sampradāya*'s sacred iconographic scheme.

An explanation for Sahajānanda's promotion of venerating a range of Vaiṣṇava divinity pairs, rather than himself as the omnipotent Parabrahman Pūrṇa Puruṣottama Nārāyaṇa, remains a point of contention between various Svāminārāyaṇa groups. The idea of Sahajānanda's complete preeminence, above even Viṣṇu or Nārāyaṇa, and as the source of all previous *avatāra* including Kṛṣṇa, was not entirely accepted within the *sampradāya* (Williams 2001: 71–82). While many adherents in the early community personally believed in the superiority of Sahajānanda, there was a hesitation to outwardly express this conviction. Previous studies note that because of the *sampradāya*'s fledgling status—compounded with opposition from other contemporaneous religious groups—the belief in Sahajānanda's divine status was underplayed by centrally placing traditionally accepted deities within the temples (Williams 2001: 74–82, 97; Kim 2009: 364). Although Sahajānanda's image was not the compositional focus within early temple spaces, it may be argued that his direct association with such divinities in textual sources nevertheless made it permissible for his form, in both literary and visual terms, to share many of the aesthetic and iconographic attributes associated with centrally venerated beings. In any case, despite these debates concerning Sahajānanda's ontological status, the adoration of his form, at least initially apart from the iconographic program of the community's foundational temples, was consistent throughout the *sampradāya*'s network, first manifesting in the extensive production of literature and poetic verses.

Seeing Divine Form in Early Svāminārāyaṇa Literature

By the second decade of the nineteenth century, the *sampradāya* generated an array of textual accounts and poetic compositions that emphasized the beauty and sanctity of Sahajānanda's physical form, along with those of other deities (most especially Kṛṣṇa). This early range of devotional texts is largely attributed to the *sādhus* of the community. Out of the dozens of renunciants who contributed their literary talent, eight in particular, known as the *aṣṭakavi* (eight poets), were especially prolific (Trivedi 2016: 192). The *aṣṭakavi* composed verses in several languages and set a framework that lyrically celebrated the philosophical trajectory of the *sampradāya*, its history, ritual calendar, and the bodily forms of its most revered figures. The emphasis on devotional image veneration, as well as the Svāminārāyaṇa theological stance of a formed godhead, no doubt served as an impetus in the creation of sectarian *mūrtipada*s (poetic verses describing sacred form) that extolled the divine forms of Sahajānanda and Kṛṣṇa. These *mūrtipada*s were also complemented by descriptions of Sahajānanda in scriptural texts that perpetuated the visualization of his historical form. Notably, every single sermon compiled within the *Vacanāmṛta*—exceeding over 270—begins with an account of Sahajānanda's appearance and dress. Thus, the collection of these works not only lauded the beauty of Sahajānanda in general terms but also provided detailed descriptions of his sartorial and physiognomic characteristics. Even as these devotional verses are Svāminārāyaṇa-specific, they nonetheless reveal a range of poetic devices familiar to the long-established corpus of Indic poetry. Out of these compositional tropes, one in particular, the *nakhaśikha*, is especially useful to consider for determining the establishment of a representational standard for the image of Sahajānanda, as both a historical figure and a divinity who embodies the idealized traits of a *mūrti*.

A well-known poetic theme, the *nakhaśikha*, literally meaning "nail to tuft," or conversely "head to toe," was commonly employed in literary passages to describe the full or partial form and physical attributes of a person.[5] The range of its application in Indic literature included subjects of courtly and sacred character, often with the aim of evoking a contemplative or even rapturous visualization of a figure. Though the use of the *nakhaśikha* was varied, it frequently conceptualized the subject by using pan-Indic signifiers of bodily excellence, many of which were fanciful rather than plausible forms. In poetry of the *sampradāya*, a salient characteristic of this literary device was the use of the conclusive *chāpa* (seal) at the end of the composition where the author completes the envisioning of the form by stating the phrase "*nakhaśikha*" or "from head to toe." The implementation of this closing expression arguably provided an authoritative, almost eyewitness inference to the description, especially when the name of the composer was recounted during its recitation.[6] One of the most well-known examples within the poetic corpus of the *sampradāya* is the eight-part *nakhaśikha* description of Sahajānanda entitled *Vandu Sahajānanda Rasarūpa*. According to sectarian hagiography, one of the *aṣṭakavi sādhu*-poets, Premānanda Svāmī, composed these verses spontaneously during an assembly in front of Sahajānanda (*Vacanāmṛta* Gaḍhaḍā II.48).[7] The composition was subsequently joined to a longer series of verses known as the *Svābhāvika Ceṣṭā* and *Līlācintāmaṇi*, also composed by Premānanda. Its contents convey a full account of Sahajānanda's physical attributes, mannerisms, and habitual daily activities, from the way he sat to the way he ate.

While the first portion of the *Svābhāvika Ceṣṭā* outlines the daily routine of Sahajānanda, the last section significantly details a complete description of his *caraṇacihna* (sacred footprint marks) and subsequently leads to the *Vandu Sahajānanda Rasarūpa* verses. Despite the fact that the *Vandu Sahajānanda Rasarūpa* composition was produced after the first Svāminārāyaṇa images were made, the idealized mode of its *nakhaśikha* format imparts a canonical quality to the description of Sahajānanda's body in accord with premodern artistic treatises.[8] Though by no means an exhaustive account of his physiognomy, the passage nonetheless blends established poetic tropes such as "teeth like pomegranate seeds" and "lotus-like eyes," with particular descriptions accounting for the number of marks on Sahajānanda's limbs and even the folds of skin on his neck and stomach (*Kīrtana Sāra* 1996: 52–5).[9] The inclusion of both types of description in the larger contemplative *Svābhāvika Ceṣṭā* compellingly suggests that the *nakhaśikha* was not only meant to facilitate the envisioning of Sahajānanda's form as an aestheticized ideal but also perhaps serve as a veritable reference source for translating his image from poetry to concrete visual works. It cannot be proven beyond doubt that such poetic works were conclusively utilized as iconographic sources for artistic works. However, given the fact that their composers—the *sādhu*-poets of the *sampradāya*—were held in great esteem, it is likely that these compositions carried a sense of tremendous authority, rendering their descriptions as possibly the only appropriate source for informing painted and sculpted imagery (Patel 2017: 58–9).[10] Moreover, the *sampradāya*'s exaltation of such extensively detailed contemplative works arguably generated an inextricable link between text and sacred form, infusing Sahajānanda's image with an indexical aura.

Padma Kaimal's examination of historical portraiture in south India recalls Wendy Steiner's emphasis on the indexical feature of portraits, as opposed to its definition of objective mirroring and recording the exhaustive peculiarities of physiognomy, which are understandably considered unreliable indicators. Steiner asserts that portraits not only serve as self-contained aesthetic forms but also—and in contrast to other art objects—"evoke a particular subject's presence" (Kaimal 1999: 64). Kaimal complements this notion by stating, "Indexicality feeds expectations of truth. In order to succeed as indices, portraits must evoke the actual person they signify" (1999: 64). In semiotic terms, Kaimal relays that one of the ways in which the link can be formed between the portrait as a sign and the living subject as the signifier is through text (as is the case with *mūrtipadas*). Though the assertion of indexicality through text is not a novel idea, in the context of Indic art (especially painting) the concept may be associated with what Molly Emma Aitken refers to as the *bhāva* (sentiment) that portraiture and its attendant text evokes, aiming "to remind the viewer of things seen and to trigger the mental sight of memory" (2010: 126). The tradition of Vaiṣṇava philosophy defines this concept as *smaraṇa*, or the remembrance of a person or deity's pastimes and qualities (Sanford 2008: 23).

This notion often manifested in the earlier spectrum of Vaiṣṇava visuality, especially in images from the Kṛṣṇa-centric Puṣṭi Mārga *sampradāya*, which produced artworks before and concurrent to the earliest Svāminārāyaṇa imagery. Specifically, the rich array of intricately painted *pichvāi*s (backdrop cloths) are fully reflective examples of such conceptual evocation, where the cyclical permanence of Kṛṣṇa's legendary actions, or *līlā*, as described in text was crystallized in the mental collective of devotional adherents and translated into visual tableaus (Krishna 2015: 37).[11] Even though such sacred images are often categorically detached from the genre of portraiture, the terms used to define them imply relational links to the function and purpose of portraits. The term *mūrti*, for example, translates directly as "embodiment," suggesting to a certain extent that they too serve as indexical or symbolic markers, though not necessarily in the pervasive visual format to which portraiture cleaves (Lefevre 2011: 63).[12]

As much as Puṣṭi Mārga images served as indices, their authority as a "historical" document in the way that portraiture is defined only existed in idealized terms. In other words, for the devotional adherent, Kṛṣṇa's narrative *līlā* served as a generative source for historical imagination (Kinsley 1979: 56–7).[13] However, as Shruti Patel argues, within the Svāminārāyaṇa world it is the earthly details of nineteenth-century Gujarat, the observed and minute articles of history associated with Sahajānanda's personhood and placement, that created the *sampradāya*'s genre of devotional narratives (see Patel this volume). Thus, unlike traditional Vaiṣṇava imagery which invites the *bhakta* (devotee) to traverse the *laukika* realm in order for devotional apperception and *līlā* to manifest, visualizations of Sahajānanda firmly ground his *alaukika* status within the earthly realm. This inversion of sorts complicates the position of Sahajānanda's image within the traditional framework of sacred Indic imagery and compels an alternative classification that permits the merger of the temporal with the eternal or the portrait with the *mūrti*. Indeed, Premānanda's *nakhaśikha* description of Sahajānanda dually expresses observation in the present tense, as well as aesthetic imagination by being specific enough in articulating an actual physical body, and yet not so mundane as to breach the standards of what constitutes divine form. Such verses point out an exceptional liminal zone where for Svāminārāyaṇa adherents the footprints of Sahajānanda, shown in Figure 9.1, can be both an actual historical document (as on the left) and a vision of the sacred, replete with all the markings of transcendence (as on the right).

In fact, dozens of Sahajānanda's *prasādi caraṇārvinda* (sanctified footprints) that survive within the *sampradāya* (as shown in Figure 9.1) are, in the devotional eye, entirely analogous to sculpted iterations associated with memorial sites that precisely show the sixteen *cihna*s (marks) or *lakṣaṇa*s (auspicious symbols) affiliated with his divine status. Thus, for devotees, both examples are potent indices fully linked to Sahajānanda's image (Paramtattvadas 2017: 125).[14] Such obscuring of categorical lines between various modes of visuality was, as Patel contends, part of "a larger cosmological refusal to see the concerns of the *laukika* and *alaukika* as divergent realms" (2017: 82). Moreover, Patel's larger study argues that the *sampradāya*'s divinization of spaces, locales, and materials

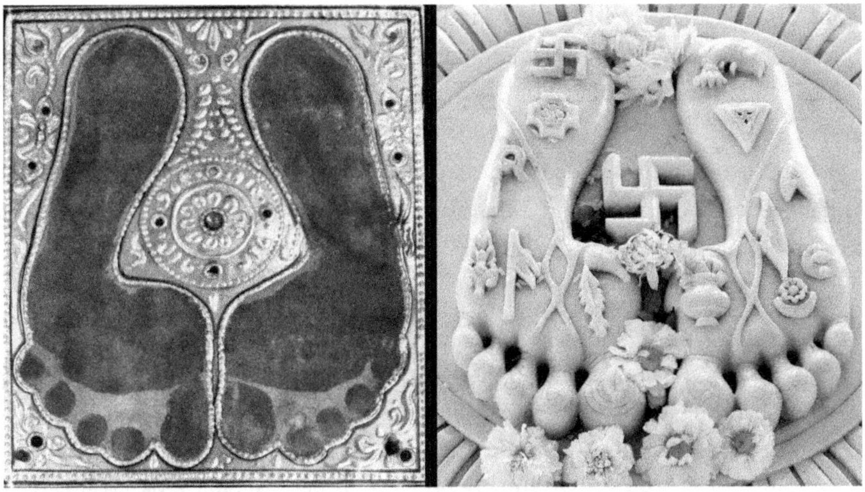

Figure 9.1 On left, *Caraṇārvinda* (footprints) of Sahajānanda Svāmī. Gujarat, *c.* 1820–30. Vermillion powder impressed on cotton. Shree Swaminarayan Mandir, Vadi. On right, Sculpted *caraṇārvinda* (footprints) of Sahajānanda Svāmī. Bochasan, Gujarat, *c.* early twentieth century. Marble. Photographs by Ankur Desai.

associated with Sahajānanda fully reflected the synthesis of these polar notions (*forthcoming* b). This fluid way of understanding Sahajānanda is not only apparent in poetic works and sanctified relics but is further evidenced by the artistic styles employed in the creation of the very first visual renderings of his form.

Creating Portrait-*Mūrti*s of Sahajānanda Svāmī

The historical record offers little information regarding the production timeline of the earliest images of Sahajānanda. In contrast, however, several sources provide relatively significant information about the artists of the *sampradāya* who were directly involved in establishing the community's aesthetic tradition and visual output. These artists may be divided into three categories: known lay devotees, known *sādhu*s, and unknown artists who were contracted from outside the community. Within the literature of the early *sampradāya*, the names of two individuals, a lay devotee named Nārāyaṇajī Hīrajībhai Suthāra and a *sādhu* named Ādhārānanda Svāmī, are the most frequently associated with the community's artistic achievements. Both were particularly skilled in the craft of *mūrti*-making (Dave and Pārikha 1984: 86–9). Suthāra along with

Ādhārānanda Svāmī are acclaimed in Svāminārāyaṇa literature for their artistic aptitude, as well as their spiritual acuity for perfectly envisioning the form of Sahajānanda (Dave and Pārikha 1984: 88).[15] In fact, Sahajānanda himself called on the skill of Suthāra to create *mūrti*s in order to facilitate image veneration across the *sampradāya*. According to the *Satsaṅgījīvanam*, an early biography of Sahajānanda completed in 1830 by the *sādhu* Śatānandamuni, Suthāra was summoned from the city of Junagadh by Sahajānanda:

> He [Sahajānandaa] decided to distribute the pictorial image of Lord Krishna to all His devotees so that individual devotees may have the pleasure of Darshan and worship Bhagwan on a daily basis. He called Naranjibhai from Junagadh and asked him, "I have heard of your expertise in making small images and drawings. I want you to prepare a cast of RadhaKrishna Dev and HariKrishna Maharaj which we can make many prints on paper." Naranji took great care and prepared two separate silver casts; one of Lord Krishna with Radha and Bhagwan Shree Hari and the other of Dharmadev and Bhaktimata accompanied by Shree HariKrishna Maharaj. Shree Hari was so pleased with both die casts that He asked Naranji Suthar to make an additional cast of Murti of Bhagwan NarNarayan Dev. O king! Naranji prepared all three casts in two months. Pleased with Naranji Suthar's devotion and effort, Bhagwan Narayanmuni rewarded him generously with a lot of wealth, new clothes and a pair of gold bangles. Shree Hari asked Adharanand swami to make hundreds of paper imprints and distributed them amongst His devotees. (Shatanand [1830] 2013: 646)

This passage is significant in so far as it is one of the first recorded accounts noting actual works commissioned directly by Sahajānanda for devotional use throughout the *sampradāya*.[16] Moreover, the text details not only the deities that Sahajānanda himself approved for image veneration among his devotees but also the format in which their *mūrti*s were to be produced and distributed. The method of creating images via metal stamps was not only common in the region of Gujarat given the prevalence of block printing traditions but, unlike stone images, was more convenient for distribution throughout the geographic domain of the *sampradāya*. Specifically, such small-scale printed and painted *mūrti*s were fully consecrated within *gharmandira* (household shrines) as well as public temple spaces.

Supplementing the initial casts described in the *Satsaṅgījīvanam*, other works show Sahajānanda in various forms as the primary subject of the composition. These examples are notable in their affirmation of the duality of Sahajānanda's image, the very same type of representation as previously discussed in the poetic corpus of the *sampradāya*. On the right side of Figure 9.2, a nineteenth-century

Figure 9.2 On left, Kṛṣṇa as Śrīnāthajī. Kota, Rajasthan, *c.* late eighteenth century. Pigment and gold on paper. Author's collection. On right, Sahajānanda Svāmī in *dvibhuja* (two-armed) form. Gujarat, *c.* mid- to late nineteenth century. Ink and pigment on paper. Shree Swaminarayan Mandir (Gopinathji Dev), Gadhada. Photographs by Ankur Desai.

painting depicts the central figure of Sahajānanda in cosmic form.[17] His appearance and dress correspond to descriptions of the supreme godhead, Parabrahman Pūrṇa Puruṣottama Nārāyaṇa, conveyed in Svāminārāyaṇa scripture. Specifically, it is detailed that this transcendent being appears in body as an effulgent, *dvibhuja* (two-armed) *sadākiśoramūrti* (the eternal youth of sixteen years) who eternally resides in his divine abode (Dave 2000: 206–10). In terms of its visual quality, the painting adheres to a certain stylistic formalism. Compressed space, exaggerated proportions, and bold and uniform contours indicate strong ties to depictions of idealized aesthetic form as found in established formats, such as the *kamangari* mode of wall painting developed in the principality of Kutch, Gujarat, around the mid-eighteenth century (Satish 2010: 22).[18] Significantly, the larger tradition of Rajput painting, particularly from the regions of Mewar and Vagad, heavily influenced visual idioms in Gujarat, including *kamangari* painting. It is almost certain that the style and its progenitors were familiar to the artists of the *sampradāya* given the fact that painters like Ādhārānanda Svāmī and Suthāra had much of their training in Kutch's capital city of Bhuj, home to a significant population of Svāminārāyaṇa adherents. Bhuj's reputation as an artistic center was cemented when the city underwent a surge of craft production under the rulership of the self-proclaimed aesthete, Rāo Lakhpatji (1741–60) (Goswamy and Dallapiccola 1983: 19–22). A patron of a variety of art forms, from fine metallurgy to painting, Lakhpatji's penchant resulted in the establishment of a local art school (Tyabji 2006: 33–4), and it is possible that in the context of this atelier, Suthāra and other Svāminārāyaṇa artists may have been introduced to visual inflections from broader regions across north and west India (Dave and Pārikha 1984: 86).[19]

Aside from formal links between such two-dimensional images of Sahajānanda and artistic styles produced in Kutch, further comparisons can be made to sacred images from other aesthetic traditions familiar to the Svāminārāyaṇa community, particularly those of the Puṣṭi Mārga *sampradāya*, which are exemplified by the image shown on the left side of Figure 9.2. The visual conventions used to depict the popular form of Kṛṣṇa as Śrīnāthajī, as shown in this late eighteenth-century painting, are paralleled in the painted depiction of Sahajānanda. Both figures with their sturdy limbs and splayed feet are postured alike in an authoritative frontal stance that bolsters their status as revered icons.[20] Considering the Svāminārāyaṇa *sampradāya*'s communal acknowledgment of the Puṣṭi Mārga community, it is likely that early Svāminārāyaṇa imagery appropriated certain stylistic elements from their artistic works (Patel 2017: 53–7).[21]

While the painted image of Sahajānanda standing frontal visually aligns with descriptions of his transcendental form, another example, a print from a metal cast attributed to Nārāyaṇajī Suthāra, portrays him as a figure styled according to the cultural specifics of nineteenth-century Gujarat (Figure 9.3). The print shows a seated figure titled as Śrī Sahajānanda Svāmī, flanked by diminutive representations of his parents, Śrī Bhaktimātā (proper right) and Śrī Dharmapati (proper left). Though Sahajānanda is holding a prayer *mālā* (rosary) and *grantha* (manuscript) in his proper right and left hands respectively—suggesting his religious nature—in all other aspects he is dressed in a manner that correlates this depiction with images of ruling elites in western India. Despite textual and material evidence affirming that Sahajānanda personally led an austere lifestyle, most visual portrayals of him overwhelmingly showcase his status as a manifest deity and sovereign (Hatcher 2020: 63; Patel *forthcoming* a and b).[22] The print shows him wearing an ornamented turban, attired in a variety of patterned fabrics and jewels, and seated on a raised platform against an embroidered *takiyā* (bolster). Contrasting the visual attributes that link this depiction of Sahajānanda with historical rulership, two notable aspects of the rendering reiterate his divine status.

Figure 9.3 Print of Śrī Sahajānanda Svāmī, with Śrī Bhaktimātā and Śrī Dharmapati, from a cast attributed to Nārāyaṇajī Hīrajībhai Suthāra. Gujarat, *c.* 1828–30. Ink and gold, on paper. Shree Swaminarayan Mandir, Vadtal. Photograph by Ankur Desai.

While the lower portion of Sahajananda's body is awkwardly compacted in a posture that is neither frontal nor in strict profile, his face and gaze, framed by a *prabāhmaṇḍala* (nimbus), is directed toward the viewer. That Suthāra utilized this convention in his representation of Sahajānanda is no unintended gesture. Molly Emma Aitken's study of Rajput painting clarifies that the convention of depicting a figure with both eyes visible was known as *do-chasmi* (two-eyes), indicating a facial position, either in three-quarter profile or fully frontal (2010: 75). The visual device was used to designate figures foreign to the Indian subcontinent. However, the exception to this rule and interpretation are depictions of divinities as icons—*mūrti*s and miraculous *svarūpa* (self-formed) images—as seen in the many artworks that centrally feature the primary Puṣṭi Mārga deity, Śrīnāthaji. The reason that iconic images retained this distinction was to facilitate and maintain an ocular link between the viewer and deity through the process of *darśan* (Aitken 2010: 277). Second, the presence of Sahajānanda's parents in the composition—a feature in several other casts made by Suthāra—significantly underscores and coalesces both his historical and transcendent identity. Sahajānanda's historical parents, Premavatī and Hariprasāda Pāṇḍe, are popularly referred to in *sampradāya* literature by their spiritual names,

Bhaktimātā and Dharmadeva, because it is believed that they were the living embodiments of *bhakti* and *dharma* (righteousness). Their placement within the composition alongside Sahajānanda, and the implicit understanding of their dual identities, restates his transcendental role as the scion and guardian of *bhakti* and *dharma*. Such iconographic details ultimately serve as an emphatic demonstration of the Svāminārāyaṇa doctrine of non-differentiation in the manifest form of the Supreme Divine (Paramtattvadas 2017: 130–1). That is, that Sahajānanda in all aspects is precisely corollary to the divine form of god present within his realm of *Akṣaradhāma* (the imperishable abode). Thus, the depiction of Sahajānanda's historical and spiritual parents situates him in his terrestrial body at the same time that it conveys his thoroughly divine nature.

In addition to Suthāra's print work, he was also charged with making a sketch of Sahajānanda from a live-sitting session, a rare incident in the entire narrative corpus of Hinduism in that a being regarded as a fully manifest deity is known to pose singularly for the purpose of a portrait (Dave and Pārikha 1984: 88, 92). The episode as relayed within the contents of the biographical work *Śrīharilīlāmṛtam* (1878) describes Suthāra's preparation of the image (*Śrīharilīlāmṛtam* IV.8.62). Notably, Vinit Vyas observes that the narrative simultaneously refers to Suthāra's rendering by the terms *chabī* (painted image or likeness) and *mūrti* (2019: 8). The dual employment of these designations fortifies the original proposal of categorizing images of Sahajānanda as both portrait and embodied sacred image. Suthāra's extant sketch shows Sahajānanda seated in profile, situated within a compacted terrace space with hanging drapery (Figure 9.4).[23] His face is set against a *prabāhmaṇḍala*. Jeweled and floral ornaments adorn his limbs and turban, and his rooted posture contrasts the mobile gesture of smelling a damask rose. While the account in the *Śrīharilīlāmṛtam* extols Suthāra's ability at capturing the likeness and beauty of Sahajānanda, the formal qualities of the sketch rather support the notion that Suthāra, again like many artists, was in fact working within the strong confines of convention. Significantly, Suthāra's portrayal was the prototype for all subsequent images of the "historical" Sahajānanda Svāmī.

Comparable to the community's distributed print images, the drawn and painted works of the *sampradāya* (including Suthāra's original portrait-*mūrti*) reveal a remarkable insistence on perpetuating a specific mode of spatial and figural articulation, recalling previous examples of Indian painting where flattened space, upturned carpets and platforms, and the preservation of compressed profiling were widely employed. The adherence to depicting Sahajānanda in a familiar setting, along with attributes and effects associated

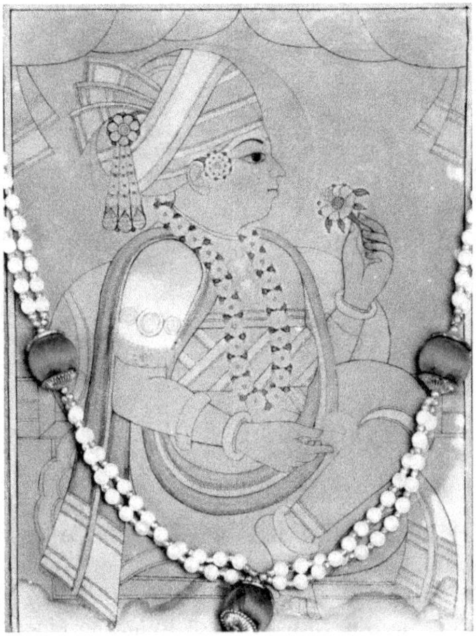

Figure 9.4 Śrī Sahajānanda Svāmī, attributed to Nārāyaṇajī Hīrajībhai Suthāra. Gujarat, *c*. 1823–8. Ink and pigment on paper. Shree Swaminarayan Mandir (Gopinathji Dev), Gadhada. Photograph by Ankur Desai.

with rulership, was not maintained due to a lack of innovation on the part of the artist. Rather, I suggest these modes were adopted in order to firmly settle Sahajānanda's image within the established lineage of elite court portraits. Indeed, a mid- to late seventeenth-century painted representation of the Basohli ruler Raja Sangram Pal (r. 1635–73), as seen on the right side of Figure 9.5, finds its form almost precisely mirrored in a nineteenth-century painting of Sahajānanda, as seen on the left side of Figure 9.5, which itself is modeled after Suthāra's master sketch.

Despite obvious differences in the facial profiles, dress, and accessories—*pāna* (betel nut quid) is held by Raja Sangram Pal while Sahajānanda bears a damask rose—the overall bearing of both figures is virtually analogous. Even as both images demonstrate an astonishing visual relation to one another, the portrayal of Sahajānanda does convey the artist's effort in creating a distinct facial type. This mimetic trace combined with the sartorial particulars of nineteenth-century Gujarat creates an overall sense of an image, or verily a portrait, that is at once individualized and yet conventional because of its clear borrowing from pre-*sampradāya* artistic traditions. It is important to reiterate that instead of indicating artistic stagnation, such appropriative efforts, including the adoption

Figure 9.5 On left, Śrī Sahajānanda Svāmī, attributed to Nārāyaṇajī Hīrajībhai Suthāra (possibly). Gujarat, *c.* 1823–8. Pigment, ink, and gold on paper. Shree Swaminarayan Mandir (Lakshmi-Narayan Dev), Vadtal. Photograph by Ankur Desai. On right, Raja Sangram Pal of Basohli. Basohli, India, *c.* mid- to late seventeenth century. Pigment and gold on paper. Bharat Kala Bhavan, Varanasi. Photograph John C. and Susan L. Huntington Photographic Archive of Buddhist and Asian Art.

of compositional strategies and iconography, were consciously implemented in order to legitimize Sahajānanda's status both without and within the devotional community.[24] In fact, Shruti Patel provides crucial evidence for how ritual, visual, and textual presentations within the *sampradāya* intentionally mirrored local patterns of rulership—all in a concerted effort to create a variant model of power and sovereignty within the region, one that donned the trappings of secular authority in order to assert spiritual authority (Patel *forthcoming* a). These endeavors are indicated in images of Sahajānanda by key visual elements, including the ubiquitous presence of a low parapet in the background, the gesture of holding a flower, the large supporting bolster, and the hanging drapery or cusped arches—all of which recall the copious examples of *jharokhā* (verandah or window) paintings of the Mughal and Rajput traditions. This former observation alone—the placement of Sahajananda's body within the space of a terrace—is significant in double measure as it simultaneously imbues the occupant of the space with temporal sovereign authority, as well as sacrality as a divinity. A. Afzar Moin reminds us that while the visual trope and performative implications of the *jharokhā* as a revelatory space is a convention that was generated in the Mughal world, it ultimately evokes earlier practices of image veneration, specifically the *darśan* of deities within temple spaces (2012: 233).

It is difficult to definitively trace the lineage of this specific mode of figural articulation to a single progenitor. Yet, a cursory examination of works that stretch further into the past and beyond the confines of the Indian subcontinent certainly lends weight to the notion that the perpetuation of certain visual elements was not arbitrary. Beyond similarities of composition and spatial arrangement, even particular gestures appear to be carried across regional and stylistic borders. Nicolas Roth makes clear that the depiction of rulers engaging in botanical olfactory enjoyment in Indic painting can be traced to Persian and Ottoman precedents (Roth 2021: 41:30-42:10). These models, both Indic and non-Indic, when juxtaposed against painted renderings of Sahajānanda, certainly call into question whether the seemingly natural act of smelling a flower was simply a documentation of an actual event or, more probable, if the gesture belonged to a perpetuated stock of poses that was used to convey the refinement and regal bearing of the sitter (Goswamy and Dallapiccola 1983: 73–4).[25] The reason that Mughal and Rajput royal court painters engaged in rich and varied visual approaches is complex, and in some cases, not entirely clear. However, in the context of Svāminārāyaṇa imagery, I suggest that the fluid borrowing of diverse artistic elements and the visual shading between Sahajānanda's earthly and divine form were employed with a conscious understanding of his singular identity as outlined in the *sampradāya*'s philosophy. The community's scriptural works unambiguously convey that the Sahajānanda with peculiar bodily marks as described in Premānanda's *nakhaśikha* is also the spotless two-armed form of Parabrahman Pūrṇa Puruṣottama Nārāyaṇa in Svāminārāyaṇa theology who appears as a golden-hued and haired youth, and whose body is composed entirely out of *satchitānanda* or "truth-consciousness-bliss" (*Vacanāmṛta* Gaḍhaḍā II.13).[26]

From a sectarian viewpoint, this understanding is further realized in key examples of consecrated sculpted images, where parallels between Sahajānanda's historical body and *mūrti* are emphatically overlapped. Installed images of Sahajānanda within the *sampradāya*'s temple sanctums visually reflect the entity of Parabrahman Pūrṇa Puruṣottama Nārāyaṇa forever enthroned in his divine abode while at the same time being incarnate in earthly, physical form as the historical Sahajānanda. An extract from the *Śrīharilīlāmṛtam* supports this notion through the continued narrative theme of the artist and sitter. In this case, a secondary incident is relayed involving the artistic efforts of Nārāyaṇajī Suthāra who endeavors to translate Sahajananda's body into sculpted form. During the construction of the Svāminārāyaṇa temple at Gadhada in 1828, Suthāra was tasked to create an image of Kṛṣṇa as the deity Śrī Gopīnāthajīdeva Mahārāja.

Figure 9.6 On left, *Mūrti* of Sahajānanda Svāmī as Śrī Harikṛṣṇa Mahārāja. Gujarat, 1824. *Pañcadhātu* alloy. Shree Swaminarayan Mandir (Lakshmi-Narayan Dev), Vadtal. On right, *Mūrti* of Śrī Gopīnāthajīdeva Mahārāja. Gujarat, 1828. Black stone. Shree Swaminarayan Mandir (Gopinathji Dev), Gadhada. Photographs by Ankur Desai.

This image, on the right of Figure 9.6, was directly modeled after the proportions of Sahajānanda, who sat for Suthāra and blessed him with the ability to constantly behold his form while executing the work (*Śrīharilīlāmṛtam* IV. 8.61). Moreover, in an earlier occurrence, Sahajānanda's own image as the deity Śrī Harikṛṣṇa Mahārāja—composed in *pañcadhātu* (five metals)—was also directly modeled after him and was installed by his own hands in the southwest sanctum of the Svāminārāyaṇa temple at Vadtal in 1824 as seen on the left of Figure 9.6.[27] In both instances Sahajānanda's body provided the *tāla* (unit) measurements for the *mūrtis*, thereby correlating his temporal physicality with the idealized, *alaukikarūpa* (transmundane form) that sacred images are associated with. While these sculpted images, along with the literary and painted examples discussed, certainly reflect a multivalency of approach, form, and function, they ultimately succeed in coalescing Sahajānanda's image in the devotional eye. For sectarian adherents, the distinctions between text, painted likeness, and abstracted sculpted form are consolidated, reflecting an understanding of Sahajānanda's identity as unified whole, where his *laukika* existence and form within the sphere of nineteenth-century Gujarat is, in fact, *alaukika*.

Conclusion

Throughout the rest of the nineteenth century, Svāminārāyaṇa image production continued to engage diverse artistic styles and methods, allowing for an adaptable and varied approach to generating Sahajānanda's form. As with his miraculous appearance in twelve ways during the *puṣpadolotsava* festival of 1816, images of Sahajānanda produced within the formative decades of the *sampradāya* are multifaceted and reflect a synthesis of diverse aesthetic histories and notions regarding sacred form. This merging of formats and approaches, then, adds complexity to the broader discourse of sacred Indic art, especially when images are not so easily defined as either portrait or *mūrti*, but rather share aspects from both parts in equal measure. Further research on the blurring between such artistic categories has the potential to yield a more incisive impression of the intricacies encountered in the study of sacred Indic imagery, especially where past modes of artistic expression persist in being reenvisioned and re-formed as religious traditions continue to evolve.

Notes

1 This essay builds on my previous explorations of Svāminārāyaṇa art and architecture. See Desai (2013 and 2019).

2 See note 47 from Patel (2017: 82).

3 Kaimal argues that portraiture and sacred images were separate genres in premodern India, even referring to portraiture's distinct, lowly status in some art treatises, such as the *Śukranītiśāra* by Śukrācārya (see note 2 from Kaimal 1995: 10).

4 I am using a modern translation of the *Vacanāmṛta*. See reference: Bhagwan (2015).

5 Allison Busch's research on the works of Braj poet Keśavadāsa (fl.1600 CE) shows that the *nakhaśikha* format was copiously used—at least in the context of Vaiṣṇava devotional poetry—by the seventeenth century. A contemporaneous treatise on poetry from circa 1601, the *Kavipriyā*, outlines the rules of *nakhaśikha* in its fifteenth chapter. According to the text, divinities should be described from bottom to top, whereas mortals are to be described from the head downward.

6 However, not all Svāminārāyaṇa *nakhaśikha* poetic descriptions feature the conclusive *chāpa*.

7 The incident of Premānanda's spontaneous composition took place on February 28, 1824. Premānanda ends the first portion of his verses with "From nail to tuft [head to toe] may the form of Premasakhi's Lord forever delight within my heart," *Vandu Sahajānanda Rasarūpa, Pada 1.*

8 By canonical, I am referring to the bank of perpetuated visual tropes found in early treatises that address figural art. The contents of these sources convey similar idealized physical traits used in Svāminārāyaṇa devotional poetry. For example, *ādhyāya* 38 of the seventh-century treatise *Citrasūtra* describes the eyes of deities as "similar to a blue lotus petal, with reddish corners, black pupils, benevolent, possessing long eyelashes . . . with their whites of the colour of cow's milk" (Mukherji 2001: 59).

9 Select verses referenced: *Vahālā tārā danta dāḍamnā bīja, chaturāī chāvtā re lol; Āvo mārā rasiyā rājīvneṇa, marama karī boltā re lol.* Interestingly, the description of Sahajānanda starts from the top of the body and thus does not adhere to the rules of *nakhaśikha* composition as outlined in the *Kavipriyā*. The adherence to this top-to-bottom direction, suitable for descriptions of humans, further complicates the notion of Sahajānanda as both a historical human figure and divine being.

10 Patel notes that many *sādhu*s often kept personal records (*vāto*) of their experiences within the community, as well as their interactions with Sahajānanda. Over time, these accounts became increasingly authoritative due to their historicity.

11 Kalyan Krishna suggests that the tradition of *pichvāi* painting possibly emerged out of narrative performance and theater. In other words, that textual sources informed performance, which in turn may have informed the depiction of *līlā* in Puṣṭi Mārga art.

12 By this I am referring to portraiture's most common approach of depicting subjects through anthropomorphic representation, often with the attendant aim at partial or full mimesis.

13 The term *līlā* is technically defined as "play" or "sport," but its definition is generally understood as all life events, actions, and mannerisms of a sacred or divine figure. In his study of Kṛṣṇa *līlā*, Kinsley implies this very notion by suggesting how the dissemination of primary *līlā* texts led to not only the sustained prevalence of Kṛṣṇa veneration but also the development of alternative histories of the deity. Thus, early compositions generated new narrative variants.

14 Paramtattvadas describes several instances in the *Vacanāmṛta* where Sahajānanda directly mentions the veneration of Parabrahman's (God's) *caraṇārvinda* in the divine abode of Akṣaradhāma. For Svāminārāyaṇa adherents, such references serve as *pramāṇa* (proof) of a formed godhead.

15 The *Śrīharicaritrāmṛtasāgara* (1871), attributed to Ādhārānanda Svāmī, is one text that relays the account of Nārāyaṇaji Hīrajibhai Suthāra. It also provides in depth details on the iconography of divinities associated with the sect.

16 Vinit Vyas also notes that the text *Satsaṅgībhuṣana*, by Vāsudevānanda Brahmacārī, mentions the circulation of portable sacred images as early as 1819 (Vyas 2019: 10).

17 Based on stylistic grounds, this painting was probably not made during the lifetime of Sahajānanda. However, extremely similar images from the early nineteenth century do exist in other temple collections. See note 20 of this chapter.

18 The term *kamangari* refers to a particular style developed by the Kamāgara Muslim caste. Originally, the caste was known for bow-making but subsequently trained in wall painting (Tyabji 2006: 90).

19 Dave and Pārikha reveal that one Devasībhai Suthāra was part of the team that worked on the Aina Mahal Palace of Rāo Lakhpatji under the direction of the court's principal artist, Rāmasiṃha Mālam. Devasībhai Suthāra was either the grandfather or grand-uncle of Nārāyaṇajī Suthāra and was also a lay devotee-artist of the *sampradāya*. It is certain that Nārāyaṇajī Suthāra, given his familial relationship to the artists of Bhuj, was especially affected by the syncretic styling and imported elements that went into the city's visual works.

20 The Shree Swaminarayan Museum in Ahmedabad houses a similar series of images printed from a metal cast attributed to Nārāyaṇajī Suthāra. These prints, which may also be compared with depictions of Śrīnāthajī, show Sahajānanda in a frontal, two-armed cosmic form with the inscriptional title of "Śrī Bhaktidharmātmajāya [the son of *bhakti* and *dharma*] Vāsudeva Svāmī." This figure is shown holding aloft two flowers and is postured in a stance similar to images of the traditionally two-armed Indic solar deity Sūrya.

21 Notably, the template of Svāminārāyaṇa ritual image veneration was directly borrowed from the Puṣṭi Mārga tradition, so much so that this influence was codified in verses 81–2 of the Svāminārāyaṇa *Śikṣāpatrī* (Williams 2001: 758–9).

22 In fact, the vast majority of Sahajānanda's sartorial descriptions that precede each *Vacanāmṛta* sermon convey that he was most often dressed in plain white garments and only modestly ornamented with flowers. Despite this, Patel argues that these descriptions, which are situated within the larger material context of the darbar-like setting in which the sermons took place, nonetheless affirm the notion of Sahajānanda's presentation as a local ruler. For a detailed overview of Sahajānanda's clothing, see Chapter 14 in Vaghela (1997).

23 The attribution of this sketch to Suthāra, though ardently confirmed by the administrative authorities of the Shree Swaminarayan Mandir, Gadhada, cannot be concretely established without further inspection. Moreover, the Shree Swaminarayan Mandir, Kalupur, possesses a large, hand-painted version similar to the Gadhada sketch, apparently dated to 1823. The Kalupur temple claims this to be the very first image of Sahajānanda created by Suthāra. However, I posit that the painting's titular inscription may be a later addition superimposed over the original border. Moreover, the assertion that the painting is the earliest image of Sahajānanda does not correspond with early sectarian narratives and known artistic practices during the nineteenth century (most often, a paper sketch would first be drafted before a large-scale painted work). Vinit Vyas has discussed the aforementioned 1823 painting (2019: 6–7).

24 Vinit Vyas reiterates this notion by pointing to the larger and pervasive practice of copying within the tradition of Rajput and Mughal painting. Vyas notes that

copying was not only enfolded into the training of artists as a way to refine their skill, but that certain visual devices were worth repeating because of their authoritative and "archetypal" status (Vyas 2019: 9, ref. note 43).

25 However, the *Vacanāmṛta* and other Svāminārāyaṇa texts do describe Sahajānanda holding flowers on several occasions (see, for example, *Vacanāmṛta* Gaḍhaḍā I.14). Nonetheless, Goswamy and Dallapiccola's foundational survey of court painting in Kutch provides several examples of individual and group dynastic portraits where the primary subjects are shown holding and smelling flowers. Goswamy and Dallapiccola note the convention's link to imperial Mughal painting (ref. Pl. I, II).

26 This venerated form of Parabrahman Pūrṇa Puruṣottama Nārāyaṇa is central in the *sampradāya*'s theology. Moreover, the bodily attributes and features of this being are appropriated from earlier references in Vedānta scripture (Dave 2000: 206). In *Vacanāmṛta* Gaḍhaḍā III.38, Sahajānanda explicitly affirms to his followers that there is no distinction between his earthly manifestation and his transcendent form as Parabrahman Pūrṇa Puruṣottama Nārāyaṇa.

27 The placement of Sahajānanda's own image within a subsidiary shrine and not the central one (and also in only one of the six early temples) has been argued to indicate a reluctance to accept the belief in his status as the ultimate godhead.

References

Aitken, M. E. (2010), *The Intelligence of Tradition in Rajput Court Painting*, New Haven: Yale University Press.

Bhagwan, S. (2015), *The Vachanāmrut: Spiritual Discourses of Bhagwān Swāminārāyan*, eds. Muktananda Swami, Gopalananda Swami, Nityananda Swami, and Shukananda Swami, trans. BAPS Sadhus, Amdavad: Swaminarayan Aksharpith.

Columbia University. *Sarapa and Nakh-Shikh Varnan: A Workshop*, Four Examples from Keshavdas (fl. 1600) provided by Allison Busch. http://www.columbia.edu/itc/mealac/pritchett/00urduhindilinks/workshop2006/keshavdas/keshavdas_index.html (accessed July 7, 2018).

Dave, K. J., and P. C. Pārikha (1984), *Svāminārāyaṇa Citrakalā: Svāminārāyaṇa Śilpa-Sthāpatyakalā*, Amadāvāda: Bhagavāna Śrī Svāminārāyaṇa Dviśatabdī Mahotsava Samiti.

Dave, R. M. (2000), *Navya-Viśiṣṭādvaita: The Vedānta Philosophy of Śri Swāminārāyaṇa*, Mumbai: Akṣara Prakāśana.

Desai, A. (2013), "From Head to Toe: Portraiture and the Sacred Image in Swaminarayan Sampraday," Paper presented at the (MAHS) Midwest Art History Society Conference, March 21–23, The Ohio State University, Columbus.

Desai, A. (2019), "The Art and Architecture of the BAPS Svāminārāyaṇa Hindu Tradition," PhD diss., The Ohio State University, Columbus.

Goswamy, B. N., and A. L. Dallapiccola (1983), *A Place Apart: Painting in Kutch, 1720–1820*, Bombay: Oxford University Press.

Hatcher, B. A. (2020), *Hinduism Beyond Reform*, Cambridge, MA: Harvard University Press.

Kaimal, P. (1995), "Passionate Bodies: Constructions of the Self in South Indian Portraits," *Archives of Asian Art* 48: 6–16.

Kaimal, P. (1999), "The Problem of Portraiture in South India, circa 870–970 A.D.," *Artibus Asiae* 59 (1/2): 59–133.

Kim, H. (2009), "Public Engagement and Personal Desires: BAPS Swaminarayan Temples and their Contributions to the Discourses on Religion," *International Journal of Hindu Studies* 13 (3): 357–90.

Kinsley, D. R. (1979), *The Divine Player: A Study of Kṛṣṇa Līlā*, Delhi: Motilal Banarsidass.

Krishna, K. K. (2015), "Pichvais: Narrative Textiles and Their Origins," in M. Ghose (ed.), *Gates of the Lord: The Tradition of Krishna Paintings*, 36–41, Chicago: The Art Institute of Chicago.

Lefebvre, V. A. (2011), *Portraiture in Early India: Between Transience and Eternity*, Handbook of Oriental Studies, vol. 25, Leiden: Brill.

Moin, A. A. (2012), *The Millennial Sovereign: Sacred Kingship & Sainthood in Islam*, New York: Columbia University Press.

Mukherji, P. D. (2001), *The Citrasūtra of the Viṣṇudharmottara Purāṇa*, New Delhi: Indira Gandhi National Centre for the Arts.

Niṣkuḷānanda, S. (2010 [1804]), *Yamdand*, Shree Swaminarayan Mandir Bhuj Kutch: Sadguru Mahant Purani Swami Dharmnandandasji & Shree Narnarayandev Printing Press.

Packert, C. (2016), "Early Swaminarayan Iconography and Its Relationship to Vaishnavism," in R. B. Williams and Y. Trivedi (eds.), *Swaminarayan Hinduism: Tradition, Adaptation, and Identity*, 240–56, London: Oxford University Press.

Paramtattvadas, S. (2017), *An Introduction to Swaminarayan Theology*, Cambridge, UK: Cambridge University Press.

Patel, S. (May 1, 2017), "Beyond the Lens of Reform: Religious Culture in Modern Gujarat," *The Journal of Hindu Studies* 10 (1): 47–85. https://doi.org/10.1093/jhs/hix005 (Accessed October 5, 2017).

Patel, S. (forthcoming a), "Networks of Power in the Nineteenth Century: The Sampradaya, Princely States and Company Rule," Unpublished paper.

Patel, S. (forthcoming b), "The Play of History: The Swaminarayan Religious Community in Modern India," Unpublished manuscript.

Roth, N. (2021, April 9), *Balsam and Betel Nut Palm: Botanical Representation in the Early Modern Deccan* [Zoom Presentation] From Malabar to Coromandel: The Future of Deccan Heritage, Art, and Culture Webinar Series. Deccan Heritage Foundation (DHF) Centre for Islamic Studies University of Cambridge and H.H. Srikantadatta Narasimharaja Waidyar Foundation.

Sanford, W. A. (2008), *Singing Krishna: Sound Becomes Sight in Paramanand's Poetry*, New York: State University of New York Press.

Satish, S. (2010), "Wall Paintings of Kutch: An Extinct Tradition," MA diss., M.S. University of Baroda.

Swami, Shatanand. (2013 [1830]), *Satsangi Jeevan*, trans. Shri Jethalal Dhanji Savani, Kalupur, Ahmedabad: Shastri Swami Hari Kṛṣṇadasji, Shri Swaminarayan Temple.

Swaminarayan, S. (1996), *Kīrtana Sāra*, Shahibaug, Ahmedabad: Swaminarayan Aksharpith.

Trivedi, Y. (2016), "Multivalent Krishna-Bhakti in Premanand's Poetry," in R. B. Williams and Y. Trivedi (eds.), *Swaminarayan Hinduism: Tradition, Adaptation, and Identity*, 191–217, London: Oxford University Press.

Tyabji, A. (2006), *Bhuj: Art-Architecture-History*, Ahmedabad, Ocean City: Mapin Publishing Gp. Pty. Ltd.

Vaghela, B. G. (1997), *Bhagavāna Svāminārāyaṇanuṃ Samakālina Lokajīvana*, Amadāvāda: Svāminārāyaṇa Akṣarapīṭha.

Vihārīlālajī Mahārāja, Ā. Ś. (2004 [1878]), *Śrīharilīlāmṛtam*, Kuṇḍaḷ: Tīrthadhāma Kuṇḍaḷdhāma tathā Śrī Svāminārāyaṇa Maṇdīra Kārelibāga-Vaḍodarā.

Vyas, V. (2019), "Śrījī nī Chabī: The Importance of Visual Culture in the Svāmīnārāyaṇ Sampradāya," Unpublished Paper.

Williams, R. B. (2001), *An Introduction to Swaminarayan Hinduism*, New York: Cambridge University Press.

Part III

Shaping the Return Look

10

Bhakti and Looking at What We Do Not Want to See

Karen Pechilis

The experience of "looking at what we do not want to see" manifests a tension in a scopic regime: The focus of the practice of looking is at odds with the horizon of what should be visible.[1] The tension alludes to "the far broader issue of visibility and invisibility, conceptualized not simply as antinomies but rather as different points on a single spectrum of the possibility of being made visible" (Bhattia and Pinney 2011: 238). The possibility of things being made visible is "a result of the practices of looking invested in them" (Bleeker 2008: 2). Intriguingly, "looking at what we do not want to see" reveals that our relationship to this practice of looking actually makes visible our own field of conventional expectations and desires—what we want to see. The point of departure for this essay is to ask why a sixth-century female *bhakti* poet-saint demands, in a verse of her poetry, that we look closely at a misshapen female figure. My identification and discussion of possible reasons will engage Indian theories in literature and in embodied practice as well as western theories of the abject and visual culture. My contention is that these lines of inquiry lead to discerning an alternative history of *bhakti* as fundamentally promoting a sustained visuality of attention to the challenging, disturbing, and avoided aspects of human social life.

In a verse attributed to Kāraikkāl Ammaiyār, the sixth-century Tamil Śiva-*bhakti* poet-saint, we are asked to gaze at a female *pēy*, a ghoulish figure whose body is the antithesis of human, and especially feminine, beauty.

> The female *pēy* has
> sagging breasts and bulging veins
> hollowed eyes and bared teeth
> ruddy down on her sunken belly
> long canines

and lanky shins on knobby ankles;
she lingers, howling, at the cremation ground.

Dancing here,
    with effortless composure
    as his matted locks radiate in all directions,
our father resides at Tiru Ālaṅkāṭu.

(*Tiruvālaṅkāṭṭu Tiruppatikam*-1, v. 1)

The context of the verse is a decad (ten verses plus a signature verse as eleventh in the set) that purports to describe, in eyewitness fashion, a wooded and menacing cremation ground in which lord Śiva dances at night. The poetess provides our field of vision. The ghoul (in the sense of one who delights in the morbid; *pēy*) is in the foreground, a subject described in detail. The figure of the dancing lord seems in the background, perhaps glimpsed by the poet over the *pēy*'s shoulder. In her other, longer poems, the gaze of the poetess fastens on Śiva, though never in this head-to-toe descriptive mode; instead, she directs our attention to his features, especially parts of his body and adornments on his body, that index his divine powers and heroic deeds. By contrast, in this verse we are compelled to look in detail at a female *pēy* in all her misshapen glory.

Literary Networks of Looking

In several ways, Kāraikkāl Ammaiyār (hereafter Ammaiyār[2]) was repurposing a cultural image. The female *pēy* was a trope in Tamil Caṅkam poetry, usually dated by scholars to several centuries prior to Ammaiyār. Caṅkam poems describe bands of female *pēy* gorging on the remains of men fallen in battle. For example, the *Puṟanāṉūṟu*, a collection of Tamil poetry (approx. first through third centuries CE) that largely focuses on themes of war and heroism, emphasizes earning fame prior to death and transport to the cremation ground. It describes the burning ground as a desolate, desiccated place where owls shriek, foxes pull apart corpses, and "demonesses" (*pēy peṇṭir*) consume the cadavers "by the light of the pyres, their bodies sending out the stench of hot meat because they have consumed the bloodless flesh" (*Puṟanāṉūṟu* 359; Hart and Heifetz 1999: 203). Verses in Ammaiyār's two decads on Tiruvalankatu represent *pēy* engaged in such activities with human bodies that have been deposited at the cremation ground, but it is a seemingly ordinary space with no overt or implied connection to the battleground of war as in the Caṅkam poetry. For this reason, Ammaiyār's description is also distinctive from a description of a female *pēy* in the late Caṅkam poem *Tirumurukkārruppaṭai*, which is likely to be contemporaneous with or later than Ammaiyār's poetry (Francis 2017: 319). In ten verses of its approximately 317 total, a female *pēy* is singled out for description as she performs her dance of victory and joy (*tuṇaṅkai*) while chewing on corpses, her distorted body indicated by her dry hair, gaping mouth, rolling eyes, live animal ornaments, pendulous breasts, and bloody fingers (see Zvelebil 1973: 126; Little n.d. vv. 47–56). Connected to war, she "frightfully sings mighty battlefield songs of conquest and destruction" (Little n.d., v. 55).

In not associating the female *pēy* with the battlefield, Ammaiyār's detailed look at her confounds the Caṅkam cultural view. In Ammaiyār's poetry, the *pēy* is contextualized by the presence of Śiva as he performs his cosmic dance. That sight elevates the cremation ground from a space simply for depositing the body as the refuse of death to a place where religious meanings of life and death are experientially grasped. This in turn brings Ammaiyār's poetry into dialogue with both Buddhist and tantric literatures, which encourage attendance at the cremation ground for such contemplation and their own correlative ritual practice (see Pechilis 2012: 67–75; Pechilis 2016). Ammaiyār's repurposing of the ghoulish image provides a distinctive view of the cremation ground as a place of religious contemplation and contestation. The cremation ground is made visible in the scopic regime of these religious practices.

As a practice of looking, the detailed description of a particular female *pēy* in Ammaiyār's verse also has kinship with the practice of looking in other Indian literatures, such as the "head-to-toe" (*nakha-śikha*) description that became a noted feature of much of the cosmopolitan Sanskrit *kāvya* (high literary poetry) and in other languages that built on Sanskrit models in the medieval period, as in the description of the women of Rajput chief Bir Singh Deo Bundela's harem, starting with the crown, in court poet Keshavdas's sixteenth-century *Rāmcandracandrikā* in Brajbhasha as discussed by Alison Busch: "The splendor where their hair is parted dazzles the heart,/like lightning flashing amid storm clouds./The vermilion-filled parts are luminous, crowned with a string of pearls."[3] Such descriptions also became a noted feature in Śrivaiṣṇava literature in Tamil and Sanskrit in the eighth to fourteenth centuries, where they were identified in commentaries as "experiences" (*anubhavas*) of images of Viṣṇu in shrines, as discussed by Steven Hopkins. He argues that in contrast to royal "head-to-toe" descriptions, devotional instances proceed from the toe of the Lord to the head, citing Deśika's fourteenth-century Sanskrit poem for Raṅganātha, the *Bhagavaddhyānasopānam* ("The Ladder of Meditation on the Lord"): "The lotus feet of the Lord of Raṅga,/exuding the perfume of the infinite Veda,/touched by the pious crowns of all the gods/and fondled by the lotus hands/of Lakṣmī and Bhū."[4] In these examples, there is a match between the physical beauty of the imagined or observed and the aesthetic experience prompted by the glorious description. The context is the power of the social affirmation, advantage, and prestige associated with beauty.

Ammaiyār's description of the female *pēy* is distinctive insofar as it does not strictly follow the head-to-toe order—she starts in the middle of the body and then alternately ascends and descends, a gaze seemingly mirroring the unbeautiful disorganization of the female *pēy*'s body. Literary descriptions of the female form did not have an uncomplicated relationship to beauty, as suggested by texts dated to earlier times nearer to Ammaiyār's period. The example of a work by Bāṇa, of the seventh century, is valuable in this regard. His *Caṇḍīśataka* praises the goddess by extolling the beauty of her foot that defeats Mahiṣa—"Toe-nails that are veritable moon-stones by reason of their self-radiant splendor"—but it also revels in the blood and destruction she causes (v. 11; Quackenbos 1917: 278). In his discussion of this poem, Friedhelm Hardy notes the salvific frame of praise to a deity, but he also links the poem to human discord, speculating that, based on the legend that Bāṇa composed this poem "when his own mistress was '*caṇḍī*', in a state of rage . . . the poem could be regarded as a prayer directly addressed to the Goddess to help him pacify his mistress, and/or as a love-letter indirectly begging his mistress to forgive him."[5] The *Mayūrāṣṭaka* of the probably contemporary poet Mayūra provides a distinctive example of this theme of "beautiful but." A young, beautiful maiden is walking: "Who is this (maiden), with beautiful limbs and wandering glance, approaching with the gait of a *haṃsa*?," but there are telltale signs that she is coming from a session of lovemaking—her garments cling to her perspiring skin, and she is redoing her hair, in which few flowers remain—she has "yielded to the power of love," and her body betrays the disarray of emerging from sexual use when looked at more closely. The poem ends on a positive note of determining her to be "surely . . . a celestial nymph, produced on earth by Brahmā," but this does not negate the poem's theme that lovemaking makes her undone (vv. 1, 2, 4, 8 in Quackenbos 1917: 72–8). These images shape narratives to intertwine the lovely and the unlovely within a positive frame, such as the righteousness of the goddess and the affirmation of love (*kama*) as a worthy human pursuit.

The corporeal misshapenness of Ammaiyār's *pēy* precludes such a sense of restoration, raising the condition identified by Arindam Chakrabarti of a "residual paradox: how the abhorrent become aesthetically arresting"

(Chakrabarti 2016: 155). In the verse, the inelegance of the bulging, sunken, and bared aspects of the *pēy*'s body contrast with the elegant dance of Śiva. This is made explicit in the verse: What I have translated as Śiva "dancing with effortless composure" is literally "dancing on the fire with cool/refreshed/composed limbs" (*aṅkaṅ kuḷirntaṉa lāṭu*), a counterpoint to the *pēy*'s "lanky shins on knobby ankles." This contrast is in the visual context of the cremation ground mentioned in the verse. Enhancing the work on *rasa* performed by K. C. Bhattacharya in the 1930s, Chakrabarti proposes "six varieties of aesthetic disgust" (Chakrabarti 2016: 159). One of his propositions specifically addresses religion: "Fourth, *the hideous can emerge as a prop for artistic relish when it is shown to be overcome by heroic, committed, or religious love*" (161; italics in the original). To illustrate this theme, he mentions the popular story "Beauty and the Beast," Tagore's *King of the Dark Chamber*, and the life stories of nuns, such as St. Catherine in Christianity and the Therīgāthā Shubha in Buddhism. In terms of the religious stories particularly, he understands them as "life-stories of nuns who did hideous things in order to test or prove their compassion" (161). In the case of Ammaiyār, the potential "proof" of her love for Śiva is not inflicting disgust on herself, as with St. Catherine drinking pus and Shubha gouging out her own eyes, but is instead lingering at the cremation ground where he dances. This lingering is conveyed through the look that seems to carefully record in other verses in the decad all of the disturbing objects found in the cremation ground, from startling predator birds, to corpses, to the female *pēy*, as though the poet performs a kind of *flaneur* of the macabre.

In other words, Ammaiyār's verse and the other verses in this decad (as well as another set of eleven along the same lines; for translation, see Pechilis 2012: 188–98) do not have the drama of "proof." Instead, the tenor is observational—a calm, encompassing view. I find two other aesthetic modes of disgust suggested by Chakrabarti more generative. The second mode, "*the hideous as the counterpoint for a shocking contrast that fascinates us*" (Chakrabarti 2016: 160), names the dynamic of seeing the *pēy* and Śiva in the same visual frame. It invites the observer to be startled by their differences, to wonder why they are in proximity, and to reflect on the location of the observer on the spectrum they suggest. The visceral aspect of this looking also needs to be addressed, to which Chakrabarti's sixth mode contributes: "*the viscerally vibrant absorption of the hideous for the sake of the sheer thrill of sensing every fold of embodied existence*" (162); however, the feel of Ammaiyār's verse under consideration, as well as across the verses on Tiruvalankatu, does not suggest a euphoria but instead an existential shudder as a resonant reckoning with embodied existence.

Visualities of the Abject

The twist in this tale is that Kāraikkāl Ammaiyār herself came to be imagined as this female *pēy* in stone and in bronze, in an interpretive act of conflation that can concretely be traced to her formidable biographer, a court minister named Cēkkiḻār who lived in the mid-twelfth century.[6]

The bronze images (Figure 10.1), two of which are dated to the thirteenth century (Chola dynasty era) and set the main principles of her iconography into the future, were designed for worship of her in Śiva temples and would be part of a set of statues of all sixty-three traditional Śiva-*bhakti* saints, so designated since the late classical era (*c.* 700–800 CE), if the temple could afford it. The placement of the image at the Śrī Kailāsanathan̲ Temple in Karaikkal, Tamil Nadu (Figure 10.1 bottom left), resembles reliefs of the dancing Śiva and Ammaiyār, such as at Rajendra Chola I's imperial temple at Gangaikondacholapuram (*c.* 1035 CE), in placing her as seated below the raised foot of the dancing Śiva Naṭarāja. There is variation across images of Ammaiyār as a *pēy*, especially in the hair and the face.[7] She can be seemingly bald or have a mass of locks, either of which can be read as a lack of assumed conventional feminine concern with appearance, in the service of religious pursuit. She can have an expression that ranges from a mild smile to a snarl. Ubiquitous features include that she is seated, she has long ear lobes (bearing tiny earrings in the MET image, Figure 10.1 top left), she has marks on her body suggesting thinness or emaciation, she has triangular breasts, narrow hips, long shins, and is playing cymbals with the hands.[8] This image too illustrates a "residual paradox: how the abhorrent become aesthetically arresting" (Chakrabarti 2016: 155), in its challenge to the canons of rendering female beauty in Indian art, in spite of its aestheticization by its use of proportionality as well as in its claim to be a portrait of the saint herself, so that we look at her, but we would not want to look like her.

In his life story of Ammaiyār, the biographer Cēkkiḻār promotes the idea that the figure of the *pēy* was understood to be repulsive by indicating that her transformation to a *pēy* signals a decisive break with her husband and family. That this break extends to the entire society is made clear in a scene in which ordinary people who view her in this form on the road making her way to Śiva's abode in Mt. Kailash are frightened by it and run away (Pechilis 2012: 203–4). Although her biographer sought to stabilize Ammaiyār's image as a saint, he destabilized her as an image of human devotion by putting her at odds with the social gaze, since ordinary people turn away and do not want to look. The onlookers in the story do not recognize the *pēy* body as saintly or sacred; that would have to be learned—from her biographer.

Figure 10.1 The many faces of Kāraikkāl Ammaiyār. Clockwise from top left: Karaikkal Ammaiyar, Shaiva Saint. Chola Period (880–1279), late thirteenth century, India (Tamil Nadu). Copper alloy. The Metropolitan Museum, New York City. CC0 1.0 Universal (CC0 1.0) Public Domain Dedication. Top right: Karaikkal-Ammaiyar, thirteenth century, Tamil Nadu. Victoria and Albert Museum, London. Used with permission. Bottom right: Contemporary reproduction image after the bronze image of Kāraikkāl Ammaiyār at the Vaṭāraṇyēśvara Cuvāmi Tirukōyil temple in Tiruvalankatu, Tiruvallar District, Tamil Nadu. This bronze was commissioned by the author to be made at Rajan Industries in Swamimalai in 2003; Author's Collection. Photo taken by the author, 2010. Bottom left: Kāraikkāl Ammaiyār at the feet of Śiva Naṭarāja at the Śrī Kailāsanathan̲ Temple in Karaikkal, Tamil Nadu. Photo taken by the author, 2009.

Today, the image of Ammaiyār is enframed by conventional Hindu piety in a brahmanic cultural network of meaning. To the Tamil Hindu public, the image of Ammaiyār as a *pēy* is primarily understood to represent a devotee of Śiva. That is the accepted and unproblematic mode of viewing the image, situating it in a category that is easily understood culturally and accompanied by known codes of behavior. For example, all of the images of the sixty-three classical Śaiva devotees are processed around the Kapālīśwarar Temple in Chennai during the major annual Paṅkuṉi Uttiram festival in March–April and Ammaiyār is within that large group. The images face backward, toward the icon of Śiva, as they are processed forward on stands by living human devotees; the mass of devotion they represent prepares the crowd for the appearance of Śiva later in the procession. They thus constitute an image of "devotion." However, one of the years I went to the festival while I was researching Ammaiyār, I noticed that her image in particular attracted devotees to light a piece of camphor on the ground in front of her image; she received several such gestures of honor, while most images had none. In such gestures, a crack is opened for the possibility of appreciating the challenge of the unbeautiful, distinguishing the image of Ammaiyār from an iterative representation of a uniform devotion to Śiva as suggested by the set, which compels us to look more closely.

In his discussion of Indian aesthetics of the repulsive, Chakrabarti notes: "Even 900 years before Abhinavagupta, Bharata distinguished between two types of hideous: *due to anxiety* (*ksobha-ja*), associated with saliva, excreta, worms, slime, dirt; and *due to agitation* (*udvega-ja*), associated with blood, entrails, corpses, and so on. A good example of the first would be the poem by Yeats called 'Crazy Jane Talks with the Bishop' that ends as follows" (Chakrabarti 2016: 157). His comment relates to a larger argument he is making that just as western theories have been used to illuminate Indian arts, the reverse can be true, because "there is no reason to freeze the ancient theories with their own local and contemporary examples" (Chakrabarti 2016: 152). Intriguingly, the distinction made by Bharata can be viewed as an apt way to characterize the difference between the views of two influential modern theorists of the abject, Georges Bataille and Julia Kristeva. These theories can be applied to investigate the visuality of the sculpture of Ammaiyār as the female *pēy*.

Bataille, who is said to be the first to theorize the abject concept, discussed it along lines that could be considered to resemble Bharata's "anxiety" distinction.[9] Bataille developed his theory under very distinct circumstances, at the time of the rise of fascism in the 1930s, and his reflections were a critique, especially "as a way of countering the 'sublimating' tendencies at work among the cultural avant-garde," including the Surrealists.[10] In his view, the abject is initiated by a tyrannical "noble" class that constitutes its "purity" by its sadistic and erotic forcing of the underclass to be unable to avoid contact with the materially abject such as filth.[11] Completely mired in these degrading circumstances, the underclass internalizes the condition: "When it ceases to be experienced as an act of exclusion to become an autonomous condition, it is then, and only then, that abjection sets in" (Lotringer 1999: 7).

It is possible to apply Bataille's theory of the performativity of the abject to Indian culture by noting that a brahmanic discourse of anxiety about everyday polluting substances emanating from select bodies (saliva, excreta) marks those bodies.[12] In an intriguing article, Akhila Vimal C. (2018) disrupts the scholarly idea that the traditional performance of Pottan Teyyam in Kerala today, in which "a performer belonging to the otherwise untouchable caste transforms into a god, often in a state of possession," constitutes a redemption—or sublimation—of the *adivasi*'s social status. She points to several factors, but I will emphasize her remarks on the disfigured bodily appearance of the performer. She asserts that both the performer's mask (*mukhapala*) and the covering of ash on the performer's body, which prevent his being burned when he lies down on the fire during the performance, look like scars, "a disfiguration that goes beyond the performance and hints at the deep-rooted social stigma." The movements of the performer's body are jerky, and even animal-like, and his speech is full of slang and unclear, such that another performer needs to "translate" it to the audience (Vimal C. 2018: 113). The drama also includes a female character, Pulachamundi, who appears in "torn and dirty clothes, wearing a stone necklace, unruly hair and body covered in mud that emphasizes the transformation of Goddess Parvati into a lower-caste woman" (Vimal C. 2018: 111). These exaggerated signs of Pulaya identity are performatively supposed to be Śiva in disguise, and the drama promotes a message of recognizing equality and thus validating the *adivasi*s. But the author argues convincingly that the body of the Pulaya, degraded by disfiguration in the drama, invalidates such sublimation. The body of "filth" is both created and maintained by religion, encoded by brahmanic anxiety and marked externally to reinforce the internalization of lesser status.

Vimal C.'s analysis cleaves the ritual's attempt to represent identity through performance. The anxiety over caste it reveals may also inform Ammaiyār's identity, but it is difficult to tell, because she does not disclose her caste in her poetry, and her biographer Cēkkiḻār explicitly locates her in a wealthy merchant and trading community. Yet the sculpted image that constitutes our vision of her retains traces of disfiguration from the feminine norm, suggesting an anxiety. As with the example of the Pottan Teyyam ritual, it is not her (the marked body's) anxiety. Ammaiyār's poetry has a meditative, self-reflexive quality to it. She expresses concerns that are religiously defined, such as seeing Śiva, accessing his grace, and distinguishing his devotees from others. In the cremation ground, she quietly observes. A gendered possibility exists: her male biographer's anxiety over a woman who is alone. Many details in his story directly ensure that her propriety is maintained (Pechilis 2014), culminating in her bodily transformation to a *pēy* that is effected by her request once she understands that her husband has remarried. Its unbeautiful nature enables her to travel freely and safely to Mt. Kailash in order to see Śiva as well as to return by his direction to the Tamil town of Tiruvalankatu, where she would witness his cosmic dance. Her biographer's anxiety produces his description of her as gazing only at Śiva as he dances, conspicuously omitting any reference at all to the cremation ground that she so elaborately describes in her poetry.

The Gaze Back: Display and Performance

Yet the sculpted image of Ammaiyār, marked by cultural anxiety, stares back. Provocatively, W. J. T. Mitchell has claimed that images ("pictures") are themselves "abject" (Mitchell 1996; reprinted with additional notes in Mitchell 2005: 28–48), beyond consideration of their subject matter. He frames the issue as what pictures themselves want:

> The painting's desire, in short, is to change places with the beholder, to transfix or paralyze the beholder, turning him into an image for the gaze of the picture in what might be called "the Medusa effect." This effect is perhaps the clearest demonstration we have that the power of pictures and of women are modeled on one another and that this is a model of both pictures and women that is abject, mutilated and castrated. The power they want is manifested as *lack*, not as possession. (Mitchell 1996: 76)

The symbolic language of the disembodied Medusa and the generic lack of the female body have been criticized as leaving out the violence done to women's bodies (Yue: 17–27), a point to which I shall return. But it does make visible assumptions of materiality and agency, especially who has the right to look. As theorized by Nicholas Mirzoeff, visuality "sutures authority to power and renders this association 'natural'" (Mirzoeff 2011: 6). Rooted in his reading of Carlyle, he considers visuality to be a regime of seeing that is controlled and naturalized by those in power. This regime precludes "the right to look" outside of the borders it enforces—that is, the source of abjection. It is by claiming the right to look, toward visualizing alternatives to the current regime, that a counter-visuality can be generated.

Situating the sculpture of Ammaiyār between Mitchell's theorizing on what images want (in the sense of both lack and desire; 1996, 2005) and Nicholas Mirzoeff's theorizing on who has the right to look (2011) enables us to see that the image is in fact gazing at us. Sadly, a destructive gesture that occurred at the St. Mungo Museum of Religious Life and Art in Glasgow in 1993 supports this point: "Only two months after the museum had opened, a visitor attacked and permanently damaged the museum's image of the Hindu god Shiva as Nataraja—the man said that he was acting in the name of Christ" (Singh 2006; see Paine 2013: 32). A 45-year-old man knocked the statue over, disabling its gaze and damaging one of its arms. The scopic regime that the museum was attempting to disrupt became visible: the Christian objects in the room had the right to look and be looked at but not the large (nearly six feet high) Hindu god. In the aftermath, the museum doubled down on its approach, leading workshops on bigotry and sectarianism guided by the notion that "a thought-provoking visit can lead visitors to question themselves and their views" (Singh 2006: 4). Or, in my terms, the programs showed that the gaze of an image has the power to make visible, and thus destabilize, a scopic regime.

What might the gaze of the sculpture of Ammaiyār be? A complicating factor is that, although Kāraikkāl Ammaiyār says that she has "joined the *pēy*" in her poetry, and her signature verses identify her as "Kāraikkāl *pēy*," does that mean that she becomes a *pēy*? The answer is debatable (see Pechilis 2012: 65–70). Her biographer Cēkkiḻār's perspective is that she does become a *pēy* at her own explicit request to Śiva ("give to me, your servant, the form of the ghouls who venerate your sacred feet," v. 49; Pechilis 2012: 203) and experiences a bodily transformation. Yet, he eschews the cremation ground that is the context in the poetry for Ammaiyār's description of the female *pēy* that her biographer and artisans who fashioned temple images take up in the first place. In her biographer's eyes, then, the image of Ammaiyār simply gazes at the dancing Śiva, which returns us to the normative visuality of devotion.

If we join the sculpture—as a self-image that she may or may not have had—with Ammaiyār's poetry, we gain a different sight. Her poems on Tiruvalankatu present themselves as in eyewitness mode, filled with descriptions of material items that suggest immersion in a socially undesirable context—a landscape that features menacing avian predators, strange rattling sounds from dried-out flora, the stark chiaroscuro of night shadows and flames encircling the eerie cremation ground, with fire and mangled body parts from corpses at its center—which seems to resonate with Bataille's emphasis on the negatively charged material context that he glosses as "filth."

However, a challenge to the Bataillean understanding of the gaze is that Ammaiyār's poetry represents her as associating largely voluntarily with the *pēy* in order to be in the fright-inducing location, where she can directly witness the dance of Śiva. To witness his dance is her rationale for being there, as suggested by her poetry, yet her poetic gaze details the inhabitants of a landscape that human society avoids and abhors. This challenges Bataille's description of the overwhelmed person's involuntary internalization of the negative social gaze. Instead of "*anxiety* (*ksobha-ja*), associated with saliva, excreta, worms, slime, dirt," the glimpse of bodily breakdown and death provided by the scene instead suggests "*agitation* (*udvega-ja*), associated with blood, entrails, corpses, and so on" (Chakrabarti 2016: 157). Here I find the theorizing of the abject by Julia Kristeva to be more generative. She posits that we carry around with us ingrained ideas and practices of proper order.[13] Through our own participation in, and maintenance of, this "symbolic order," we create what we sense is a stable identity. We understand, for example, the meaning of death in a conceptual framework that supports life. But when confronted by the materiality of death—a corpse—our symbolic order is threatened by the impossibility of assimilating the corpse: it lies in mute contradiction to our attempts to contain or exclude it. When this occurs, she theorizes, the subject and object distinctions we carry around with us break down in the face of the visceral realization of death and its ever proximity to life. That this realization is not a resolution—we remain alive, though challenged—is the experience of the abject (Kristeva 1982: 3–4, 65–6). This suggests an existential shudder, and the elements of the cremation ground that Ammaiyār describes—creepy animals and plants, chiaroscuro, corpses—are a visual inducement of the shudder. The shudder makes the symbolic order palpably visible.

For Kristeva, such an experience of the abject in the past was explored by religion, with its sacred "at the limits of social and subjective identity," but now is engaged by contemporary art, especially literature (Kristeva 1982: 26; see 17–26). In her view, a writer, especially a poet, explores ways in which language is structured over our deepest fears:

> any practice of speech, inasmuch as it involves writing, is a language of fear. . . . Not a language of the desiring exchange of messages or objects that are transmitted in a social contract of communication and desire beyond want, but

> a language of want, of the fear that edges up to it and runs along its edges. . . . We encounter this discourse in our dreams, or when death brushes us by, depriving us of the assurance mechanical use of speech ordinarily gives us, the assurance of being ourselves, that is, untouchable, unchangeable, immortal. But the writer is permanently confronted with such a language. (Kristeva 1982: 38)

This is a way of understanding the complexity of the *bhakti* gaze that looks out at us from the figure and the poetry. Although Kristeva wants to believe that religion can "purify" the abject, Vimal C.'s analysis of the brahmanic traditional performance of Pottan Teyyam challenges that connection. *Bhakti* is better described by Kristeva's insistence that the experience of the abject alters what we think we know and radically challenges us to see things in a different way.

The display of art objects holds potential for this challenge. The museum mode is to decontextualize objects from their cultural detail and recontextualize them with an eye toward chronology, object aesthetics, and programmatic concerns. In the case of the Ammaiyār sculpture, its gaze becomes spotlighted by such a technique, which opens possibility. If brought to a viewer's attention, this could challenge the viewer to ask and imagine what the object sees, rather than simply what the viewer sees. As Renée Hoogland proposes, aesthetic experience is the possibility of "an expressive event in which both the subject and the object of perception enter into a force field that is constituted in and by their encounter," which she argues is "a process of alteration, or a force field, whose consequences are neither pregiven nor unambivalent" (Hoogland 2014: 15).

Contemporary artists are directing the challenge of the abject's gaze toward identity and social justice concerns.[14] In her article "Queering Abjection," Jayne Wark argues, drawing on the theorizing of Julia Kristeva and Judith Butler, that attention to the abject can promote social change: "Butler's call for a reworking of abjection as a force for political agency and resignification resonates with Kristeva's opinion that 'abjection is eminently productive of culture. Its symptom is the rejection and reconstruction of languages'" (Wark 2016: 37, quoting Kristeva 1982: 45). In particular, Wark views lesbian-themed art as displays that foreground and thus undermine the social abjection of select bodies, such as lesbian bodies, by "invoking" the two theorists' "conceptions of [the abject's] potential for psychic and social transformation" (Wark 2016: 48). That is, seeing lesbian bodies overtly displayed in art creates the possibility of reckoning, recognition, or acceptance.

The gaze back to society is dramatized in the moving arts such as film, dance, and theater. In her pioneering research on visuality and theatrical performance, Maaike Bleeker points out the paradox of theatrical staging: "The staged character of the theatrical event makes it by definition antithetic to modernist notions of authenticity and truth, thus condemning the theatre to presentational strategies that, in order to convince as true and authentic, have to be aimed at obscuring or erasing traces of its own condition of being staged" (Bleeker 2008: 3). Building on Lehmann's discussion of the transformation from dramatic theater, which emphasizes representation, to postdramatic theater, which emphasizes "the relationship between what is staged and the modes of perceiving of the audience" (Bleeker and Germano 2014: 365), she directs our attention to the "relationality of vision" between "the body seen and the body seeing" (Bleeker 2008: 4). The aim is to shift the analysis from what the drama is saying to what it is doing: "Events can be staged in ways that confirm the beliefs that an audience already has, or in ways that propagate beliefs that the audience is stimulated to adopt. They can also be constructed in ways that destabilize systems of belief, and draw attention to how such systems mediate in the ways in which we relate to what we encounter" (Bleeker and Germano 2014: 365).

A recent example of a dance-drama on the life of Ammaiyār provides a case study. In 2012, the dance-drama *Katyayani's "O,"* in part exploring the life story of Kāraikkāl Ammaiyār (the other part was devoted to Rabi'a of Basra), was performed in Delhi.[15] My interest is in the ways in which the portion on Ammaiyār upends received expectations in terms of both the narrative content and the optics of the performance, piercing the scopic regime, and therein calls attention to the relationality between performer and seer (Bleeker's term, contrasted with the passivity of spectator, 2008: 18). In the first place, the subject of the dance-drama is a saint, but it is not a pious treatment as per earlier "mythologicals" films (for an example, see later in this essay) or contemporary drama akin to their modality (see an example in Pechilis 2019). Instead, the dance-drama's field of vision is informed by feminism, following the outlines of Cēkkiḻār's biographical story yet constructing a different perspective that does not remain at the level of inviting the audience to watch but instead calls attention to the agency of the seer. The dramatized saint's gaze back to us mediates this perspectival shift.

The biographer's dominant and now conventional version of her life story embeds Kāraikkāl Ammaiyār in a domestic drama: she and her husband argue over a mango that she secretly gave to a Śaiva mendicant, and when she tries to replace it with a mango she spontaneously receives from Śiva, her husband grows fearful and departs. The contemporary dance-drama retains the narrative frame of a domestic dispute but shifts the meaning to speak to a present-day concern: men's violence toward women's sexuality. In the dance-drama, but not the biography, Ammaiyār's husband accuses her of marital infidelity. This is a radical, sexualized departure from the biography, one that her biographer labored to foreclose. The contemporary dance further pushes the theme by situating the consequences of the husband's departure in a modern discourse of sexual harassment: after he flees, the dancer portrays the abandoned Ammaiyār as the victim of numerous unwanted sexual advances by strange men, dramatized by a masked male dancer actually grabbing her in an embrace while a voice-over provides numerous snippets of town gossip as well as beckoning calls of men. She throws off the man, screaming a curse, "to hell for you to betray the beauty that drove me," an intriguingly reflexive statement that she angrily repeats several times. Her anger at men's "betrayal" of her beauty challenges the male entitlement to approach, proposition, and assume possession of women by labeling them as selfishly unjust and violent in response to a woman's appearance. At the same time, this modern "Kāraikkāl Ammaiyār" raises the issue of her own investment in her beauty, implicitly critiquing its outsized role in the trajectory of her life toward marriage and her habitation of wifehood.

This moment of awareness precipitates her transformation to a *pēy* or ghoul-like creature. To the loud, rhythmic beat of drums and cymbals and bathed in red light, the dancer performs a strenuous dance to represent her *tapas* (or austerities) in the cremation ground. As the culmination of her transformation, the dancer appears in a monotone leotard and shorts, and ash falls from above to bathe her: this is her transformation to a *pēy* (Figure 10.2). At this moment, Śiva appears in human-like form, they dance while having a brief (voice-over) conversation, in which Ammaiyār says that she has "seen enough of this world" and asks to be taken to his heavenly abode, Mount Kailasha in the Himalayas. But Śiva tells her that "there is no Kailasha other than this world." She persists, asking "What kind of world?" and Śiva urges her to "let us transform this burning earth into the Kailasha of your imagination."

"What kind of world" indeed? It is an indeterminate question that is not directly answered by the narration of the dance-drama but instead hangs in the air, inviting the seer to engage it. The voice-over redefines the field of the dance-drama as "the world," well beyond a narrow story of one female saint. What has the dance-drama provided us with to see this world? We can think back to the scene of the abandoned Ammaiyār, faithful to her husband and Śiva yet physically and verbally accosted by lascivious men. In this manner, the dance-drama introduces elements that are not part of the traditional story but that relate to concerns and experiences today. The scene calls attention to focalization—how something may be seen between what is seen and who is seeing. To describe

Figure 10.2 Shilpika Bordoloi as Kāraikkāl Ammaiyār in *Katyayani's "O,"* conceptualized and directed by Sohaila Kapur, 2012.

this concept, Mieke Bal uses the granite relief of the Descent of the Ganges/ Arjuna's Penance in Mahabalipuram, Tamilnadu (Figure 10.3):

> This example illustrates quite clearly the theory of focalization. Incidentally, it also suggests that, and how, narratological concepts are relevant for the analysis of visual narrative. We can view the bas-relief as a (visual) sign. The elements of this sign—the standing Arjuna, the standing cat, the laughing mice—only have spatial relations to one another. The elements of the fabula—Arjuna assumes a yoga position, the cat assumes a yoga position, the mice laugh—do not form a coherent significance as such. The relations between the sign, the relief, and its contents—the fabula—can only be established through the mediation of an interjacent layer, the vision of the events. The cat sees Arjuna. The mice see the cat. The spectator sees the mice who see the cat who has seen Arjuna. And the spectator sees that the mice are right. Every verb of perception—to see—in this report indicates an activity of focalization. Every verb of action indicates an event. (Bal 2017: 135)

The assessment of the scene in *Katyayani's "O"* as "our world" is left to the viewer, though from the character's point of view the experience is deeply disturbing: she yells at the man/men, and in the final scene with Śiva she complains that in this world, "all human desires are burnt in this stinking cremation ground," to which he replies, as previously noted, that "we" could transform the world. The

Figure 10.3 The Descent of the Ganges or Arjuna's Penance rock relief at Mahabalipuram, Tamil Nadu (seventh to eighth century CE). The cat appears in a yogic posture under the lead elephant's tusks. Upward left diagonally from the cat is the yogic figure identified with Arjuna. Photo by the author, 2015.

dance-drama enables attention on the violence toward women and its limitations on the realized potential of women in the world.

The larger cultural context at the time was in the process of focusing attention toward violence against women. The performance context of the *Katyayani's "O"* dance-drama suggests a cosmopolitan audience for its revisioning of Ammaiyār's story: it was staged in India's national capital and rendered in English by both the dancers' speaking plus voice-over that accompanied the dance. At the capital, and across India, women's groups had been pressuring for the cultural and legal recognition of sexual violence as a crime (Kannabiran 2010; Singh and Butalia 2012). The Nirbhaya rape and murder, and the mass demonstrations in protest, took place about six months after the dance performance. Initiated in its wake, the Fearless Collective of artists, led by Shilo Shiv Suleman, began to create collaborative street art murals that sought to reclaim public space for affirmative visual "messaging to evoke the safe and sacred world we want to inhabit" (Fearless Collective). Active critique continues to call out politicians and the public for dismissively labeling incidents of sexual harassment as "eve-teasing" (Dasgupta 2017). Legal changes include the 2013 Sexual Harassment of Women at Workplace Act (Prevention, Prohibition and Redressal, popularly known as the "POSH Act").

Such reframing of the poet-saint's life story is a counter-narrative of *bhakti* since classical expressions of devotion do not overtly challenge the violence toward women animated by patriarchal social structures. Classically, devotion is an acceptable form for select few women to transgress patriarchal norms; if they were subjected to violent discipline, such as the poet-saint Mīrābāī by the royal family she married into, what is remembered in the life story is the validation of her devotion that her survival proved. The dance-drama's contemporary interpretation suggests an alternative history of *bhakti*, one that uses the imposed vulnerability of women in classical sources as a "representational archive" (Singh 2014) to demand that society change today.

The dance-drama picks up on the abject imagery of Ammaiyār's poetry and refocuses it. The radical nature of the dance-drama's gesture is instantiated by its image of a young Ammaiyār as a *pēy* (Figure 10.2). Though none of the sculptural images of Ammaiyār code her as old, a performance iconography of her image had been previously established by a Tamil "mythologicals" film classic on her life story as represented by Cēkkiḻār, A. P. Nagarajan's 1973 *Karaikkal Ammaiyar*, starring the notable actress and singer K. B. Sundarambal. This film presents the transformation of Ammaiyār from young woman (played by the actress Lakshmi, who was about twenty years old at the time) to *pēy* as a miracle that is visually manifested by age. The film shows the young Ammaiyār, dressed in a blue saree, praying to Lord Śiva to remove her beautiful body that day; next, the film shows an image of lightening accompanied by a clap of thunder; then, an older woman has replaced the young woman. The older woman (K. B. Sundarambal, who was over sixty years old) has gray hair and the pronounced three white lines on her forehead of a staunch Śaivite. She wears an unadorned ochre-colored saree and walks with a staff; all of these traits resonate with cultural images of a sage.[16] This influential depiction of Ammaiyār continues to be used in contemporary dramas (Pechilis 2019). The *Katyayani's "O"* dance-drama retains the youth of Ammaiyār, her *bhakti* transforming the vulnerable body of a woman alone to the empowered body of a woman with the conviction of her own worth.

Bhakti poet-saint Ammaiyār's poetry and the contemporary interpretation of her life story compel society to look at what it does not want to see. The bronze sculptures that represent her remind us that she has a gaze that is both direct and indeterminate. The sculpture's disruption—or aesthetic encounter as a "violent embrace" in Hoogland's analysis—is illuminated by theorizing emotions and their relation to the challenge of the abject. With it, we can imagine an alternative history of *bhakti*, one that prioritizes visuality and asserts the right to look. The scopic regime it is up against is revealed by the dominant visuality of *bhakti* today.

The digital age has produced a "convergence" of production, consumption, and response that creates a "remix culture" (Fagerjord 2009), more commonly called a "participatory culture." Two recent studies of the presence of *bhakti* poet-saints on YouTube, Neelima Shukla-Bhatt's study of Narasinha Mehta (2014) and Lakshmi Subramanian's study of Mīrābāī (2018), show this participatory culture in action. In an analysis of both performances of Narasinha Mehta's songs and comments in response to them, Shukla-Bhatt reveals an "inspirational popular culture in cyberspace" (2014: 237). Subramanian argues that viewers' affective responses are to the fore in YouTube video renderings of Mīrābāī's songs. Both studies suggest that devotional participation is creating a contemporary convergence of meaning that has in its scope heritage, identity, and positivity. Outside of that lens is the radical counter-narrative of a feminist interpretation of a poet-saint and its direct confrontation of the oppression of women today. A clip from the 2012 dance-drama discussed herein exists on YouTube, but it is not tagged with "Kāraikkāl Ammaiyār" and is thus unaccounted for in the dozens of YouTube sites relating to her that come up on a search, such as the 1973 film starring K. B. Sundarambal; music, especially songs from that film, which differ from the poet-saint's own compositions; Tamil conference talks on her life story; and footage of the annual "mango festival" held in Kāraikkāl Ammaiyār's honor annually in summer.[17] The sculpture's gaze, as understood from Ammaiyār's own poetry as well as its dramatization in a contemporary dance, sees through this celebratory mode, for those who do not want to look away.

Notes

1 Hal Foster on "scopic regime": "the difference between the terms [vision and visual] signals a difference within the visual—between the mechanism of sight and its historical techniques, between the datum of vision and its discursive determinations—a difference, many differences, among how we see, how we are able, allowed, or made to see, and how we see this or the unseen therein. With its own rhetoric and representations, each scopic regime seeks to close out these differences: to make of its many social visualities one essential vision, or to order them in a natural hierarchy of sight" (1988: ix).

2 Note that the title Kāraikkāl Ammaiyār translates to the lady/mother/saint from the town of Kāraikkāl. Ammaiyār on its own is too generic to refer specifically to the poet-saint unless contextualized by the initial use of her full title.

3 See the discussion in Busch (2011: 44–6 and 69–72); quote is from 71.

4 Hopkins (2002: 136–8), quoted verse from 157. As Hopkins notes, "One of the most widespread, though little studied, descriptive devices in Indian literature is the sequential description of a god or goddess, a hero or heroine, from foot to head or head to foot (*pādādikeśāḥ*, *āpādacūḍānubhavam*, or *nakha-śikhā*, literally 'toenail to topknot' for Krishna *tribaṅga*). The actual origin of such limb-by-limb descriptions is far from clear." He points to the early examples of the *Puruṣa sūkta* (Ṛg Veda 10.90); the description of the body of the Buddha in the *Lakkhaṇasuttāna* of the *Dīgha Nikāya* (*c.* 3 BCE) and the *stotras* of Mātṛceta, the *Catuḥśataka*, and the *Śatapañcaśatika* (*c.* 150 CE); the Pāli *Therīgāthā* verses of Bhikkhunī Ambapālī and those of Bhikkhunī Subhā (*c.* fifth century); Bāṇa's *Caṇḍīśataka* of the seventh century, and the *Pañca Śasti* (500 verses on the Goddess Kamākṣī of Kanchipuram) of his perhaps contemporary, Mūka (Hopkins 2002: 136).

5 Hardy (1994: 284); see also 282–3. Hardy calls Quackenbos's translation "rather stilted" (1994: 577, n.9). Sukumari Bhattacharji (1980: 17) agrees on Bāṇa's confluence of forms: "One, however, cannot help feeling that his Candi differs very little from the heroines of his prose romances."

6 A stone frieze image that resonates with the iconography of Kāraikkāl Ammaiyār appears under the foot of the Śiva Naṭarāja in the southwest corner niche of the outer wall of Rajendra Chola I's temple at Gangaikondacholapuram, which, completed in 1035 CE, predates Cēkkiḻār's narrative.

7 Some sculptures of Ammaiyār depict her as a young woman, prior to her association with and assumed transformation to a *pēy*. Examples would be the stone image in the shrine to Kāraikkāl Ammaiyār at the Somanātha Temple in Karaikkal, the bronze image of her (in a full set of sixty-three) at the Kāsi Viśwanathan Temple in Kumbakonam, and the image of her for a contemporary full set of the sixty-three saints I saw at a *sthāpati*'s (artisan's) workshop in Swamimalai in 2003 that he was preparing to ship to a temple in Singapore. Such images depict her standing.

8 This sculptural conflation of poet and *pēy* does seem to follow the poet's description of "the female *pēy*" as having the elements described in the poem (reproduced earlier): sagging breasts, bulging veins, hollowed eyes, bared teeth, a sunken belly, long canines, and lanky shins on knobby ankles—with the artisan emphasizing knobby knees for more pronounced visual effect. That there remains a bit of slippage in the sculptures' (Figure 10.1, specifically the images from the Metropolitan Museum, the Victoria and Albert Museum, and the author's reproduction copy) conflation of poet and *pēy* is visually suggested by the figure in the active process of chiming the hand cymbals; this is the poet, who keeps the rhythm of Śiva as he dances "with effortless composure/as his matted locks radiate in all directions." This is distinct from the poet's description of the female *pēy* as one who "lingers, howling, at the cremation ground" described in this verse, as well as the *pēys*' wild gestures and lack of language that other verses describe (Pechilis 2012: 69–72).

9 "In 1934 Bataille was the first to conceptualize abjection. He wrote the text 'L'abjection et les formes misérables' [Abjection and miserable forms], which was left incomplete and belonged to his *Essays on Sociology*" (Georgelou 2014: 27).

10 Lotringer (1999: 3). This article provides an incisive interpretation of Georges Bataille's brief writing on the abject, including Bataille's resonances with fascism. A translation of Bataille's reflections into English by Yvonne Shafir, "Abjection and Miserable Forms," appears in the same book (actually a book publication of a journal) on pp. 8–13.

11 Bataille (1999: 11), Lotringer (1999: 7).

12 "Bataille's definition of abjection was unprecedented. Detaching the concept from any specific substance, social situation, cultural determination, racial or biological distinction, he defined it by its own performativity. People don't just become abject because they're treated like a thing, but because they become things to themselves" (Lortinger 1999: 7).

13 I focus on later stages of the experience of the abject and not on Kristeva's reformulation of Lacan's mirror stage to describe the genesis of the experience of the abject.

14 Kristeva is not supportive of the use of the abject for identity politics, which her interviewer Sylvère Lotringer characterizes as an "optimization of the abject in the United States." In part, she views the verbal as preserving the ambiguity of the abject in contrast to the visual:
"I find that, in a way, the verbal art, insofar as it eludes fetishization, and constantly raises doubt and questioning, the verbal art lends itself better perhaps to exploring these states that I call states of abjection. From the moment that you establish it in a sort of image or something representable, salable, exposable, capitalizable, you lose it" (Kristeva 1999: 30).

15 *Katyayani's "O"* was sponsored by ICCR (Indian Council for Cultural Relations) and held at its headquarters, Azad Bhavan, I.P. Estate, New Delhi on the 18th of May 2012, and funded by the Ministry of Culture. The dance-drama was directed by Sohaila Kapur and choreographed and performed by Gilles Chuyen and Shilpika Bordoloi. The dance-drama offered linked profiles of Rābi'a of Basra and Kāraikkāl Ammaiyār insofar as the dancer transformed her costume onstage at the conclusion of the former profile to initiate her performance of Kāraikkāl Ammaiyār. The Rābi'a portion was scripted by Sohaila Kapur and the Kāraikkāl Ammaiyār portion was written by H. S. Shivaprakash and conceptualized and directed by Sohaila Kapur. *Katyayani's "O"* was one of two dance-dramas on female devotional saints that were performed in New Delhi that year. Later that same year, Madhu Kishwar staged a dance-drama about female saints, *Talking to God in the Mother Tongue*, on 6–9 November 2012 at Azad Bhavan as part of the sixth edition of the Delhi International Arts Festival, 20 October–10 November 2012, at which the story of Kāraikkāl Ammaiyār was danced by acclaimed Chennai dancer Lakshmi Vishwanathan.

16 An earlier filmic precedent exists. K. B. Sundarambal played Avvaiyar, a classical Tamil female sage, in the 1953 film *Avvaiyar*, directed by Kothamangalam Subbu, where she is made up to look older (including gray hair), and she is dressed in exactly the same way.

17 Available at https://www.youtube.com/watch?v=9nCoHqs1ZEQ—*Katyayani's "O"* published by mahimjunction. Last accessed June 3, 2022.

References

Bal, M. (2017 [1985]), *Narratology: Introduction to the Theory of Narrative*, 4th ed., Toronto: University of Toronto Press.

Bataille, G. (1999 [1993] [1934]), "Abjection and Miserable Forms," trans. Yvonne Shafir, in Sylvère Lotringer (ed.), *More and Less*, 8–13, Brooklyn: Semiotext(e)/Autonomedia.

Bhattacharji, S. (1980), "A Survey of Sataka Poetry," *Indian Literature* 23 (5)/Facets of Poetry: 12–40.

Bhatti, S., and C. Pinney (2011), "Optic-Clash: Modes of Visuality in India," in Isabelle Clark-Decès (ed.), *A Companion to the Anthropology of India*, 223–40, Malden: Wiley-Blackwell.

Bleeker, M. (2008), *Visuality in the Theatre: The Locus of Looking*, Basingstoke and New York: Palgrave Macmillan.

Bleeker, M., and I. Germano (2014), "Perceiving and Believing: An Enactive Approach to Spectatorship," *Theatre Journal* 66 (3): 363–83.

Busch, A. (2011), *Poetry of Kings*, New York: Oxford University Press.

Chakrabarti, A. (2016), "Refining the Repulsive: Toward an Indian Aesthetics of the Ugly and the Disgusting," in A. Chakrabarti (ed.), *The Bloomsbury Research Handbook of Indian Aesthetics and the Philosophy of Art*, 149–65, London: Bloomsbury Academic.

Dasgupta, P. (2017), "Why Are We Still Calling Sexual Harassment 'Eve-Teasing' in India?" *Huffpost India*, July 5, 2017. https://www.huffingtonpost.in/2017/07/04/why-are-we-still-calling-sexual-harassment-eve-teasing-in-indi_a_23015316/ (accessed October 1, 2020).

Fagerjord A. (2009), "After Convergence: *YouTube* and Remix Culture," in J. Hunsinger, L. Klastrup, and M. Allen (eds.), *International Handbook of Internet Research*, 187–200, Dordrecht: Springer. https://doi.org/10.1007/978-1-4020-9789-8_11 (accessed October 1, 2020).

Fearless Collective. https://fearlesscollective.org/ (accessed May 30, 2022).

Foster, H., ed. (1988), *Vision and Visuality*, Dia Art Foundation; Seattle: Bay Press.

Francis, E. (2017), "The Other Way Round: From Print to Manuscript," in V. Vergiani, D. Cuneo, and C. A. Formigatti (eds.), *Indic Manuscript Cultures through the Ages:*

Material, Textual, and Historical Investigations, 319–52, Berlin: De Gruyter, https://doi.org/10.1515/9783110543100-011 (accessed October 1, 2020).

Georgelou, K. (2014), "Abjection and Informe: Operations of Debasing," *Performance Research* 19 (1): 25–32.

Hardy, F. (1994), *The Religious Culture of India*, Cambridge: Cambridge University Press.

Hart, G. L., and H. Heifetz (1999), *The Four Hundred Songs of War and Wisdom: An Anthology of Poems from Classical Tamil: The Puranānūru*, New York: Columbia University Press.

Hoogland, R. (2014), *A Violent Embrace: Art and Aesthetics after Representation*, Durham: Duke University Press.

Hopkins, S. (2002), *Singing the Body of God*, New York: Oxford University Press.

Kannabiran, K. (2010), "Feminist Deliberative Politics in India," in A. Basu (ed.), *Women's Movements in the Global Era: The Power of Local Feminisms*, 119–56, Boulder: Westview Press.

Katyayani's "O" (2012), Profiled on the Television Show State of Culture, hosted by Sohaila Kapur. Posted June 27, 2012, https://www.youtube.com/watch?v=9nCoHqs1ZEQ (accessed October 2020).

Kristeva, J. (1982 [1980]), *The Powers of Horror: An Essay on Abjection*, trans. L. S. Roudiez, New York: Columbia University Press.

Kristeva, J. (1999 [1993]), "Fetishizing the Abject," trans. J. Herman, in S. Lotringer (ed.), *More & Less*, 15–35, Brooklyn: Semiotext(e)/Autonomedia.

Little, L. (n.d.), "Tirumurugarruppadai or 'Guide to Lord Murugan.'" http://murugan.org/texts/tirumurukarruppadai_layne_little.htm#world (accessed October 1, 2021).

Lotringer, S. (1999 [1993]), "Les Miserables," in S. Lotringer (ed.), *More & Less*, 2–7, Brooklyn: Semiotext(e)/Autonomedia.

Mirzoeff, N. (2011), *The Right to Look: A Counterhistory of Visuality*, Durham: Duke University Press.

Mitchell, W. J. T. (1996), "What Do Pictures 'Really' Want?" *October* 77: 71–82.

Mitchell, W. J. T. (2005), *What Do Pictures Want? The Lives and Loves of Images*, Chicago: University of Chicago Press.

Paine, C. (2013), *Religious Objects in Museums: Private Lives and Public Duties*, London: Bloomsbury Academic.

Pechilis, K. (2012), *Interpreting Devotion: The Poetry and Legacy of a Female Bhakti Saint of India*, London: Routledge.

Pechilis, K. (2014), "Devotional Subjectivity and the Fiction of Femaleness: Feminist Hermeneutics and the Articulation of Difference," *Journal of Feminist Studies in Religion* 30 (2): 99–114.

Pechilis, K. (2016), "Bhakti and Tantra Intertwined: The Explorations of the Tamil Poetess Kāraikkāl Ammaiyār," *International Journal of Dharma Studies* 4 (2). https://doi.org/10.1186/s40613-016-0024-x.

Pechilis, K. (2019), "Bhakti's Visualities of Connection in the Arts Today," *The Journal of Hindu Studies* 12 (3): 142–67. https://doi.org/10.1093/jhs/hiz009.

Quackenbos, G. P. (1917), *The Sanskrit Poems of Mayūra,* edited with a translation and notes and an introduction, together with the text and translation of Bāṇa's *Caṇḍīśataka*, Columbia University Indo-Iranian Series, Vol. 9, New York: Columbia University Press.

Shukla-Bhatt, N. (2014), *Narasinha Mehta of Gujarat: A Legacy of Bhakti in Songs and Stories*, New York: Oxford University Press.

Singh, H. (2014), *The Rani of Jhansi: Gender, History, and Fable in India*, Delhi: Cambridge University Press.

Singh, K. (2006), "Bigot Busters: Tackling Sectarianism," *Interpret Scotland* 14: 4.

Singh, N., and U. Butalia (2012), "Challenging Impunity on Sexual Violence in South Asia: Beginning a Discussion," *Economic and Political Weekly* 47 (28): 58–63.

Subramanian, Lakshmi C. (2018), "Mirabai Sings on YouTube: The Transmission of a Poet-Saint in the Age of Digital Devotion," in M. Balaji (ed.), *Digital Hinduism: Dharma and Discourse in the Age of New Media*, 69–86, Lanham: Lexington Books.

Vimal C., A. (2018), "Performing Disfiguration: Staging of Relationalities in Pottan Teyyam," *Performance Research* 23 (8): 108–14.

Wark, J. (2016), "Queering Abjection: A Lesbian, Feminist and Canadian Perspective," in R. Arya and N. Chare (eds.), *Abject Visions: Powers of Horror in Art and Visual Culture*, 30–50, Manchester: Manchester University Press.

Yue, G. (2021), *Girl Head: Feminism and Film Materiality*, New York: Fordham University Press.

Zvelebil, K. V. (1973), *The Smile of Murugan: On Tamil Literature of South India*, Leiden: E.J. Brill.

11

Mīrā's Iconography

From Miniature to Movie

Heidi Pauwels

Introduction: Mīrā's Iconographical Types

Perhaps north India's most famous devotee is Mīrābāī (*c.* 1500–48). A sixteenth-century Rathor princess from Merta, she was married into the Mewar royal house but gave up everything for her devotion to Kṛṣṇa and went on extended pilgrimages to eventually disappear in the Kṛṣṇa temple in Dwarka (Taft 2002 and 2009). Many sets of narratives, hagiographical and folk, nationalist and Rajput, have grown up around her persona (Hawley and Juergensmeyer 2004: 119–33). This chapter is about the meaning that has been invested in Mīrā over time as expressed in visuals and how those relate to such narratives told and songs sung in her name.

At the outset of her evocative 2002 documentary *A Few Things I Know about Her*, Mumbai-based filmmaker Anjali Panjabi orders a Mīrā image from a vendor of god-images. As she does so, she ventures the question: *āp ko mālūm hai ki Mīrā dikhtī kaisī hai?* "Do you know what Mīrā looks like?" The answer is in the negative, but the salesperson assures her that upon ordering, she will receive the proper image if she brings in a photo. The question is in the present tense: What images of the evanescent woman-devotee do people have in mind around the turn of the twenty-first century? The answer is significant: it allows for the devotee to bring in her own concept according to which images can be shaped. Likewise, the focus of this chapter is on the multiple Mīrā images today, with the understanding that they are built on past perceptions. To fully grasp present memory, we have to ask also how it came about. What follows then is an investigation into how Mīrā's visual image has evolved over time in different contexts. The chapter explores the dynamic relationship between *bhakti* and history—from royal court to nationalism to consumerism—as revealed through changing images anchored to the ways her songs were transmitted and her story was told.

Visual and aural memories are closely intertwined. Mīrā is after all most famous as a devotee-singer. For many such saints, or *bhakta-kavi*s, iconographic conventions have spread across visual media, from painting and sculpture to chromolithograph, over theater and popular film. The importance of sound for the latter is clear, but also the former is often inscribed with poetry. Mīrā's songs are employed in a ritual context inclusive of singing in front of images in the temple or the household shrine. Images then are imprinted with songs that invoke a characteristic devotional mood or *bhāva* for the saint. What are such moods associated with Mīrā?

Devotional literature and film scholar Philip Lutgendorf has defined the "Mira trope" that is frequently cited in film (2012: 176). He distinguishes two aspects, renunciation and resistance, the former marked iconographically by the plain sari, whether white signifying widowhood or yellow indicating asceticism. Her musical instrument, whether *tanpura* or the one-stringed *iktārā* of the itinerant *yogi*, reinforces the renunciation theme. Lutgendorf insightfully argues it may also evoke resistance given the ambiguity of the *yoginī*, the woman ascetic (177). Still, it is difficult to make the case that contemporary iconography of Mīrā signifies insubordination.

Mīrā's overall visual appearance today is not one of defiance, her pose is rarely strident. Rather, she is usually depicted as meekly seated, bent over her instrument with veil drawn modestly to cover her hair, as is the case for the *mūrti* of Mīrā sold in the bazaar by vendors like the one encountered by Anjali Panjabi in the documentary. Or Mīrā may be depicted seated in front of her *mūrti*, in the privacy of her *pūjā* room, absorbed in playing her instrument or engaged in worship. One trend-setting example of this type is on the cover of a 1930 special slim booklet *Bhakta Nārī*, "Woman Devotee," brought out by the influential Gītā Press of Gorakhpur's Hanumān Prasād (Figure 11.1).

There is a submissive quality to this stance, usually interpreted as self-denying dedication and subservience to God. In popular posters, indeed, Kṛṣṇa is never far off, whether as her deity (*mūrti*) or as a vision-like appearance, hovering somewhere in the background. Scholar of *bhakti* J. S. Hawley has discussed how the widely read *Amar Citra Kathā* comic version *Mirabai* that appeared in 1971 (ACK no. 36) portrays the saint "transformed into a paragon of general female virtue, a good model for character building for the young middle-class Indians of the late twentieth century" (1995: 108). The comic edits out her fearless defiance

Figure 11.1 Cover of the 1930 booklet *Bhakta Nārī* by Hanumān Prasād Poddār. Gītā Press, Gorakhpur. Accessed at Internet Archive March 2021, https://archive.org/details/BhaktaNariGitaPressGorakhpur/page/n1/mode/2up; Public Domain CC0 1.0 Universal.

of societal norms in favor of "domesticating Mira" (109), as illustrated in two adjacent scenes, a color one with Mīrā serving her husband at her "daytime job" and a lower-key one of Mīrā in dark silhouette worshipping her deity in her spare time, so to speak (110). Only after the death of her husband does the deity come to the foreground. Hawley insightfully draws attention to the discrepancy between the images and the text.

Contemporary posters show a fair amount of variation but strikingly little that reminds of fearlessness or even defiance. The closest is the popular image of her drinking the poison cup that her persecutors sent her. Sometimes these images contain references to her defiant song *Rāṇojī the zahara diyau mhe jāṇī* "Rāṇā, you gave me poison to drink, I know" (Caturvedi 1983: 111 no. 38). Even so, there is no stridency in her eyes or pose. Rather, she is portrayed as oblivious to her environment, totally absorbed in Kṛṣṇa, the deity in front of her. Another type of poster shows Mīrā dancing in ecstasy, intertwined with an "imaginary" partner, Kṛṣṇa, or with Kṛṣṇa's vision in the background. Often this is set in the privacy of her shrine. Even when these images are accompanied with reference to her more defiant songs, such as *paga ghūngharu bāndha mīrā nācī*, "Mīra dances defiantly, anklets fastened on her feet," the image does not portray her as boldly insolent but rather in a trance. Her eyes are closed, for she is immersed in her chosen deity. The transgression here would be in the eye of the voyeuristic beholder. A good example from the aforementioned booklet *Bhakta Nārī* is its multicolor image of Mīrā playing her instrument in a temple setting with a shaft of light coming in, a "spotlight" as it were from heaven. This image is accompanied by a line of poetry where Mīrā calls herself a loyal slave or *cākara* (Poddar 1930: 5).[1] While Mīrā's stories always mention her defiance, as do several of her songs, the images instead portray her in conformity with conventions of female modesty.

As I started out on writing this essay, a quick internet search googling recent images of Mīrā rendered a fair number of posters of Mīrā in a pose I had not been aware of before, cradling her Kṛṣṇa image or even an actual little baby Kṛṣṇa, as if it is a doll. The puzzling prevalence of this image forms a striking contrast with the way Mīrā has evolved in western New Age circles, where her spirituality has been foregrounded to the extent that "(a)ny sense of Krishna as an image is gone," only his energy remains (Hawley's afterword in Bly and Hirschfield 2004: 94, see also Martin 2010).

How did it happen that headstrong Mīrā is depicted so demurely, her fervent *bhakti* depicted as that of a girl for a doll? Did her early iconography show more of her obstinate resistance? There are few premodern Mīrā portraits but an explosion of popular paintings at the time of the nationalist movement that has continued unabated in post-independence times. I will first investigate whether we can detect an evolution over time in her portrayals in paintings and posters, from Rajput court and folk depictions to nationalist ones. Subsequently, I will focus on nationalist movies that depict Mīrā, paying attention to evolving story lines as well as iconography. And finally, I will trace the proclivity in contemporary Indian popular poster art to portray the relationship with her Lord by focusing on the treatment of her image like a doll. To explain this new popular pose, I will again muster evidence from movies, both devotionals about Mīrā and secular ones referencing her imagery. The key question behind this investigation is how emotional communities have evolved around her changing images.

Miniature to Postal Stamp: From Defiance to Compliance?

Notwithstanding her fame, there appear to be very few early depictions of the princess-devotee. Perhaps this is related to the fact that there are very few manuscripts exclusively devoted to her work (on the latter, see Hawley 2005: 98–115). The majority of illustrations for editions of Mīrā's poetry are not actually inscribed as being her portrait. Rather, they depict anonymous "women suffering separation" (*virahiṇī*) or playing a musical instrument. The latter often are marked as depictions of musical Rāgas, such as Rāg Toḍī, conventionally rendered as a musician with an admiring deer approaching her. Thus, the exquisite 1810 Guler painting on the cover of 1989 *Manushi* special on women *bhaktas* is Mīrā by association only. There is no inscription. Still, it tells us something about the perception of her persona: the centrality of her suffering, narrowed as love-sickness, and of her voice as a singer-musician.

Around the turn of the twenty-first century an inscribed portrait of Mīrā from a private collection came to light, published in a catalogue of music and dance-themed Indian paintings (Masselos, Menzies and Pal 1997: 60, fig. 99b) and used as the frontispiece illustration of the poetic transcreations of her poetry by Bly and Hirshfield (2009). It depicts a richly adorned woman clad in red with long loose black hair, mid-stride as she balances two lamps, one in each hand. The rectangular format of the painting (22 × 9.5 cm) is rather unusual and raises suspicion that perhaps it was lifted out of context. One suspects in particular that something toward which the lady was moving was cut off to the right. The inscription below identifies the scene: *Mīrā bhakti karai chai* or "Mīrā doing *bhakti*" and provides a date: 1838 (1895 VS).[2] Scribbled in, squeezed to the left, is the name of the painter Premjī of Citaur (*Cītoṛ kau Chatāro Pemjī chai*). These inscriptions look like later additions, which casts doubt on the identification with Mīrābāī.

The same 1997 catalogue (61, fig. 99a) also contained an image of folk visual perceptions of Mīrā in the form of a double-page from an illustrated book on Mīrā's life. The colophon in red on the first folio identifies it as *Mīrābāī kī ādi anta kī kathā* written down in Kota by a scribe named Sukhlāl. The catalogue estimates it to date from the late eighteenth or early nineteenth century. The upper half of each page contains hagiographical text with quotes of Mīrā's songs, the lower panel has the illustration. This set depicts on one page the Raṇachoḍa image with a group of mostly women worshippers inside a temple. Perhaps Mīrā is the lead figure, or she has already been absorbed in the image, as the text tells us, leaving only her garment for the brahmins to find when they enter. Indeed, the deity is adorned in the same red fabric as the saris of the ladies worshipping. On the other page, the text above quotes a variant of her aforementioned song: *Rana ju zahar dīyau main jānī* "the Rāṇā gave me poison to drink, I know." In the illustration, the Rāṇā and his courtiers are shown plotting against Mīrā in the men's quarters of the palace. A small delegation is seen setting out to take a cup to Mīrā, who in the women's quarters is shown as about to drink the poison cup in the presence of her ladies-in-waiting. Rosary in hand, Mīrā raises the cup to one of the ladies, who is also holding a cup. Her facial expressions are not defiant, rather serene.

Such illustrated manuscripts seem to have been popular, another one is displayed in the Mīrā Smārak Museum in her hometown Merta, where an enlarged modern version of the poisoning scene is also painted on the wall.[3] One wonders whether these texts were part of the oral tradition of reciting Mīrā's life story, or *Janam Patrī*, as described by Parita Mukta (1994: 112–14, 233–4) and Nancy Martin (1999), or perhaps of the *Mīrā Parcī* or "Introducing Mīrā" type of written literature, which included in some versions Mīrā's songs (Bhāṭī 1984: 15). This may be a fruitful area of research to pursue to bring to light new images from a premodern folk tradition, perhaps related to the performance traditions with *phaṛ* or illustrated scroll of the Pābūjī and Devnārāyan traditions. Strikingly, in this folk milieu the oral and visual are intertwined, story, song, and image work together to create the appropriate mood or *bhāva*.

The edition of *Mīrā Parcī* also includes an image (from the Caupāsanī collection in the Rajasthānī Shodh Sansthān of Jodhpur) purported to portray Mīrābāī and her cousin Jaymal worshipping a Cārbhujā (four-armed) deity (facing p. 16).[4] This looks like a cult image of the type called *manoratha*, a souvenir painting of the patron with the image of the deity. Usually, these are taken home after a pilgrimage undertaken as a vow, hence the name. Such images are very popular for the Vallabhan deity of Śrīnāthjī in Nathdwara (Lyons 2004: 104). In that sectarian milieu, *manoratha* paintings are attested from the mid-eighteenth century onward and continue to be popular today (Ambalal 1987: 80 and examples 96ff.). No work has been done on non-Vallabhan traditions as of yet. Unfortunately, there are no legible inscriptions in the reproduction of the purported Mīrā *manoratha*, so the identification is as yet uncertain.

The paucity of actual inscribed pre-nineteenth-century Mīrā portraits could be explained by purported adverse reactions by her in-laws in Mewar to her public expression of her devotion to the detriment of family honor, as argued by Warwick University social studies scholar Parita Mukta (1994, see also Martin 2000: 165–6). Notwithstanding such hostility from Sisodiya Rajputs, Mukta found and published in her book one inscribed miniature painting featuring Mīrābāī from a book *Darśanoṃ kī kitāb* from the Udaipur Palace Library itself (1994: facing 92, Plate I). This image is inscribed with her name and shows her in a palace setting, singing in front of the deity, his eyes meeting hers. Interestingly, it is dated from around 1900, by which time a "rehabilitation" of sorts of Mīrā as a nationalist icon was taking place. Mīrā specialist scholar Nancy Martin has highlighted how a group of Marwari Rajasthani scholars worked to puzzle out Mīrā's history together with twentieth-century Shyāmaldās, the nationalist counter-historian to nineteenth-century colonial James Tod (Martin 2000: 169–71). Shyāmaldās was initially commissioned to do so by the Rāṇā of Mewar, even though the latter was still hostile to commemorating the woman who had brought shame to his family (Martin 2000: 165). Eventually, Mīrā's religious fame prevailed and in 1955 in the very Cittaur fort, a temple was declared Mīrā's. Images of her and Kṛṣṇa have since been installed there (Mukta 1994: facing 93, Plates XVIII–XIX).

The project recovered Mīrā as Rajput and nationalist heroine and eventually culminated in the issuing of a postage stamp in 1952. This was part of the series "Saints and Poets," which also included Kabīr, Tulsīdās, and Sūrdās. Certainly, this demonstrated her pride of place in the new Indian nation's "mystic" Hindu tradition.[5] Mīrā is clad in white and holding a rosary, conforming to the favored timid pose of surrender to Kṛṣṇa (Figure 11.2). This humble posture is reinforced by the poem chosen in the booklet to accompany the stamp:

Figure 11.2 Ministry of Communications, Government of India, 1952; a commemorative postage stamp on Saints and Poets: Mira, fifteenth to sixteenth century; India Postage Stamps; 1 October; https://postagestamps.gov.in/Stamps_List.aspx; Government Open Data License GODL.

Mhaṇe cākara rākho jī
Cākara rahasūṃ bāga lagāsūṃ, nita uṭhi darasaṇa pāsūṃ
Bindrāvana kī kuñja galina meṃ, govinda līlā gāsūṃ
[Let me be Thy servant, O'Lord:
I shall serve Thee and tend Thy garden
And (as my reward) see Thy face every day:
Of Thee, shall I sing in the lanes
And bowers of Bindraban.]

The biblical-sounding translation evokes the mode of servitude (*dāsya*) rather than Mīrā's usual sweet intimacy (*mādhurya*), as does the choice of poem with the refrain using the word *cākara*, "servant," a term with a connotation of loyalty and dependence on the master who provides for the needs of the servant.[6]

The booklet also clarifies the stamp was "adapted from a painting in the House of Kishangarh." It seems to be based on a redrawing of a detail of a painting that is currently the earliest painting depicting Mīrābāī that has been published.[7] The Rathor court of Kishangarh sponsored the original, possibly by the hand of the famous painter Nihālcand at some point in the middle decades of the eighteenth century. The then crown prince Sāvant Singh (1699–1764) frequently commissioned Nihālcand paintings to match his own work composed under the pen name Nāgarīdās. One of his hagiographical works, *Pad-prasaṅg-mālā* or "Garland of anecdotes around songs," contained five sections (*prasaṅgas*) devoted to Mīrā's life contextualizing six of her songs with anecdotes from her life (Pauwels 2006). This confirms the appreciation of Mīrābāī among her Rathor kinsmen well before the anticolonial Rajput reappraisal (Pauwels 2010b).

The stamp's Mīrā image then is excerpted from a larger scene. To understand its significance, it is important to consider the full painting, which represents a group of *bhaktas* in the interior of a temple or shrine, not unlike the one portrayed on the illustrated folk manuscript referred to above. Seated toward the back is a man who plays the *dholak*, which gives the impression of a *bhajan* session, yet the singing seems to have been momentarily paused. Mīrā, whose head is haloed, is rather awkwardly positioned among the white-clad women devotees, all like her with rosaries in hand. She is not playing her instrument, but one of the women behind her holds it for her. In contrast to the stamp's adaptation, this Mīrā is stretching one arm in front of her, turning upside down a small item. Is it a cup that she is showing to have emptied? Perhaps the scene depicts Mīrā drinking the poison cup, an incident related in Nāgarīdās's *Pad-prasaṅg-mālā*

(15). It could be part of a series illustrating the Mīrā chapters in this work, a courtly counterpart to the folk one mentioned earlier. What is significant is that the stamp has cut off Mīrā from the context of the story's defiance of authority. At the same time, it has adapted her pose to one of pious rosary-recitation (*japa*). This conforms to the aforementioned 1971 *Amar Citra Kathā* comic's perspective, described by Hawley as a "domesticating" project in service of the nation (1995: 109). The new postcolonial nation was keen to subdue strident *bhakti* heroines into loyal citizens. Once independence was realized, defiance became compliance.

What had happened in between the mid-eighteenth-century Kishangarhi and the mid-twentieth-century philatelic portrayal of Mīrā? In the course of the nineteenth century some impactful changes in the visual regime of Mīrā depictions must have taken place. Surprisingly, the Mīrā theme was not picked up by the influential painter Rājā Ravi Varmā or his press' chromolithographs.[8] The Bengali modernist school on the other hand was interested in Indian "mystics." Abanindranath Tagore's student Kshitendranath Majumdar produced an elegantly attired long and lanky Mīrā playing her instrument in front of her deity, a rather east Indian Buddha-looking Kṛṣṇa (now in Allahabad Museum). Another of Tagore's students in Vadodara, Nandalal Bose, working on the murals of the Gaekwad family's cenotaph called Kīrti Mandir, represented a white-clad Mīrā engaged in solitary *pūjā*, her deity nowhere to be seen, but her songs inscribed in the borders, including the one with reference to the drinking of the poison cup.[9] Meanwhile, Gandhi interpreted Mīrā as exemplary for his project of "righteous resistance" or *satyāgraha*, as a strong heroine who would stand her morally superior and nationalist ground (Kishwar and Vanita 1989: 86–7). But feminists who denounced Gandhi's reworking of Mīrā for the nation may be right: in the end his interpretation of Mīrā resulted into "conversion of her subversion into submission, her dissent into consent, and her marginality into a given" (Martin 2012). Images we see appear in this period from Gujarat include those by Kanu Desai of the Gujarat Vidyāpīṭh founded by Gandhi, who had studied under Nandalal Bose at Shantiniketan. In the words of Parita Mukta, his images "insidiously feed into the notion of woman as seductive in her chastity" (1989: 98).[10] Desai was also active in film, designing sets, and as artistic director for, among others, the Mīrā-inspired *Jhanak Jhanak Pāyal Bāje* (1955; discussed in Lutgendorf 2012). There seems to be a close connection between the Gandhian images and the movies, in particular, though not limited to "devotionals."

Nationalist Mīrā in the Movies

Popular from the beginning of cinema in India, the genre of the "devotional" also called "Saint Film" (Rajadhyaksha and Willemen 1999: 204) highlights the saints of the *bhakti* movement. It focuses on emotion with frequent close-ups that invite the viewer to intimacy with God through the medium of the saint whose life is portrayed. Yet, at the same time, many of these early movies carry a strong progressive agenda, befitting the central idea that love trumps ritualism. Devotionals were often based on theatrical performances and reworked literary material, recasting for their purposes both hagiographic writings about and devotional songs by the saint featured. Already silent films were screened with an accompanying score that involved songs, but the advent of sound afforded the possibility to fully exploit featuring the famous songs of the saints of India.

Starting from the colonial period, religious movies were suffused with sociopolitical meaning. Some call "the father of the Indian movie" "Dādāsahib" Dhundhiraj Govind Phalke a "high priest of this new bhakti" that was politically strident (Kaul 1998: 187–90). While that may be an overstatement, it is clear that in the heat of the independence movement, devotional movies were read as a metaphor for political events.[11] A Gandhian example is Kanjibhai Rathod's 1921 movie *Bhakta Vidur Dharma Vijay* ("The devotee Vidur, Virtue's Victory"), whose eponymous mythological hero appeared clad in Gandhi-cap and *khaddar* shirt. The silent movie was screened with an accompanying musical score that included a strident nationalistic song in praise of the *charkha*, or spinning wheel (Rajadhyaksha and Willemen 1999: 244). That same year, Rathod also made *Meerabai* (Rajadhyaksha and Willemen 1999: 197), which was followed by Phalke's own *Sant Meerabai* in 1929. While neither of these films have survived, and no stills or even posters or announcements are currently available, likely these Mīrā movies too sent nationalist messages.

The advent of sound meant that each region would focus on casting its saints in their own vernacular. The link with local theatrical musicals was very close. Mīrā's case managed to supersede such regional boundaries and broke language barriers. For instance, Bengali cinema initially produced devotionals about Bengali saints with progressive messages. Thus, New Theatres in Kolkata scored a first hit with a movie on the famous fifteenth-century Bengali saint, *Chandidas* (1932, dir. Debaki Bose). Based on a musical (by Aparesh Chandra Mukherjee, Rajadhyaksha and Willemen 1999: 255), it stressed the love of the brahmin saint for a washerwoman, striking a progressive chord. It was so successful that it had a Hindi remake by cameraman Nitin Bose with the beloved singer-actor

K. L. Saigal in the lead.[12] This movie became the New Theatres' first Hindi hit (Rajadhyaksha and Willemen 1999: 259), which opened the way for the big-budget film *Meerabai* (1933), simultaneously shot in Bengali (dir. Hiren Bose and Basanta Chatterjee, with Chandrabati Devi and Durgadas Bannerjee) and in Hindi as *Rajrani Meera* (dir. Debaki Bose) with Durga Khote and Prithviraj Kapoor in the lead roles (Rajadhyaksha and Willemen 1999: 257).[13] A still of the movie shows Mīrā (Khote) clinging romantically to the chest of her Kṛṣṇa (Kapoor) on the steps of the *jagamohana*, or interior shrine of the temple.[14] The hierarchical relation is emphasized as he is standing a step higher than she is, but still the romantic aspect of their relationship is apparent. This was about to change.

Similarly, in Maharashtra, Prabhat Studios was famous for its devotionals about Marathi saints. The trailblazer director Rajaram Vankudre Shantaram[15] made in 1935 the movie *Dharmatma* (originally named *Mahatma*) on the sixteenth-century Eknāth (Rajadhyaksha and Willemen 1999: 262; van Skyhawk 2001). The lead was played by Bal Gandharva, who had been famous as a female impersonator in the theater. In the wake of this success, the Marathi *Sadhvi Mirabai* came out in 1937, directed by Baburao Painter, based on a play of Gandharva's Nāṭak Maṇḍalī (Rajadhyaksha and Willemen 1999: 52).[16] Bal Gandharva starred as Mīrā, iconographically portrayed as white-clad, judging from the two sung fragments available.[17] In the first one, Mīrā sings in front of her outcaste *camār* Guru Raidās, indicative of the progressive agenda of this devotional.[18] While Bal Gandharva as Mīrā takes a self-assured stance in declamation, even in front of her guru, still deference is stressed to her mother-in-law, whose feet she respectfully stoops to touch in the second fragment. That a cross-dressing actor played the saint Mīrā did not attract negative comments at the time.

It seems not to have been a problem either for Muslim actresses to perform the role of the Hindu saint, as in 1932 a Hindi *Meerabai* (dir. Ramnik Desai) featured in the title role the actress Zubeida, who had been famous for her role in the first talkie, *Alam Ara*.[19] In 1940, Mukhtar Begum, the second wife of the playwright Agha Hashar Kashmiri,[20] starred in a Punjabi *Matwali Meera* along with the stage actor Fida Husein as Raidās (Hansen 2011: 290–1). Many devotional movies of this time were anticommunalist in tone. Thus, the 1942 *Bhakta Kabir* (dir. Rameshwar Sharma), with Bharat Bhushan in the title role, was advertised as "Kabir kills communal bogey" (Dwyer 2006: 89–90). Movie personnel's religious affiliations in Mīrā movies drew criticism only in the heat of Partition in 1947, when the Muslim director W. Z. Ahmad directed *Meera Bai* (Dwyer 2006: 175 n. 58).

Figure 11.3 Bilingual poster of the Punjabi film *Matwali Mira*, directed by Prafulla Roy with Mukhtar Begum in the title role, produced by studio Shree Bharat Lakshmi Pictures, 1940.

Figure 11.4 Mīrā fondles her image. Screenshot from the Tamil film *Meera*, directed by Ellis R. Dungan, produced by T. Sadasivam at studio Chandraprabha Cine, 1945.

Figure 11.5 Domestic scene with Bhoj (Vinod Khanna) and Mīrā (Hema Malini) sewing an outfit for her deity. Screenshot from the Hindi film *Meera*, directed by Gulzar, produced by Premji 1979.

Figure 11.6 Young Mīrā (Aashika Bhatia) and her Giridhar from the Hindi TV serial *Meera*, directed by Mukesh Kumar Singh, produced by Sagar Pictures, aired 2009–10 on NDTV's Imagine channel.

The interest in the Mīrā theme throughout the 1930s may also be partially explained by the fashion of Rajput costume dramas common in films of that period. It is at this time that the centrality of the *mūrti* for Mīrā becomes visually foregrounded. A promotional film poster of *Matwali Meera* shows Mīrā doubled up, as a child and as an adult, looking up as she holds on to the feet of the Kṛṣṇa deity (Figure 11.3). This is on par with a roughly contemporaneous illustration in the influential nationalist lawyer Bankey Behari's publication on Mīrā printed by the Gītā Press in Gorakhpur in 1937, which showed Mīrā in a very similar position (99).[21] A preoccupation becomes apparent in this period with the devotee in a subordinated position clasping the feet of the deity.

South India too in the 1930s and 1940s produced a plethora of devotionals on south Indian *bhaktas*, but here too, Rajasthani Mīrā proved popular. *Bhakta Meera* was directed in Tamil in 1938 by Y. V. Rao, after the major success (up to Ceylon) of the devotional *Chintamani* the year before. In Telugu, *Meerabai* came out from Navyakala Film Studio in 1940, directed by B. N. Rao.[22] The booklet of the latter featured a still with Mīrā clinging to the feet of her deity, similar as the contemporaneous movie in the north (Figure 11.7). It appears then that complete submission, even clinging to her god in the form of the deity-image, was characteristic for the way Mīrā was visualized in this period.

This success in the south paved the way for the most successful Mīrā movie of all, Chandraprabha Cine's production in Tamil in 1945, directed by Ellis R.

Figure 11.7 Promotional poster for the Telugu film *Meerabai* directed by B. N. Rao, produced by studio Navyakala Films, 1940.

Dungan.[23] The film's status as a classic is in no small measure, thanks to the lead role being taken up by the charismatic Karnatic classical singer M. S. Subbulakshmi, who sang the lyrics to great effect.[24] It was a hit with all-India appeal and a Hindi version followed in 1947. Its premiere was attended by Lord Mountbatten as well as Pdt. Javaharlāl Nehru (Rajadhyaksha and Willemen 1999: 304). *Meera* was instrumental in establishing a canon of eighteen Mīrā *bhajans*. Its story is close to the Mīrā story as told by the aforementioned Bankey Behari (1937), featuring a mostly understanding husband and stressing the success of Mīrā's songs at the Mewar court and among common people alike. The climax is Mīrā's absorption in the deity at Dwarka, which features a backdrop highly reminiscent of the Kishangarhi painting, with dark temple interior and a diverse group of devotees engaged in *bhajan* in her company.

This movie starts with a scene from Mīrā's youth (Subbulakshmi's daughter Radha played the young Mīrā), where a holy man, Rūpa Gosvāmī, visits her parental house, keen to meet the great devotee whose birth he had been made aware of by a shooting star. Little Mīrā's grandfather Dūdā introduces her to the Svāmī, but she has only eyes for the image brought along by the visitor, which comes to life for her, during the collective *bhajan* session at court. After her mother has told her a bedtime story about Kṛṣṇa, she has a dream in which she dances in the moonlight with the handsome young Kṛṣṇa (played by a female actor). When Kṛṣṇa disappears in the dream, she wakes up disturbed and sneaks out of the bedroom, only to be reassured when she finds the holy man's Kṛṣṇa image where she had seen it earlier. She fondles it in delight (Figure 11.4), before taking it with her to bed.

The following morning, grandfather Dūdā and Rūpa Gosvāmī find her happily asleep with the deity in her arms. These visuals are the first to establish the portrayal of Mīrā as a child treating the deity as if it were a doll, but they are balanced with Mīrā's dream vision, where she dances with Kṛṣṇa as a romantic partner. The many *bhajan* scenes in this movie invite the viewer, if not to sing along, at least to partake in the community of the devout, or *satsaṅga*. Sarojini Naidu quite astutely had introduced the Hindi version as an invitation of the north to join the south in this devotional community led by the glamorous, yet modestly shy Subbulakshmi. This national community-building *Meera* movie remained an unrivaled mainstay for the next three decades, even though some other movies tried to cash in on the success.[25]

The Trope of Little Mīrā's Doll

Dungan's use of traditional images of Mīrā worshipping her *mūrti* in the course of daily ritual care, as well as that of the romantic "dream vision" with an adult Kṛṣṇa, was complemented with the strikingly new visual of little Mīrā holding on to her deity as if to a doll. In classical aesthetic *rasa* terminology, this bespeaks a shift from *dāsya* or "servitude" and *mādhurya* or "erotic love" to the *vātsalya* or "motherly love" type. A similar phenomenon, with a special devotion to the Bāl Gopāl or young child Kṛṣṇa image, is noted for contemporary Bengali women's preoccupation with household shrines by anthropologist Ashlee Andrews (2019: 225 and 232). How did the "little Mīrā with doll" trope become so prominent in the visual landscape? I will trace this development through Mīrā's depiction in film productions and associated posters and booklets. Here, as elsewhere, "the dominance of the 'nation' in scholarly analysis of the ocular modern" is unhelpful (Holt and Pechilis 2019: 129), or at least it does not explain the phenomenon. While attention on nationalist politics behind early devotional movies is important, it needs to be balanced with attention to "implicit connections by investigating the intertwining of individuality, aesthetics, performance, and the aura of shared-community identity" (Holt and Pechilis: 130).

To be sure, the motif of Mīrā's attachment to her deity, her *mūrti* of Kṛṣṇa as a child, is not new. Already in 1712 the hagiographer Priyādās alluded to Mīrā's request to take "Giridhāralāla," the *mūrti* she had worshipped in her paternal home, with her in her wedding palanquin (*ḍolā padharāya*). Her mother assented to this request at the emotional time of *vidā*, the ceremonial lament at the bride's departure after the wedding (Rūpkalā 1977: 715). In 1762, the Marathi hagiographer Mahīpati proffered a variant, as he told of Mīrā's childhood desire to marry Kṛṣṇa and her father's bestowing her a *mūrti* to perform *sevā* for. Scandal ensued because of her ecstatic singing in front of holy men, but here it is her parents who saw themselves forced to offer her the poison cup (*Bhakta-vijay*, chapter 38, Phaḍke 1974: 295–304). By the nineteenth century, Rajput reconstruction narratives, such as Devī Prasād's 1898 version, elaborated on the *mūrti* as playmate in her youth, but only as a first phase, after which her devotion matured due to the loss of her husband, father-in-law, and father in short order (Martin 2000: 169–70).

Among the early Mīrā devotionals in independent India was Shree Bharat Lakhsmi Pictures' 1949 Hindi film directed by Prafulla Roy, entitled *Giridhar Gopal ki Meera*. This film continued the focus on the preoccupation of the child Mīrā with her deity, as it featured a song *mohe byāh gaye giridhari bālpane men* "Giridhari married me in childhood."[26] This is not to say that the trend was mono-directional. At the same time, the adult Mīrā continued to be glamorized. In 1950, Ranjit Movietone brought out Kidar Sharma's fascinating Mīrā-themed *Jogan*. This is not a devotional but the story of a village-returned urban atheist (*nāstik*) student (Dilip Kumar), who becomes fascinated with a Mīrā-inspired religious mendicant (glamorously played by Nargis).[27] This movie is permeated by the audio of Mīrā songs, in the voice of Geeta Dutt, yet the image of Kṛṣṇa remains out of focus for the first fifty or so minutes of the film, fitting the *nāstik*'s perspective. The main poster for the film features Dilip with Nargis who holds her musical instrument in one hand and not an image of Kṛṣṇa but a book in the other.[28] This movie, though, was strictly speaking a "social."

Old-fashioned devotionals followed, like another *Rajrani Meera* (dir. G. P. Pawar) in 1956. Its poster featured the traditional Mīrā singing and playing her instrument as if conjuring up a vision of Kṛṣṇa.[29] A Bengali *Mirabai* followed in 1960, directed by Gunamoy Bandhyopadhyay with the Bengali actress Anubha Gupta. In 1976, a color movie, Satish Kumar's *Meera Shyam*, featured the first actual movie poster I am aware of with a grown-up Mīrā holding her image in her arms as if it were a doll,[30] which was foreshadowed by the child-Mīrā doing likewise in Dungan's 1945 film.[31] For the soundtrack, Mīrā's songs were performed by playback singers Lata Mangeshkar and Asha Bhonsle. One would expect this film to have become a classic, but it was upstaged by Gulzar's 1979 movie *Meera*, with music arranged by Pandit Ravi Shankar. Notwithstanding a lukewarm initial reception, Gulzar's movie was the one that became the classic. It was for many years a staple for Doordarshan programs on Kṛṣṇa-related religious holidays. Is it coincidental that this is also a landmark movie for the popularity of the Mīrā-with-doll image we are tracing?

The main driving force behind the making of the movie was the lead actress Hema Malini, who was inspired by her family guru from Poona, Mīrādāsī (Gulzar 1979: 32). Yet the director himself pursues an overall historical approach that evinces an ambiguous attitude toward the miracles.[32] Gulzar's movie draws in interesting ways on the popular hagiographic and *bhajan* traditions of Mīrā.[33] Through his contextual placement of Mīrā's songs, the director invites the viewer to read in new meanings that often undermine the conventional ones. Remarkably, the viewer's sympathy does not go out to Mīrā, whose devotion frequently comes over as excessive. At times Gulzar belittles Mīrā's preoccupation with her deity, suggesting comparison to a little girl's play with a doll. A scene from early on in her married life shows Mīrā sewing a little turban for her Kṛṣṇa image (Figure 11.5). As her husband Bhoj, played by the handsome Vinod Khanna, finds her engaged in this occupation, he teases her: "You seem a real housewife today?" She replies in kind: "I am turning Kṛṣṇa into a Rajput. 'Dress like the locals,' they say" (*jis deś rahnā, vahī bheṣ pahnnā*; Gulzar 1979: 109). Mīrā's husband then mentions he heard from her friend Lalitā that she composes devotional songs and sympathetically asks her to share one with him. This could be a chance to share her devotion with her husband. Yet Mīrā instead insults him by choosing to sing a song to the effect that she does not care whether the Rāṇā gets angry, she cares only about her Kṛṣṇa (Gulzar 1979: 109). This song is one of Mīra's classics of defiance addressed to the powerful "Rāṇā," the ruler of Mewar, but here it has been turned into a housewife's (misguided) insistence on privacy, when her husband tries to be understanding of her emotional world. Gulzar has literally domesticated the message through contextualizing with a petty conjugal conflict, in the process detracting from the saint's radical devotion.

Behind the initial banter, the audience senses Bhoj's deeper sadness. Mīrā's sewing a miniature outfit looks like preparing an outfit for a little baby to come setting up the expectation of a tender scene between future parents-to-be. This is thwarted by Mīrā's inability to let go of her premarital fixation on her *mūrti*, and the viewer is led to sympathize with her husband's disappointment at her inability to grow up, leave "dolls" behind, and be interested in actual children. At the end of the movie, during her final trial this is articulated in the accusation of her not fulfilling her duty as a wife to produce offspring (Gulzar 1979: 147).

Such strengthens the impression that by conventional standards of womanhood, Mīrā is a failure.

The marital discord was already foreshadowed in the wedding night scene. Here too, Bhoj is portrayed as a sensitive and concerned groom. He is aware that his new bride had been married off against her wishes to cement a political alliance between traditional enemies: her Rathor and his Sisodiya family. When he arrives in the bedroom, he gently inquires how she is doing. Mīrā bluntly blurts out that she will not be able to make him happy. She is committed to keeping her end of the contract to set a political example but forswears a personal relationship with him. Bhoj presumes out loud that this is due to her ingrained hatred as a Rathor for a Sisodiya, but Mīrā answers:

> "That is not the reason . . . the reason is, my own belief, my love."

Bhoj misunderstands:

> "You love someone else?"

This misunderstanding, that Mīrā is in love with another mortal man, is played to the amusement of the audience:

> "Is he Rathor?"
> "No"
> "Sisodiya?"
> "No"
> "So, who is he?"
> "The one who was my playmate in childhood, whom I grew up with, that's the one I love, him only . . ."
> "So why didn't your parents marry you to him?
> "I did get married"
> "To him? Who is he?"
> "Kṛṣṇa"
> "Kṛṣṇa who?"
> "That one, whose *mūrti* I've brought with me."

Bhoj bursts out laughing, but Mīrā remains serious. Bhoj puts the *mangal-sūtra* around her neck:

> "That is a wedding of your soul, and this . . . Give me your word, as long as you live, you won't take it off your body." (Gulzar 1979: 99–100)

Here, Gulzar is repurposing a dialogue from a script he wrote just a few years earlier for Hrishikesh Mukherjee's 1971 *Guddi* ("The Doll"). That movie centered on the infatuation of the eponymous young girl (Jaya Bahadur) with the movie star Dharmendra (played by the actor himself). Guddi herself compares her love for the movie star to Mīrā's for Kṛṣṇa (Lutgendorf 2012: 184–6). The whole movie revolves around the heroine outgrowing her childish obsession with a film idol so as to forge a proper marital bond with a "suitable boy." Foreshadowing the wedding night in *Meera* is a scene in *Guddi* where the heroine tells the hero that she cannot marry him because she loves someone else. He presses her to reveal his rival's identity, much like Bhoj does in *Meera*, and she confesses she is in love with Dharmendra, the movie star. Like Bhoj, the hero bursts out laughing, belittling her puerile preoccupation with the film idol, contrasting with their more adult relation. In view of the earlier explicit comparison with Mīrā's love for Kṛṣṇa, Gulzar's reprise of this dialogue in *Meera* seems quite deliberate. In effect, he portrays Mīrā's love for Kṛṣṇa as an immature girl's obsession, like that of a girl for a doll (as evoked by the title of the movie referenced, *Guddi*). The concern seems to be that Mīrā's example through phantasies of romanticized love might lead young girls astray from proper matrimony.

This ambiguity about the woman-saint whom Gulzar's film ostensibly celebrates may bespeak a broader societal consensus that the normative matrimonial ideal should not be relegated to secondary place. The Bollywood climate of the 1970s can be characterized as defensive of the sexual economy of the middle-class upper-caste extended family (Prasad 1998: 170–5).[34] Gulzar's Mīrā's childish obsession with Kṛṣṇa seems to have become lodged in the collective memory of filmmakers and audiences alike. It is echoed even in a cricket movie like Chandani Kulkarni's 2008 *Meerabai Not Out*, which contains echoes of Gulzar's view of Mīrā's love as immature. At the beginning of that movie, the narrator sets up a comparison of Kṛṣṇa-infatuated Mīrā with cricket-besotted heroine of the movie, also named Meera:

> Those who whole-heartedly wish something can't be "out," whether they want god Kṛṣṇa himself or cricket, or whether they are Mewar's Mīrābai or our Meera Achrekar, living near Shivaji Park.

This comparison is underscored with a shot of a Mīrā poster dissolving into one of the heroine on her scooter. While the movie subsequently gets off on another track, at a crucial point, it returns to Mīrā with a scene parallel to the wedding night in Gulzar's *Meera* and the confession of love for the movie star in *Guddi*. When the Meera in Kulkarni's movie is asked in marriage by her socially superior boyfriend, she confesses that she has a prior love. Upon her suitor's nervous inquiry, she confesses that her heart's love is not Kṛṣṇa but near-homonymous cricket. Here too the groom-to-be bursts out laughing. This scene feels like a subconscious rerun of the earlier ones. The denouement shows the girl's extreme preoccupation with cricket nearly ruining her. This Meera chooses to attend a cricket game just before the ceremonial celebration (*muhurt*) of her betrothal. When she is late for the occasion, the fiancé's rich family feels insulted and calls off the wedding. Needless to say, in the end all is cleared and she too can reach that *summum bonum* of the middle-class heroine, blissful hypergamic matrimony. Still this bespeaks the lingering unease in the filmmaker's mind, and presumably that of his audience, with girls' Mīrā-like fixation on other than matrimonial concerns, be it cricket, moviestars or Kṛṣṇa idolization.

The doll trope is most clearly articulated on television in a series called *Meera*, produced by Sagar Pictures and aired on NDTV 2009–10.[35] Like Gulzar's film, it was promoted as a costume drama with lavish sets, signaling the subject was approached more like a "historical" and one with a decidedly consumerist overabundance of jewelry and accessories at that. This Sagar brothers' production too follows Gulzar in foregrounding Mīrā's preoccupation with her Kṛṣṇa as that of a child for a doll. The theme song of the series comes back again and again to the line *sāṃvale guḍḍī se vah khelī* "she played with a dark-hued doll." The promo stills of the series feature the young Mīrā, playing with her Kṛṣṇa image (Figure 11.6), and in the song, she refers to her *mūrti* as a "doll" on several occasions. In contrast to Gulzar's preoccupation, the filmmakers' agenda is not to show Mīrā outgrowing her fixation. Rather, it seems part of an effort to bring the sixteenth-century heroine closer to the twenty-first-century viewer of consumerist Hindutva India. Mīrā's family is portrayed as one of those upper-caste and upper-middle-class ones that are featured in prime-time soap series, with attitudes recognizable to the contemporary viewer, just a more than lavish lifestyle. For instance, they show solicitous deference toward their family guru Raidās, who is consulted for important matters, such as the naming of the baby girl. His caste identity is not stressed.

The first episode shows the young child Mīrā asking her parents for a doll to marry in imitation of her servant-friend Lalitā, who behaves as an exemplary little housewife toward her own doll. Mīrā's doting parents are amused and indulge her wish. They set off to the bazaar, as modern parents would to the mall. Little Mīrā gets to take her pick among a consumer's dream collection of male dolls. Her selection of a Kṛṣṇa image for her doll-groom comes over as rather random, though a subsequent visit to the guru imbues the choice with more mystic gravitas. Her parents invite the guru to a lavish wedding ceremony for their daughter with the doll, like typical parents of that class, keen to capitalize on an occasion to show off their wealth. It is hard to avoid the impression that this Mīrā is a pampered girl whose parents (and everyone else around her) cater to her every wish.[36]

In this television series, Mīrā's story transforms, true to the medium, into a melodrama-like soap series focusing on mother and daughter-in-law (*sās-bahu*) relations. Following the conventions of such scenarios, Mīrā ends up devoted to her young husband, with conflicts squarely attributed to her in-laws' machinations. This affects even the diction of Mīrā's *bhajans*. Thus, on the eve of an evil plot of her in-laws that will send her husband into war, she sings in front of her image: *tuma sanga prīta na toṛo jī* "Please do not break up my togetherness with my love." This is a plea for Kṛṣṇa to protect her husband, her love (*prīta*), and bring him back safely from the battlefield.[37] Such constitutes a fascinating permutation of the more usual diction of the refrain *tuma sanga prīta na toṛūṃgī* "I will not give up my togetherness in love for you." The slight adjustment completely turns the meaning upside down: from Mīrā's insistence that she will love Kṛṣṇa even if he turns away from her to her asking his help to bring her husband home. The rehabilitation of Mīrā as a proper *pativratā*, or woman devoted to her husband, is clearly underway on the small screen.

In conclusion, while Mīrā's story and her songs show both submission to god and defiance to the outside world, visually the submission prevails. Her pose in popular culture has remained meek and submissive, even through the nationalist movement when she was upheld as a symbol of resistance against the colonizer. In the course of the twentieth century, portrayals of Mīrā evolved in the direction of ever-stronger attachment to her *mūrti*. Earlier visions' *mādhurya*, where Mīrā was romantically intertwined with her god are still there to be sure, but many posters now tend to show *vātsalya*, Mīrā's mothering, cherishing her deity as a doll. Movies, whether devotional or "social" using the Mīrā trope, highlight increasingly Mīrā's child play with a Kṛṣṇa doll, which is sometimes marked as a childish preoccupation standing in the way of a mature relationship with her real-life husband. This can be interpreted as part of an irenic effort to hold her up as a positive role model for girls while avoiding interference of any form of idolization with wifely duties. The husband comes first, and if not, ultimately Mīrā comes to grief. Popular culture's portrayal of the depth of her devotion turns into idolization, rendered ever shallower as hagiography conforms to the genre of the soap series in an increasingly consumerist societal context.

Notes

1 Interestingly, the booklet also included a Muslim saint, Rabia. Later on, Yusuf "Bangalorewala," the Muslim illustrator of the aforementioned comic on *Mīrā* in Pai's *Amar Citra Kathā* series, also reported to have been inspired by this female saint (Hawley 1995: 120).

2 The modern rendition of the consonant cluster *-kt-* in *bhakti* may indicate it was a later addition.

3 For a picture of the latter, see https://www.inditales.com/mirabai-birthplace-merta-rajasthan/. See also the 2002 documentary by Anjali Panjabi, where turning the leaves of one such a book, she pauses briefly on a striking illustration of Mīrā assaulted by snakes. This was part of an exhibit in the Mehrangarh Library in Jodhpur (Anjali Panjabi, personal communication, May 10, 2021).

4 It could be the Merta Cārbhujā Nāth deity, purportedly portrayed in a similar image (published in Purohit 1996: facing p. 32). Alternatively, it might be the image at Dwarka.

5 The series also included the Indo-Muslim poet Ghālib, so there is at least a token gesture toward a composite spirituality.

6 The booklet provides only the refrain and first verse of Mīrā's song numbered 35 in Caturvedī 1983; its multiple variants are given in Tivārī (1974: 183–6).

7 Haidar (1995: 138–9); plate 125 (photo by R. Skelton). I am grateful to Navina Haidar for providing me with a colored copy of the plate from her dissertation. A detail of the painting is also reproduced on the cover of the popular edition of Mīrā's works (Caturvedī 1983) and appears in Prabhāt 1965, who specifies it depicts the time of the fire ritual (*āratī ke samay*). Mīrā's bust was redrawn and issued as the stamp (Haidar 1995: 139 n. 143).

8 Varmā traveled in Rajasthan and as guest of the Mewar Rāṇā even visited Cittaur in 1901. While in his diaries he mentions the legend of Padmāvatī and made a sketch that is a study for her likeness (Neumayer and Schelberger 2005 and 2003), Mīrā does not come up. Perhaps he was preoccupied with dynastic themes because he was invited to paint portraits of Rāṇā's ancestors.

9 For images, see https://ramaarya.blog/2017/05/31/vadodara-kirti-mandir-nandalal-bose/ (accessed January 31, 2021).

10 By Mukta's assessment, Gandhian activist, painter, and editor Ravishankar Rawal too "depicted woman as seductive through her chastity" (1989: 99).

11 For a critique of the nationalist interpretation of Phalke's films, see Schulze (1998).

12 Saigal had a stage actor past, including playing Sītā in Rām-līlā performances as a child growing up in Jammu.

13 Again, we see overlap of personnel with the theater, Kapoor being very active in Shakespeare performances at the Grant Anderson Company at the time.

14 Available online at http://i3.cinestaan.com/image-bank/1500-1500/70001-71000/70071.jpg (accessed January 31, 2021).
15 Shantaram also had been an actor in a theater group (Rajadhyaksha and Willemen 1999: 178).
16 See https://indiancine.ma/CKX/info (accessed January 31, 2021).
17 Two clips are available on the internet, one where Bal Gandharva sings songs by Sūrdās https://www.youtube.com/watch?v=tS3ZmC1ZHDw, and another by Mīrā in Marathi https://marathisangeetnatakblog.wordpress.com/2020/03/25/25-march-2020-the-sangeet-natak-and-cinema-part-2-bal-gandharva-and-the-first-talkies/ (accessed January 31, 2021).
18 The iconography of Mīrā's relationship with the Dalit *camār* guru is an interesting topic that deserves to be investigated in its own right.
19 See indiancine.ma/BAH/info (accessed January 31, 2021).
20 See https://indiancine.ma/DCS/info (accessed January 31, 2021).
21 Accessible via Internet Archive at https://archive.org/details/dli.ernet.2527/page/n127/mode/2up (accessed March 21, 2021).
22 See https://indiancine.ma/CNH/info and https://indiancine.ma/DCU/info, resp (accessed January 31, 2021).
23 A full-length Tamil version of the movie can be watched at https://indiancine.ma/EEZ/info (accessed January 31, 2021).
24 She had already worked with Dungan in 1940 for his *Sakuntalai*, see https://indiancine.ma/AKOZ/info (accessed January 31, 2021).
25 Already mentioned above was W. Z. Ahmad's 1947 *Meerabai*, and a Gujarati movie of the same name was directed by Nanabhai Bhatt (father of Mahesh Bhatt), starring his wife Neena in the same year, see https://indiancine.ma/EUF/info (accessed January 31, 2021).
26 See https://indiancine.ma/FLL/info (accessed January 31, 2021).
27 I am grateful to Gayatri Chatterjee for introducing this movie to me. I will publish a fuller analysis elsewhere.
28 See https://anuradhawarrier.blogspot.com/2018/06/jogan-1950.html (accessed January 31, 2021).
29 See https://meerabaiofmerta.blogspot.com/2019/04/film-rajrani-meera-1956.html (accessed January 31, 2021).
30 See poster image at https://www.cinestaan.com/movies/meera-shyam-4565/images (accessed June 15, 2022).
31 The aforementioned *Amar Citra Kathā* comic series also features Mīrā holding the image in that way in the 1986 issue on Guru Ravidas (issue no. 350), Hawley (1995: 125).
32 Gulzar's film has a lot in common with Hermann Goetz's book on Mīrā (published first in 1956 [1966]; see Martin 2000: 174–5).

33 I have analyzed both in more detail elsewhere, see Pauwels (2010a: 45–67; 2007: 99–120).

34 Lutgendorf suggests that the theme may betray unease with feminine renunciation, which needs to be subordinated to patriarchal society. Yet at the same time it also constitutes a meta-reflection on the world of commercial cinema (and middle-class bourgeoisie) as a shadow-world of cheap dreams (2012: 188–90, 193–4). That is certainly true for *Guddi*.

35 The official website is https://web.archive.org/web/20090729054139/http://www.ndtvimagine.com/shows/showdetails.php?id=130

36 The July 27, 2009, episode; https://www.youtube.com/watch?v=cavjQQPBKGE (accessed January 16, 2021).

37 October 9, 2009, episode; http://www.dailymotion.com/video/xar831_meera-9st-october-part1hq_shortfilms (accessed January 29, 2011).

References

Ambalal, A. (1987), *Krishna as Shrinathji: Rajasthani Paintings from Nathdvara*, Ahmedabad: Mapin.

Andrews, A. N. (2019), "Gopāl Is My Baby: Vulnerable Deities and Maternal Love at Bengali Home Shrines," *Journal of Hindu Studies* 12 (2): 224–41.

Behari, B. (1937), *The Story of Mira Bai*, 2nd ed., Bombay: Bharatiya Vidya Bhavan.

Bhāṭī, N. S., ed. (1984), *Mīrābāī rī Paracī va Paracī Kāvya*. Paramparā 69–70, Jodhpur: Rājāsthānī Shodh Sansthān.

Bly, R., and J. Hirshfield (2009), *Mirabai*, Boston: Beacon.

Caturvedī, P. (1983), *Mīrābāī kī Padāvalī*, Prayāg: Hindī Sāhitya Sammelan.

Dwyer, R. (2006), *Filming the Gods: Religion and Indian Cinema*, London: Routledge.

Goetz, H. (1966), *Mirabai, Her Life and Times*, Bombay: Bhāratīya Vidyā Bhavan.

Gulzār (1979), *Mīrā: Kathā, moṃtāj, anusandhān aur paṭkathā*, New Delhi: Rādhāklhihā, mo:śan.

Haidar, N. (1995), "The Kishangarh School of Painting c. 1680–1850," PhD diss., Oxford University.

Hansen, K. (2011), *Stages of Life: Indian Theatre Autobiographies*, Ranikhet: Permanent Black.

Hawley, J. S. (1995), "The Saints Subdued: Domestic Virtue and National Integration in Amar Chitra Katha," in L. Babb and S. Wadley (eds.), *Media and the Transformation of Religion in South Asia*, 107–34, Philadelphia: University of Pennsylvania Press.

Hawley, J. S. (2005), *Three Bhakti Voices: Mirabai, Surdas and Kabir in Their Times and Ours*, New York: Oxford University Press.

Hawley, J. S., and M. Juergensmeyer (2004), *Songs of the Saints of India*, New York: Oxford University Press.

Holt, A. R., and K. Pechilis (2019), "Contemporary Images of Hindu *Bhakti*: Identity and Visuality," *Journal of Hindu Studies* 12: 129–41.

Kaul, G. (1998), *Cinema and the Indian Freedom Struggle*, New Delhi: Sterling.

Kishwar, M., and R. Vanita (1989), "Poison to Nectar: The Life and Work of Mirabai," *Women Bhakta Poets: Manushi* 50–2: 75–93.

Lutgendorf, P. (2012), "The Mira Trope in Mainstream Hindi Cinema: Three Examples from Notable Films," in S. Cavaliere (ed.), *Gurumala. Proceedings of the Seminar in Honour of Shyam Manohar Pandey*, 123–43, Naples: Annali dell'Università degli Studi di Napoli "L'Orientale."

Lyons, T. (2004), *The Artists of Nathadwara: The Practice of Painting in Rajasthan*, Ahmedabad: Mapin.

Martin, N. (1999), "Mīrā Janma Patrī: A Tale of Resistance and Appropriation," in N. K. Singhi and R. Joshi (eds.), *Religion, Ritual and Royalty*, 227–6, Jaipur: Rawat.

Martin, N. (2000), "Mirabai in the Academy and the Politics of Identity," in M. Bose (ed.), *Faces of the Feminine from Ancient, Medieval and Modern India*, 162–82, New York: Oxford University Press.

Martin, N. (2010), "Mirabai Comes to America: The Translation and Transformation of a Saint," *Journal of Hindu Studies* 3: 12–35.

Martin, N. M. (2012), "Mirabai," *Oxford Bibliographies Online*. DOI: 10.1093/OBO/9780195399318-0070.

Masselos, J., J. Menzies, and P. Pal, eds. (1997), *Dancing to the Flute: Music and Dance in Indian Art*, Sydney, Australia: Art Gallery of New South Wales.

Mukta, P. (1989), "Mirabai in Rajasthan," *Manushi* 50–52: 94–9.

Mukta, P. (1994), *Upholding the Common Life: The Community of Mirabai*, New Delhi: Oxford University Press.

Neumayer, E., and C. Schelberger (2003), *Popular Indian Art: Raja Ravi Varma and the Printed Gods of India*, New Delhi: Oxford University Press.

Neumayer, E., and C. Schelberger (2005), *Raja Ravi Varma, Portrait of an Artist: The Diary of C. Raja Raja Varma*, New Delhi: Oxford University Press.

Pai, A. (1971), *Mirabai*, Mumbai: Amar Chitra Katha.

Panjabi, A. (2002), [Documentary], *A Few Things I Know about Her*, Government of India: Film Division.

Pauwels, H. (2006), "Hagiography and Reception History: The case of Mīrā's Padas in Nāgrīdās's Pada-prasaṅga-mālā," in M. Horstmann (ed.), *Bhakti in Current Research 2001–2003*, 221–4, New Delhi: Manohar.

Pauwels, H. (2007), "*Bhakti* Songs Recast: Gulzar's Meera Movie," in H. Pauwels (ed.), *Indian Literature and Popular Cinema: Recasting Classics*, 99–120, London: Routledge.

Pauwels, H. (2010a), "Who Is Afraid of Mirabai? Gulzar's Antidote for Mira's Poison," in D. Dimitrova (ed.), *South Asian Religion in Film and Literature*, 45–67, New York: Palgrave McMillan.

Pauwels, H. (2010b), "Rāṭhauṛī Mīrā: Two Neglected Rāṭhauṛ Connections of Mīrā," *Journal of Hindu Studies* 14 (2–3): 177–200.

Phaḍke, V., ed. (1974), *Śrībhakta Vijaya*, Puṇẽ: Yaśavanta Prakāśana.
Poddar, H. P. (1930), *Bhakta Nārī*, Gorakhpur: Gītā Press.
Prabhāt, C. L. (1965), *Mīrābāī: Śodh Prabandh*, Bombay: Hīrāgranth Ratnākar.
Prasad, M. M. (1998), *Ideology of the Hindi Film*, Delhi: Oxford University Press.
Purohit, C. (1996), *Bhaktimati Mīrāṃbaī*, Kishangarh: Śrī Nimbārkācārya Pīam.
Rajadhyaksha, A., and P. Willemen (1999), *Encyclopaedia of Indian Cinema*, 2nd rev. ed., London: Oxford University Press.
"Rūpkalā" Bhagvānprasād, Sītārām Śaraṇ, ed. (1977 [1903–1909]), *Gosvāmi Nābhājī kṛt Śrī Bhaktamāl: Śrī Priyādāsjī praṇīt ṭikā-kavitta, Śrī Sītārāmśaraṇ Bhagvānprasād Rūpkalā viracit Bhaktisudhāsvād tilak sahit*, Reprint. Lucknow: Tejkumār Book Depot.
Schulze, B. (1998), "The First Cinematic Pauranik Kathanak," in V. Dalmia and T. Damsteegt (eds.), *Narrative Strategies: Essays on South Asian Literature and Film*, 50–66, Leiden: CNWS.
Taft, F. (2002), "The Elusive Historical Mira," in L. Babb, V. Joshi, and M. Meister (eds.), *Multiple Histories: Culture and Society in the Study of Rajasthan*, 313–35, Jaipur: Rawat.
Taft, F. (2009), "Six Incarnations of Mirabai," in V. Joshi and S. Singh (eds.), *Culture, Polity, and Economy*, 163–72, Jaipur: Rawat.
Tivārī Bhagavāndās (1974), *Mīrāṃ Kī Prāmāṇik Padāvalī*, Allahabad: Sāhitya Bhavan.
van Skyhawk, H. (2001), "Saint, Cinéma et dharma: Ekanāth et les intouchables au temps the V. Śāntārām," in F. Mallison (ed.), *Constructions hagiographiques dans le monde indien: Entre mythe et histoire*, 325–33, Paris: Librairie Honoré Champion.

Contributors

Ashlee Norene Andrews is Assistant Professor of Religion at the University of North Carolina at Greensboro, where she teaches courses in South Asian religious traditions, gender and embodiment, and theory and method in the study of religion. She is currently finishing her manuscript, *Ma Prays for Us at Home: Valuing Hindu Women's Domestic Worship as Reproductive Labor.* This book draws from ethnographic research Dr. Andrews completed in Kolkata, India, and Chicago, Illinois, and argues that the domestic shrine traditions that Bengali Hindu women maintain in India and the United States are a form of reproductive labor crucial to the sustenance of Hindu traditions and subjectivities, and of profound value to the women who perform them as an affective, relational, maternal, and home-making labor.

Richard H. Davis is Research Professor of Religion at Bard College, New York. His publications include *Lives of Indian Images* (1997) and *The Bhagavad Gita: A Biography* (2015). He has also written a catalogue of early Indian chromolithograph prints, *Gods in Print: Masterpieces of India's Mythological Art* (2012). His current projects are a cultural history of religions in early India and a study of the early history of religious prints in modern India.

Ankur Desai is an independent scholar and archivist at the John C. & Susan L. Huntington Photographic Archive of Buddhist and Asian Art. His specializations include Indic temple architecture and religious iconography, and his current research interests focus on religious imagery from western India during the early modern period.

John Stratton Hawley—informally, Jack—is Claire Tow Professor of Religion at Barnard College, Columbia University. His most recent books on India's *bhakti* traditions are *A Storm of Songs: India and the Idea of the Bhakti Movement* (2015), *Sur's Ocean* (with Kenneth Bryant, 2015), a poem-by-poem commentary called *Into Sur's Ocean* (2016), and a revised, enlarged edition of *Sūrdās: Poet, Singer, Saint* (2018). His book *Krishna's Playground: Vrindavan in the 21st Century*

(2020) has recently been translated into Hindi as *Kṛṣṇa Līlābhūmi* (2022). Jack has been a Guggenheim Fellow and a Fulbright-Nehru Fellow, and is a member of the American Academy of Arts and Sciences.

Amy-Ruth Holt is an independent scholar and art historian, who has taught at Washington & Lee University, the University of Alabama, Birmingham, and the Ohio State University, Newark. Her research interests include the arts and architecture of southern India, modern media imagery, and Hindu material culture. She has published a variety of essays in edited volumes and articles in the *Journal of Hindu Studies*, including a coedited issue with Karen Pechilis, "Contemporary Images of Hindu *Bhakti*: Identity and Visuality" (2019), "Symbols of Political Participation: Jayalalitha's Fan Imagery in Tamil Nadu" (2019), and "A Secular Tamil Saint? Karunanidhi's Use of Divine Imagery in Dravidian Politics" (2016).

Murad Khan Mumtaz is Assistant Professor in the Art Department at Williams College. His research focuses on Indo-Muslim devotional expression in the early modern period. By combining art history with textual analysis, he examines the cultural contexts within which Islamicate devotion was experienced and patronized in South Asia. His forthcoming book is titled *Faces of God: Images of Devotion in Indo-Muslim Painting.*

Shruti Patel is Assistant Professor of History at Salisbury University, and most recently she was an American Association of University Women (AAUW) American Postdoctoral Research Fellow and Visiting Scholar at Tufts University (2021–2) completing her book project. Her research interests are in the history of colonial, princely, and postcolonial India, ethics and power, intellectual history and religious identities, working with textual, visual/material, and ethnographic materials. She has published in the *Journal of Hindu Studies.*

Heidi Pauwels is Professor in the Department of Asian Languages and Literature at the University of Washington in Seattle, WA. She has published on sixteenth-century Krishna Bhakti (*Krishna's Round Dance Reconsidered* 1996 and *In Praise of Holy Men* 2002), compared classical Sanskrit, early modern Hindi and contemporary film and television retellings of the stories of Sita and Radha (*The Goddess as Role Model* 2008), and two volumes on Kishangarh art and poetry: *Cultural Exchange in Eighteenth-century India* (2015) and *Mobilizing Krishna's World* (2017). A third volume, *India's Mona Lisa,* is forthcoming from Cambridge University Press. She has recently coedited a special issue of the *Journal of the*

Royal Asiatic Society on vernacular views of Aurangzeb (with Anne Murphy, 2018) and of *South Asian History and Culture* on fifteenth-century Gwalior (with Eva De Clercq, 2020).

Karen Pechilis is a historian of religions who is Chair and Professor in the Department of History at Drew University. She teaches courses in world history, gender and history, and religion and history. She has served as director of the Humanities Program in the College and Director of Arts & Letters in Drew's Caspersen School of Graduate Studies. Her research explores critical perspectives on devotional religion that engage history, arts and letters, experience, and gender; recent publications include the monograph *Interpreting Devotion: The Poetry and Legacy of a Female Bhakti Saint of India* (2012), the coedited (with Barbara Holdrege) volume *Refiguring the Body: Embodiment in South Asian Religions* (2017), and a journal special issue coedited with Amy-Ruth Holt, "Contemporary Images of Hindu *Bhakti*: Identity and Visuality," in the *Journal of Hindu Studies* (2019).

Shandip Saha is Associate Professor of Religious Studies at Athabasca University in Edmonton, Canada. His primary research has been on the patronage of the Vallabha Sampradāya and other north Indian religious devotional communities under the Delhi Sultanate and the Mughal Empire. His other research interests revolve around the stylistic changes in the performance of devotional music by professional classical and nonclassical performers in the Indian subcontinent.

R. Jeremy Saul is Lecturer in Religious Studies at Mahidol University, Bangkok. His research examines Indian shrines for deities that have become popular for miracles in recent history, particularly in Rajasthan and adjacent areas. His current book project highlights the role of merchants known as Marwaris in the propagation of shrines and newly acclaimed miracle deities in the recent era of economic liberalization and Hanumān and Ram-centered Hindu activism. His most recent articles/chapters are "Navaratri as a Festival of Hanuman and Male Asceticism" (2021) and "Merchants, Ritualists, and Bifurcated Hanumans: A Cultural History of Miracle Deities in Rajasthan" (forthcoming).

Index

Note: References to images and captions are in bold.

'Abd al-Ḥaqq Muḥaddith-i Dehlavī 145
'Abd al-Raḥmān Chishtī 23, 150
'Abdullāh Kheshgī 150
abject 30, 261, 278–9
  gaze 270–3
  visuality 266–70
Ācārya 119–20, 125–7, 164, 169, **175**, 178, 188, 203, 213, *see also* Vallabha
Advaita Vedānta 71, 213–14, 230, 237
  Vivekananda Vedanta Society 71, 79
aesthetics 10–11, 22, 57–9, 89, 236, 268, 273, 298, *see also rasa*
agency 2–3, 9, 16, 19, 90, 92, 114, 184, 214, 218, 270, 273–4
Agrawal 85, 89, 99
Agroha 89, 99
Ahmad, W. Z. 295
Ahmedabad 21, 108, 115–18, 120, 122–7, 129–31, 175, 177–80
Ajmer 143
Akhbār-ul akhyār 145
Akshar Bhuvan 120, **121**, 124–5, 128
alaukika 28, 165, 180, 236, 242, 252
Amar Chitra Katha (*Amar Citra Kathā*) (comics series) 9, 286, 293
ancestor 18, 65–8, 72, 75, 78–9, 81, 89, 92, 96, 101, 118
Andhra Pradesh 88, 219, 223–4
aniconic 87, 93, 97, 222–3
anubhava 263
archive 20, 108–11, 118–24, 127, 250, 278, 287
artifact 21, 25, 128
ascetic
  advice from 104
  Bābā Lāl Das 150–1
  and Dārā Shikoh 156
  and Hanumān 92, 99, 101–2
  and Kabīr **143–4**, 147, **153**–4, 156, 159
  and Kamāl **143–4**, 154, 156, 159
  and Mīrā 30, 286
  and Nityānanda 222
  Śaiva 104, 274
  and Sūrdās 206
  and Svāminārāyaṇa *sampradāya* 110, 113–15, 117–18, 120, 122–3, 127, 129
authenticity 15–16, 18–21, 118, 129, 274
avatāra 89, 147, 238

Bābā Farīd Ganj Shakar 138
Bagchi, Anand Prasad 49
bairāgī 150–1
Bālājī (Hanumān or Pañcmukhī Hanumān) 19–20, 85–105
  Ghata Mehandipur Bālājī **97**–9
  Icchāpūṛn Bālājī 85, **86**–93, 102–5
  Mehandipur Bālājī 94, **95**
  Salasar Bālājī **92**, 101–2
Bal Gandharva 295
Bangalore (Karnataka) 210, 218, 222
baniyā 164, 167, 179–80
Battal 45–7, 50, 53
beauty 29–30, 156, 159, 198, 227, 239, 248, 261, 264–6, 275
Behari, Bankey 296–7
Bengali American 8, 17–18, 63–81
Bengali Association of Greater Chicago (BAGC) 68
bhajan 141, 200, 205, 226–7, 292, 297–8, 300, 304
Bhakta Meera (1938 Tamil movie) 296
bhakti visualities (*bhakti* visuality) 6, 43, 65–6, 68, 81
bhāva 12, 165–6, 170, 241, 286, 290
biography 6, 151, 193, 214, 222, 244, 275
Biswas, Nabakumar 49
Bose, Nandalal 293
Brijbasi & Sons **190**, 191–3
bronze images 266, **267**, 268

Calcutta Art Studio 17, 48–52, 56–8
caraṇacihna (sacred footprint marks) 240
caraṇārvinda (footprints) 116, **119**–20, 126, 242, **243**
caste 6, 30, 68, 114, 141, 152, 154, 225, 269, 295, 302–3
chakra 27, 213–30
chala 54, **55**, **56**
Chandraprabha Cine 296
chatrī **116**
Chaudhriwas Dham 99–100
Chishtī 4, 23, 138, 143, 145, 150, 154, 159
Chitra Silpi Company 46
Chore Bagan Art Studio 17, 47
citrajī 14, 24, 164–7, **168–9**, 170–81
Cittaur 291
Columbus, Ohio 27, 210–30
cremation grounds 262–3, 265, 270–2, 275–6

Dabistān-i mazāhib 151, 153
dance
  contemporary dance-drama 6, 273–9
  and Kṛṣṇa 199
  and Mīrā 288–9, 297–8
  and returning the gaze 28–30
  and Sahajānanda 117
  of Śiva in cremation ground 262–3, 265, 270, 272 (*see also* Śiva Naṭarāja)
Dārā Shikoh 23, 142–5, 150–3, 156
darśan
  and *bhakti* 7, 10, 13–15
  and *citra seva* 170, 175–8
  and God-prints 17
  and home shrines 66–7, 72
  and *jharokhā* 250
  and *naẓar* 7, 15
  and Nityānanda's *ānanda darśan* 217, 225–6
  and *prasādi* 111, 120
  and Sahajānanda 235, 237, 247, 250
  and Shree Swaminarayan Museum 21
Dharmakuḷ 125–6
Dharmendra 302
diaspora 18, 67, 76, 82 n.3, 130, 218–19, 225
distributive materiality 112–15
dohā 147, 149, 161
domestic worship (*bārir pūjā*) 63
Dungan, Ellis R. 296–9
Durgā 17, 43, 48, 51, 53–4, **55–6**, 78, 80
Dwarka 119, 285, 297

electrotyping 43, 46
enchantment 111, 117, 127–8

familial 65–7, 74–6, 80–1
faqīr 145, 148–9
festival
  Bālājī 88
  citra sevā (Puṣṭi Mārga) 24, 113, **168**, 169–70, 172, 176, **177**, 179
  Durgā Pūjā 48, 54–5, 57
  images 212
  mango 279
  Paṅkuṉi Uttiram 268
  puṣpadolotsava 235, 253
  Sahajānanda 28
Few Things I Know about Her, A (2002) 285
film 2–3, 16
  Bālājī 93
  and *darśan* 7
  Kāraikkāl Ammaiyār 274, 278
  Mīrā 285–303
  Nityānanda 210, 224–6
  and the return look 28–31
five elements 146, 223
focalization 275–6, **277**

Gadhada 122–3, 245, 249, 251–2
Gandhi, Mohandas Karamchand 132, 293–4
Gaṇeśa 48, 50–1, 54, 73, 214–15, 217
Garh Mahal 168
gaze
  abject 273
  bhakti 273, 278–9
  and *darśan* 7, 10, 13–15
  depiction of blindness 188
  erotic 15
  female 3, 29–31, 261–2, 264, 271–4
  filmic 7
  goddess 54
  guru 226–7, 247
  image 270–1
  male 29

and *naẓar* 7, 15, 26
neutral 29
scholarly 67–8
social 266
Ghata Mehandipur Bālājī temple 96–7, 99
Ghazal 141
ghoul, *see pēy*
Giridhar Gopal ki Meera (1949 Hindi movie) 299
Gītā Press, Gorakhpur 286–7, 296
Gokulnāth 167, 171
Gopīnāth 167, 171, 251–2
Gorakhnath 144
Govardhanlāl 24, 168, 172–4, 176–7, 179
Government School of Art, Calcutta 49
Guddi (1971 movie) 301–2
Gujarat
baniyā community 164, 167, 179–81
and images of Mīrā 293
and images of Sahajānanda 28, 235–53
Shree Swaminarayan Museum 21, 108
and the Svāminārāyaṇa *sampradāya* 108–30, 235–7
Gulzar 296, 299–303
guru, *see also sadhu*
and Bālājī 95–100
and *bhakti* 2–4, 7–8, 14, 18, 25–8
and home shrines 65, 71
and immateriality 26–8
and Kabīr 146–7, 151
and Mīrā's iconography 295, 300, 303
Paramahaṃsa Nityānanda 209–30
and Puṣṭi Mārga 165, 189
and Svāminārāyaṇa *sampradāya* 127

Haji Muhammad Naushā 23, 146–9
ḥaq (*ḥaqīqa*) 139, 147, *see also* Truth of Certainty; Truth-Reality
Ḥasanāt ul-ʿārifīn 144–5, 150
"head-to-toe," *see nakhaśikha*
heart 11–12, 80, 94, 98, 105, 147, 215, 238, 263, 302, *see also sahṛdaya*
Hindu Art Studio 46
home shrine 2–3, 8, 14, 17–18, 63, **64**–9, **70**, **72**, 74, **75**, **77**, **79**–81, 166, 169
Houston, Texas 223–4

Icchāpūrṇ Bālājī 19–20, **85**, 86, 88, 94, 101–5, *see also* Bālājī
iconicity 7, 25, 188
iconography
Bālājī 85, **86**
Bengali religious culture 53
cover image 8
Durgā Pūjā Shrine 17, **55–6**
god and goddess 218–19
Kabīr **140**, **143–4**, 154, **157**, **158**, **160**
Kālī 44, **45**, **47**, **52–3**
Kamāl **143–4**, **155**, **158**, 159
Kāraikkāl Ammaiyār 266, **267**, 278
Mīrā 285–**8**, **291**, **293**, **295**, **296**–**7**, 306 n.18
Nityānanda **211**, **214**, 219–20, **221**–2
royal devotees and saints 212
Sūrdās 186, **187–8**, 189, **190**–3, 199–201, **204–5**, 206
Svāminārāyaṇa 237–43, **247–50**
identity
abject 269, 272–3
Bengali American women 18, 66, 73–6, 81
devotional 19, 53, 279, 298
Durgā 55–7
Kabīr 153
Kamāl 158
Kāraikkāl Ammaiyār 271
Marwari 19, 87, 93
Mīrā 298, 302
Nityānanda 210, 219, 222, 224, 227, 230
performance 278
Pulaya 269–70
Sahajānanda 236, 247, 251–2
Sūrdās 24, 188–9, 199
Sūrsāgar 195
Svāminārāyaṇa *sampradāya* 109, 113, 115, 118, 235
temple community 18–19
immigrant 68–70, 73–4, 80–1
Indic (as used in this volume) 4
internet 3, 6, 16, 24–5, 27, 186–91, 193, 200, 204, 212, 224–5, 288
ISKCON 191–2

Jadrup 144–5
jaulāhā 152

Jhalawar 167–8
Jhanak Jhanak Pāyal Bāje (1955 movie) 293
jīvan mukti 216, 222, 228, 230
Jogan (1950 movie) 299
Jubilee Art Studio 46

Kabīr 137–9, **140–2**, **143**, **144–52**, **153–6**, **157–8**, 159, **160**–1
Kabīr Panth 141
Kajla Dham 99–100
Kālī 17, 43–4, **45**, **47**, 48, 57, 69, 75, 78–80
  Kṛṣṇa-Kālī 50–1, **52**, **53**
Kalighat 17, 43–8, 50, 52–4
Kali Yuga 85, 90, 102, 106
Kamāl Das 23, 137, 144, 154, **155**–6, **157–8**
Kansaripara Art Studio 46
Kāraikkāl Ammaiyār; Ammaiyār 29–30, 261–6, **267**, 268–80
Kashi 154
Kasur 150
Khanna, J. B. 41, 48
Khanna, Vinod 296, 300
Khazīnat ul-aṣfiyā' 150
Khote, Durga 295
Kishangarh 6, 167, 172, 292–3, 297
Kota 168–9, 171–2, 245, 289
Kṛṣṇa
  in Amar Singh *Sūrsāgar* 197–204
  and *bhakti* 12–13, 15, 30, 41
  blue color 8
  child form of 25, 187, **188**–9, **190**–1, **192**, 194–5, 206, 212, 298–304
  in Kalighat painting 44
  Kṛṣṇa-Kālī 43, 48–51, **52**–3, 57
  and Marwari temples 98–9, 102
  and Mīrā 30–1, 285–8, 293, 295, **296**, **297**–304
  in Nityānanda's temples 215, **216**
  and Puṣṭi Mārga 8, 24, 28, 164–7, 169–74, 178–9, 241–2
  and Sahajānanda 28
  in Svāminārāyaṇa *sampradāya* 237–9, 241–2, **245**, 246, 251–2
Kubera **104**, 105
Kulkarni, Chandani 302
Kumar, Dilip 299

Lakṣmī 41–2, 50, 54, 89, 105, 118, 199, 264
Lakṣmīnārayaṇ Dev Gādī 118
Lāl Dās 145
laukika 28, 165, 180, 236, 242, 252
līlā 12, 133, 199, 241–2, 254 n.13, 292
  Śrīharilīlāmṛtam 235, 248, 251–2
liṅga 22, 217, 223
lithography 43, 45–6
Loī 159, **160**
Los Angeles, California 27, 191, 218, 222–4

Ma'ārij ul-wilāyat 150
mahārāja 8, 24, 164, 168–9, 171–2, 174, **175**–7, 179–80, 251, **252**
Māhavidyās 48
Mahiṣāsuramardinī 48, **55**–**6**, 264
maṇḍala 210, 219, 226, 228
  prabāhmaṇḍala 247–8
manoratha 11, 24, 183, 290
  popular style 178, **179–80**
  traditional style 176, **177**
Marwari 19–20, 85, 87–102, 105–6, 291
material (materiality; material culture)
  and the abject 269, 272
  as archive 110–12, 118–24
  and *bhakti* 5, 85, 87, 94–5, 106, 109–10
  and *darśan* 13–14, 120
  as distributive 112–18
  and immateriality 1–2, 26–8, 210–13, 217–24
  and Indic devotion 2, 90
  and interdisciplinarity 9–10
  and media 224–8
  and memory 16–21, 76–7
  and museum 124–31
  as *prasādī* 120, **121**
  and visuality 9–10, 26, 90–1, 110, 164–6, 228–9, 237 (*see also laukika* and *alaukika*)
Matwali Meera (1940 Punjabi movie) 295, **296**–7
meditation (Life Bliss Meditation) 210, 215, 219, 222–3, 227–9
Meera (1945 Tamil movie; 1947 Hindi remake) 31, **296**, 299
Meera (1979 Hindi movie) 31, **296**, 299

Meera (2009–10 TV series) **296**, 303
Meerabai (1921 silent movie) 294
Meerabai (1932 Hindi movie) 294–5
Meerabai (1933 Bengali-Hindi movie) 295
Meerabai (1940 Telugu movie) 296–7
Meera Bai (1947 Hindi movie) 295, 297
Meerabai Not Out (2008 Hindi movie) 302
Meera Shyam (1976 Hindi movie) 299
Mehandipur 19–20, 87–8, 94–7, 99–100, 106
Merta 285, 290
Mewar 25, 171, 173, 195, 197–8, 200, 202–4, 206, 245, 285, 290–1, 297, 300, 302
Mīnāṭcī 219–20, 223–4, 226–7
Mīrā 7, 29–31, 278–9, 285–6, **287**, 288–90, **291**–5, **296–7**, 298–304
Mirabai (1960 Bengali movie) 89, 295, 299
miracle 3, 20, 85, 87–91, 93–6, 98–106, 217, 278, 300
Mir'āt ul-asrār 150
Mīr Kalan Khan 158–9
Moṭā Mahārāj Śrī 125–9
Mughal 23, 26, 90, 141–3, 145, 156, 159–60, 174, 250–1
Mu'īn al-Dīn Chishtī 143
Mukhtar Begum 295–6
Mullā Shāh 144
multiplicity (*śleṣa*) 212, 228
mūlvar **214**, 222
Munshi Raziuddin 138, 145, 147–50, 159, 161
mūrti
  and home shrines 63, 72–3
  and Mīrā 286, 296, 298, 301–4
  and Nityānanda 218–20, 222, 227
  and portraiture 237, 241–2, **247**, 248, **252**, 253
  and the Puṣṭi Mārga 165–6
  and Sahajānanda 14, 28, 108, 110, 236–7, 240, 242–53
Murugaṉ 210, 215, 219, **220**, 226–7
muvaḥḥid (muvaḥḥidān) 144–6, 151

Nāgarīdās 292
nakhaśikha (*nakha-śikha*) 239–42, 251, 253 n.5, 254 n.9, 263, 280 n.4
Nargis 299
Narnārayaṇ Dev Gādī 21, 118–20, 122–7, 129–30
Nathdwara 24, 164, 168–9, 171–4, 176, 178, 290
National Art Gallery 46
naẓar 7, 15, 26
nīm qalam 152
nirguṇa 111, 138, 144, 222–3
nirvāṇa 147
Nityānanda (or Nithyananda), Guru Paramahaṃsa 27, 210, **211**–20, **221**–8, **229**–30

Oneness Capsule 27, 210, 226–7
Oriental Studio 46

pandal 54–5
participation 4–5, 10, 15, 19, 65–7, 71, 74, 76, 80, 272, 279
Pārvatī 211, 217–19, 222
patua 17, 43–5, 53
Persianate 139, 142, 144–5, 147, 151, 153, 156, 158, 160–1
pēy 29–30, 261–6, **267**, 268, 270–2, 275, **276**, 278, 280 n.8
Phalke, Dhundhiraj Govind 294
pichvāi **179**, 182 n.6, 241, 254 n.11
pīr 148, 151
portraits
  and *bhakti* 22
  as embodiment and energy 8, 25–8, 213
  human and divine 212
  and iconicity 25
  and indexicality 22, 241–2
  of Kabīr and Kamāl 152–60
  of *mahārājas* 24, 174, 176
  and *manorathas* 176–8, **179**, **180**
  and media 14, 224–8
  of Mīrā 285–304
  and *mūrti* 14, 110, 236–7, 242–53
  in photographic style 24, 173
  self-portrait 27, 30, 210, 213, **214**, 217–29, 266
  of Sūrdās 186–206
practices of looking 1–3, 7, 9, 11, 13–15, 17, 26, 261
  immaterializing portraits 2, 15, 25–8, 31

materializing memory 2, 15–21, 31
mirroring portraits 2, 15, 21–5, 31
shaping the return look 2, 15, 29–31
Prahlad Singh Tipanya 160
prasādīnī jagyā 111, **116**, **123**
prasādīnī vastu 111–12, **119**
pratimā 222–3, 228
pūjā
bārir pūjā 63
and *darśan* 14
Durgā Pūjā 17, 43, 48, 51–8
at home shrines 18, 63–78
and Mīrā 286, 293
in the Nityānanda temple 215–17, 220, 228
in the Puṣṭi Mārga 165–6
Puṣṭi Mārga (Puṣṭimārg) 23–4, 28, 109, 113–14, 164–81, 182 n.3, 188, 202, 204, 213, 241–2, 246–7

Qādirī 146
qawwālī 23, 138, 147–9, 154, 161

Rādhā 51–3, 98, 102, 173, 199, **216**, 238, 244
Raidās 295, 303
Rajput 6, 89, 91–2, 105, 164–81, 245, 247, 250–1, 263, 285, 288, 290–2, 296, 299–300
Rajrani Meera (1956 movie) 295, 299
Rāma 20, 85, 87–90, 92–5, 100, 102–3, 105, 215, **216**
Ramakrishna 71, 78–9
Ramalingkum, M. 42
Rāmānand 145, 151–2
Rāmāyaṇa 87, 99, 103, 105, 194
Rao, B. N. 296–7
rasa
bhakti rasa 12–15
dāsya rasa 292, 298
disgust 13, 265
mādhurya rasa 292, 298, 304
prem rasa 12, 147
śanta rasa 13
and Sufism 12, 22–3, 26, 32, 147–8
vātsalya rasa 202, 206, 298, 304
Ratangarh temple 19, 88, 96–100
Rathod, Kanjibhai 294
recollection (*smṛtī*; *smaraṇa*) 112, 241
ritual
and the abject 30, 263, 269–70
and *bhakti* 5–6, 13, 23–4
and *darśan* 14–15
and guru 27, 100, 218, 226–30
and hereditary rights 92, 99
as a marketplace 18
and miracles 96–9
as *sevă* 164–71
and women's home shrines 65–83
Roy, Prafulla **296**, 299
Rūpa Gosvāmī (Rūpa Gosvāmin) 12, 297–8

sādhu 120, 235–6, 239–41, 243–4, 254 n.10, *see also* guru
Sadhvi Mirabai (1937 Marathi movie) 295
saguṇa 15, 108, 161, 222
sahaj 147
Sahajānanda Svāmī 14, 20–1, 28
images of 235–58, **245**, **247**, **249**, **250**, **252**
materiality of 108–34, **116**, **119**, **121**, **123**
sahṛdaya 11–12
Sai Baba 73
Śaiva Siddhānta 213, 229
Śakta 48, 53, 57
śakti 27, 78–9, 96, 102, 213, 215, 217, 223, 227
Salasar 19–20, 87–8, 91–102, 106, *see also* Bālājī
samādhi
living enlightenment 226
memorial 104
San Jose, California 27, 220, 222–4, 231 n.11
Sant Meerabai (1929 silent movie) 294
Sarangpur (Salangpur) 122
Sarasvatī 50, 54, 78–9
Sarasvatī, Dayānanda 172
sat 147
Satī (goddess) 43–4, 50
Rānī Satī 93
satsaṅga 27, 123, 159, 200, 205, 217, 224–6, 298
scopic regime 14, 30, 261, 263, 271, 274, 279, 280 n.1
Seattle, Washington 223–4
sevā 14, 24, 67, 164–74, 176–81, 182 n.5
by Mīrā 299

Shah Jahan 23, 26, 143
Shantaram, Rajaram Vankudre 295
Sharma, Indra 191–3, 205–6
Sheikh Taqī 150
Shree Swaminarayan Museum 108–31, **125**
siddha (*siddhi*) 27, 216–17, 222, 225–30
ṣifāt 149
Singhal, J. P. 41–2, 58–9
Śirdi Sai Baba (Shirdi Sai Baba) 215, **216**, 229
Śiva
  Ānandeśvara-Ānandeśvarī **211**, 215, 218–22, 226–7, 229, 230
  Ardhanārīśvara 218, 226–7
  and *chakra*s 215
  Dakṣiṇāmūrti 215, 221–3, 229–30
  in dance-drama 274–6
  in disguise 269
  and Gaurī 50
  and Kālī 48, 50
  Mahādeva 48, 50, 55, 57, 213, 231–2
  Naṭarāja 223, 262–3, 265–6, **267**, 270–2, 280 n.6
  Sadaśiva 213, 223
  and Satī 50
  Śiva-*bhakti* 15, 261, 266
  Śiva-Śakti 102
  and Umā 55
  U.S. temples 223–4
Śrīnāthjī 24, 27, 164, 167, **168**, 169–78, **179**–81, 182 n.4, 290
Subbulakshmi, M. S. 297–8
sufi (Sufism)
  and *bhakti* 5, 23
  Chishtī 4, 138
  and Hindu and Muslim 4
  Indo-Muslim 4
  and Kabīr 137–61
  and Kamāl 149–59
  Persian and Urdu sources 23
  poetry 5
  and portraits 26
  and *rasa* 12
  and Sūrdās 187
Suhrawardī 150
Sūrdās (Sūr) 186–206, **187**, **188**, **190**, **192**, **196**, **203**, **204**, **205**
Sūrsāgar 25, 195–204, **196**
Svāminārāyaṇa *sampradāya* 27, 108–31, 235–53
svarūpa 24, 164–78, 182 n.5

Tagore, Abanindranath 293
Tagore, Rabindranath 265
Tamil, *see also* Kāraikkāl Ammaiyār
  Caṅkam 262
  film 31, 278, **296**
  gods 219–20, 231 n.9, 270
  guru/sage 27, 210, 282 n.16
  iconography 218, **267**
  language 4–5, 213, 217, 263, 279
  Mahabalipuram 276, **277**
  Śiva-*bhakti* 5, 15, 30, 261, 268
  temples 22, 219, 223–5, 266, **267**
Tantra (tantric) 26, 27, 48, 95, 107 n.4, 173, 212–13, 216–19, 226–9, 263
tawḥīd 137, 145
ṭhākurghor 68–9
tilak 156, 189
Tirupati 89, 105, 219
Truth of Certainty 146
Truth-Reality 139, 141, 147, 149
Turk 146–7

Udaipur 25, 169, 177, 182 n.4, 188, 195, 197, 200, 202, **203–4**, 205, 290
umbrella, *see chatrī*
Unity of Being 149, 152

Vadtal **116**, 119–20, **121**, 122–4, 127, 235, **247**, **250**, **252**
Vaiṣṇava (Vaiṣṇavism)
  Bengali 53, 57
  Bengali Gauḍīya 12
  Marwari 20, 85–107
  nakhaśikha 263
  Svāminārāyaṇa 108–9, 237–8, 241–2
  tilak 156, 189
  tulsī beads 189
  Vallabha *sampradāya* 164, 181
Vallabha (*sampradāya*; Vallabhācarya) 8, 23–4, 164–85, 188–9, 202–3, 290, *see also* Puṣṭi Mārga
Varma, Raja Ravi 41–2, 48, 58, 59 n.2, 293, 305 n.8

Verma, Kalicharan **188**, 192, 205–6
vigraha **214**, 220, 222
visuality
  and art history 9
  and *bhakti* 4, 6, 13, 43, 65–8, 81, 106, 109, 261
  and cinema 14–15
  as a comparative category 1–2, 7, 10
  counter-visuality 9, 270–1
  and *darśan* 7, 14, 66
  as historical 3–4
  Indic 2–4, 9, 10
  as materializing memory 16–21
  as mirroring and immaterializing portraits 21–8
  as modern 2–4, 87, 91, 106
  and museum 14–15
  and *rasa* theory 11
  and religion studies 10
  as shaping the return look 28–31
  and theater 273–4

wife 8, 50, 52, 55, 69, 159, 160, 198, 275, 295, 300, 303, 304
women
  Bengali American 8, 17–18, 63–84, 298
  images of 8, 51, 99, 179–80, 198–200, 202, 217, 263–4, 270, 289–90, 292, 304
  violence against 6, 30, 270, 274–5, 278–9
woodblock printing 43, 45–7, 54, 56, 59 n.3

yantra **214**, 223, 228
yaqīn 146–7
yoga 51, 276
  Nithya Yoga 27, 210, 216–17, 223–5, 227, 230 n.4
  yogaḍaṇḍa 206

ẕāt 149, 152

www.ingramcontent.com/pod-product-compliance
Lightning Source LLC
Chambersburg PA
CBHW071801300426
44116CB00009B/1167
9781350214224